The Politics of the Periphery in Indonesia

The Politics of the Periphery in Indonesia

Social and Geographical Perspectives

Edited by
Minako Sakai, Glenn Banks
and
J. H. Walker

NUS PRESS
SINGAPORE

© 2009 NUS Press
National University of Singapore
AS3-01-02, 3 Arts Link
Singapore 117569

Fax   : (65) 6774-0652
E-mail : nusbooks@nus.edu.sg
Website : http://www.nus.edu.sg/nuspress

ISBN 978-9971-69-479-1 (Paper)

All rights reserved. This book, or parts thereof, may not be reproduced in any form or by any means, electronic or mechanical, including photocopying, recording or any information storage and retrieval system now known or to be invented, without written permission from the Publisher.

National Library Board Singapore Cataloguing in Publication Data

The politics of the periphery in Indonesia: social and geographical
   perspectives / edited by Minako Sakai, Glenn Banks and J. H. Walker.
   – Singapore: NUS Press, c2009.
   p. cm.
   Includes bibliographical references and index.
   ISBN-13: 978-9971-69-479-1 (pbk.)

   1. Central-local government relations – Indonesia.   2. Decentralisation in government – Indonesia.   3. Indonesia – Politics and government – 1998-
   I. Sakai, Minako, 1963-.   II. Banks, Glenn.
   III. Walker, J. H. (John Henry), 1958-

JS7193.A3
320.4598049 – dc22   OCN308886646

Cover: An eating stall in Martapura of South Kalimantan (Photograph Minako Sakai).

Typeset by: International Typesetters Pte Ltd
Printed by: Vetak Services

Contents

List of Tables, Figure and Illustrations	vii
Acknowledgements	ix
Abbreviations	xi
Contributors	xiv

Introduction: The Place of the Periphery   1
Minako Sakai, Glenn Banks and J. H. Walker

1. State, Region and the Politics of Recognition: Towards Cosmopolitan Models of Political Integration   14
 Joel S. Kahn

2. Patrimonialism and Feudalism in the *Sejarah Melayu* (Raffles MS 18)   39
 J. H. Walker

3. Creating a New Centre in the Periphery of Indonesia: Sumatran Malay Identity Politics   62
 Minako Sakai

4. Indonesia, Aceh and the Modern Nation-State   84
 Anthony Reid

5. Problems of Integration: West Sumatra's Place in Indonesia   101
 Audrey R. Kahin

6. Beyond Economic Imperatives: 117
   Resources, Identity and Conflict in the Asia-Pacific
   Glenn Banks

7. Social Identity and Access to Natural Resources: Ethnicity 134
   and Regionalism from a Maritime Perspective
   Dedi S. Adhuri

8. Violence and the Construction of Identity: Conflict 153
   between the Dayak and Madurese in Kalimantan, Indonesia
   Mary Hawkins

9. National Legitimacy through a Regional Prism: Local 173
   Pilgrimage and Indonesia's Javanese Presidents
   George Quinn

10. Papuan Nationalism: Christianity and Ethnicity 200
    Richard Chauvel

11. Indonesian *Adat* Communities: Promises and Challenges 219
    of Democracy and Globalisation
    Leena Avonius

12. Chinese Indonesian Identities: Challenging Homogenising 240
    Discourses
    Charles A. Coppel

13. "More Indonesian than the Indonesians": A Chinese- 254
    Indonesian Identity
    David Reeve

14. Indonesian Identity after the Dictatorship: Imagining 274
    Chineseness in Recent Literature and Film
    Paul Tickell

Bibliography 296

Index 325

List of Tables, Figure and Illustrations

Tables

3.1	Locations of DMDI Workshops and Major Events in Indonesia	66
7.1	Ministry of Agriculture Decree No. 392/1999 on Marine Zoning for Fisheries	136
7.2	Some Conflicts between Fishermen in Indonesia (2000–2)	142

Figure

7.1	The Kei Islands	137

Illustrations

3.1	Renovated Benteng Kuto Besak, Palembang	69
3.2	Advertisement for Malay Dance Festival held in Palembang, 2004, profiling the then governor of South Sumatra Province	71
3.3	DMDI Workshop, Pekanbaru, Riau, Dec. 2007	76

Acknowledgements

Various people offered us valuable assistance in producing this volume. We thank the University of New South Wales at ADFA campus for providing us with financial assistance in organising the workshop entitled "National Integration and Regionalism in Indonesia and Malaysia" in 2002. Susan Cowan, Margaret McNelly, Taufiq Tanasaldy, Ahmad Kusworo and Taufiq Prabowo assisted us in organising the conference. In particular, Taufiq Tanasaldy and Paul Tickell offered valuable help throughout this project. The editors thank especially Charles Coppel for his strong encouragement and personal support for this project. Minako Sakai wants to express her appreciation to Cornell University and the National University of Singapore where she worked on the finalisation of this volume as a Visiting Fellow in 2006.

Abbreviations

ADFA	Australian Defence Force Academy
AIPP	Asian Indigenous Peoples Pact
AMAN	Aliansi Masyarakat Adat Nusantara (Alliance of the Indigenous Peoples of the Indonesian Archipelago)
ASEAN	Association of Southeast Asian Nations
Baperki	Badan Permusyawaratan Kewarganegaraan Indonesia (Body for Consultation on Indonesian Citizenship)
BK	Bung Karno (Sukarno)
CIA	Central Intelligence Agency
CSIS	Centre for Strategic and International Studies
CoW	Contract of Work
DMDI	Dunia Melayu Dunia Islam (The Malay and Islamic World)
DPR	Dewan Perwakilan Rakyat (People's Representative Council)
DPRD	Dewan Perwakilan Rakyat Daerah (Regional People's Representative Council)
ELSHAM	Lembaga Studi dan Advokasi Hak Asasi Manusia (Institute for Human Rights Study and Advocacy)
GAM	Gerakan Aceh Merdeka (Free Aceh Movement)
GAPENA	Gabungan Persatuan Penulis Nasional Malaysia (Federation of National Writers Associations of Malaysia)
GDP	Gross Domestic Product
GKI	Gereja Kristen Injil (Evangelical Christian Church, Papua)
GKII	Gereja Kemah Injil Indonesia (Tabernacle Bible Church of Indonesia)

GMNI	Gerakan Mahasiswa Nasional Indonesia (Movement of Indonesian Nationalist Students)
GMPKM	Gerakan Masyarakat Peduli Kebudayaan Melayu (Movement of People Who Care about Malay Culture Foundation)
Golkar	Golongan Karya (Functional Groups, a political party)
Hankam	Pertahanan and Keamanan (Defence and Security)
HIV-AIDS	Human Immunodeficiency Virus-Acquired Immune Deficiency Syndrome
IAIN	Institut Agama Islam Negeri (State Institute of Islamic Studies)
ICG	International Crisis Group
ICMI	Ikatan Cendekiawan Muslim Indonesia (Association of Indonesian Muslim Intellectuals)
IKSEP	Institut Kajian Sejarah dan Patriotisme Malaysia (Malaysian Institute of Historical and Patriotism Studies)
ILO	International Labour Organisation
IMT-GT	Indonesia-Malaysia-Thailand Growth Triangle
INS	Indonesische Nederlandsch School (Indonesian Dutch School)
IWGIA	International Working Group on Indigenous Affairs
KTP	Kartu Tanda Penduduk (citizen identity card)
LMD	Lembaga Musyawarah Desa (Village Consultative Council)
Masyumi	Majelis Syuro Muslimin Indonesia (Consultative Council of Indonesian Muslims)
Monas	Monumen Nasional (National Monument)
MMSD	Mining, Minerals and Sustainable Development
MPR	Majelis Perwakilan Rakyat (Indonesian Parliament)
NASA	National Aeronautics and Space Administration
Nasakom	Nasionalis Agama Komunis (Nationalism, Religion, Communism)
NFS	Nucleus Estate/Small-holder Scheme
NGO	Non-governmental Organisation
NII	Negara Islam Indonesia (Indonesian Islamic State)
NRM	Natural Resource Management
NU	Nahdlatul Ulama (Revival of Religious Scholars)
OPM	Organisasi Papua Merdeka (Free Papua Movement)
OXFAM	Oxford Committee for Famine Relief
Pari	Partai Rakyat Indonesia (Party of Indonesian Citizens)
PDIP	Partai Demokrasi Indonesia–Perjuangan (Indonesian Democratic Party Struggle)

PDP	Presidium Dewan Papua (Papuan Presidium Council)
PDRI	Pemerintah Darurat Republik Indonesia (Republic's Emergency Government)
Permesta	Perjuangan Semesta (Total Struggle)
Permi	Persatuan Muslimin Indonesia (Union of Indonesian Muslims)
PERZIM	Perbadanan Muzium Melaka (Museum Corporation of Melaka)
PKI	Partai Komunis Indonesia (Indonesian Communist Party)
PNI	Partai Nasional Indonesia (Indonesian Nationalist Party)
PNI (Baru)	Pendidikan Nasional Indonesia (Indonesian National Education)
PPP	Partai Persatuan Pembangunan (United Development Party)
PRC	People's Republic of China
PRRI	Pemerintah Revolusioner Republik Indonesia (Revolutionary Government of the Republic of Indonesia)
PSI	Partai Sosialis Indonesia (Indonesian Socialist Party)
PSII	Partai Sarekat Islam Indonesia (Indonesian Islamic Union Party)
PT	Perseroan Terbatas (Limited liability company)
PTPN	PT Perkebunan Nusantara (State Plantation Company)
RMS	Republik Maluku Selatan (Republic of South Maluku)
SARA	Suku, Agama, Ras dan Antar-golongan (Ethnicity, Religion, Race and Class)
SBY	Susilo Bambang Yudhoyono
SKP	Sekretariat Keadilan dan Perdamaian (Justice and Peace Secretariat)
SM	*Sejarah Melayu* (Raffles MS 18), Malay Annals
TNI	Tentara Nasional Indonesia (Indonesian Armed Forces)
UN	United Nations
UMNO	United Malays National Organization
UNDP	United Nations Development Programme
UNWGIP	United Nations Working Group on Indigenous Populations
VOC	Verenigde Oostindische Compagnie (Dutch East India Company)
WALHI	Wahana Lingkungan Hidup Indonesia (Friends of the Earth Indonesia)
WNI	Warga Negara Indonesia (Indonesian citizens)

Contributors

Dedi S. Adhuri (d.adhuri@cgiar.org) is a scientist at Policy, Economics and Social Sciences, WorldFish Center, Penang, Malaysia. He is also affiliated to the Maritime Study Group (MSG) at the Research Center for Society and Culture, Indonesian Institute of Sciences (LIPI) in Jakarta. With the Maritime Study Group, he has carried out intensive research on marine resource management (communal marine tenure, fisheries conflict, co-management).

Leena Avonius (leena.avonius@helsinki.fi) is Senior Researcher at Asia-Pacific Studies, Renvall Institute, University of Helsinki. She received her Ph.D. in anthropology at Leiden University in 2004. Her current research focuses on human rights discourses in Indonesia.

Glenn Banks (G.A.Banks@massey.ac.nz) is Associate Professor, Development Studies at Massey University. He taught human geography at University of New South Wales at ADFA until 2008. He has been researching the large-scale mining sector in Papua New Guinea since the late 1980s, focusing on issues of the social impact, development and conflict, local economic development and applied policy development in the context of resource management and local communities.

Richard Chauvel (richard.chauvel@vu.edu.au) teaches in the School of Social Sciences at Victoria University in Melbourne, His research interests are in the history and contemporary politics of eastern Indonesia, particularly Papua and Maluku, and in Australia's relations with Indonesia. His recent publications include *Constructing Papuan Nationalism: History, Ethnicity and Adaptation*.

Charles A. Coppel (c.coppel@unimelb.edu.au) is a Principal Fellow in the School of Historical Studies at the University of Melbourne. He has been researching the ethnic Chinese in Indonesia for more than four decades. His publications include *Indonesian Chinese in Crisis* (1983), *Studying Ethnic Chinese in Indonesia* (2002) and the edited volume *Violent Conflicts in Indonesia: Analysis, Representation, Resolution* (2006).

Mary Hawkins (m.hawkins@uws.edu.au) is a Senior Lecturer in the School of Social Science, University of Western Sydney. She is a social anthropologist who has worked for the World Bank, AusAID and UNDP. In recent years Mary has developed her long-standing interest in the formation of ethnic and other identities to encompass globalisation and emergent global identities. Her most recent publications include *Global Structures, Local Cultures* (2006) and *Race and Ethnicity* (with Farida Fozdar and Raelene Wilding, 2008).

Audrey R. Kahin (arkahin@yahoo.com) was managing editor of Southeast Asia publications at Cornell University and co-editor and editor of the journal *Indonesia* from 1978 to 1995. Her most recent publications include *Rebellion to Integration: West Sumatra and the Indonesian Polity 1926–1998* (2000); and *Historical Dictionary of Indonesia*, 2nd ed., with Robert Cribb (2004).

Joel S. Kahn (j.kahn@latrobe.edu.au) is an Emeritus Professor in the Sociology and Anthropology Program at La Trobe University. He has published widely on the themes of peasant economy, development, modernity, globalisation, culture, and identity in Southeast Asia in comparative perspective. His most recent book is *Other Malays: Nationalism and Cosmopolitanism in the Modern Malay World*. He is currently researching forms of religious experience and secularism in Asia and Europe.

George Quinn (George.Quinn@anu.edu.au) is Head of the Southeast Asia Centre in the Faculty of Asian Studies, ANU, where he teaches Indonesian and Javanese. He is author of *The Novel in Javanese* (1992) and *The Learner's Dictionary of Today's Indonesian* (2001). A companion study to his chapter here, "Throwing Money at the Holy Door: Commercial

Aspects of Popular Pilgrimage in Java", appears in the edited volume *Expressing Islam: Religious Life and Politics* (2008).

David Reeve (d.reeve@unsw.edu.au) a Senior Visiting Fellow at the University of New South Wales, has been visiting Indonesia since 1969, as a diplomat, historian, researcher and language teacher. He was a founding lecturer in Australian Studies at Universitas Indonesia in 1984–87, and Resident Director of the ACICIS program at UGM and UMM in 1997–99. He has published on Indonesian politics and history, Australian and Indonesian perceptions of each other. He is working on a biography of Ong Hok Ham.

Anthony Reid (ariar@nus.edu.sg) is a Professor at the Asia Research Institute, National University of Singapore, of which he was foundation director (2002–07). He has taught and researched Southeast Asian history at the University of Malaya (1965–70), ANU (1970–99), and UCLA (1999–2002). His more recent books include: *An Indonesian Frontier: Acehnese and other Histories of Sumatra* (2004); *Imperial Alchemy: Nationalism and Political Identity in Southeast Asia* (forthcoming); and as editor or co-editor: *Việt Nam: Borderless Histories* (2006); and *Islamic Legitimacy in a Plural Asia* (2007).

Minako Sakai (m.sakai@adfa.edu.au) is a Senior Lecturer in the School of Humanities and Social Sciences, University of New South Wales at ADFA. She is a social anthropologist and has published on post-regional autonomy identity politics and the impact of Islamisation on social structure and identity construction in Sumatran communities. She is the editor of *Beyond Jakarta: Regional Autonomy and Local Societies in Indonesia* (2002).

Paul Tickell (p.tickell@adfa.edu.au) teaches Indonesian at the University of New South Wales at ADFA. He has held similar positions at Monash, Flinders and the University of Western Australia. His major research interests lie in the cultural politics of late colonial Indonesia.

J. H. Walker (j.walker@adfa.edu.au) teaches politics at the University of New South Wales at ADFA. He is the author of *Power and Prowess: The Origins of Brooke Kingship in Sarawak*. He has published articles about Sarawak history and political culture in journals such as *RIMA*, *Modern Asian Studies*, *Theory and Society*, *Borneo Research Bulletin* and *Australian Religion Studies Review*.

INTRODUCTION

The Place of the Periphery

Minako Sakai, Glenn Banks and J. H. Walker

Indonesia's Extremities

Viewed from space at night, Indonesia assumes a different profile from its familiar intricate pattern of islands, coasts and mountains.[1] Java positively glows with an incandescent light, southern central Sumatra is a radiant oasis, and Bali is an intense spot of heat. The rest of the archipelago is marked by an inky darkness splattered only occasionally by the lights of provincial capitals and other isolated points of illumination. In many senses such a view reflects the spread of economic and political power across Indonesia as it has been since Independence: the locus of political power and debate centred on Java, with some small pockets of influence outside this core. Like other external views of the earth,[2] there is more that can be read into such a speckled view of Indonesia by night. For one, many of the other isolated points of illumination are related to major resource projects and areas—the Freeport mine and Sorong oilfields in Papua, fires and developments in Kalimantan, and the flaring of oil and gas in Aceh. And for another, the unbounded nature of the dispersion of night lights across the region (especially as markers of inclusion and exclusion) brings home the socio-political construction of national boundaries, and the continuities and relationships across these boundaries—with the Malay Peninsula, the Malaysian states on Kalimantan, across the Papuan border into Papua New Guinea, and even into northern Australia. Of course peripheries exist in the social as much as the physical sense: through the (from space, at night) unseen dynamic tensions of exclusions and marginality, and this volume seeks to engage with these social, cultural and political margins along with, indeed often in association with, the physical frontiers of the Indonesian nation. In these ways, then such a conceptualisation provides a productive image with which to open a volume concerned with the margins (the darker extremities) of Indonesia.

The particular configuration of an (en)lightened core and darker extremities has provided a backdrop to post-Suharto moves towards decentralisation and regional autonomy. And yet this has always presented a fragile state of affairs, one that is fiercely guarded through the lens of Indonesian nationalism. The effects of this nationalistic political imperative are not contained within the state, but like night-time continuities, can ripple outwards to affect relationships with neighbours. One high profile recent example was the granting by the Australian government in March 2006 of temporary visas to 42 asylum-seekers from Papua Province, Indonesia. They arrived in northern Queensland in January and claimed that they were seeking refuge in order to escape abuses by the Indonesian military against the Papuan population, who were operating under the pretext of suppressing the Papuan secession movement. Angered, Jakarta interpreted the Australian decision as evidence that Australia was questioning the territorial integrity of Indonesia. In protest, Jakarta recalled its ambassador from Canberra in late March and bilateral relations between the two countries became strained. Responding to this development, Canberra altered its migration procedures, which in turn, sparked protests from the Australian public who accused Jakarta of meddling with Australia's internal affairs. The subsequent security cooperation treaty between Canberra and Jakarta in November 2006 explicitly highlighted the fact that both states will respect each others' territorial integrity and sovereignty.

This is just one recent event in which Indonesia showed extreme sensitivity in relation to the recognition of its territorial integrity. The independence of Indonesia was achieved only after fighting against Western (predominantly Dutch) colonialism, and ever since, "once independent, forever independent" (from the lyrics of "Independence

Day", *Hari Merdeka*) has encapsulated the strong nationalist sentiment promoted among Indonesians by the state. The nation-building project has committed significant resources (material, financial and intellectual) to create, support and promote the unity of the nation through, among other ways, national history writing projects.

The side effect of the political importance attached to territorial integrity and nationalism in Indonesia is that it has also affected intellectual frameworks. As elsewhere, Indonesian nationalism has promoted academic studies bound by territorial boundaries and country-based studies as the main framework of intellectual reference. In the broader Southeast Asian context, Thongchai Winichakul has openly criticised the domination of country histories in this body of work. Instead he has advocated "postnational histories", which should as their starting point, challenge the assumption of the national essence.[3] History at the interstices, he states, is "the history of locations and moments between being and not being a nation, becoming and not becoming a nation".[4] In such projects, the periphery naturally occupies a central place.

In the case of Indonesia, academics have paid much attention to the exploration of tensions between central and local actors.[5] For example, prominent secession movements such as the Organisasi Papua Merdeka (OPM, Free Papua Movement) and Gerakan Aceh Merdeka (GAM, Free Aceh Movement) have been a focus as they have posed an immediate threat to the national integration of Indonesia. The relationship between these 'difficult' provinces and the development of post-Suharto regional autonomy has been well documented.[6] Away from these hot spots, the tension between national integration and local identity has been a more low-key affair, traditionally studied by anthropologists.[7]

The fall of Suharto in 1998, followed by the plan to implement regional autonomy in 2001, was not only a major political event in Indonesia, but also affected how academics have approached analysis of the country. This is because regional autonomy has opened up new discursive areas in which power relations between the central government and the periphery, as well as between regions, can be negotiated.

The central government's devolution of power to local governments (primarily through Law 22/1999 and Law 25/1999) was the central mechanism by which this process occurred. Driven initially in large part by the necessity to placate Aceh and Papua, the aim of this heightened regional autonomy is to bring more accountability to the local levels and develop policies to reflect local interest. Law 22/1999 has also increased interest in reviving local institutions of governance. During the New Order, Suharto introduced a unitary village system to replace various local governance systems. Responding to the new opportunities, for example, the West Sumatran traditional governance unit, *nagari*, was revived.[8] Other regions and political and civil leaders also started to call for reviving local identity and tradition, including Islamism, in order to receive popular support. During the New Order, Javanese culture was closely associated with Indonesia through the national use of Javanese batik and Javanese words. Reviving local identity and customs has produced power struggles at the local level, where newly empowered local power brokers are concentrating on policies that promote the economic interests of their respective regions.[9]

A number of recent edited volumes have highlighted emergent local power politics and their dynamic relationships with the central government.[10] These books have generated a new research area by focusing on the local power brokers and various actors in addition to political leaders, reflecting a close collaboration between political scientists and anthropologists. The focus of these collections has been on contemporary case studies from across Indonesia highlighting the institutional development related to governance, and the role of emergent local elites and their power patronages within the boundaries of Indonesia.

The contribution of this volume to the current exploration of local power politics is twofold. First, it looks into border regions with Indonesia's immediate neighbours. By expanding the focus of interest transnationally to Malaysia (and to a lesser extent Papua New Guinea) for comparison, and by examining the links across Indonesia's peripheral border regions, the issue of national integration across Indonesia can be tested at the 'interstices' as Winichakul has suggested.

Secondly, the essays in this book expand the search for an understanding of the forces behind the tensions between the peripheral regions and the centralist state. In order to advance this, we have incorporated historical constructions of the periphery and their relationships with 'states' in addition to contemporary case studies. The chapters also traverse issues ranging from identity, resource access, religion and the Chinese Indonesian population in order to explore how these have affected a sense of belonging to, and consequently relations with, the nation.

Through this approach, this volume engages with a number of academic debates taking place beyond Indonesian studies. The first of these seeks to bring 'periphery regions', long buried under centralised national discourses, to the front of this new research trajectory. Calls for a refocus on regions rather than states are not only taking place in the field of Southeast Asian studies, but also in European and African studies. The post-World War II independence movements that spread through Southeast Asia, however, produced some of the strongest exemplars of modern nation-states, with the nation-building projects (internal and external) of Singapore, Indonesia and Malaysia generating states which, until recently, had seemed models for the transfer of the Western ideal to the developing world. As Joel Kahn (Chapter 1) and others note though, the universalist values that underpinned the civic rhetoric of unity during the New Order never completely encompassed the identities and aspirations of large segments of Indonesia's citizenry. The fall of the New Order has led to outbursts of local frustration, community organisations and regional aspirations, but not in a simple, homogenous way. It is the very diversity of these responses from the periphery, and their origins and profound implications for understandings of 'the state', the citizen and the 'region' which this volume draws on to produce insights into the transformation of the Indonesian state and nation.

Peripheral Places and Peoples?

In the Indonesian context and as reflected in this volume, *region* refers to a particular area which has or is actively creating itself as a distinctive socio-political entity. Here we are responding to the recent work[11] which highlights the centrality of people, social and economic networks, and social movements to the construction of peripheries and regions. This volume explores how the people in the Indonesian archipelago (particularly in the periphery) have negotiated, created or are trying to form a region as a distinctive entity against the nation—even beyond the nation—and are seeking to locate and secure the region through organic, local, bottom-up processes in the face of concerted efforts by the centre to integrate them into the modern nation. Regionalism here thus refers to a shared localised vision and strategy to create such a distinctive entity, and one that has to be centred, so to speak, in the Indonesian periphery.

In considering the distinctive features of a region, the state remains one of the key reference points, even if as an organisational counterpoint. Our approach is to critically examine possible paradigms of national integration rather than assuming anticolonial nationalism as the sole possible framework. Joel Kahn rightly points out in his chapter in this volume that the "anticolonial struggle aims to replace racially or culturally alien rulers with indigenous ones". However, a serious problem became evident in postcolonial Indonesia as 'Indonesian-ness' (like 'Malay-ness') was far from universally agreed or homogeneous. A central question which cuts across the region, and this volume, is: Who precisely belong to or are perceived to belong to (and by implication who and where is peripheral to) an imagined 'Indonesia'?

Indonesia and the Malay World

Colonialism and postcolonial nationalism have been the basis of the current geographical configuration of Indonesia and its neighbours. As the nocturnal satellite view suggests, there is nothing natural about these boundaries and the peripheries they create. In this regard, it is important to bring back into focus the existence of the Malay world, which stretches across insular and peninsular Southeast Asia. The precolonial Malay world consisted of a series of overarching and interrelated trading networks that lasted until the consolidation of European colonialism over island Southeast Asia in the nineteenth century. This marked the beginning of the division and domination of the region by the Western colonial powers, and the much more recent solidification of these boundaries under postcolonial nationalism. John H. Walker (Chapter 2) productively revisits the issue of peripheral regions in indigenous historical court chronicles by examining the role that regions played in the internal politics of the Malay courts. Walker claims that the periphery did play a significant role in Malay politics despite the common perception that Malay sovereignty was based on a centralised, absolutist ideology.

The notion of the Malay world still dominates the minds of political leaders across Indonesia, Malaysia and the Philippines, despite the creation of separate postcolonial nation-states. The Malay and Islamic World Movement is one of the emergent socio-economic forces designed to unite the Malays against the waves of globalisation, based as Minako Sakai (Chapter 3) suggests on shared identity and the common understanding that Malays have been marginalised by these processes. While the uniting of the Malays across the Strait of Melaka under the banner of *Melayu Raya* (Greater Malaya) was a failed political movement in the postcolonial nation-making process, it is still present in the minds of the Malays as an important socio-political possibility in the contemporary world, and one that seeks to negate social and geographic peripheries.

National Integration and the Region

How did the postcolonial states affect the position of the peripheral regions? This is a central question linked to the current political tensions in Indonesia. It is important to underline the fact that "most Indonesians outside Java experienced 'state' in its modern sense only in the form of an alien imposition" as Anthony Reid (Chapter 4) suggests. The alien nature of the Indonesian state is directly linked with the recurrent problems surrounding Aceh and Papua. Particularly in the case of colonial Papua, eastern Indonesians held the middle and lower positions in the civil administration, police and education, and Papuans felt that they were mistreated and discriminated against by the Indonesians even before Papua became a part of independent Indonesia as Richard Chauvel (Chapter 10) argues. Their Melanesian appearance and Christian beliefs further marginalise the Papuans from the Malay Muslim population of Indonesia. Ethnicity and religious differences however, are only a partial explanation for regional impulses. We need to acknowledge that even in geographically less 'peripheral' regions such as West Sumatra, with its Malay Muslim population, people have also found it difficult at times to belong to a centralised Indonesian nation, as Audrey Kahin (Chapter 5) points out. The West Sumatran revolt was a nationalistic movement by a people who had long upheld an egalitarian republican model for Indonesia and were subsequently aggrieved by their perception of 'peripheral' treatment.

Who Owns the Resources?

The most intense regional conflicts in Indonesia are all located away from the centre, an unruly periphery that represents a centrifugal axis that seeks to spin power and authority out from Java. The two most critical in terms of the future of the nation are clearly the Aceh rebellion and the struggle over autonomy in Papua. These two, along with Kalimantan (and in recent memory, East Timor) share the characteristic of being 'resource-rich' provinces, blending a potent combination of some or all of oil, minerals, timber, natural gas and marine resources.[12] These conflicts in the resource-rich provinces have been interpreted recently by observers through the lens of the global literature on resource curses and conflict.[13]

The 'resource curse' literature developed from the late 1980s in response to the growing awareness that countries 'blessed' with natural resources were, as a group, performing worse in terms of economic development than those without abundant natural resources.[14] It is noteworthy that

Indonesia was regarded as a model for the translation of resource rents into development. By the late 1990s, the global literature (albeit rather focused on Africa) was making a further claim—that a high dependence on natural resources was not only a poor route to economic development, but gave rise to a greater likelihood of internal or civil conflict.[15] Aceh and Papua, two high profile, resource-rich and conflict-ridden Indonesian provinces, were now viewed as exemplifying this pattern. In one of the more contentious claims in this literature, Paul Collier and Anne Hoeffler have argued that resource conflicts were driven primarily by 'greed' (a greater share of resource rents) than by ethnic or regional 'grievance' (in spite of the rhetoric that typically accompanies such conflicts).[16]

However, the role of resources in generating conflict in Indonesia's periphery and elsewhere is clearly contingent on a range of other factors.[17] Examples of conflicts over resources from contemporary Indonesia illustrate that struggles over resources (local–state, local–corporate or local–migrant) are fundamentally entwined with issues of local resource control, sovereignty and identity (Dedi Adhuri, Chapter 7).[18] The economic motives in such conflicts are simply one component (most readily understood and applied by observers) of what are essentially *moral* conflicts about the right to access, control and utilise resources for many communities in Indonesia, especially those at the periphery. It is community identity and security, not necessarily greed that drives these conflicts, as discussed by Glenn Banks (Chapter 6). And it is tensions between community identity and resource control that bring these communities and regions into conflict with the Indonesian state. The imposition of new rules from the centre regulating and allocating access to local resources is in this sense as much an assault on local and regional identity as it is on the resources themselves. The national laws allowing all Indonesians to have access to the sea, while laudable in protecting this right, can create tensions between the different types of 'locals', as Adhuri points out.

Transmigration programmes are aimed at reducing the population concentration in Java and simultaneously developing the 'underdeveloped, frontier periphery' outside Java: they have a distinctive regional logic and expression. Transmigration, started by the Dutch and continued by the Indonesian government, saw the resettlement of large numbers of Javanese to Sumatra, Kalimantan and Papua, alongside various development programmes. Kalimantan has abundant tropical forests and the Suharto regime promoted the timber industry to investors to generate national revenues. As result, the indigenous Dayak population were displaced in their homeland and forced to compete with the new transmigrants, particularly those from Madura. Control over and competition for access to resources then led to violent conflicts between the Dayak and some of the migrant Madurese as Mary Hawkins (Chapter 8) shows.

National Cultures or Local Cultures

Why does local culture matter and how has national integration influenced local identities and cultures? After the fall of Suharto, there was strong criticism directed at the apparent domination of Javanese culture in Indonesia. There is good evidence, for example, that Javanese culture has influenced the national discourses of political legitimacy in Indonesia as George Quinn (Chapter 9) argues. References to Javanese political prophecies and visits to sacred sites have been frequently used to legitimise the political authority of the Indonesian presidents. On the other hand, such localised Islamic cultural practices have increasingly alienated the groups who have distinctive cultural and religious traits such as Christian Papuans (Richard Chauvel, Chapter 10). Again, the turning point in Indonesia was the fall of Suharto in 1998. In the ensuing power vacuum, traditional customary communities (*masyarakat adat*) decided to raise their voices to challenge the domination of state power in social development. Having in the past been coerced into serving the 'national' development interest, *adat* community leaders formed a national association, AMAN (Alliance of the Indigenous Peoples of the Indonesian Archipelago), in order to strengthen and re-centre customary law, *adat*, in the nation-state. The development of such an association was both regional and national as Leena Avonius (Chapter 11) shows. National and global networks of NGOs played an important role in the establishment of this organisation, but the disappearing media coverage of AMAN over time suggests that cultural unity across Indonesia's regions remains an elusive goal.

Where do the Ethnic Chinese Belong?

Chinese Indonesians, as Charles Coppel (Chapter 12) demonstrates, have been singled out as an ethnic group which did not legally belong to the imagined new Indonesia: they were situated clearly on the social and cultural periphery. And yet in many ways this was clearly a politically motivated and marginalising positioning: although Bahasa Indonesia is the national language, symbolising the unity of the state, it is less commonly used than regional languages such as Javanese and Balinese by most Indonesians. Rather it is Chinese Indonesians who typically speak Indonesian at home more frequently than 'indigenous' Indonesians. Despite this, and their long sojourn in the Malay-Indonesian archipelago, the allegiance of Chinese Indonesians to the Indonesian nation and state has often been questioned. Consequently, they have been targeted as 'others' and frequently been the subject of culturally, economically, politically and racially motivated violence. Such views have created a pitfall in the academic discourses by essentialising Chineseness in Indonesia as the single other, as Coppel argues. He proposes new research directions including biography to counter such homogenising discourses.

Responding to this call, David Reeve (Chapter 13) highlights the biography of a renowned Chinese Indonesian historian, Ong Hok Ham, who was an expert on the Dutch East Indies. Ong went through a series of periods in which he actively chose to be 'Indonesian' in various ways. In this sense, contrary to the political and discursive alienation of Chinese Indonesians from 'Indonesian-ness', individual Indonesian Chinese can be "more Indonesian than the Indonesians", as Reeve puts it.

During the New Order regime, Chinese Indonesians and their identity were silenced and displaced from the public domain. However, along with political openness, the Chinese Indonesian identity has moved in from the periphery and even been strongly featured in Indonesian literary works by non-Chinese Indonesians, as shown by Paul Tickell (Chapter 14), who also demonstrates the increasing plurality of Indonesian Chineseness.

Conclusion

The genesis of this volume was a series of regular lunch-time conversations among Sakai, Walker and Banks at the University of New South Wales at ADFA (Australian Defence Force Academy) campus café in 2001. Sakai had worked on contemporary anthropological studies on Indonesia, and became more intrigued by the emergent socio-economic and nascent political development across the Strait of Melaka, bridging Sumatra and the Malay Peninsula. Walker's historical research interest intersected with the regions which are currently known as Indonesia, Malaysia and Brunei. Banks' research focused on community access to resources, particularly in the context of mining in Melanesia, and has highlighted the absence of comparative studies across the colonial relic that is the border between Papua New Guinea and the Indonesian province of Papua.[19]

Our conversations evolved into reflections on the existing disproportionate focus on national boundaries and significant lack of scholarly works which highlight the peripheral, sub-national and cross-border regions. In seeking to correct this, we organised a workshop titled National Integration and Regionalism in Indonesia and Malaysia (NIRIM) in November 2002 at our campus. The current volume has evolved from this and retains our strong joint interests on Indonesian margins, and the relationship between the peripheries, the adjoining neighbours and the Indonesia centre.

The processes of identity formation at the periphery involve continual negotiation, accommodation, incorporation and imagining of 'community', as this volume explores. These imaginings and negotiations, like all such dialectics, have taken place against a backdrop of national political, social and economic change. As the cases in this volume illustrate, however, the context is no longer (if it ever was) contained within the nation: the influences stretch further. Powerful international referents and actors including international NGO movements and multinational resource corporations are strongly involved, and these become incorporated into local imaginings of place and community, shaping responses from peripheral regions and groups towards national, centralising pressures. What is striking in these examples is the complexity of the processes, and the incessant negotiations between and with actors at various levels—between peripheries and multiple centres, and among groups and communities within the national polity. History and history-making at the interstices is not straightforward.

This volume brings together the perspectives of a diverse group of scholars (historians, anthropologists, geographers and political scientists) who are able, through their empirically-based studies of the interplay between the centre and the periphery, to provide telling insights into the historical, geographical and anthropological dimensions that underpin identity and region-making processes in contemporary Indonesia. We hope that this volume provides a prism through which observers will be better able to understand the dynamic transformations occurring at Indonesia's social and geographic periphery.

Notes

1. See, for example, the NASA Visible Earth website, Earth at Night scenes at <http://visibleearth.nasa.gov/view_rec.php?id=1438>.

2. D. E. Cosgrove, "Contested Global Visions: One-World, Whole-Earth, and the Apollo Space Photographs", *Annals of the Association of American Geographers* 84, 2 (1994): 270–94.
3. T. Winichakul, "Writing at the Interstices: Southeast Asian Historians and Postnational Histories in Southeast Asia", in *New Terrains in Southeast Asian History*, ed. A. T. Ahmad and Tan L. E. (Athens, OH: Ohio University Press, 2003), pp. 3–29.
4. Ibid., p. 11.
5. See A. Kahin, *Rebellion to Integration: West Sumatra and the Indonesian Polity* (Amsterdam: University of Amsterdam Press, 1999) and I. Amal, *Regional and Central Government in Indonesian Politics* (Yogyakarta: Gadjah Mada University Press, 1992) for tensions between regional governments and the central government. M. Malley, "Regions: Centralization and Resistance", in *Indonesia beyond Suharto: Polity, Economy, Society, Transition*, ed. D. K. Emmerson (Armonk: M. E. Sharpe with the Asia Society, 1999), pp. 71–105, presents a good overview of the relations between the central government and regions during the New Order period.
6. R. McGibbon, *Secessionist Challenges in Aceh and Papua: Is Special Autonomy the Solution?*, Policy Studies no. 10 (Washington, D. C.: East-West Centre, 2004); A. Sumule, "Swimming against the Current: The Drafting of the Special Autonomy Bill for the Province of Papua and its Passage through the National Parliament of Indonesia", *Journal of Pacific History* 38, 3 (2003): 353–69.
7. See A. L. Tsing, *In the Realm of the Diamond Queen: Marginality in an Out-of-the-Way Place* (Princeton: Princeton University Press, 1993), M. M. Steedly, *Hanging without a Rope: Narrative Experience in Colonial and Postcolonial Karoland* (Princeton: Princeton University Press, 1993), and R. S. Kipp, *Dissociated Identities: Ethnicity, Religion, and Class in an Indonesian Society* (Ann Arbor: University of Michigan Press, 1993) for ethnographic accounts of national integration and identity in the outer islands of Indonesia.
8. F. Benda-Beckmann and K. Benda-Beckmann, "Recreating the Nagari: Decentralisation in West Sumatra", Max Planck Institute for Social Anthropology Working Paper no. 31, 2002, <http://www.eth.mpg.de/pubs/wps/pdf/mpi-eth-working-paper-0031.pdf>.
9. M. Sakai and E. Morrel, "Reconfiguring Regions and Challenging the State? New Socio-economic Partnerships in the Outer Islands of Indonesia", in *Asia Reconstructed: Proceedings of the 16th Biennial Conference of the ASAA, 2006*, ed. A. Vickers and M. Hanlon (Canberra: ASAA and Research School of Pacific and Asian Studies, Australian National University [ANU], 2006).
10. E. Aspinall and G. Fealy, eds., *Local Power and Politics in Indonesia: Decentralisation and Democratisation* (Singapore: Institute of Southeast Asian Studies [ISEAS], 2003); M. Erb, P. Sulistiyanto and C. Faucher, eds., *Regionalism*

in Post-Suharto Indonesia (London and New York: RoutledgeCurzon, 2005); D. Kingsbury and H. Aveling, eds., *Autonomy and Disintegration in Indonesia* (London: RoutledgeCurzon, 2003); H. Schulte Nordholt and G. van Klinken, eds., *Renegotiating Boundaries: Local Politics in Post Soeharto Indonesia* (Leiden: KITLV Press, 2007); R. H. McLeod and A. J. MacIntyre, eds., *Indonesia: Democracy and the Promise of Good Governance*, Singapore: ISEAS, 2007); and M. Sakai, ed., *Beyond Jakarta: Regional Autonomy and Local Societies in Indonesia* (Adelaide: Crawford House, 2002).

11. A. Hurrell, "Regionalism in Theoretical Perspective", in *Regionalism in World Politics: Regional Organization and International Order*, ed. L. Fawcett and A. Hurrell (Oxford: Oxford University Press, 1995), pp. 37–73.

12. As noted earlier, these peripheries were at the centre of the post-Suharto political debates around regional political autonomy and decentralisation.

13. For example, A. Rosser, "Escaping the Resource Curse: The Case of Indonesia", *Journal of Contemporary Asia* 37, 1 (2007): 38–58; M. Z. Tadjoedin, "A Future Resource Curse in Indonesia: The Political Economy of Natural Resources, Conflict and Development", CRISE Working Paper no. 35, Oxford: Oxford University, 2007.

14. See R. Auty, *Sustaining Development in the Mineral Economies: The Resource Curse Thesis* (London: Routledge, 1993); J. Sachs and A. Warner, "The Curse of Natural Resources", *European Economic Review* 45 (2001): 827–38.

15. P. Collier, "Economic Causes of Civil Conflict and their Implications for Policy", World Bank, 15 June (2000); M. Ross, "The Political Economy of the Resource Curse", *World Politics* 51, 2 (1999): 297–322.

16. P. Collier and A. Hoeffler, "Greed and Grievance in Civil War", *Oxford Economic Papers* 56, 4 (2004): 563–95.

17. See G. Banks, "Linking Resources and Conflict the Melanesian Way", *Pacific Economic Bulletin* 20, 1 (2005): 117–23; L. Horowitz, "Daily, Immediate Conflicts: An Analysis of Villager's Arguments about a Multinational Nickel Mining Project in New Caledonia", *Oceania* 73 (2002): 35–55; R. Hayter, T. J. Barnes and M. J. Bradshaw, "Relocating Resource Peripheries to the Core of Economic Geography's Theorizing: Rationale and Agenda", *Area* 35, 1 (2003): 15–23.

18. See also L. Visser, "Remaining Poor on Natural Riches? The Fallacy of Community Development in Irian Jaya/Papua", *Asia Pacific Journal of Anthropology* 2, 2 (2001): 68–88.

19. C. Ballard, "Citizens and Landowners: The Contest over Land and Mineral Resources in Eastern Indonesia and Papua New Guinea", in *Mining and Mineral Resource Policy Issues in Asia Pacific: Prospects for the 21st Century*, ed. D. Denoon *et al.* (Canberra: ANU, 1997), pp. 76–81.

CHAPTER 1

State, Region and the Politics of Recognition: Towards Cosmopolitan Models of Political Integration

Joel S. Kahn

[T]here is a value system that cannot be compromised, and that is the values that we praise. And if the values are good enough for our people, they ought to be good enough for others, not in a way to impose because they are God-given values. They aren't United States created values. These are values of freedom and the human condition and mothers loving their children.[1]

If we may believe the current *communis opinio* in political philosophy and sociology, the liberal nation-state as we know it is rapidly becoming an endangered species. While not yet extinct, it is at least in decline or seriously challenged. Two broad processes have been identified as driving this development.... First, the nation-state's position as the predominant unit of social organization is eroded from the outside by the gathering forces of globalisation and the shift of the locus of power from the national to the supra- and transnational levels. Second, the nation state's legitimacy, authority and integrative capacities are also weakened from within by the increasing pluralisation of modern societies, while the liberal, universalist values that undergird it are challenged by claims for special group rights (or exemptions from duties) by a multitude of groups emphasizing their cultural difference from the rest of society. The normative evaluation of these—real or supposed—trends differs widely. Some explicitly welcome them as opportunities on the road to a postnational, multicultural utopia, others envisage a nightmare of social disintegration, 'balkanization', and intercultural conflict.[2]

Regionalism: An Indonesian Dilemma?

For a large number of observers both inside and outside Indonesia, that nation's chief dilemma lies in how it should go about "managing" the fallout from an often fiercely contested, and in some circumstances extremely dangerous, regional politics. There is a large and growing body of analysis of the regional conflicts that have marked the period of transition to a post-New Order state. Indeed, a number of the chapters in this volume, by offering detailed analyses of particular instances of regional conflict and violence, contribute significantly to our understanding of the magnitude of Indonesia's regional dilemma.

The themes of recent analysis range from detailed documentation to more reflective writing, covering the situation both in internationally known hot spots such as Aceh, Papua, Maluku (the Moluccas) and Kalimantan (Indonesian Borneo), to regions less well known to outsiders.[3] This literature has focused on a variety of questions and themes. What are the causes of the apparent resurgence of regional loyalties and conflicts given the by now rather long history of apparently successful Indonesian nation-building? Why does "regionalism" sometimes lead to conflict and deadly violence? Are the underlying causes of regionalism really geographically or spatially determined, as the term implies? Or is regional conflict at base about something else? Are regional conflicts easily reducible to differential access to resources? Or, given that regional sentiment so often seems to crystallise around differences of religion and culture, should they instead be explained in terms of an intensified politics of recognition in the Indonesian context?[4]

What about the transnational dimensions of identity formation? Are they new? And how should we evaluate them? In the aftermath of the Bali and Jakarta bombings, what is the likelihood that regional conflicts in Indonesia will become entangled in global ones, particularly the evolving clash between "Islam" and "the West"?

Finally, can "good governance" be achieved in Indonesia in such a way as to further democratisation and the spread of basic human rights, reduce the level of violence, prevent Indonesian conflicts from themselves becoming further entangled in global ones without sacrificing the cosmopolitan possibilities inherent in translocalism? Are the current policies of the post-New Order state effective ways of mitigating violence? Or are they perhaps to some extent even implicated in it? In other words, should we not have expected that the emergence of a modern liberal state committed to reform, openness, democracy, and the accompanying commitment to human rights, regional autonomy and the rights of indigenous peoples in the regions—all of which were rather brutally suppressed in the Suharto era—would in fact have led to a reduction in the levels of regionally-based violence?

At one level each of Indonesia's regional conflicts is a product of unique circumstances, and hence each of these questions might well be answered differently depending on the circumstances. In Maluku, for example, the origins of conflict appear to lie in a perception on the part of indigenous Christian elites that Muslims were displacing them in local and regional government. This in turn drew local contests between Christians and Muslims into a broader "translocal" conflict in which Islamic movements, often based in Java, were drawn into what they took to be a defense of the rights of local Muslims. Here then religious identity has been the central issue, while the grounds of conflict were the contest for political office. In Kalimantan, violence seems to have broken out as a consequence of indigenous Dayak resentment of the greater commercial success of immigrant groups, and more generally of what they perceive to be the pillage of their land and resources by outsiders. But it is not all immigrants, or even all Muslim immigrants, who have been the target, but instead a particular group of Muslim immigrants from Madura. Hence while Maluku may appear to be the site of a clash of religions, Kalimantan seems instead to have witnessed the outbreak of an identity politics that is more ethnically based. And in the former the stakes are political office, while in the latter they are more purely economic.

The situation in Aceh is different again. Here there was a clash between vying nationalist visions, one Indonesia-wide, the other premised on an alternative, Acehnese, nation. The stakes here were control of a sovereign state apparatus, control that would also deliver not so much ownership of local resources, but the revenues that flow to the state from foreign-owned extractive industries.

The analyses of and debates over the nature, causes and implications of particular regional conflicts in Indonesia must therefore engage with a diversity of unique political, economic, historical, geographical and cultural circumstances. And in each case extralocal as well as local factors came into play, raising questions even about whether "regional" adequately describes what is going on here. Nonetheless, such conflicts when taken cumulatively have led some to ask whether Indonesia is in fact on the path to becoming a "failed state" incapable of ensuring the integrity of the nation, at least in the form it took when Indonesians achieved their independence from their colonial rulers, with all that this may imply for regional, indeed global, peace and security.

Given that questions about the integrity of the Indonesian nation, and the capacity of the post-Suharto state to maintain it, are increasingly in the air, there is some value in taking a step back from the specific circumstances of individual outbreaks of violence that have marked the recent history of Indonesia to examine the phenomenon of "national integration" more broadly. When this is done it becomes evident that at least ostensibly similar processes have marked transitional phases in the history of modern nation-states in other places and times and that, as the quote from Koopmans and Statham at the start of this chapter suggests, recent challenges to such integration are by no means unique to Indonesia. Indeed the life of all modern nations appears to have been marked by contests over what it is that generates the integrity of the modern nation, the glue that holds together its diverse and potentially competing classes, cultures and communal groups, and even over whether the nation-state in general has a future in a world increasingly characterised by universalising globalisation on the one hand and particularistic identity politics on the other. Far from such conflicts being exceptional, then, it may be that the modern nation-state has always been and is now everywhere a contested entity, even in the supposed heartlands of political modernity. One analyst has gone so far as to suggest that:

> The only plausible conclusion to be drawn today is that even in modern Europe the nation-state is nothing but a theoretical scheme, even an invention.... It is apparent that the doctrine of the nation-state, even when it is related to the concept of the political nation, can only temporarily hold together internal social and political fissures—fissures that result partly from historical coincidence and the deliberate, forcible integration which normally characterized the birth of the state. Sooner or later comes the backlash.[5]

Are the processes in Indonesia most often described as "regional", entirely unique or, when taken together, unique to Indonesia? Are they rather a manifestation of a fatal weakness in particular kinds of nation-state entities and/or particular projects of national integration? Are they endemic to the nation-states of the region, or globally in the current historical conjuncture? Indeed, are such conflicts manifestations of deep flaws within the modern nation-state *tout court*? And is "regionalism", with its underlying assumption about some necessary connection between state, nation and territory an adequate means of characterizing the main faultiness within the Indonesian nation?

Questions such as these suggest that there may be some value in attempting a kind of broader contextualisation of both the diversity of "regional" conflicts in Indonesia and the analyses that have been offered of them within broader historical trends and more general debates over the phenomena of nationalism and postnationalism. This chapter attempts such a contextualisation by focusing specifically on the idea of national integration and of challenges to it. It does so in part by locating the phenomenon within the broader region of which the territory of modern Indonesia forms a part, and by examining the Indonesian case in the context of broader issues and debates over the formation, and future, of modern nation-states. Of particular interest here is the relevance of comparisons with the histories of nationalism and state formation not just in northwestern Europe (so often used as the yardstick against which "third world" states are measured, and found wanting) but in other post-imperial formations in places like southern, central and eastern Europe and the Middle East. In what follows I want to pursue this goal of contextualising regional conflict in Indonesia by problematising the issue of nation-building, and more specifically, through a critical examination of the fairly widespread assumption that the best antidote to "tribalisation"—of which Indonesia's regional conflicts appear to be a particular type—is to pursue nation-building projects that are culturally neutral, that is, based on universal principles of national integration.

Rediscovering Universalism: "Civic Nationalism"

As the quotation from George W. Bush with which I began suggests, there is a growing body of opinion that universalistic and universalising modes of political integration are the best means of combating the "tribalism" that has characterised all levels of politics—regional, national and global—in recent decades.

It is important to note that this discovery of the merits of political universalism is not restricted to intellectuals and politicians of the political "right". Although there are obvious differences between the views of the American political elite and those of both liberals and Marxists, in certain fundamental respects they all share a commitment at least to the possibility of universal values in general, and the need for discourses and practices of political integration that are in some sense neutral to differences of culture, religion, gender, and sexuality, in particular.

It is equally important to understand that this dedication to modern universalism, while it may be a response to historically particular political and intellectual circumstances—the collapse of the Soviet empire and the re-emergence of nationalism in the former Eastern bloc, the perceived "excesses" of multiculturalism and identity politics in the United States, the flow of "new immigrants" into Western Europe and the rise of "cultural racism", the emergence of what Huntington called a "clash of civilisations" on a global scale, together with the frustration of many intellectuals with what they take to be the theoretical excesses of postcolonial and multicultural theory in the humanities and social sciences—is better understood as a re-discovery of universalising trends and tendencies from earlier periods of modern political and intellectual history.[6]

In one sense these debates are long-standing. Certainly they go back to the founding of both the American and French republics, and their origins may well lie in earlier liberal, or even imperial traditions. But a more recent time when attachment to universalistic modes of political integration appeared to achieve something like global reach is the period after the Second World War, when the majority of liberal intellectuals and, more importantly, liberal and/or westernised political elites in both the West and the former colonial world, generally assumed that the building of successful modern communities—national or otherwise—depended on establishing genuinely universal group loyalties and institutions that treated all citizens equally regardless of religion, race and cultural/ethnic affiliation. To pursue the alternative—to base the modern polity, corporation or local community on so-called primordial ties and the institutional traditions of particular cultural or religious groups, or to grant rights on the basis of membership of particular groups—would be to set off on a road to fragmentation, conflict, instability, stagnation and even communal violence.

In what has come to be recognised as a classic expression of the problem of nation-building for the newly independent states of Africa, Asia and the Middle East, the anthropologist Clifford Geertz wrote of the "crystallization of a direct conflict between primordial and civil sentiments". The problem posed by the co-presence within the nation of these competing loyalties, Geertz argued, was that they were "of the same general level" that is they were "on the same level of integration". They therefore "threaten to undermine the nation itself" because they "involve alternative definitions of what the nation is, of what its scope of reference is". Primordial political discontent, wrote Geertz, "wants not just Sukarno's or Nehru's or Moulay Hasan's head, it wants Indonesia's or India's or Morocco's".[7] The challenge faced by newly independent states seeking to bring their peoples into a world marked by economic growth, political modernisation and social stability, according to Geertz, was to find a way of superimposing an "unfamiliar civil state, born yesterday from the meager remains of an exhaustive colonial regime" upon the "fine-spun and lovingly preserved texture of pride and suspicion and…somehow contrive to weave it into the fabric of modern politics".[8] This process Geertz termed the "integrative revolution".

Various terms have been used to describe the implicit distinction between "good" and "bad" forms of political integration at work here[9]: civic, liberal, republican, patriotic, universalist, French on the one hand versus organicist, ethnic, nationalist, primordial, particularist, German on the other.[10] Most such observers have agreed that particularistic or ethnically based nationalist projects were precisely what had brought Europe to the brink of catastrophe, and that they would in all likelihood have the same results in the former colonies. It was therefore incumbent upon modern states everywhere to rededicate themselves to classical "civic" models of nation-building. It is significant in this regard that most Marxist intellectuals, and political elites in socialist states, shared with their liberal counterparts an attachment to universalistic models of social integration, although here obviously it was communism that provided the basis for a universalising, culturally neutral, discourse and polity.

There are two significant ways in which Indonesia is a case in point. First, there is a strong sense in which both the dominant trends within the movement for national liberation and the various post-independence governing elites in Indonesia have dedicated themselves to universalistic principles of national integration. Second, there is a strong perception on the part commentators on and observers of the Indonesian political scene, that when this has not been the case—when the state has abandoned its commitment to universalism and religio-cultural neutrality for particularistic goals (usually those derived from the cultural presuppositions of the dominant, Javanese, ethnic group)—that this has been responsible for the variety of forms of conflict, fragmentation and violence of which events of post-1998 are a part.[11]

The more recent dedication to universalistic forms of political integration on the part of George W. Bush and his circle of advisors then takes up and modifies many of these earlier assumptions about the causes of political conflict and violence within nation-states, and the best means of preventing or overcoming them.

Is the problem of Indonesian regionalism, and the challenge that it poses to national integrity, and now increasingly also global security, to be understood in terms of the failure of the Indonesian state to reject all forms of religio-cultural particularism, and to engage in practices and policies that are truly informed by universalistic principles of good governance? More generally, is the history of modern state formation and nation-building—a history of both "successes" and "failures"—best understood in terms of this divide between universalism and particularism? Should we be persuaded by the arguments from either "left" or "right" that in some kind of universalism lies the answer to successful political integration at the local/regional, national or even global level?

It is certainly not my intention here to reject the quest for universal models of political integration out of hand. Instead, my more general aim is to argue for the possibility of alternatives to current understandings of political universalism. But to see that there are alternatives, we need to problematise existing visions of universalistic political integration by pointing to a number of difficulties in at least some of their presuppositions. Specifically, I want to look more closely at:

- The issue of the "content" of the nation, and especially the assumption that particularistic nationalism has always been reactionary or retrograde.
- The issue of ethnicity, and the assumption that ethnic challenges to nationhood are invariably particularistic.
- The presumption that culturally neutral forms of national integration are desirable or even possible.

The Content of the Nation

Contrary to what many advocates of civic forms of nation-building seem to believe, it appears to have been the homogeneity of the nation that constituted the central problematic not just for "reactionary forces" but for intellectuals, political activists and elites sympathetic to projects of national emancipation, particularly in Europe after the French Revolution.

National particularity and homogeneity therefore constitute a bedrock of the classical problematic of modern nationalism:

> For a nationalist, the nation without a state is incomplete; so is the state without a nation. Thus the aim of all national movements since the early nineteenth century has been to establish a nation-state, expressing the idea both of individual self-determination and of the sovereignty of the people. From the point of view of the national movements, the nation-state alone embodied progress, modernity, and a break with the *ancien régime*.[12]

A key presupposition of modern nationalism is that the modern state in some sense represents the will of the people, and that it does so precisely because it, and its functionaries, are of the people. The centrality of a concern for the content of the nation, and in particular that the nation should be racially/culturally homogeneous, therefore constitutes to one degree or another the problematic of all modern nationalisms, including emancipatory nationalisms, since these presume that freedom and equality are only possible when they can be guaranteed by a sovereign nation-state within which the functionaries of the state are truly representative of the people. And to be representative, they have to be of the same "nationality" as the populace. Only in this way can they truly be seen to represent the will of the people for emancipation. Typically, emancipatory nationalism posits an intimate relation between the uniqueness of the culture of their nations and universal emancipatory objectives by linking the two. The argument here is that some set of cultural values and predispositions provides the best vehicle for instilling democratic values more broadly. The centrality of a concern for the content of the nation, and in particular that the nation should be racially/culturally homogeneous, therefore, constituted the problematic not just for reactionary/counter-modernist nationalism.

Anticolonial liberation movements, almost by definition, were informed by such assumptions about national homogeneity. For merely to aspire to liberation from colonial rule presupposed that there existed a radical racial and/or cultural distinction between ruler and ruled in the colonial context.[13] Whatever universal aims they might therefore have had—such as sovereignty and democracy—anticolonial struggles aimed precisely to replace racially or culturally-alien rulers with indigenous ones. And they did this because it was presumed that only when the holders of state power share in a common indigenous/non-Western "culture" with the people could the state represent the emancipatory aspirations of the people.

Of course, with the benefit of hindsight, we can see just how potentially problematic such assumptions of racial or cultural homogeneity in fact were—hence leading us almost inevitably now to see the nation, particularly the nation in former colonies, as an invented, constructed, or in Anderson's felicitous terms, an "imagined" community. We can with hindsight more easily see how the "problem" of the modern Indonesian nation-state, for example, is precisely the problem of how to create a modern state that represents the will of the people, when the "people" are not in fact homogeneous but diverse—hence the contradiction that, while it may be especially acutely felt in places like Indonesia, turns out to be endemic to the whole system of nation-states where homogeneity is only ever an ideal, never an established fact.

Nonetheless, as the history of democratic/emancipatory nationalisms clearly shows, a commitment to national particularism does not inevitably bring forth counter-modern reaction, racial exclusion or a history of "ethnic cleansing", as advocates of culturally-neutral discourses and practices of nation-building seem to believe.

An Ethnic Challenge to Modern Nationhood?

This leads us to question the assumption that the most significant challenge to national integration stems from the essential artificiality of particular nations when they have been imposed on top of a real diversity of cultures and languages. Such is the view of many who presume that nation-states are bound to fail either when the nation is culturally diverse or when dominant ethnic groups govern culturally diverse nations. In Indonesia, in particular, there are those who would attribute the current fragmentation to the coming to the surface of older cultural "faultlines"—Dayak in Kalimantan, Acehnese in northern Sumatra, Papuan in Irian, etc.[14] From this perspective the current crisis in Indonesian national integration is seen to be the inevitable result of this central problem of Indonesian nationalism.

There are, however, significant difficulties with the view that certain states, including Indonesia's, are weak or flawed because of the artificiality of the nation, in contrast to the diversity of its constituent *ethnie*. Many have pointed to the flaws in "primordial" visions of cultural identity on which this way of problematising Indonesian nationalism is based. Recent critiques of "cultural essentialism" suggest that national communities, if they are indeed imagined, are no more imaginary than are other forms of community that presume some degree of cultural homogeneity. After all, contemporary Malaysia is not beset by cultural conflicts between Malays, Javanese, Sumatrans, eastern Indonesians and the like. Here a similar cultural mix of indigenous and immigrant peoples who, at least before they were divided by the territorial boundaries of the British and Dutch colonial empires, formed part of a single, if internally highly diverse, culture area in (pen)insular Southeast Asia, solidified into a single racial/ethnic block known as the Malays, suggesting that the separate regional cultural identities surfacing in Indonesia are not doing so because of objective primordial cultural divisions.

Indeed it can be argued that those cultural and religious groups implicated in the various regional conflicts, are themselves also imagined, and in many cases imagined rather recently.[15] Some analysts have contended that the "multicultural" model of Indonesian diversity is a product of New Order forms of governance,[16] while studies of the colonial period actually suggest that a number of current cultural and religious "communities" were actually constituted during the colonial period, making "ethnicity" and "nationalism" in Indonesia contemporary, rather than historically-sequenced developments.[17] This is all the more true when we see that the political aspirations of many of Indonesia's cultural and religious minorities are no less universal than those of the state.

Indonesia's regional dilemma cannot, therefore, be explained merely by referring to the presence within the nation of a diversity of religious and cultural groups pursuing purely particularistic cultural agendas. It would be more plausible to suggest that the "tribalisation" of Indonesia into what often appear to be warring religious and cultural "communities" is a precipitate of modern state and nation-building projects rather than being an adequate characterisation of patterns of religio-cultural diversity in the precolonial period. At the very least, it can be argued that Indonesia's current politics of cultural and religious recognition are contemporaneous with the development of an Indonesian national imaginary—in no meaningful sense do they precede it—and, moreover, that they are as likely as nationalism to use a language of universal rights (if only of the universal right to cultural or religious recognition).

The Presumption of Cultural Neutrality

This leads to a consideration of the difficulties with the idea of a pure form of national integration that underpins appeals to the superiority of "civic" nationalism. As we have seen, many analysts of modern nationalism have made distinctions between civic and ethnic forms of national integration, arguing that the former, because they are neutral with respect to cultural and religious difference, are more inclusive, and hence less likely to generate a politics of recognition on the part of excluded and marginalised groups.[18]

The legitimacy of this project of building a modern universalist state on contractual as opposed to primordial ties can, however, be questioned. Central to such a questioning is the conviction that the key polarities on which the case for the integrative revolution rested were in fact false ones, and that both civic and primordial/ethnic models of integration were equally implicated in the development of homogenising beliefs and practices that, by suppressing diversity, were equally detrimental to social integration in the long run.

The sociologist John Hall expresses this sensibility in the following terms:

> Ethnic nationalism's search for social homogeneity scarcely looks liberal. [Yet p]urportedly morally superior civil nationalism, where choice replaces blood so as at least to allow the possibility of integration, may well be no better: French revolutionary nationalism brutally assailed minorities, with the rigidity of that republican tradition leading to an on-going contemporary crisis caused merely by the wearing of scarves in school. Must we agree about everything? Or is it possible to imagine a civil nationalism, allowing for the recognition of diversity within a more neutral frame?[19]

While still holding out the possibility of more "neutral" forms of nationalism, this nonetheless suggests that what must be subjected to critical scrutiny is the distinction between existing contractual (culture-free) patriotisms and primordial loyalties—between universalist and particularist institutions—and whether such a distinction can be upheld in theory or in practice. If not, is the homogenising project of "civic" nation-building any less problematic than classical modern nationalism? The ways in which George W. Bush elides universal and American values in the quote with which I began points to the difficulty in drawing a line between the universal and the particular.

More sympathetic than some recent critics of the differentiation of civic and ethnic nationalisms, Aviel Roshwald has nonetheless found it difficult to make hard and fast distinctions between the nationalisms of eastern and central Europe and the Middle East in the early years of the twentieth century on these grounds, suggesting instead that:

It is my sense that more interesting questions can be posed about the nature and evolution of nationalist ideologies if one thinks of ethnic and civic elements as cohabiting uneasily and competing, with one another within any given construction of national identity.[20]

With knowledge of the possibility of such entanglements of civic and ethnic elements in mind, it is interesting to note how even the most "progressive" of nationalists could not avoid thinking in particularistic ways:

> [M]any nationalist intelligentsias were deeply divided over how to balance and integrate the civic and ethnic dimensions of collective identity. Masaryk's realists, the Yugoslav activists, the PPS, the liberal wing of the CUP, among others, all emphasized shared political values as cardinal attributes of national community. The leadership of each of these movements regarded its own ethnic group's culture, and language (Czech, Croatian, Polish, Turkish) as a medium for the dissemination of progressive, universal values among the population of the ethnic group itself as well as among culturally, linguistically, and/or historically related nationalities (Slovaks, Serbs, Ukrainians, Kurds and Arabs, respectively). The articulators of these programs tended to be blind to the discriminatory potential or cultural-imperialist implications of their own ostensibly tolerant and egalitarian philosophies.[21]

There are in fact good reasons why such a distinction is difficult to uphold, particularly in practice. In this regard we would do well to take note of the critique offered of universalising modernist discourse as a whole by the sociologist Peter Wagner. Taking issue with those who see in America the manifestations of a purer form of modern life than that which operates in the "Old World", Wagner makes a telling critique of all such universalising projects. The treatment of America as the terrain of modernity "uncontaminated" by history and tradition, leads to a judgement of America as superior to Europe in a technical-economic and socio-political sense, but at the same time as inferior in a moral and philosophical sense.

Wagner's focus on America is important to our theme in a number of ways, not least because, as our opening quote from Bush suggests, America is currently the source of the most authoritative (by dint of its military power) version of the case for universal values. But here I am especially concerned with the way Wagner exposes the critical flaw thrown up by such an encounter with America. Wagner writes that all such approaches

> have in common a double intellectual move. They first withdraw from the treacherous wealth of sensations that come from the socio-historical world to establish what they hold to be those very few

indubitable assumptions from which theorizing can safely proceed. And subsequently, they reconstruct an entire world from these very few assumptions. Their proponents tend to think that the first move *decontaminates understanding*, any arbitrary and contingent aspects being removed. And that the second move creates a *pure image* of the world, of scientific and/or philosophical validity from which then further conclusions, including practical ones, can be drawn. (Whatever dissonance there may be between sensations and this image will then be treated as the secondary problem of the relation between theory and empirical observation).[22]

But such an operation is bound to fail, Wagner argues, because concepts like autonomy and rationality, so central to the modernist interpretation of the world

> are never pure, or merely procedural and formal, never devoid of substance. As a consequence, they cannot mark any unquestionable beginning, and doubts can be raised about any world that is erected in their foundations, that is, about the consequent second move.[23]

We can see why this should be so by looking a little more closely at the very concept of universalism within the human and cultural sciences, since never is a discourse labelled universalistic fully inclusive of the human species in its entirety. Instead so-called universalism is inevitably grounded in an understanding of what it is that constitutes the human essence, whether conceived in religious, biological or terms, that almost from first principles must adjudge some human beings as somehow more fully or completely human than others. It would, for example, be an exceptional universalist who did not view children as at least not yet fully capable of exercising mature human reason, and hence deny them certain rights that their "human-ness" would otherwise entitle them to, such as freedom to cross busy roads without assistance. As this example suggests, to say that universalism is not genuinely inclusive of the whole of the human species is not necessarily to find it morally faulty. It is only to note that particular historical/cultural presuppositions will inevitably be called upon to account for, and act on the very real diversity of humanity. It is clearly this characteristic of so-called universalism that enables some forms of universalism at the same time to be racially exclusive, something that postcolonial and feminist theorists have clearly shown.[74]

If there can be no "pure" universalism, uncontaminated by history and culture, then it is not surprising that all formulations of civic nationalism as somehow culturally neutral can always be shown to be inflected by particularistic "ethnic" nationalism. The American tradition of "civic" discourse upon which George W. Bush draws is a clear case in point. It builds on a republican compromise among the range of Protestant sects that dominated the political life of the colonies—"universal" with respect to denomination, but clearly also particularist, and hence exclusivist with respect to others. Why else, for example, should those of broadly Protestant background have so universally constituted immigrants from southern and eastern Europe and Asia as "alien" from the end of the nineteenth century, if American republicanism was really neutral with respect to all humans regardless of culture and religion? Bush's rhetoric is an attempt to take us back to a time before liberalism American-style broadened out to become inclusive of Irish, Italian, Jewish, and Chinese Americans, to name those groups who were apparently found to be most alien by late nineteenth-century American republicans.[25]

This all suggests that the current (re)turn to "civic" models of community-building, whether national or otherwise, should best be understood as the renewal of a modernist project of abstraction or reification, the goal of which is to root out the influence of all cultural particularity. John Hall wonders whether there might be forms of national integration that are somehow more "neutral" than those currently pursued in places like France. Perhaps he, like all other advocates of a "civic" nationalism abstracted from all culture and history might better accept that real human beings are always also inevitably cultured beings, and that any project that seeks somehow to "disembed" them from their cultural milieux will inevitably be problematic at the very least.

Cosmopolitanism or Cosmopolitanisms

Are there alternative models of social and political integration that do not buy into the sterile, and one might suggest inevitably power-saturated discourses of cultural neutrality? In the last part of this chapter I want to explore the concept of cosmopolitanism, particularly as it has been revised in recent social and political theory, as one such possibility.[26]

Writing of the origins of Immanuel Kant's notion of cosmopolitan right (*ius cosmopoliticum*), Anthony Pagden shows how it took shape at a time when the long-standing western concept of civilising empires was under attack and in decline. Deriving from classical times, the project of empire had always been intimately connected with the project of exporting to the ruled the way of life—*civitas*—of the rulers. In Pagden's words:

Implicit in the European conviction that, with time, all the peoples of the world would become—and, indeed, *had* to become—Europeans was the claim that the peoples of the non-European world had an obligation to surrender a portion of their livelihood, and in most cases their political autonomy, in exchange for the inestimable goods which their conquerors had brought them.[27]

Kant's notion of a cosmopolitan order was probably the best known, and certainly most widely cited alternative, described by Pagden as "a confederated world-system ... divided by climate, culture and language, but united in its legal and political objectives...." Only such a system, Kant believed, "would be capable of ensuring world peace and of providing the necessary guarantees for the continuing future development of mankind".[28]

Laudable as it might be, what might the difficulties be in "reviving", and most importantly in implementing, Kant's cosmopolitan ideal two centuries after it was formulated? It must be noted at the outset that there will be fundamental objections to any suggestion of a return to Kantian ideals, objections sharpened in recent decades as a consequence of the pervasive impact of poststructuralism, feminism, multiculturalism and postcolonialism in the field of Kant studies just as elsewhere in the humanities and social sciences. We must acknowledge the force of Michel Foucault's argument, first sketched out in *The Order of Things* (1973), about the problematic nature of the conceptualisation of "man" on which the modern "human sciences" are based. Specifically the suggestion here is that Kant is unable to demonstrate the independence (to thought) of the category "humanity", which is nonetheless crucial to his whole project. Flowing from this is the contention that Kant's project is fatally flawed because of what can be called the exclusionary assumptions underpinning his concept of "man", namely that it is so heavily inflected by particular assumptions about the nature of mature human reason that it inevitably judges women, non-Europeans, and even the European masses as in some sense incompletely human (in short, Kant's racism, sexism and classism completely undermines the claim to universalism upon which his philosophical/anthropological system is based).[29]

The internationalisation of the nation-state system in the period of decolonisation doubtless changes the parameters of the problem, although it might be argued that these make the Kantian problematic more rather than less pertinent. Kant almost certainly failed to appreciate the depth of influence of cultural factors and cultural identities although he did take some such affiliations (national, but even subnational) as significant.[30] But neo-Kantians have attempted to rectify this by building on Kant's insights to examine the implications of the presence within the global system of what they call competing doctrines of the good embedded in what at least appear to be irreducibly different "cultures".[31]

It must also be recognised that what is sometimes rather loosely termed cultural globalisation has involved a progressive detachment of the links between "culture" and "territory"—phenomena that in Kant's time were firmly conjoined in emancipatory nationalism. Recent attempts to recover and revise classical understandings of a cosmopolitan political order now need to take account of the fact that, far more typically, identity politics are "deterritorialised", something that a global confederation of republics clearly does not address.[32]

But while such revisions of the Kantian paradigm can and have been advanced, at the risk of overgeneralising it can be argued that few recent defenders of a notion of a normative cosmopolitanism take seriously the proposition that any such concept will always be universalising and particularizing, and therefore inevitably inclusive and exclusionary, at the same time. Indeed, I would suggest that the late twentieth century advocates of a normative cosmopolitanism may be guiltier than was Kant himself of propagating racially and culturally-exclusionary categories of universal human reason. Perhaps because students of international jurisprudence and political theory—most of whom seem still to envisage the possibility of culturally neutral (and thereby truly universal) practices, institutions and values—dominate the debate, the current normative discourse on global governance may be serving to blind us to the possibility that culturally embedded forms of cosmopolitanism are already in existence outside, indeed even within, the so-called Western world.

In contrast to such normative forms of cosmopolitan discourse, in recent years the argument has been increasingly advanced that not only is there no necessary contradiction between cosmopolitan sensibilities on the one hand and ethnicity, cultural particularism and nationalism on the other, but that in fact cosmopolitan practice may always be "grounded" or "rooted" in the experiences of particular "ethnic" groups.[33] Take the case of the Minangkabau in West Sumatra. The Minangkabau are not especially exemplary in the ways they think about insiders and outsiders living in the territory of West Sumatra or outside it. West Sumatra certainly does not have a monocultural society, given the presence there of other ethnic and religious groups—Javanese, Chinese, Mentawaian, Batak, European (residents or agents of Western political and economic interests), Christians, etc.—about whom the Minangkabau are perhaps as apt as anyone else to voice "racist" sentiments. Moreover, Minangkabau constantly hold each other up to idealised standards of what it means to be Minangkabau and Muslim, and judge both others and each other lacking, thereby excluding at different times those who are seen not to conform to idealised notions of maleness and femaleness, as well as children and/or marginal social groups even in village society.

At the same time West Sumatra is relatively peaceful, relatively free of the sometimes-horrendous conflicts that beset other regions of Indonesia—such as Timor, West Papua, Aceh, Maluku—about which we hear a great deal more. (Given the reports in the West on Indonesian violence one might be forgiven for assuming that in this sense the region is not typical of the nation as a whole). This is, of course, not only the case for West Sumatra, but for many other regions of modern Indonesia. In spite of the many stories that find their way into the global media—and indeed these days into the anthropological discourse on Indonesia, which currently appears to share the world's fascination for suffering and death—in most parts of Indonesia a diversity of races, religions, etc., live side-by-side in relative harmony even as they may be "constantly offending one another".

Is this "relative peace" (a better term than Kant's idea of "perpetual peace" in such circumstances) the result of the imposition by the nation-state or external powers or international institutions of the "rule of law", the principles of good "global governance" based on republican principles? Hardly. Instead I would suggest that a certain cosmopolitanism governs the practices of localised individuals and institutions, everyday interactions between individuals and groups, popular cultural activities, forms of economic relations, and institutions of village government. In other words at the level of the "popular"[34] something like genuine cosmopolitan practice takes place, even though it may be "contaminated" by the particularities of time, place and culture.

Could one go further to argue that in instances where a breakdown of such cosmopolitan coalitions has taken place—in Aceh, West Papua, Kalimantan, Maluku—more often than not this has been precisely a result of the imposition from above (by the Indonesian state, outside powers and institutions) of disembedded, supposedly universal, culturally neutral forms of power, jurisprudence, and the like?

Taken together, these points lead to a view of cosmopolitanism that differs fundamentally from the one which sees it as an abstract, disembedded orientation to the world grounded in a naturally-given and hence universal human rationality that can only be operationalised through the mechanisms of audit. Instead it points to an embedded and pluralised cosmopolitanism, one that is not given in advance, but produced as an outcome of a project never to be finished; a cosmopolitanism of liberty rather than discipline.[35]

In a further contrast with received notions, cosmopolitan is no longer viewed as an identity standing above or outside all others, but instead refers to identities that are culturally specific and hence diverse, and at the same time outward reaching and relational. To quote Kant, the cosmopolitan emerges in groups

> existing successively and side by side, who cannot *do without* associating peacefully and yet cannot *avoid* constantly offending one another. Hence they feel destined by nature to [form]...a coalition in a *cosmopolitan* society...—a coalition which, though constantly threatened by dissension, makes progress on the whole.[36]

Now it becomes evident that all forms of cosmopolitan practice—practice that "cannot content itself with the study of what makes each people different but must be oriented from the start to what they have in common"[37]—inevitably begin with culturally inflected presuppositions about what it is that constitutes that common humanity. At the same time, in practice, cosmopolitan ideas will also inevitably generate notions of radical alterity, as those presuppositions come under the challenge of human diversity. Perhaps unchallenged, there is no reason for the cosmopolitan to revise his or her notion of human essence, no reason not to proceed with the assumption that diversity is evidence of "perversity" in one form or another—as evidence that the bearers of difference are either redeemably or irredeemably not, or not yet, fully capable of human reason.

Yet, precisely because all such universalist ideals are informed by particular, culturally inflected notions of human essence, they are not in principle immutable. There is no logical reason why they should take the form that they do. The question then becomes: how do such changes come about, how do exclusionary narratives become inclusive (while doubtless now in turn defining new exclusions)? It seems equally clear that the answer does not lie at the level of will. The resolution in other words is not a philosophical one. It will instead be shaped by existing power relations and embedded in particular conflicts that are at the same time over the authenticity of cultural representations and the right to represent, that is speak on behalf of, particular groups.

Conclusion

The search for cosmopolitan alternatives to both "ethnic" and "civic" forms of political integration may not perhaps strike observers of Indonesia's often violent "politics of recognition" as of any direct relevance to the day-to-day problems being experienced by people caught up in regional, and national, cycles of violence. But it does, I hope, serve as a warning that to rush to the judgement that Indonesia is any more a failed state than any other brings with it dangers, particularly in the current climate of global opinion within which intervention in the affairs of nation-states in the name of "universal values" is an all too real possibility. It may also serve as a warning to Indonesia itself, that a pretence to religious and cultural neutrality in the face of ongoing regional conflicts may not be the way to go, especially when the state is viewed, in many cases justifiably, as no abstract, neutral entity standing above and outside "civil society". Instead agents of the Indonesian state, including the Indonesian military, have always and inevitably been both partisan and involved in a diversity of ways in all the significant so-called regional conflicts from Aceh to Irian.

Finally, to those outside observers and analysts of the Indonesian scene who would question what might seem an overly theoretical approach to the problems of Indonesian regionalism, let me merely conclude with two observations. First, there is the ethical and methodological question that all outside analysts of a place like Indonesia need to ask themselves: and that is no matter how insightful their analysis, what is their point? What possible value or meaning can there be in apparently dispassionate—or even passionately committed—external analysis of the Indonesian situation? Part of the answer to this question, I believe, must involve both a reflexive consideration of the meaning of "academic" analysis and a means of situating one's own approach within the problem under analysis and not as some offstage reflection upon it. I see this elaboration of the concept of cosmopolitanism precisely as an attempt to deal with this issue.

A second reason to initiate a search for what one author has called "actually existing cosmopolitanisms"[38] in places like Indonesia is that it is not we alone, or even most importantly, who bring a cosmopolitan perspective to bear on Indonesian events and processes. The key question is how and under what circumstances might what might be called (misleadingly) "indigenous" cosmopolitan practices have developed in Indonesia itself, if only better to understand the circumstances under which these sometimes fail. Only in this way can we specify the underlying causes of regionalism in contemporary Indonesia, and thus predict the likelihood of either a fracturing of the nation-state or the closer integration of various social groups into the one nation.

Notes

I am particularly grateful to Clive Kessler, Ken Young and to the editors of this volume for comments and suggestions on an earlier draft of this chapter. I would also like to acknowledge La Trobe University and the Australian Research Council for their financial support of the research project on "Asia Pacific Cosmopolitanisms" out of which this chapter arises.

1. *The Age*, "US President George Bush in an Interview with Bob Woodward", 20 Aug. 2002, p. 12.
2. R. Koopmans and P. Statham, "Challenging the Liberal Nation State? Postnationalism, Multiculturalism and the Collective Claims of Migrants and Ethnic Minorities in Britain and Germany", *American Journal of Sociology* 105, 3 (1999): 652.
3. For a selection of such work see International Crisis Group (ICG), "Communal Violence in Indonesia: Lessons from Kalimantan", ICG Asia Report no. 18, 27 June 2001; N. L. Peluso and M. Watts, eds., *Violent Environments* (Ithaca: Cornell University Press, 2001); G. Acciaioli, "Grounds of Conflict, Idioms of Harmony", *Indonesia* 72 (2001): 81–113; C. Manning and P. V. Dierman, eds., *Indonesia in Transition: Social Aspects of Reformasi and Crisis* (Singapore: ISEAS, 2000); A. Smith, "Is Indonesia Breaking up?" *New Zealand International Review* 26, 5 (2001): 19; D. Kingsbury and H. Aveling, eds., *Autonomy and Disintegration in Indonesia* (London: Routledge Curzon, 2003); R. W. Hefner, ed., *The Politics of Multiculturalism: Pluralism and Citizenship in Malaysia, Singapore, and Indonesia* (Honolulu: University of Hawai'i Press, 2001); E. Aspinall and G. Fealy, eds., *Local Power and Politics in Indonesia: Decentralisation and Democratisation* (Singapore: ISEAS, 2003).
4. The use of the term derives from the work of the Canadian philosopher Charles Taylor. See, for example, C. Taylor, *Multiculturalism and "The Politics of Recognition": An Essay by Charles Taylor*, ed. A. Gutmann (Princeton: Princeton University Press, 1994).
5. See P. Alter, "The Rhetoric of the Nation-State and the Fall of Empires", in *The Habsburg Legacy: National Identity in Historical Perspective*, ed. R. Robertson and E. Timms (Edinburgh: Edinburgh University Press, 1994), p. 202.
6. I have made this argument about the rediscovery of modern universalism in more detail in J. S. Kahn, *Modernity and Exclusion* (London: Sage, 2001).

7. C. Geertz, "The Integrative Revolution: Primordial Sentiments and Civil Politics in the New States", in *The Interpretation of Cultures*, ed. C. Geertz (New York: Basic Books, 1973 [1963]), p. 261.
8. Ibid., pp. 268–9.
9. See further P. Chatterjee, *Nationalist Thought and the Colonial World* (London: Zed Books, 1986).
10. See further A. Appadurai, "Patriotism and its Futures", *Public Culture* 5, 3 (1993): 411–29; L. Dumont, *German Ideology: From France to Germany and Back* (Chicago: University of Chicago Press, 1994); J. Habermas, "Citizenship and National Identity: Some Reflections on the Future of Europe", in *The Nationalism Reader*, ed. O. Dalibour and M. R. Ishay (Atlantic Highlands: Humanities Press, 1995), to name a few.
11. See, for example, D. Bourchier, "Lineages of Organicist Political Thought in Indonesia", doctoral dissertation, Monash University, 1996; M. Pabotinggi, "Indonesia: Historicizing the New Order's Legitimacy Dilemma", in *Political Legitimacy in Southeast Asia: The Quest for Moral Authority*, ed. M. Alagappa (Stanford: Stanford University Press, 1995), pp. 224–56.
12. Alter, "Rhetoric of the Nation-State", pp. 197–8.
13. An example precisely of the ways in which colonial and anticolonial discourses were mutually constitutive.
14. The term "faultline" is used in this way in the Indonesian context by Vivienne Wee in her paper, "Political Fault-Lines in Indonesia: Atavistic Movements in Riau, Aceh and Beyond", presented at the panel on Political Fault-lines in Southeast Asia: Premodern Atavisms in post-Colonial Nation-States, Annual Meeting of the Association for Asian Studies, Chicago, 22–25 Mar. 2001.
15. The use of the category "Dayak" to mobilise the indigenous peoples of Borneo against immigrants from Madura, for example in the conflicts in Kalimantan relies on a discursive merging of a large number of "tribal" identities (and also the exclusion of others) that is of relatively recent origins (see M. Hawkins, this volume, and also Y. Maunati, "Contesting Dayak Identity: Commodification and the Cultural Politics of Identity in East Kalimantan", doctoral dissertation, La Trobe University, 2000).
16. See J. Pemberton, *On the Subject of 'Java'* (Ithaca: Cornell University Press, 1994); and Aspinall and Fealy, *Local Power and Politics*. I have argued that Indonesia's multicultural model of ethnic diversity has been the result of a fairly long-standing discursive strategy of 'culturalising' differences of wealth, status and power [see J. S. Kahn, "Culturalizing the Indonesian Uplands", in *Transforming the Indonesian Uplands: Marginality, Power and Production*, ed. T. Li (Amsterdam: Harwood, 1999), pp. 79–103].
17. For the case of the Minangkabau, see J. S. Kahn, *Constituting the Minangkabau: Peasants, Culture and Modernity in Colonial Indonesia* (Oxford: Berg, 1993); for a study of cultural and religious identity formation in colonial Sulawesi, see

A. Schrauwers, *Colonial "Reformation" in the Highlands of Central Sulawesi, Indonesia, 1892–1995* (Toronto: University of Toronto Press, 2000).

18. It is worth noting that there is a 'developmentalist' version of this paradigm, by which I mean the view of nation building as primarily about the 'development' of different sub national groups located on a temporal axis ranging from less to more 'developed'. The underlying assumption relevant to national integration, here, is that 'development', conceived as a universal, culturally neutral process, will ultimately result in a homogeneous nation when all groups share equally in development. The focus on development as a form of nation-building and national integration has clearly been prevalent in Indonesia, as well as elsewhere in (pen)insular Southeast Asia. For an analysis of developmentalist discourses in Malaysia, see Khoo K. J., "The Grand Vision: Mahathir and Modernisation", in *Fragmented Vision: Culture and Politics in Contemporary Malaysia*, ed. J. S. Kahn and Francis L. K. Wah (St. Leonard's: Allen & Unwin, 1992), pp. 44–76; for Singapore, see, for example, Chua B. H., *Communitarian Ideology and Democracy in Singapore* (London and New York: Routledge, 1995).
19. J. A. Hall, "How Homogeneous Need We Be? Reflections on Nationalism and Liberty", Review Essay, *Sociology* 30, 1 (1996): 163–71. An earlier critique of the pretence of cultural neutrality, and the exclusions generated by French republicanism is found in H. Lebovics, *True France: The Wars over Cultural Identity 1900–1945* (Ithaca: Cornell University Press, 1992).
20. A. Roshwald, *Ethnic Nationalism and the Fall of Empires: Central Europe, Russia and the Middle East, 1914–1923* (London: Routledge, 2001), p. 6.
21. Ibid., p. 68.
22. P. Wagner, "The Resistance that Modernity Constantly Provokes: Europe, America and Social Theory", *Thesis Eleven* 58 (1999): 43. Emphasis in original.
23. Ibid.
24. Uday Mehta, for example, demonstrates how nineteenth-century British liberals were able to conclude that Indians were not yet capable of mature human reason, hence justifying the postponement of the democratic rights to which they would otherwise have been entitled. See U. Mehta, "Liberal Strategies of Exclusion", in *Tensions of Empire: Colonial Cultures in a Bourgeois World*, ed. F. Cooper and A. L. Stoler (Berkeley: University of California Press, 1997), pp. 59–86. A somewhat similar argument has been made to demonstrate how Enlightenment political philosophy could be both universalist and patriarchal at the same time. See, for example, C. Pateman, *The Problem of Political Obligation: A Critique of Liberal Theory* (Cambridge: Polity Press, 1985).
25. A more detailed account of this critique of universalism in general, and the American republican variant of it in particular, is found in Kahn, *Modernity and Exclusion*.

26. See, for example, D. Held, *Democracy and the Global Order: from the Modern State to Cosmopolitan Governance* (Cambridge: Polity, 1995); M. Nussbaum, "Patriotism and Cosmopolitanism", in *For Love of Country: Debating the Limits of Patriotism*, ed. M. C. Nussbaum and J. Cohen (Cambridge, MA: Beacon Press, 1996), pp. 3–17, and the various contributors to S. Pollack *et al.*, "Cosmopolitanisms", *Public Culture* 12, 3 (2000); M. Featherstone *et al.* eds., "Special Issue on Cosmopolis", *Theory, Culture and Society* 19, 1–2 (2002); S. Vertovec and R. Cohen, eds., *Conceiving Cosmopolitanism: Theory, Context, and Practice* (Oxford: Oxford University Press, 2002).
27. A. Pagden, "The Genesis of 'Governance' and Enlightenment Conceptions of the Cosmopolitan World Order", *International Social Science Journal* 50, 155 (1998): 8.
28. Ibid.: 13.
29. For examples of such critiques, see S. Mendes, "An Honest but Narrow-Minded Bourgeois?", in H. Williams, ed., *Essays on Kant's Political Philosophy* (Chicago: University of Chicago Press, 1992); K. Waters, "Women in Kantian Ethics: A Failure of Universality", in *Modern Engendering*, ed. B.-A. Bar On (Albany: Suny Press, 1994); B. Hermann, "Could it be Worth Thinking about Kant on Sex and Marriage?", in *A Mind of Our Own*, ed. L. Anthony and C. Witt (Boulder: Westview, 1997); D. Harvey, "Cosmopolitanism and the Banality of Geographical Evils", *Public Culture* 12, 2 (2000): 529–64; and P. Melville, "Kant's Dinner Party: Anthropology from a Foucauldian Point of View", *Mosaic* 35, 2 (2002): 93–109.
30. Hill, for example, argues that Kant's views need to be modified, but without any essential refutation, by acknowledging that respect for someone as a human being includes respecting that what they value is partly a product of their being embedded in "intertwining networks of cultures and subcultures" as well as "cross-currents of contrary social influences". Kant's views clearly manifest an overemphasis on the autonomy of individuals that was characteristic of his times. Hill goes on to argue that as a modern Kantian one "should not overestimate the irresistibility of these cultural bonds by assuming that reflective persons can never see good reason to set aside a part of their heritage". See T. E. Hill Jr, *Respect, Pluralism, and Justice: Kantian Perspectives* (Oxford: Oxford University Press, 2000), p. 73.
31. I am thinking here particularly of the debate over the possibility of intercultural communication joined most notably by Rawls, Rorty, Habermas and others (see, for example, various contributions in R. Kearney and M. Dooley, *Questioning Ethics: Contemporary Debates in Philosophy* (London: Routledge, 1999).
32. For examples, see the chapters by Ulrich Beck, Stuart Hall and Rainer Bauböck in *Conceiving Cosmopolitanism: Theory, Context and Practice*, ed. S. Vertovec and R. Cohen (Oxford: Oxford University Press, 2002).

33. See, for example, K. A. Appiah, *Cosmopolitanism: Ethics in a World of Strangers* (New York: W. W. Norton, 2006); R. Fine, "Taking the 'Ism' out of Cosmopolitanism: An Essay in Reconstruction", *European Journal of Social Theory* 6, 4 (2003): 451–70: P. Werbner, "Global Pathways: Working Class Cosmopolitans and the Creation of Transnational Ethnic Worlds", *Journal of Ethnic and Migration Studies* 28, 1 (1999): 119–33; R. Werbner, "Cosmopolitan Ethnicity: Entrepreneurship and the Nation: Minority Elites in Botswana", *Journal of Southern African Studies* 28, 4 (2002): 731–53 and various contributors to *Anthropology and Cosmopolitanism: Rooted, Feminist, Demotic, and Vernacular Perspectives*, ed. P. Werbner (Oxford: Berg, 2008).
34. Popular is used here in a distinctive sense to distinguish this kind of practice from both 'exemplary' or 'high' modernism and so-called 'subaltern' consciousness on the other (see Kahn, *Modernity and Exclusion*). I am not therefore suggesting that intercommunal relations in West Sumatra are governed by 'traditional' institutions and practices, since such relations have emerged as part of modern processes of migration, global tourism, commodification, the rule of a modern state, etc.
35. This way of describing modernity is derived from Peter Wagner. See P. Wagner, *A Sociology of Modernity: Liberty and Discipline* (London: Routledge, 1994). A case has been made that Kant himself in his "pre-critical" phase actually came much closer to such an approach than is normally assumed. See the important study by J. H. Zammito, *Kant, Herder, and the Birth of Anthropology* (Chicago: University of Chicago Press, 2002). Although he is using the term "cosmopolis" in a different way, Toulmin makes a similar contrast between Renaissance and Enlightenment approaches to the "facts" of human diversity. See S. E. Toulmin, *Cosmopolis: The Hidden Agenda of Modernity* (New York: Free Press, 1990).
36. Kant, *Anthropology from a Pragmatic Point of View*, p. 191.
37. A. W. Wood, *Kant's Ethical Thought* (Cambridge: Cambridge University Press, 1999), p. 199.
38. The phrase comes from an unpublished paper by J. N. Brown, "Rooted in the Global, Routed through the Local: Cosmopolitanism in Liverpool's Age of Sail", presented at the Conference on Place, Locality and Globalisation, Center for Local, International and Regional Studies, University of California, Santa Cruz, 28 Oct. 2000.

CHAPTER 2

Patrimonialism and Feudalism in the *Sejarah Melayu* (Raffles MS 18)

J. H. Walker

From the introduction of Guided Democracy until the collapse of the New Order, Indonesian governments have strived to establish and maintain a strong centralised state to subsume the country's fissiparous local and regional identities. Equally, in Aceh, West Papua and East Timor, strong regional identities provided a source of political action which threatened and, in the case of East Timor, overcame centralised authority. As the range of chapters in this volume illustrates, however, the hegemonic pretensions of the Indonesian state have been subverted and negotiated by regional identities and loyalties in many ways short of demands for independence. Indeed, local and regional loyalties and identities have provided important, even essential, counterpoints to centrist states.

Hegemonic claims by the state, and attempts by populations to evade or resist such claims, have a long history in the archipelago. This study seeks to explore how both processes were expressed in Indonesia's more distant past. The subject of this study is the seventeenth-century Malay court text the *Sejarah Melayu*, or Malay Annals (Raffles MS 18).[1] Often analysed as asserting royal absolutism in precolonial Malay political culture, the text of the *SM* also represents the way in which centralised royal authority was challenged by the importance of regional and family-based identities, and royal responses to such challenges.

Although Winstedt considered that the Raffles 18 recension published by Brown was completed around 1536, scholars are now inclined to date its completion to 1612.[2] Intended as a central legitimising text for the Melaka-Johor rulers, forced from their capital a century earlier by the Portuguese, the *SM* was written "to vindicate a claim to greatness: of the dynasty, the Bendahara, and the realm as a whole; and, most importantly, to provide a mythically based, a truly sacral, code of political conduct by which this greatness could be retained or restored".[3] Although other texts also provide important insights into Malay conceptualisations of power and identity, few enjoy the *SM's* central place in Malay historical consciousness or match its sophistication and subtlety. Roolvink's identification of more than 20 versions collected in the archipelago both suggests that the *SM* enjoys an almost unrivalled status in the Malay world and testifies to its widespread prestige amongst precolonial Malays.[4]

Scholars have long emphasised the extent to which the *SM* is concerned to promote a totalising discourse of kingship, a discourse which stressed the authority of rulers and the obedience of subjects. P. E. de Josselin de Jong suggested in 1964 that the political ethic propounded by both the *SM* and a related text from a court on the northeast coast of Sumatra, the *Hikayat Raja Raja Pasai*, was "the subject's unquestioning loyalty and submission to his king, and his avoidance at all costs of the unforgivable sin of *derhaka*". For de Jong, Malay rulers were not constrained by any force within their realms. Pointing to the narratives in the *SM* concerning the fall of Singapore and of Melaka, de Jong argued that misrule or injustice by the ruler was avenged by forces from without the realm.[5] Similarly, Zainal Abidin proposed that Malay ideas about *daulat* (divine attributes of Malay kingship) and *derhaka* provided the conceptual keys to reading the *Sejarah Melayu*, writing of the Malay ruler that "*daulat* endows him with many rights and privileges, places him above his society, beyond reproach and criticism ... *daulat* also entails unquestioning loyalty from his subjects".[6]

Timothy Moy expanded this understanding, writing that the "Raffles MS 18 presents the reader with a pre 1612 concept of a monarchic, status society in which the ruler has absolute pre-eminence as focus of all social and political activity and loyalty".[7] In 1974, however, Walls struck a discordant note by suggesting that textual concerns with *derhaka* and loyalty in the *SM* were susceptible to more ambiguous readings than scholars had allowed. Walls noted that

> Over and over in the text Malay subjects speak of *derhaka* ... as if it were an unthinkable evil, something that rulers and subjects alike just naturally assume Malays never do because it is counter to their *"adat"*, their "custom", and would thus bring shame on them or their families. And yet at the same time they are being presented as virtually universally accepted principles of Malay society, one gets the impression that the text is in actuality seeking to establish them as such more than reflecting an already existing situation.[8]

In support of his argument, Walls pointed out that throughout the text views extolling loyalty "are defended; reasons are given why they should be observed; various arguments, some implicit and others explicit, set forth their basis and justifications".[9] Far from being assumed, the principle of unquestioned loyalty to the ruler, Walls suggested, was being propounded.

Walls did not pursue the implications of this insight, but a similar interpretation has more recently been offered by James Scott, who queried

> Why should the court chronicles take as one of their major themes the condemnation of treason? My assumption is that it was precisely because it was the key problem of Malay statecraft....the frequency with which *durhaka* was censored [sic: censured?] in the chronicles is an excellent indication of how frequently it actually jeopardised the survival of Malay kingdoms. It is a case of "Methinks the Lady doth protest too much...."[10]

Although treason is not the focus of this paper,[11] Walls's and Scott's arguments about *derhaka* raise broader questions concerning the precolonial Malay world, encouraging further exploration of the sources of power and identity in Malay society. If rulers were not unambiguous or unchallenged fonts of status, position, power and identity, what other sources and conceptualisations of loyalty and allegiance competed with them? If, as Anthony Reid argued, the "exalted rhetoric of Southeast Asian rulers was always in tension with the tenuousness of their power base",[12] what rival loyalties, identities and motivations did rulers have to overcome, absorb or accommodate?

Rhetoric of Melakan Kingship in the *Sejarah Melayu*

Zainal Abidin identified five sources of "supreme authority" for Melakan rulers: their claimed descent from Iskander Dzu'l-Karnain (Alexander the Great); their status under Islam as God's shadow on earth; *daulat*; their possession of the sacral, royal regalia of Melaka; and the compact between their progenitor, Sri Tri Buana, and Demang Lebar Daun.[13] Of these, I want here to explore the impact of the compact, which perhaps has been the most important of the five in the promulgation of royal absolutism.

On being sighted with his two brothers on Bukit Seguntang Mahameru, the Melakan progenitor, Sri Tri Buana, was recognised as descended from the world-ruler, Raja Islander Dzu'l-Karnain, and thus as a proper sovereign for Palembang. His arrival was sufficient to cause grain in the surrounding rice-fields to turn into gold, a sure sign of his *daulat*. So unambiguous were his claims to sovereign authority, that the ruler of Palembang, Demang Lebar Daun, abdicated, handing his city over to Sri Tri Buana, whom he then served as Prime Minister.

Although legitimising the dynasty through this reference to its magical and sacral origins might have underpinned absolutist claims to authority, the transfer of sovereignty from Demang Lebar Daun to Sri Tri Buana was achieved through a compact between the two. The compact, and the consequences of its being broken, are key themes in the narrative, central to debates about the nature of Malay royal authority. It is therefore worth discussing the episode at length. Demang Lebar Daun addressed Sri Tri Buana:

> Your Highness, the descendants of your humble servant shall be the subjects of your Majesty's throne, but they must be well treated by your descendants. If they offend, they shall not, however grave be their offence, be disgraced or reviled with evil words: if their offence is grave, let them be put to death, if that is in accordance with Mohammedan law.

To which Sri Tri Buana agreed, requesting of Demang Lebar Daun, "that your descendants shall never for the rest of time be disloyal to my descendants, even if my descendants oppress them and behave evilly". Demang Lebar Daun consented, but with an essential *proviso*. "Very well Your Highness. But if your descendants depart from the terms of the pact, then so will mine." To this, also, the king agreed, thus surely undoing his earlier attempt to preclude the imposition of such conditions.[14]

Although the compact is often cited as evidence of the absolute authority of Malay royalty, such interpretation depreciates the importance of Demang Lebar Daun's final proviso. An alternative reading of this episode might conclude that Demang Lebar Daun extracted the ruler's agreement to his subjects' repudiating their ruler if he were to break his oath to treat them justly. The annalist thus established an ambiguous claim for royal authority and preserved socially-constructed constraints on the arbitrary use of royal power. As Zainal Abidin observed, the contract "contradicts the popular assumption that the Sultan must be obeyed at all times, that he must be accorded a blind loyalty, and that any disobedience will be regarded as *derhaka*". Zainal Abidin suggested instead that the compact showed "that the authority of the Sultan prevailed to the extent that he exercised it fairly and in the interests of the people".[15]

Yet, having described the making of the compact so carefully, the annalist proceeded immediately to misrepresent it, ignoring the implications of that final concession extracted by Demang Lebar Daun.

> And that is why it has been granted by Almighty God to Malay rulers that they shall never put their subjects to shame, and that those subjects however gravely they offend shall never be bound or hanged or disgraced with evil words. If any ruler puts a single one of his subjects to shame, that shall be a sign that his kingdom will be destroyed by Almighty God. Similarly it has been granted by Almighty God to Malay subjects that they shall never be disloyal or treacherous to their rulers, even if their rulers behave evilly or inflict injustice upon them.[16]

Thus the annalist provided two versions of the compact, the second, absolutist version effectively undermining the original, social contract by making the ruler accountable not to his followers, but to God.

The annalist, himself, explored this ambiguity through the testamentary admonitions (*wasiat*) that were the subject of Walls's study. In royal admonitions to heirs, Walls found that the

> heirs are variously enjoined to refrain from coveting the goods and wives of their subjects and to live in concord with their brothers; to heed the counsel of their advisers, control their anger and their greed, and faithfully perform their religious duties; to cherish and forgive the offences of their subjects and to be concerned foremost with religious matters; to be diligent in religious matters, refrain from confiscating the goods of others, rule with justice, consult the ministers of state, and limit the death penalty only to those infractions for which it is mandatory in Muslim law.

As Walls observed, "what emerges is a reciprocity of obligations" between rulers and subjects.[17] Rulers who behave unjustly will be punished, but the source of their travail will be divine. Justice is not presented as a human construct, but elevated to God.[18]

Although this principle, which sought to make the ruler responsible to God rather than to his subjects, smacks of royal absolutism, the annalist seemed, again, to equivocate. Nobles might not oppose their ruler, but nor need they serve him. When Tun Perak was not appointed to high office, he withdrew from the court and established himself at Klang. Eventually the ruler, at the urging of the people of Klang, appointed Tun Perak to govern them. Still later, Tun Perak's success at Klang provoked the ruler to invite him back to court, "And taking sireh from his bowl he gave it to Tun Perak, saying, 'You are wasted at Klang, Tun Perak! You must come and live in the city'."[19]

The annalist seemed concerned that the implications of Tun Perak's career not be overlooked. In his *wasiat*, Tun Perak, by then entitled Bendahara Paduka Raja, urged his family to "do your duty to your Raja, forgetting not what the divines tell us, that a just prince is joined with the Prophet of God like two jewels in one ring. Moreover the Raja is as it were the deputy of God." These injunctions, which propound royal absolutism, are no sooner uttered, than subverted. Tun Perak turned to his sons,

> Tun Zainal "Abidin, if you fail to obtain office at court, go and dwell in the forest, for shoots and leaves make a good enough meal for a man with a small appetite!" And to Tun Pawah the Bendahara said, "Dwell not in the city, Pawah! Go dwell on some river reach that the scum which floats down the river may turn into gold for you". And then to Tun Isak he said, "Isak, seek not your livelihood in the Raja's audience hall!" Such were the last injunctions of Bendahara Paduka Raja to his family; not after the same fashion to all of them but as was appropriate to each.[20]

Although, as Walls suggested, the author might, in these episodes, be "referring to the general decline in the fortunes of the Sultanate after the fall of Malacca",[21] the effect of Tun Perak's career and *wasiat* is to undermine royal claims to absolutism. In these episodes, the ruler is neither the only source of identity and power, nor even the preeminent one. The course of Tun Perak's own career, rather than any compulsion to serve the ruler, is offered as a model for future conduct.

It is not just, as Tun Perak implies, that capable men will attract their own reward. It is important to note also the extent to which Tun Perak's removal from the court demonstrated the ruler's dependence on attracting talented officials or the support of powerful feudatories. Notwithstanding the rhetoric of royal absolutism, Malay rulers recognised the challenge of attracting (and maintaining the loyalty of) followers. Sultan Ala'u'd-din had cause to reflect in the *SM* that "subjects are like the roots and the ruler is like the tree'; without roots the tree cannot stand upright...."[22] Several hundred years later, Sultan Mahmud of Palembang told a Dutch official that it "is easy for a subject to find a lord, but it is often difficult for a lord to find a subject, much less maintain one".[23] As Scott observed of a later period of Malay history:

> With a sparse population and a scattering of many petty kingdoms jockeying for clients, the would-be follower was in a fairly enviable position. The objective of an ambitious ruler was to prevent his Malay retainers from running off individually or in groups to settle under the protection of another, competing *datok* or sultan.[24]

The difficulty which rulers could face in attracting and maintaining a following was a widely accepted and clearly articulated element in relations between rulers and ruled, and an important constraint on arbitrary or unjust royal behaviour. The career of Sri Tri Buana, in this as in other matters, is exemplary: "And Sri Tri Buana became famous as a ruler; and all mankind, male and female, came from every part of the country to pay homage to him, all of them bringing offerings for his acceptance."[25]

Local informants told Pires that, when Mohammed Iskander Shah settled at Melaka, he "strove to populate the land. He acted justly, wherefore people came from other places to live and settle there."[26] The ruler's own status reflected the size and splendour of his following. The Batara of Majapahit decided to marry his daughter to Sultan Mansur Shah after he "perceived how clever Sultan Mansur Shah was and how he excelled all other princes in everything that he did, *and how well-bred and sharp-witted were his followers*".[27] Even the glory of Iskander Dzu'l-Karnain is represented partly in terms of his entourage. He is described as having "princes, divines and theologians, chiefs, warriors and men of valour, gathered around the throne, whilst behind the king were his closer retainers and trusted henchmen".[28]

Patrimonialism and Feudalism

Machiavelli noted that the "kingdoms known to history have been governed in two ways: either by a prince and his servants, who, as ministers by his grace and permission, assist in governing the realm; or by a prince and by barons, who hold their position not by favour of the ruler but by antiquity of blood".[29] This distinction relates less to the "antiquity of blood" than to whether the notables were appointed by the ruler, and were dependent on and answerable to him, or whether their position reflected their own primacy over a distinct community within the polity. The two types of position reflected different relationships between the ruler and the chief or official, and between the chief or official and the subject people. *Feudal* rulers depended for power on the support of *chiefs* and the chiefs' capacity to mobilise their subject peoples in the ruler's support. In a *patrimonial* polity, officials derived their authority from the ruler, who mobilised the support of his population and was able to absorb any independent sources of power he confronted.

The distinction between feudal and patrimonial systems is well established in social science literature.[30] It enables the delineation of processes whereby the ruler's authority and power expanded and contracted; where the balance of power moved from the centre to the periphery or *vice versa* or, even, to rival centres. The challenge for rulers was to impress or overawe autonomous chiefs sufficiently, so that they sought to define themselves as expressions of the ruler's will, as his officials. The conundrum facing officials was whether to seek to improve their status through the service of a ruler, or to convert their dependent, reflected status into more autonomous chieftaincy or, even, independent rulership.

Distinguishing between chiefs and officials, between feudal and patrimonial authority, establishes ideal types. In most polities, both roles occurred, sometimes enacted by the same individual. But these ideal types also represent historical experience, allowing scholars to analyse changes in the nature of power through centuries. For example, Anthony Reid identified three distinct periods in the history of Aceh: the years prior to 1589, when the Orang Kaya dominated a succession of weak rulers; 1589–1636, when Acehnese rulers reformed their realms to concentrate power in their own hands and succeeded in reducing the Orang Kaya; and the period following 1636, which saw the decline of central power and the reemergence of a powerful chiefly class able to dominate the court.[31] Barbara Andaya has suggested that the largely autonomous power exercised by Perak chiefs in the nineteenth century represented recent developments. In the previous century, titleholders had been far more dependent on powerful Perak rulers for their position and rank.[32] Similarly, the *SM* represents patrimonial ideals as being contested by feudalising tendencies and, furthermore, provides insights into the strategies available to rulers seeking to establish, maintain or restore royal authority.

Structure of Power in Melaka

Titleholders in the Melaka sultanate were ordered into four grades, in multiples of four. Immediately below the ruler ranked his ministers, the Bendahara, Temenggong, Sri Nara 'diraja and Laksamana. They took precedence above 8 officials who, in turn, ranked above a further 16 titleholders. Positioned below the 16 were 32 district chiefs.[33] This ideal ordering of status and power positions reflected the court's desire to replicate Hindu-Buddhist cosmology, and thus underpinned and emphasised the ruler's hegemonic claims. It was an essential element of the totalising discourse of Malay kingship. In ranking district chiefs so lowly, however, the court might have sought to preclude the emergence of rival centres on its periphery. In this ideal representation, district chiefs, however powerful, could increase their precedence only through royal favour. This concern to contain the status of those who governed the periphery suggests that they were perceived by the court to pose real threats to its own pre-eminence. Far removed from the court, the chiefs of the periphery could too easily assert their autonomy, and become the focus for local dynastic loyalties.

Sandhu and Wheatley described Melaka as a galactic patrimonial state, with the city surrounded by a number of "patrimonial benefices" and dominating more distant tributary kingdoms.[34] Certainly, the SM seems to emphasise patrimonial ties, rather than feudal or segmentary relationships, as ideal. The power to absorb the sovereignty of other rulers, by virtue of descent from Iskander Dzu'l-Karnain, is a key feature of Melakan rulership. When Demang Lebar Daun, the ruler of Palembang, brought the three princes down from Bukit Si-Guntang Mahameru, "every ruler from every part of the country came to pay his respects to them". One brother was taken to rule at Minangkabau, one to Tanjong Pura, whilst the third, from whom the Melaka rulers traced their descent, assumed the rule of Palembang after Demang Lebar Daun abdicated to make way for him. For Demang Lebar Daun, the opportunity to serve the Iskander-descended prince, Sri Tri Buana, overrode his own claims to sovereignty.[35] The Queen of Bentan was no less able to resist the centripetal attraction of Sri Tri Buana, installing him as her heir, and thus consigning her own family to the status of his retainers.[36]

Patrimonial ideals are also evident in the text's emphasis on the importance of being in the presence of the ruler. Having entered the entourage of Sri Tri Buana, Demang Lebar Daun is concerned to position himself close to its centre. Access to the ruler is to be preferred to control over provinces, however rich. When Sri Tri Buana decides to leave Palembang, Demang Lebar Daun tells him "If your Majesty goes, I will accompany you, for I must not be parted from your Highness."[37]

Feudalising Tendencies and Patrimonial Responses

Although patrimonial ideals are so heavily promoted, it is clear from the text that power and identity in the Melaka sultanate were also subject to countervailing feudal tendencies. Ironically, it is precisely in the rulers' role as the font of titles that patrimonial ideals are most vigorously contested by feudalising pressures.

Although titles derived from the ruler, it is clear that the descendants of titleholders sought to assert their right to be considered for succession to particular titles. Title-giving remained the ruler's prerogative, but his freedom of action was constrained by a widespread recognition that first consideration should go to members of particular families. When Bendahara Puteh died Sultan Mahmud Shah assembled "Those who were eligible to be made Bendahara."[38] According to Wilkinson, four of the nine assembled were sons of Bendahara Tun Perak, four were sons of Bendahara Sri Nara 'diraja and one was the son of Bendahara Tun Puteh.[39] A similar constraint seems to have governed succession to the Laksamana title. Although Hang Tuah was not succeeded as Laksamana by his son, he was succeeded, successively, by his two sons-in-law.[40] When Sri Rama died (in the reign of Sultan Mahmud Shah) his son was appointed to the title with the same rank.[41] The development of heritable claims on titles inhibited the ruler's discretion in their allocation, since his choice became restricted to a small group of possible claimants. This limitation of the ruler's choice of titleholders to those qualified by descent represents a significant diminution of the patrimonial ideal.

The *SM* records several responses to such developments. Since there were usually a number of possible claimants for a title within a family, competition for appointment could become intense. Would-be successors needed to attract the ruler's attention, thus reinforcing his centrality. When Hang Tuah was succeeded by his son-in-law, Hang Khoja, his other son-in-law, Hang Nadim, abducted the daughter of the Bendahara of Pahang in an attempt to win Sultan Mahmud Shah's attention and approval.[42] The emergence of two lineages with claims on the Bendahara title, whether part of a deliberate royal strategy or not, also increased the ruler's centrality by creating for him opportunities for mediation and reconciliation.[43]

A more radical response was for rulers to create less formal networks of association outside the framework established by title hierarchies. The creation of an inner, informal grouping of untitled confidantes, more clearly dependent on royal patronage, reasserted a patrimonial ideal in opposition to titles claimed partly by right of descent. Cross-cutting and, even, confronting the court's formal and visible structures, the development of informal groupings of favourites around the ruler potentially reinvigorated his discretion and autonomy. The distinction between formal titleholders and favourites is prefigured in the description, already quoted, of Iskander Dzu'l-Karnain's retinue, which included "behind the king ... his closer retainers and trusted henchmen".[44] Pires's informants told him that Sultan Mansur Shah had "raised men from nothing", citing in particular his appointment of a Kling as Comptroller of the Exchequer and his preferment of a "cafre" from Palembang.[45]

It is clear from the *SM* that, during the reign of Sultan Ahmad, tensions between titleholders and favourites reached crisis point. Ahmad "had no great liking for the chiefs". Instead of favouring the formal titleholders of his court, Ahmad preferred the company of Tun 'Ali Hati, Tun Mai Ulat Bulu and Tun Muhammad Rahang, thirteen other young men and, even, his slaves. "They", we are told, "were his companions in sport and pastime".[46] The *SM* records that, after the fall of Melaka, Sultan Ahmad's favourites treated the Melakan ministers and officials with insolence. When Ahmad's father, Sultan Mahmud Shah heard of Ahmad's behaviour, he ordered his son's death in order to reassume the rulership. Mahmud Shah's reassumption of the rulership was accompanied by a reassertion of pre-eminence by those qualified by descent to dominate the court. The Bendahara had died following the fall of Melaka. Mahmud Shah appointed the late Bendahara's son as Bendahara Paduka Raja, while Bendahara Paduka Raja's son, Tun Isak, was given the title Paduka Tuan. The detail with which the episode is recounted suggests the important role that the discontent of titleholders with the influence of royal favourites had played in Sultan Ahmad's overthrow.[47]

Centre and Periphery

Notwithstanding the desire of rulers to surround themselves with entourages, and of followers to seek places at court, the administration of realms required the appointment of officials to govern areas outside the capital. When Demang Lebar Daun decided to follow Sri Tri Buana from Palembang, he appointed his younger brother to administer the city.[48] Similarly, the *SM* recounts how Sultan Iskander Shah, after he was expelled from Singapore, arrived at Sening Ujong on the peninsula, and "perceiving that this was a good place he left a minister there—which is why the place has a minister to this day...."[49] Following Melaka's defeat of the Siamese ruler of Pahang, the SM recounts that the Melakan ruler dispatched the Sri Bija 'diraja to govern Pahang.[50]

The administration of peripheries and their integration into a patrimonial framework created particular tensions for Melaka. On the one hand, provincial officials were appointed by the centre to maintain its interests: outlying districts existed in the realm to maintain and serve the centre. On the other hand, however, it is clear that successive rulers accommodated localised identities based on geographical communities. Indeed, peripheral populations were mobilised on the basis of localised communal identities. For example, when the Bendahara built a new palace for Sultan Mansur Shah, the populations of various outlying areas were allocated specific responsibilities, so that the men of Bentan Karangan collected the material, the men of Panchur Serapong built the *balai* (audience hall) with help from the people of Buru, the pavilion was built by men from Suir, waiting rooms by the people of Sudar and Sayong, the drum hall by the population of Apong and the outhouses by men from Merba.[51]

Outlying districts seem to have been governed on one of three possible bases. Some districts were awarded to support holders of particular titles, passing with the title to successive incumbents, some were allocated to titleholders or individuals at the ruler's pleasure, whilst a third category appear to have been hereditary holdings of particular families.[52] Bentan was the Bendahara's appanage "by custom", whilst Sungei Raya "was by custom the fief of the Laksamana".[53] When Tun Pikrima was created Paduka Tuan, he was awarded Buru as a fief.[54] Examples of hereditary fiefs are less common in the SM. When Sultan Mansur Shah was leaving Majapahit, he sent Hang Tuah to ask the Batara for Siantan. The Batara agreed, so that Siantan "became the territory of the Laksamana, for himself and those that came after him".⁵⁵ When the Sri Bija 'diraja, who was based at Singapore, was executed, "the fief of Singapura" was given to his son.⁵⁶

Although the apparent infrequency of hereditary fiefs might indicate the operation of a patrimonial idea, it would be unwise for scholars to assume that Melakan notables necessarily considered fiefs to be so entirely in the gift of the ruler. Since titleholders in Melaka increasingly seem to have been drawn from a very few, interrelated patrilineages, most holders of fiefs were probably appointed in succession to close relatives. Over time, their families are likely to have begun to conceive of their rights to fiefs, no less than their rights to titles, as a function of descent and kinship. They are likely to have begun to develop feudal in place of patrimonial sensibilities.

This suggestion draws support from other representations in the *SM* of the resilience of kinship as a source of identity and loyalty. It is clear from the text that family loyalties were sometimes sufficiently strong to outweigh the obligations nobles owed to their ruler. For example, when Sultan Mahmud Shah sought to appoint Laksamana Nadim to lead the fleet against the Maharaja of Lingga, "the Laksamana was unwilling to go and sought to be excused on the ground that Maharaja Isak was his kinsman". Although the Ruler was displeased with the Laksamana, he acquiesced.⁵⁷ When Sultan Ala'u'd-din asked Tun Narawangsa to bring the Sri Agar Raja back from Perak, Tun Narawangsa sought to be excused because the Raja Perempuan of Perak was his niece and "with her I am but a servant".⁵⁸ Conversely, Sultan Mahmud Shah suggested that Paduka Tuan be sent to bring Tun Aria Bija 'diraja to court precisely because Paduka Tuan and Tun Aria Bija 'diraja were brothers-in-law. Both Sultan Mahmud and Paduka Tuan seem to have considered that this connection, rather than royal fiat, would encourage Tun Aria Bija 'diraja's compliance. In order to increase his influence over Tun Aria Bija 'diraja, Paduka Tuan decided to take his wife, who was Tun Aria Bija 'diraja's sister, with him.⁵⁹

The most extreme example of family loyalty undermining the obligation to serve the ruler is provided by a dialogue between Sri Nara 'diraja and his brother, Tun Narawangsa. When, after the fall of Bentan to the Portuguese, Sultan Mahmud Shah and the Sri Nara 'diraja met Tun Narawangsa, Sri Nara 'diraja said, "Come with me, for the Ruler is here." And Tun Narawangsa answered, "The Ruler we have with us; well and good. But if my wife falls into the hands of the Franks, is that good?" The Sri Nara 'diraja tells his brother that he can return good for evil, since the Ruler had killed their father, but he added, "Moreover am I not your brother? Have you the heart to abandon me?"[60] Although this episode might indicate the damage to the Sultan's prestige that defeat by the Portuguese had inflicted, it demonstrates also that matrimonial and family ties were not subsumed or replaced by the demands of patrimonial kingship.[61]

It was not just, however, that noble families developed hereditary claims over particular areas, or that family members maintained for each other loyalties which the authority of rulers could not overcome. In the episode already cited concerning Tun Perak, the text provides evidence also of areas on the periphery initiating leadership roles for nobles in order to secure their community's interests, apparently in opposition to the ruler. Although he was the eldest son of Bendahara Sriwa Raja, Tun Perak was given no appointment at court. He therefore withdrew and settled at Klang. The *SM* recounts that

> when after a while the people of Klang discarded their headman, they went and presented themselves before the Raja in Malaka to ask for another. And when Sultan Muzaffar Shah asked them whom they wanted, they replied, "If it please your Highness, it is Tun Perak that we crave should be given to us as our headman". Their request was granted and Tun Perak was made headman of Klang.[62]

Three important elements need to recognised in this narrative. First, that the people of Klang "discarded their headman". Secondly, that their having done so is not presented as remarkable, nor are the people of Klang apparently apprehensive for the consequences of their actions. Far from fearing the ruler's response, they calmly presented themselves before him to ask that he appoint Tun Perak, the man of their choosing, as their new headman. And, finally, their ruler did so. The episode appears to subvert patrimonial ideals and the rhetorical claims of the ruler. Not only local leadership, but the ruler's own role as the font of titles and honour, are presented as socially constructed. His action is presented as a function not just of the will of ordinary people, but by the will of ordinary people with a *localised* sense of identity and community.

Another episode which suggests the primacy of regional-based identity over centralised power systems has been cited by Wilkinson. Sultan Mansur Shah ordered the death of the headman of Sening Ujong, and "As a result of this the Sening Ujong people would not come out of their country any more."[63] Although it would be incautious to draw too much from such scarce evidence, such evidence should not be ignored.

The *Hikayat Raja Raja Pasai* also represents regional resistance to royal authority. When Merah Silu became a Muslim, some of his followers refused to convert, "So they fled to the upper reaches of the river Pasanagan."[64] Their resistance seems to have been enduring, since Pires subsequently noted that the Pasai rulers "have been unable to convert the people of the interior". Pires also described conflict between the Pasai court and the producers of export commodities, who "sometimes disagree with Pase because of the crops of pepper, silk and benzoin; but they affirm that in the quarrels their wishes prevail over Pasai".[65] The *Hikayat Banjar* represents both the resistance of outlying populations and the concern of rulers to overcome it. It describes how the ruler ordered his official, Aria Magatsari, to subjugate the river districts of Tabalung, Balanan and Petaka and their neighbouring hillsides. When Aria Magatsari brought the chiefs of these areas to the court "with *gifts* of homage", the ruler addressed them:

> Rural chiefs, I place you under Aria Magatsari, who will be your governor. Every year you must come and bring your tribute *of you own accord*, without waiting for us to come upstream and collect it. Do not be negligent, for then you will certainly incur chastisement.[66]

Additionally, scholars have found indications of identity-based resistance in other historical records of Malay states. In 1717, the ruler of Jambi was constrained to agree to a contract with the local Minangkabau community which guaranteed Minangkabau property and people from seizure, allowed them to live under Minangkabau rather than Jambi law, limited the corvee labour demands that could be placed on them and exempted them from royal tolls and from the expectation of making expensive gifts to the ruler.[67]

Centres or Peripheries

One further set of relationships between Melaka and outlying districts needs to be considered: Melaka's emergence at the head of a network of subsidiary realms, whose own rulers acknowledged the Melaka ruler's pre-eminence. Melakan regional dominance was created through four processes: recognition of the Melakan ruler's overpowering grandeur, the dispatch of surplus princes to create new realms, conquest and marriage ties. Often, Melakan dominance was maintained over subordinate realms by a combination of several or all of these factors.

The *SM* records a number of cases of rulers doing obeisance voluntarily to Melakan rulers. The Rajas of Rekan, Terengganu and Maluku were all described as performing homage at Melaka.[68] The Raja of Kedah came to pay homage to Sultan Mahmud Shah, requesting in return a drum of sovereignty.[69] Similarly, following his conversion to Islam, the Siamese ruler of Patani sent an official to pay homage to Mahmud Shah on his behalf. In return, Mahmud Shah entitled the ruler Sultan Ahmad Shah.[70] These voluntary submissions in the SM are exemplary, recalling the career of Sri Tri Buana and demonstrating the irresistible, immutable attractions of the Iskander-descended ruler.

Voluntary recognition by other rulers of Melakan pre-eminence was an ideal which did not preclude the Melakan court's forcing its claims on other realms, however. The existence of the court of Pagar Ruyong in the Minangkabau highlands, ruled by the descendants of Sri Tri Buana's elder brother, and themselves Iskander-descended, constituted a continual affront to Melaka's hegemonic claims. Although Pagar Ruyong itself was beyond the strategic reach of Melaka, its outlying dependencies, especially those ruled by junior branches of the Pagar Ruyong ruling family, were more vulnerable to Melakan ambitions. The object of Melakan aggression against such realms was to detach them from the orbit of Pagar Ruyong and integrate them into the Melakan hierarchy.

When the Siak ruler, who was descended from the rulers of Pagar Ruyong, refused to acknowledge Melakan overlordship, Sultan Mansur Shah dispatched forces to conquer him. Although Mansur Shah's forces killed the Siak ruler, Maharaja Permaisura, they took his son back to Melaka, where Mansur Shah married him to his daughter and created him Sultan Ibrahim of Siak.[71] Not all of the Iskander-descended ruling families absorbed into the Melakan hierarchy retained their positions, however. After Sultan Ala'u'd-din of Melaka conquered Kampar, he displaced its ruler in favour of his own son, Menawar Shah.[72]

Barbara Andaya has drawn attention to the unsettling effects of ambitious, portionless members of Malay royalty in power relations in the Malay world in the eighteenth century.[73] As the fate of Kampar suggests, this problem also is represented in the SM and comprised an important catalyst for the expansion of Melakan power through the creation or annexation of realms for Melakan princes. Although Sultan Mansur Shah initially dispatched the Sri Bija 'diraja to govern Pahang following its conquest, he subsequently recalled that official, dispatching instead his own son, Raja Muhammad, as ruler.[74] The rulers of Pahang subsequently seem to have been ranked second only to those of Melaka in the hierarchy of rulers that Melaka maintained. The closeness of family connections was fostered through a series of marriages. Melakan rulers both took wives from the Pahang branch of the family, and supplied Pahang rulers with wives from amongst their own daughters.[75]

It is in the creation of lesser realms for kinsmen that tensions in the *SM* between patrimonial and feudal ideals are exposed most obviously. Subsidiary rulers, however inferior to their Melakan overlords, maintained territorial and population bases for their power distinct from that of Melaka. Like the Iskander-descended princes from Pagar Ruyong, subsidiary rulers from the Melakan ruling family embodied a constant potential challenge to the Melakan ruler's primacy. Melakan rulers sought to resolve this tension by maintaining and publicly enacting their superiority over their kinsmen. When Sultan Muhammad of Pahang had Tun Telanai of Terengganu killed for doing homage to Melaka, the Melakan ruler sent his Laksamana to Pahang. The Laksamana's followers killed a cousin of Tun Telanai's assassin, precipitating the Sultan of Pahang to send hurried and renewed obeisance to Melaka.[76] Melakan rulers also enacted their claims to superiority over their Pahang cousins not just by exacting obeisance from them, but by sending officials from Melaka to install successive heirs as sultans.[77]

Melakan rulers also sought opportunities to demonstrate their power over their kinsmen ruling at Siak and Kampar. When Sultan Ala'u'd-din of Melaka heard that Sultan Ibrahim of Siak had executed a man without referring the case to Melaka, he sent the Laksamana to rebuke the Siak ruler: "Do you think it is permitted to put people to death without sanction from Malaka? Are you going to be a law unto yourselves here in Siak?"[78] Kampar, too, was represented as being kept in strict subservience to the Melakan court. On Sultan Menawar Shah's death, his son, Raja Abdullah travelled to do homage to the Melakan ruler, Mahmud Shah. Mahmud Shah proclaimed Abdullah Sultan of Kampar and married him to his daughter.[79] Although Perak had been founded by a dispossessed son of Sultan Mahmud Shah, without Melaka's support or sanction,[80] the SM records that the Perak ruler, too, eventually acknowledged to his brother in Melaka that he did "obeisance to him and am the recipient of his bounty".[81] The emphasis which the SM places on the continued performance of obeisance by lesser rulers, and the right of successive Melakan rulers to install and entitle heirs, suggests the ongoing concern of Melakan rulers to maintain and demonstrate their primacy, and to resist pressures from the periphery towards segmentation.

Pires's account confirms the complex difficulties encountered by Melaka in controlling its regions and periphery. Pires distinguished between independent realms, realms with rulers subservient to the Melakan ruler, and settlements under the governance of Melakan "mandarins" or other officials. Thus Lide, which had been part of the kingdom of Pedir, had succeeded in asserting and maintaining its independence.[82] It seem likely that Pires reflected indigenous understandings in distinguishing between kingdoms (*reinos*) and lands (*terras*).[83] Siak, Kampar, Indragiri, Lingga and Pahang were all ruled by kings under Melakan overlordship.[84] With, perhaps, the still recent failure of Pedir to maintain its claims over Lide in mind, Sultan Ala'u'd-din was reported to have detained the rulers of Kampar, Indragiri and Pahang at his court.[85] The status of Rokan and Purim seems to have confused Pires. He described them as Melakan vassals under mandarins,[86] but subsequently claimed that Rokan had its own king under Melakan overlordship, whilst "Purjm" was governed by a Sheikh.[87] The country between Kampar and Indragiri, which used to have its own king, was described as being under a mandarin who was a Melakan vassal.[88] Tengkal, also, which adjoined Indragiri, "has no king or mandarin. It is a county which is obedient to Malacca as a tributary".[89]

Conclusion

The complex array of power relations between Melakan rulers, their titled officials, chiefs and subsidiary kings suggests that Malay royal power and authority was conceived and realised in more diverse forms than some writers have allowed. Although the *SM* seems to present patrimonial ties as ideal, underpinning, as they would, royal absolutist pretensions, the annalist seems to have been unable to ignore other sources of action, which derived from dynastic and regional loyalties and identities. Although the identification of feudal elements in Melakan domination of outlying areas partly reflects technological constraints on the expansion of government, feudalising tendencies at the court itself suggest that patrimonial absolutism was not beyond effective challenge, expanding and contracting in response to the wide-ranging demands from power conflicts and realignments.

Centrist and authoritarian values and claims by states have a long tradition in the Indonesian Archipelago. But if the values and complexities recorded in historical narratives such as the *SM* can be believed, so too do resistance and evasion by local communities.

Notes

1. "Sejarah Melayu or Malay Annals", trans. C. C. Brown, *JMBRAS* 25, 2–3 (1952). For a romanised edition of the Malay text, see *Sejarah Melayu: The Malay Annals MS*. Raffles No. 18, romanised by A. R. Haji Ismail (Kuala Lumpur: MBRAS repr. no. 17, 1998), pp. 65–313. Although I am aware that the title, *Sejarah Melayu*, is a European imposition and that the text should be more correctly referred to as *Sulalat al-Salatin*, the work is almost always cited as *Sejarah Melayu*. An important recent exception to this convention in H. Chambert-Loir, "The *Sulalat al-Salatin* as Political Myth", *Indonesia* 79 (April 2005): 131–60.
2. For discussions see R. Roolvink, "The Variant Versions of the Malay Annals", *Bijdragen tot de Taal-, Land- en Volkenkunde* 123 (1963): 310–11; C. Walls, "Legacy of the Fathers: Testamentary Admonitions and the Thematic Structure of the Sejarah Melayu", doctoral dissertation, Yale University, 1974, p. 130 and C. H. Wake, "Melaka in the Fifteenth Century: Malay Historical Traditions and the Politics of Islamisation", in *Melaka: The Transformation of a Malay Capital c 1400–1980*, ed. K. S. Sandhu and P. Wheatley (Kuala Lumpur: Oxford University Press, 1983), vol. II, p. 130; Vladimir Braginsky, *The Heritage of Traditional Malay Literature: A Historical Survey of Genres, Writings and Literary Views* (Leiden: KITLV Press, 2004), pp. 92–103.
3. P. E. de Josselin de Jong, "The Character of the 'Malay Annals'", in *Malayan and Indonesian Studies: Essays Presented to Sir Richard Winstedt on his Eighty-fifth Birthday*, ed. J. Bastin and R. Roolvink (Oxford: Clarendon Press, 1964), p. 241.
4. Roolvink, "The Variant Versions of the Malay Annals", p. 301.
5. Josselin de Jong, "The Character of the 'Malay Annals'", p. 239. For the relationship between the *Sejarah Melayu* and the *Hikayat Raja Raja Pasai*, see A. Teeuw, "Hikayat Raja Raja Pasai and Sejarah Melayu", in *Malayan and Indonesian Studies*, ed. Bastin and Roolvink; and P. L. A. Sweeney, "The Connection between the Hikayat Raja2 Pasai and the Sejarah Melayu", *JMBRAS* 40, 2 (1967): 94–105.
6. Z. A. b. Abdul Wahid, "Sejarah Melayu", *Asian Studies* 6, 3 (1966): 446.
7. T. J. Moy, "The 'Sejarah Melayu' Tradition of Power and Political Structure: An Assessment of Relevant Sections of the 'Tuhfat Al-Nafis'", *JMBRAS* 48, 2 (1975): 64.
8. Walls, *Legacy of the Fathers*, p. 97.
9. Ibid., p. 98.
10. J. C. Scott, "Freedom and Freehold: Space, People and State Simplification in Southeast Asia", in *Asian Freedoms: The Idea of Freedom in East and Southeast Asia*, ed. D. Kelly and A. Reid (Cambridge: Cambridge University Press, 1998), p. 51.

11. For discussion of the representation of treason in the *Sejarah Melayu*, see J. H. Walker, "Autonomy, Diversity and Dissent: Conceptions of Power and Sources of Action in the *Sejarah Melayu* (Raffles MS 18)", *Theory and Society* 33 (2004): 213–55.
12. A. Reid, *Southeast Asia in the Age of Commerce. Vol. 2: Expansion and Crisis* (New Haven: Yale University Press, 1993), p. 202.
13. Z. A. b. A. Wahid, "Power and Authority in the Melaka Sultanate", in Sandhu and Wheatley, *Melaka*, pp. 101–4.
14. Brown, "Sejarah Melayu or Malay Annals", p. 26.
15. Wahid, "Power and Authority in the Melaka Sultanate", p. 103.
16. Brown, "Sejarah Melayu or Malay Annals", p. 27.
17. Walls, *Legacy of the Fathers*, pp. 28–9.
18. Ibid., p. 102.
19. Brown, "Sejarah Melayu or Malay Annals", pp. 64–6.
20. Ibid., p. 119.
21. Walls, *Legacy of the Fathers*, p. 36.
22. Brown, "Sejarah Melayu or Malay Annals", p. 124.
23. B. W. Andaya, *To Live as Brothers: Southeast Sumatra in the Seventeenth and Eighteenth Centuries* (Honolulu: University of Hawai'i Press, 1993), p. 194.
24. Scott, "Freedom and Freehold", p. 51.
25. Brown, "Sejarah Melayu or Malay Annals", p. 26.
26. Tomé Pires, *Suma Oriental of Tomé Pires: An Account of the East from the Red Sea to Japan, written in Malacca and India in 1512–1515*, trans. and ed. Armando Cortesao (London: Hakluyt Society, second series, no. 89, 1967), p. 238. The *Hikayat Raja Raja Pasai* also reported of Majapahit, "The Emperor was famous for his love of justice. The empire grew prosperous. People in vast numbers thronged the city". A. H. Hill, trans., "Hikayat Raja Raja Pasai", *JMBRAS* 33, 2 (1960): 140.
27. Brown, "Sejarah Melayu or Malay Annals", p. 80 (emphasis added).
28. Ibid., p. 14.
29. Niccolò Machiavelli, *The Prince and the Discourses* (New York: Modern Library, 1950), p. 15.
30. R. Bendix, *Max Weber: An Intellectual Portrait* (New York: Anchor Books, 1962 [1960]), pp. 334–81. See also B. Anderson, "The Idea of Power in Javanese Culture", in *Language and Power: Exploring Political Cultures in Indonesia*, ed. B. Anderson (Ithaca: Cornell University Press, 1982), pp. 17–87. It is important to emphasise that I do not use the term 'feudal' either in its medieval European context, which refers to land tenure and service, or in the context in which it is sometimes used in contemporary Malaysia. The relationships between ruler and ruled which some contemporary Malaysian intellectuals criticise as 'feudal' were, in fact, patrimonial.

31. A. Reid, "Trade and the Problem of Royal Power in Aceh, Three Stages: c 1550–1700", in *Precolonial State Systems in Southeast Asia*, ed. A. Reid and L. Castles (Kuala Lumpur: MBRAS monograph no. 6, 1975), p. 46.
32. B. W. Andaya, "The Nature of the State in 18th Century Perak", in Reid, *Precolonial State Systems*, p. 35.
33. K. S. Sandhu and P. Wheatley, "From Capital to Municipality", in Sandhu and Wheatley, *Melaka*, vol. II, p. 511. The *Hikayat Raja Raja Pasai* also distinguished ministers (*mentri*), senior officials (*orang besar-besar*), courtiers (*sida-sida*) and chiefs (*hulubalang*). A. H. Hill, "Introduction" to "Hikayat Raja Raja Pasai", p. 30.
34. Sandhu and Wheatley, "From Capital to Municipality", p. 509.
35. Brown, "Sejarah Melayu or Malay Annals", p. 25.
36. Ibid., p. 29.
37. Ibid., p. 28.
38. Ibid., p. 134.
39. R. J. Wilkinson, "The Malacca Sultanate", *JMBRAS* 13, 2 (1935): 22–67.
40. Brown, "Sejarah Melayu or Malay Annals", p. 171.
41. Ibid., p. 125.
42. Ibid., p. 145. Conversely, when Sri Awadana failed to perform his allocated duties to the ruler's satisfaction, Sultan Mahmud Shah commented, "If it should come to the turn of Sri Awadana to be Bendahara, may God take our life". Ibid., p. 188.
43. See, for example, the account of the conflict between Tun Perak and Sri Nara 'diraja. Ibid., pp. 66–7. The development of family and factional rivalries, and their repercussions for the exercise of power in Melaka, are discussed by both Wake and Bowen, and need no further elaboration here. Wake, "Melaka in the Fifteenth Century", pp. 128–62; J. R. Bowen, "Cultural Models for Historical Genealogies: The Case of the Melaka Sultanate", in Sandhu and Wheatley, *Melaka*, vol. I, pp. 162–79.
44. Brown, "Sejarah Melayu or Malay Annals", p. 14.
45. *Suma Oriental of Tomé Pires*, p. 249.
46. Brown, "Sejarah Melayu or Malay Annals", p. 166.
47. Ibid., p. 170. Henri Chambert-Loir has recently suggested that Sultan Ahmad's reign was invented in the *Sejarah Melayu* to remove blame from his father, Sultan Mahmud Shah, for defeat by the Portuguese. Acceptence of Chambert-Loir's arguments would not affect this section of my analysis because I am concerned, not with *events* in Melakan history, but with the *values* expressed in the narrative about Melakan history. Chambert-Loir, "The *Sulalat al-Salatin* as Political Myth", pp. 150–60.
48. Brown, "Sejarah Melayu or Malay Annals", p. 28.
49. Ibid., p. 51.

50. Ibid., p. 92.
51. Ibid., p. 88.
52. Compare this with Donald Brown's analysis of Brunei's provincial structure. Brown noted three types of territorial administration: *kerajaan*, which comprised the appanages of the sultan; *kuripan*, which were allocated to officials, and *tulin*, which were held by hereditary right. D. E. Brown, *Brunei: The Structure and History of a Bornean Malay Sultanate* (Brunei: Brunei Museum, 1970), pp. 79–85.
53. Brown, "Sejarah Melayu or Malay Annals", pp. 86 and 156.
54. Ibid., p. 108.
55. Ibid., p. 82. Although the text is ambiguous, it does seem to indicate that Siantan became a family possession rather than an appanage to the Laksamana title.
56. Ibid., p. 125.
57. Ibid., pp. 176–7.
58. Ibid., p. 195.
59. Ibid., p. 182.
60. Ibid., p. 190.
61. Such episodes might support Tony Day's assertion of the importance of family and kinship rather than state structures in Southeast Asian history. See T. Day, "Ties that (Un)Bind: Families and States in Premodern Southeast Asia", *Journal of Asian Studies* 55, 2 (1996): 384–409.
62. Brown, "Sejarah Melayu or Malay Annals", p. 64.
63. Quoted by R. J. Wilkinson, "The Pengkalan Kempas 'Saint'", *JMBRAS* 9, 1 (1931): 134–5.
64. Hill, "Hikayat Raja Raja Pasai", p. 120.
65. *Suma Oriental of Tomé Pires*, p. 143.
66. J. J. Ras, ed., *Hikayat Bandjar: A Study in Malay Historiography* (The Hague: Martinus Nijhoff, 1968), p. 241 (emphasis added).
67. Andaya, *To Live as Brothers*, p. 155.
68. Brown, "Sejarah Melayu or Malay Annals", p. 115.
69. Ibid., p. 137.
70. Ibid., p. 152.
71. Ibid., pp. 96–7.
72. Ibid., p. 122. Wolters has also suggested that Melaka's acquisition of Indragiri seems to have been motivated by rivalry with Pagar Ruyong, whose dependency it had been. O. W. Wolters, *The Fall of Srivijaya in Malay History* (Kuala Lumpur: Oxford University Press, 1975 [1970]), p. 170.
73. B. W. Andaya, "The Role of the Anak Raja in Malay History: A Case Study from Eighteenth Century Kedah", *Journal of Southeast Asian Studies* 7, 2 (1976): 162–87.

74. Brown, "Sejarah Melayu or Malay Annals", p. 98. Muhammad was his father's favourite son and intended heir in Melaka until one of his followers killed the son of the Bendahara in retaliation for an accidental insult. Ibid., pp. 97–8.
75. For examples, see ibid., pp. 113 and 193.
76. Ibid., pp. 115–6.
77. For example, see ibid., p. 144.
78. Ibid., pp. 117–8.
79. Ibid., p. 133.
80. Ibid., p. 193.
81. Ibid., p. 204.
82. *Suma Oriental of Tomé Pires*, p. 141.
83. Ibid., p. 163, fn 1.
84. Ibid., pp. 149, 156 and 262.
85. Ibid., p. 251.
86. Ibid., p. 149.
87. Ibid., p. 262.
88. Ibid., p. 152.
89. Ibid., p. 153.

CHAPTER 3

Creating a New Centre in the Periphery of Indonesia: Sumatran Malay Identity Politics

Minako Sakai

Introduction

This chapter examines the revival of transnational Malay identity (*serumpun Melayu*) and related cultural symbols across Sumatra following regional autonomy introduced in 2001. The coastal areas of Sumatra are a traditional homeland of Malay Muslims who largely share cultural traits with the Malay Muslims in peninsular Malaysia. Although Sumatra has large deposits of natural gas, oil and minerals, its economy has lagged significantly behind Jakarta's, resulting in resentment against Jakarta-centred development. In order to challenge Jakarta as the centre of Indonesia's economic and political networks, Sumatran leaders have started to identify Malaysian Malays as alternative counterparts in order to create a new economic node spanning the Strait of Melaka.[1] As I show in this chapter, numerous events epitomising the rising importance of a transnational Malay identity have taken place in the Sumatran provincial capitals of Medan, Padang and Palembang, where representations of Malayness had been relatively subdued since Indonesian independence.

In the case of Riau, while Malayness was hitherto debated and negotiated as part of the discourse of Riau identity, rather than linked to a wider transnational Malay identity, local politicians have recently turned to using an inclusive definition of Malayness in order to lead cross-strait economic development projects.

In view of these recent developments, I will examine why Malayness, and in particular, a transnational Malay identity, has suddenly become an appealing notion in Sumatra's urban centres. I argue that the recent interest in *serumpun Melayu* in Sumatra is a response to the end of centralistic governance in Indonesia and the New Order policies which had concentrated power in Jakarta, marginalising Sumatran and other Indonesian Malays. Consequently, Malay identity and cultural symbols in Sumatra had become almost extinct. Indeed, during the New Order, *serumpun Melayu* cultural affinities and movements of Malays across the Melaka Strait were deliberately suppressed and obstructed by a government bent on enforcing the notion of a strongly unified Indonesian republic.[2]

My focus in this chapter is how decentralisation has opened up new opportunities for Sumatran Malays to speed up the island's economic development. In particular, I will highlight how local Malay politicians have identified the substantial Malay populations of the neighbouring nations of Malaysia and Singapore as potential new partners, and are now capitalising on their shared Malayness to attract investment.

In doing so, however, I am not asserting that "Malayness" has only one interpretation in Sumatra. An interesting contrast to the discourse of Sumatran Malay politicians is that of school-age children in the Riau Archipelago who perceive Malayness as backward and boring while "Jakarta" is closely associated with dynamism and democratisation.[3] Instead, what I wish to highlight here are the varying socio-political contexts that have affected the meaning of Malayness.[4] As Alan Rew and John Campbell state, identity is shaped "in relation to the significant Other".[5] Malayness in contemporary Indonesia fits this model of a fluid and situational identity. There is no single agreed definition of what constitutes being a Malay, and it is precisely because of its elusiveness and inclusiveness that local politicians and intellectuals are now able to promote an inclusive Malay identity. In an era of regional autonomy, provincial leaders are seeking new investment avenues and partners. I argue too that the sudden increase in interest in Malay culture movements by local politicians reflects an attempt to create a new centre in a decentralised Indonesia where new power dynamics may be negotiated. Now that Jakarta no longer has unchallenged economic, cultural and political dominance, local politicians and leaders in the Indonesian periphery are keen to challenge the centrality of Jakarta and increase their own power.

In the following section, I will discuss a series of organised events in various provincial capitals in Sumatra, all of which aim to revive various attributes of Malayness, including *serumpun Melayu* identity. In passing, it may be worth noting that each of these cities claims or is trying to establish itself as the centre of the Malay Islamic world in Indonesia. I will then analyse the stated aims and motivations of individuals leading these activities, and will explore what it means to be a Malay in Sumatra in a decentralised Indonesia.[6]

The Malay and Islamic World Movement (DMDI)

Calls to revive *serumpun Melayu* derive from local as well as outside groups. The main external advocate of Malay-based economic, social and cultural collaboration is Malaysia. In a country whose so-called *bumiputra* (indigenous) population is just over 50 per cent, Sumatran Malays are perceived as close kin, sharing the same cultural roots. *Serumpun*, meaning derived from a common stock or family, is often used by Malaysian as well as Sumatran Malays to reflect their shared roots. While Malay Muslims had dominated the region's economy and culture for centuries, European colonialism and the subsequent creation of postcolonial nation-states left most Malay populations in the archipelago economically weak minorities in various home countries. Aiming to revive the glory of its past, the Malaysian state of Melaka initiated the Dunia Melayu Dunia Islam (DMDI, henceforth, the Malay and Islamic World Movement) in 2000, under the leadership of its chief minister, Datuk Seri Haji Mohd Ali bin Mohd Rustam. Responding to this call, most provincial governors of Sumatra attended the first Malay and Islamic World Movement convention on 18–21 October 2000 in Melaka in association with leading Malay studies organisations in Malaysia, including the Institut Kajian Sejarah dan Patriotisme Malaysia (IKSEP, Malaysian Institute of Historical and Patriotism Studies), Perbadanan Muzium Melaka (PERZIM, Museum Corporation of Melaka) and Gabungan Persatuan Penulis Nasional Malaysia (GAPENA, the Federation of National Writers Associations of Malaysia). As declared at the convention, the aims of the Malay and Islamic World Movement include:

1. To become the reference point on socio-cultural and economic aspects of the Malays for the Malay world;
2. To revive Melaka's past as an Islamic centre;
3. To promote tourism to Melaka; and
4. To create stronger ties among the Malay and Islamic communities in the world.[7]

Datuk Ali bin Mohd Rustam's rationale for initiating the Malay and Islamic World Movement was that the Malays had been divided and marginalised with the consequence that they were economically weak, leaving their cultural heritage almost extinct.[8] He was also concerned that the division of Malay Muslims would prevent Malays from competing against the Europeans who may interfere with the Malay world.[9] His hope for the Malay and Islamic World Movement was thus to rectify this by bringing all Malays together to recreate cultural and business networks across the Malay Islamic world. With this intention, he had approached international Malay community leaders, including some from Sri Lanka, Singapore, Brunei and Indonesia. In Indonesia, his invitation was favourably received by Indonesian provincial governors as it came after the fall of Suharto when moves toward regional autonomy were under way and when regional leaders were looking for new economic partners. Thus, Indonesian counterparts agreed to participate in the annual convention in Melaka, which is expected to become a meeting place for Malays to rekindle their cultural and emotional ties. In order to strengthen the Malay and Islamic World Movement network, the Indonesian delegates also agreed to host a workshop every year to discuss their annual plans.

The Malay and Islamic World Movement consists of nine bureaus (socio-cultural, youth, women, education, religion, science and technology, information technology, economy and tourism) which plan collaborative activities in the Malay world. One of its most influential individuals is Dr Datuk Abdul Latif Abu Bakar, who led the socio-cultural bureau of the movement since the beginning, is a professor of media studies at the University of Malaya, and holds the second highest position in GAPENA. Since 2001, he has also been the director of Melaka's tertiary arts college (Institut Seni Malaysia Melaka), set up to develop the local arts community and teach Malay music, dance and crafts. In my interview with him in February 2002 in Melaka, he explained that the Malays, who had been separated because of colonialism, need to unite to compete against Europe and other political and economic powers. He explained that GAPENA, led by Professor Datuk Ismail Hussein, has always conducted activities to forge ties amongst the Malays both inside and outside Malaysia and that the Malay and Islamic World Movement was a natural next step. As the head of the Movement's socio-cultural bureau, he has organised numerous gatherings of cultural figures across the Malay world, ranging from Madagascar and South Africa to Indonesia, resulting in numerous publications. Datuk Abu Bakar was strongly influenced by the vision held by Ibrahim Yaacob, a Malayan Malay who had promoted the idea of uniting the Peninsula with Indonesia prior to the declaration of independence by Sukarno and Hatta. He commented that "Facing the waves of globalisation which may be negative and might extinguish Malay identity, it is appropriate for the Malay stock to strengthen their values, customs and cultures together."[10] It is in this context that the Malay and Islamic World Movement seeks to play a key role in ensuring that Malay identity endures.

How far have the Malay and Islamic World Movement activities expanded in Indonesia? As shown in Table 3.1, since 2001 Malay and Islamic World Movement gatherings have been held almost annually in Indonesia, and the hosts now include not only Sumatran provinces, but also West Kalimantan. Despite a criticism raised officially by Indonesian delegates at the Bukit Tinggi meeting in 2003 that the Movement's aims remain ambiguous, participating provincial leaders seem interested

TABLE 3.1

Locations of DMDI Workshops and Major Events in Indonesia[11]

Year	Location, Province	Event
2001	Palembang, South Sumatra	Workshop
2002	Medan, North Sumatra	Workshop
2003	Bukit Tinggi, West Sumatra	Workshop
	Pangkal Pinang, Bangka Belitung	Cultural festival
2004	Bengkalis, Riau	Cultural festival
2006	Pontianak, West Kalimantan	Workshop
2007	Pekanbaru, Riau	Workshop, cultural festival and official
	Jambi	inauguration of the DMDI secretariat in Jambi
2008	Aceh	Official inauguration of the DMDI secretariat in Aceh, cultural festival and workshop

in continuing despite the costs of hosting a workshop or event. This may be because the workshops provide a rare opportunity for hosts to display their generosity and promote their cities and provinces directly to participants.[12] Significantly, as the Movement's president, Melaka's chief minister attends each event, accompanied by Malaysian Malay business leaders: past meetings have resulted in memoranda of understanding on joint economic and cultural projects.[13]

What is intriguing is to explore why the notion of transnational Malayness has suddenly attracted the attention of regional politicians in the Malay-dominated provinces of Indonesia. I will now trace how this phenomenon has emerged in several Sumatran provincial capitals, analysing how local power politics has been connected with various attempts to revive Malayness in Palembang, Padang, Medan and Pekanbaru.

Palembang

There was a strong sense of cultural inferiority to the rest of Indonesia when I first conducted my research in the highlands of Palembang and surrounding areas of South Sumatra between 1994 and 1996. There was a widely held notion that South Sumatra did not have a distinctive symbol comparable to the Javanese courts, West Sumatran domestic architecture, or the colourful temples of Bali. The regional pinnacle of glory was traced back to the maritime Hindu-Buddhist kingdom of Sriwijaya, which had thrived between the seventh and eleventh centuries, but was regarded as second best in comparison to the Javanese kingdom of Majapahit, according to the head of South Sumatra's Department of Tourism in the mid-1990s.[14]

A more recent symbol of Malay heritage and culture in the South Sumatran capital of Palembang was its defunct sultanate. However, there was little local interest in the sultanate since it was abolished by the Dutch in 1825. Its most famous figure, Sultan Mahmud Badaruddin II had attacked the Dutch a number of times but in 1821 was exiled to Ternate. History textbooks depict Sultan Mahmud Badaruddin II as a local Indonesian nationalist hero in line with the dominant national history-writing discourse, and both Palembang's international airport and provincial museum are named after him. Until recently, however, Palembang did not have visible icons to evoke this royal Malay past.[15] As well, in ethnically heterogeneous South Sumatra the authority of the sultans had not strongly permeated into the highlands, and creating a

South Sumatran identity focusing on a glorious court-based past was no easy task. Furthermore, the political status of Palembang's native Malays (*wong Palembang asli*) had been relatively weak, and they had not done much to raise their cultural profile.

After the fall of Suharto, however, these Palembang Malays were among those who responded to calls to boost local culture and pride in the new context of regional autonomy. Looking for local values led to a public discussion of the restoration of the *Simbur Cahaya*, the code of conduct based on *adat* (customary) law operating during the time of the sultanate, with a plan to revive cultural traditions around 2000.[16] This debate took place alongside the successful renovation of the Sultan of Palembang's Grand Mosque (Mesjid Agung).

In addition, the activities of a local organisation, Kerukunan Keluarga Palembang (KKP, the Association of Palembang Families) became more prominent after the fall of Suharto. This organisation was formed in the late 1980s so that Palembang natives would remember their traditional culture and use their local language, which was a dialect of Malay, with pride. According to the Association's head, Kgs Roni Hanan, a native of Palembang and a successful business person, Palembang natives were being left behind and marginalised in their hometown by migrants. His aim was to strengthen the identity (*jati diri*) of Palembang natives by teaching the younger generation their customs and language. With this vision, in 1999 the Association started the Palembang Darussalam Festival, to be held annually during the fasting month to showcase the greatness of Palembang as the centre of the Malay Islamic world. The festival started as a low-key event mainly attended by locals[17] but has gradually grown; it received strong support from the provincial government in 2003, when it was attended by several celebrated Islamic clerics, including Dai Sejuta Umat (K. H. Zainuddin MZ). Roni Hanan, told me that he was hoping that the political and economic position of native Palembang people would strengthen as their unique culture and customs gained more respect.[18] By 2004, the festival had become one of the major events in Palembang during the fasting month, attracting participants from outside the city.

It was in this context that South Sumatran governor Rosihan Arsyad, keenly contesting for a second term and engaging in profile-raising activities, organised the first Malay and Islamic World workshop in Indonesia in 2001.[19] During his governorship he also managed to successfully bid to host the National Sports Week (PON) in 2004. His efforts overlapped with Megawati Sukarnoputri's presidency (July 2001 to October 2004), when her husband, Taufik Kiemas, a native South Sumatran, was also said to be keen to improve Palembang's image by refurbishing some key urban areas of the city prior to the opening of the games. The games attracted visitors from outside the region and were a good venue for promoting the province's business and tourism potential. The city's key historic buildings, including the Grand Mosque, and Benteng Kuto Besak, the remains of the Palembang sultanate's fort located next to the Mosque along the Musi River, were given a facelift. Despite their direct connection to Palembang's sultanate, until 1998 such buildings and areas had been neglected. Furthermore, promoting Palembang as the Malay Islamic centre was receiving popular support. The governor and the provincial tourism body spent a large sum of money accommodating the delegates and visitors from other provinces at Swarna Dwipa Hotel, at the time one of Palembang's best hotels.[20]

As the host of the first Malay and Islamic World Movement workshop in Indonesia in May 2001, governor Rosihan Arsyad's keynote speech was in line with one he had delivered in Melaka in 2000. In his speech, he frequently used the term *serumpun Melayu* or one Malay stock.

FIGURE 3.1
Renovated Benteng Kuto Besak, Palembang (Photograph Minako Sakai)

He emphasised that the Malays had lost their unity and became scattered due to Western colonialism. With the end of the colonial era, the Malay peoples obtained sovereignty; some became part of an independent country, while others became a part of a state where Malays remained a minority. Arsyad viewed that Palembang had close historical ties with Melaka and Singapore and he felt that the people of South Sumatra had been called upon to be involved in an effort to unify *serumpun Melayu* following the first convention in 2000 in Melaka.

He identified four sectors as being crucial to the efforts to unify the Malays and to enhance the process of regional autonomy which had started in January 2001: education and religion; culture and tourism; investment and trade; and information and transportation. Other relevant specialists were invited to present papers at this convention. The majority of the speakers were politicians and officials from various countries (mainly Indonesia and Malaysia) who addressed issues of a practical nature, for example, destinations for regional tourism.[21]

At this workshop in Palembang, there was much discussion of the tourism potential of Bukit Seguntang, the hill where Iskandar Zulkarnain (Alexander the Great), the legendary ancestor of the Malay peoples, had descended. In addition, South Sumatra Province planned to renovate the banks of the Musi River as a waterfront resort, including the restoration of the Palembang fort. Until the beginning of 2000, the area was used as a minibus terminal, and frequented by vegetable traders. The roads were poorly paved, becoming muddy and wet during the rainy season. Within a few years, however, the provincial government transformed the riverside into a nicely paved waterfront entertainment area with some trendy restaurants. The provincial government also started an annual Malay dance and arts festival in 2002 to promote Palembang as a tourist destination. In December 2004, the third Malay dance and arts festival, attended by guests from Brunei and Malaysia, was held at the recently renovated Musi riverbank. The annual festival continues to attract local attention and guests were plentiful at the opening ceremony in 2006.[22] In 2008 the Musi Tourism Board was established by the provincial government to promote tourism to South Sumatra and organise numerous cultural events throughout the year; its executive board included native Malays from Palembang.[23] The renovated Malay heritage sites have become a focus of the video clips in the province's tourism campaigns.

With the increased interest in Malay culture in Palembang and revival of sultanates in other regions in Indonesia, the resurrection of the

FIGURE 3.2

Advertisement for Malay Dance Festival held in Palembang, 2004, profiling the then governor of South Sumatra Province (Photograph Minako Sakai)

Palembang Sultanate itself took place on 9 March 2003 in Palembang.[24] Drs Raden Haji Muhammad Sjafei Prabu Diradja, SH, a policeman and at the time also a member of the provincial parliament, was installed as Sultan Mahmud Badaruddin III. The resurrection of the sultanate was clearly with reference to other more prosperous regions in Indonesia and Malaysia which have preserved a strong Malay cultural identity. However, soon after the restoration, a controversy began, and continues, in the local media about the new Sultan's legitimacy and the authenticity of his genealogy.[25] The dominant view among local intellectuals was that the Palembang Sultanate had ended under the Dutch, and resurrection under any circumstances was not legitimate.

As these episodes suggest, reviving Malayness and promoting Palembang as Sumatra's Malay Islamic centre involves various actors who are trying to renegotiate power within local, national and global contexts and gain access to future development projects. Now let us turn to Padang.

Padang

West Sumatra is the heartland of the Minangkabau—a people with a strong ethnic identity and sense of tradition. The combination of a strong belief in Islam and unique matrilineal tradition in Minangkabau culture has attracted the attention of many local and foreign scholars. The Minangkabau are also widely known as emigrants: many have settled outside West Sumatra where they largely engage in small-scale trade.

After the fall of Suharto, West Sumatran local politicians and others began to emphasise their identity as Malays and encourage research to substantiate the shared roots of the Minangkabau and the Malays. One good example is the Gerakan Masyarakat Peduli Kebudayaan Melayu (GMPKM, the Movement of People Who Care about Malay Culture Foundation), which was set up on 7 July 2000 in Padang with the full support of West Sumatra's provincial governor at the time, Zainal Bakar, and local academics. Its chairperson and founder was a Partai Golongan Karya (Golkar, Functional Groups) member of the provincial parliament, Marizal Umar. The aim of this foundation is to lead and strengthen the cultures of the Malays of the Indonesian provinces of West Sumatra, North Sumatra, Riau, Jambi, South Sumatra, West Kalimantan as well as Malaysia, Singapore, Brunei, southern Thailand and the southern Philippines.

Based on this vision, the Foundation organised two seminars in 2002 which involved local academics substantiating the case for a Minangkabau-Malay identity. The first one was a seminar to critically examine Malay cultures in the past, present and future, and held in Padang in January 2002. The second seminar, held in March of that year, and entitled "Investigating the footsteps between Malay and Minangkabau through Language and Culture", was supported by the Department of Local Literature, Faculty of Letters at the University of Andalas in Padang and was held on campus.[26] In 2002 the Foundation also received 600 million rupiah from the provincial government in support of these events. However, the seminars did not attract much interest outside Padang: one member of the Foundation attributed this to the fact that they had not been advertised widely enough. In order to improve this situation and to present Padang as the centre of the Malay world, the Foundation held a Malay stock cultural festival to showcase dancing and singing by delegates from Sumatra, Kalimantan, Singapore, Brunei and Malaysia in December 2002.

According to Marizal Umar, the movement was sparked by the realisation that although Malays had once been progressive and united, they had been left behind and scattered across regions due to their colonial experience. During the Suharto era, in particular, Malays never attained high positions in government, and Indonesian political culture was heavily influenced by the Javanese. As a result the Minangkabau people no longer remember that they are a part of the wider Malay world. When I asked the chair for his definition of Malays, he implied that it was the task of academics to investigate and elaborate: as a politician he was there to provide opportunities for intellectuals to develop their ideas and he collaborated with local academics on issues relating to Minangkabau-Malay relations.[27]

The head of the Department of Regional Literature at the University of Andalas, Dr Media Sandra Kasih, was one of the Foundation's chief collaborators and supported Marizal Umar's view that anti-Javanese sentiments were behind the resurgence of Malay culture movements.[28] While undertaking her doctoral studies in Malaysia, she became conscious of the cultural ties between Malays in that country and the Minangkabau. After returning to Padang, she started to reflect further about the relations between the Malays and Minangkabau and wanted to organise a seminar on this issue with her colleagues. Her interests matched those of the Foundation, and they collaborated in organising the Minangkabau-Malay seminar held in March 2002.[29] As a continuation of this seminar, she was preparing to set up a research centre for Malay studies at the university financed by Malaysia's Dewan Bahasa dan Pustaka (Institute of Language and Literature) in order to promote the study of Malay literature. She held the view that people of Malay stock were everywhere—including West Sumatra, where Malay identity is inclusive. She strongly opposed the view that Riau Malays were the only genuine Malays and that the Minangkabau were not part of the Malay world.

Responding to the interest in inclusive Malayness in West Sumatra, the provincial government hosted the third Indonesian Malay and Islamic World Movement workshop in Bukit Tinggi in 2003. Hopes for further collaboration with the Malay Islamic world were high, despite, as mentioned earlier, some criticism about the ambiguity of the movement's aims. However, with the sudden deaths of two of its key pro-Malay advocates, Marizal Umar in 2002 and Media Sandra Kasih a few years later, followed by corruption charges against the then governor, Zainal Bakar, the advocates for Malayness in West Sumatra have lost some momentum.

Medan

Malayness in North Sumatra since the creation of the Republic of Indonesia has been a tricky issue. The sultans of the northeast coast of Sumatra were extremely wealthy since they leased out their land to the Dutch; but they were doomed by the "social revolution" (1945–46) when many Malay aristocrats were killed.[30] The awkwardness surrounding Malay identity in North Sumatra was further compounded during Sukarno's *Konfrontasi* (Confrontation) with Malaysia. The North Sumatran Malays who were related to various royal families in Malaysia felt torn between the Indonesian state and their cultural affinity with the Malays in Malaysia; Konfrontasi was seen as a test of their loyalty to the Indonesian state. With the dark memory of the revolution, North Sumatra's Malays were fearful of allegations that they were traitors.[31]

Such fears have contributed to the low profile of the Malays in this region. The four sultanates—Langkat, Serdang, Deli and Asahan—were not well known and it was in this context that the Majelis Adat Budaya Melayu Indonesia (Indonesian Malay Customs and Cultural Assembly) was formed in 1971 in order to unite the four royal families.[32]

It is therefore not surprising that North Sumatran Malays have also not been politically significant. Despite the glorious past of the Malay rulers, post-Independence provincial governorships had been occupied by non-Malays until 1998, when Tengku Rizal Nurdin was elected.[33] A member of the Serdang aristocracy, he was supportive of reviving Malayness and organised the second Indonesian Malay and Islamic World Movement workshop in 2002 in Medan to boost the province's profile within the Malay region. He was on the executive council of the Malay and Islamic World organisation, and enthusiastically led the push for Malay Islamic values in North Sumatra.[34] The Malays in North Sumatra strongly feel that they have been marginalised in their own homeland, a view often expressed, for example, by Tuanku Luckman Sinar Basyarsyah II, a prominent historian at North Sumatra University, as well as the current Sultan of Serdang.[35]

The role of sultans as the leaders of the Malays and proponents of Malay culture was highlighted during a major land dispute case against PT Perkebunan Nusantara II (PTPN II, State Plantation Company). Those who claimed land rights, including the sultans, undertook a series of demonstrations against the governor of North Sumatra. As a result of their struggle, 450 out of 50,000 hectares were released from PTPN II's concession areas and returned to the community. Yayasan Melayu Raya (Great Malay Foundation), established on 20 March 2003, headed by the four sultans, aims to use the returned land to enhance the welfare of the Malays in East Sumatra as well as elsewhere. The foundation intends to establish a Malay Centre, which will have educational institutions, a hospital, and a cultural centre to which Malays will have free access. The secretary of the Yayasan Melayu Raya, O. K. Saidin, stated that such opportunities would rectify the current marginalisation of North Sumatran Malays.[36]

Despite a series of activities to strengthen Malay culture in North Sumatra, the death of Tengku Rizal Nurdin in September 2005 in a plane crash seems to have set back the tide of reviving Malayness.

Riau

Riau, with its abundant oil and mineral deposits, is one of Indonesia's resource-rich territories. Identifying the ownership of this territory has never been an easy task since the region has multiple ethnic groups, including recent migrants, and contested territorial boundaries. Local elites jockeying for power have been constantly debating who the native people are and consequently who should control the province's natural resources. The breaking away of the Riau Archipelago from the mainland Riau Province in 2002 is one recent example of how the resource issue dominates local politics. Here I will briefly recount some major events in Riau's local politics, most of which are closely linked to identity politics in the Indonesian periphery. In this process, until recently, the focus was not so much about identifying Malayness per se as defining Riau natives in order to determine who legitimately owns Riau.[37]

Since Riau is ethnically heterogeneous, defining Malayness—and claiming indigeneity—on the basis of being descendants of the Malay sultanate has not been a successful strategy. For example, the first example of the politicisation of Malayness in Riau was in the movement to restore a Riau Sultanate after the declaration of Indonesia's independence. Seeing an opportunity to restore the sultanate, which had been abolished in 1911, Riau Malays called themselves "True Born Riau Malays" (*Melayu Riau Sejati*). However, this movement failed as it was seen as anti-nationalist and furthermore did not receive support from the non-Malay peoples of the province.[38]

The next example of the politicisation of Riau identity was the Riau Movement in the 1950s, which led to the separation of Riau Province

FIGURE 3.3

DMDI Workshop, Pekanbaru, Riau, Dec. 2007 (Photograph Minako Sakai)

from Central Sumatra, which comprised Jambi, West Sumatra and Riau in 1958.[39] The movement emphasised a "Riau Malay" identity to create the special territory of Riau Province, separate from West Sumatra and Jambi. This movement, and subsequent creation of Riau Province, shows that the key element in Riau identity is a sense of territorial belonging, rather than ethnicity.[40] Since the establishment of Riau Province, local politicians have focused on creating a Riau identity in order to define and guard their territory. Key government positions were often occupied by ethnic Javanese and Minangkabau and negative stereotypes of ethnic Malays were prevalent up until the late 1980s.[41] Ethnic Malays were politically and economically marginalised in their homeland. This began to change in the 1990s when Malays started to assert their ethnic identity through literature,[42] but the movement did not gain momentum because many local leaders were more focused on protecting Riau's resources against control by Jakarta-based and other neighbouring ethnic groups.

The conflict surrounding access to natural resources and increasing numbers of newcomers such as Minangkabau migrant traders were the driving force behind the formation of the Riau independence movements. In early 2000, the Second Riau People's Congress (Kongres Rakyat Riau II)[43] was organised in Pekanbaru and the participants opted for the independence of Riau from Indonesia over special autonomy.

In order to front up to the central government as a united Riau, leaders of the Riau Independence movement, for example, Tabrani Rab and Al Azhar, have used inclusive definitions of Malays within Riau in order to include non-Muslim indigenous ethnic people. Riau has a number of isolated ethnic groups, such as Sakai and Petalangan, whose homeland encompasses the province's key resource areas.[44] Both Tabrani Rab and Al Azhar are academics and political leaders in Pekanbaru who have actively publicised Riau Malay identity. In order to incorporate non-Muslim ethnic groups and their resource-rich homelands into Riau, Tabrani Rab and Al Azhar advocated that the core essence of Malayness is not based on Islam, but a common history and boundaries within the province. To reflect the heterogeneity of Riau's populace, the proposed Federal Republic of Riau acknowledged Christianity, animism and Buddhism in addition to Islam as recognised religions. On the other hand, in order to seek support from ethnic Malays, the republic also intended to promote and empower Riau Malay culture and values.[45]

The challenge for the Riau independence movement, however, came not only from Jakarta but from within Riau itself. People in the Riau Archipelago felt exploited by those on the mainland, and some leaders began making efforts to establish a Riau Archipelago Province, separate from the mainland. Their efforts finally led to official approval of the new Riau Archipelago Province in 2002 and its formation in 2004.[46] Those who fought for the creation of the Riau Archipelago Province justify their territorial claim on the basis of the Riau Sultanate, which flourished from the eighteenth to the twentieth centuries and included the Riau Archipelago, present-day Singapore and Johor but not mainland Riau. When a war broke out in 1722 between the aristocratic Malays of the Riau Archipelago and Raja Kecik from Johor, the defeated Raja Kecik withdrew to the mainland near Pekanbaru where he established the Siak Kingdom.[47] Furthermore, the archipelago was often economically viable without the mainland. In their view, the Riau Archipelago, rich with natural resources (sand from Bintan and Batam, tin from Singkep and Karimun and natural gas from Natuna) has been milked as a cash cow by the central government and the provincial government of Riau, and local residents were forced to accept nominal compensation in exchange for their precious land.⁴⁸ Economic development, particularly infrastructure, lagged as the provincial capital of Riau Province was in Pekanbaru on the mainland. While the governor of Riau Province refused to endorse the formation of the new province, Indonesia's Minister of Internal Affairs gave his in principle support, and the Dewan Perwakilan Rakyat (DPR, People's Representative Council, the lower house of legislature) in Jakarta officially endorsed the plan in September 2002. In 2004, Riau Archipelago became Indonesia's 32nd province and its first governor, Ismeth Abdullah, was elected in 2005.⁴⁹

Due to local politics, the official response to the assertion of Riau's status as the centre of an inclusive Malay Islamic or *serumpun Melayu* world was delayed compared with initiatives from Padang, Medan and Palembang.⁵⁰ However, along with recent increased interest in the fate of the marginalised Malays in their various homelands, particularly since the implementation of regional autonomy in Indonesia,⁵¹ the Riau provincial government has taken several measures to promote Riau as the centre of the Malay world. For example, the provincial government launched a development mission statement called Riau Vision for 2020 in which it stated its aim to become the centre of the Malay Islamic world.⁵² As a step to achieving this goal, a new governor of Riau Province, elected in 2003, Rusli Zainal, became the head of the newly formed Governors' Forum to represent Sumatra in the regional economic Indonesia-Malaysia-Thailand Growth Triangle (IMT-GT) in 2005. Despite a history of failed programs, Sumatran governors have begun to see the benefits of being part of the IMT-GT, which they hope will create a new centre in their own region, in collaboration with counterpart Malay regions.⁵³ One of the first steps was to launch a regional airline. During the New Order, Sumatran airline routes were designed to connect provincial towns to Jakarta; provincial air travel routes connecting Sumatran cities were extremely limited. In order to change this, Riau Airlines was launched in 2002, flying to Sumatran cities and Melaka from Pekanbaru.⁵⁴ In order to advance their 2020 vision, the provincial government also encouraged cultural leaders and academics to gather to discuss a proposal to recommend Malay as one of the United Nation's official languages in December 2007.⁵⁵

Conclusion

Based on my discussion of the motivations and aims of specific cases of reviving Malayness in various parts of Sumatra, several factors which have affected the resurgence of interest in Malay ethnicity emerge. The first factor is the absence of an absolute centre in post-Suharto Indonesia. The power of Jakarta and Javanese cultural hegemony are increasingly in decline in post-Suharto Indonesia and the power vacuum is noticeable to local elites, all of whom aim to make their province or region "the centre". As Vivienne Wee succinctly points out, in post-Suharto Indonesia, "there is no longer one relationship between the centre and periphery or even one centre and one periphery. There are multiple attempts to be the centre, there are multiple peripheries, and there are multiple interactions between all these."[56] The absence of an absolute centre/Jakarta is a most attractive context for local elites who want to create an economic and cultural centre in their respective regions, which had languished on the margins of Indonesia for nearly half a century.

In relation to this, the second factor is a popular expectation that regional autonomy will transfer power to native sons or so-called *putra daerah*, instead of to newcomers such as migrants from other parts of Indonesia. The Malays who had been marginalised in their homeland are looking for an opportunity to boost their status and power through the *serumpun Melayu* identity. A similar case of popular expectations fuelled by regional autonomy were demonstrated by the ethnic conflicts which broke out between the Dayak and the Madurese in Central Kalimantan in 2001 (see Hawkins, Chapter 8, this volume). For the Dayak, this was a long-awaited opportunity to become masters of their own land.[57]

The third factor is ongoing Islamisation in Indonesia, which particularly influenced the country's urban middle class. Political Islam was never fully successful during the Suharto era, but Islamisation was steadily permeating into the lives of the urban middle class. In the 1990s Suharto recognised the surge of popular interest in Islam and gave support to the formation of the Ikatan Cendekiawan Muslim Indonesia (ICMI, Association of Indonesian Muslim Intellectuals) and recruited some Muslim politicians to his cabinet in 1994. This change in Jakarta certainly affected popular perceptions of Islam across Indonesia: there was a surge in Islamic fashion and an increase in the number of pilgrimages before the economic crisis. Increasingly, middle-class women in Sumatran Malay cities started to wear Malay-Muslim clothes for social gatherings and many Muslim fashion shows were held in Sumatra. Islamic book publishing is also thriving in Indonesia.[58] In this context, such Islamisation is also strengthening Malay Islamic identity, bridging the territorial gap between Indonesia and the Malay world.

Regional autonomy has enabled provincial governments to seek economic ties with immediate neighbours without sponsorship from Jakarta. Furthermore, regional government heads now see a lucrative opportunity for collaboration in trade, education, communication and tourism. Suharto's Indonesia provided a direct transport and communication system between the peripheries and Jakarta as the single centre, but links among and within those peripheries remained weak.[59] Transport networks between Jakarta and the regions have been far more developed than the connections between or within the regions. Malay culture movements and their aims to establish alternative networks of communication and education are certainly a backlash against New Order era policies.

Notes

1. See M. Sakai and E. Morrell, "Reconfiguring Regions and Challenging the State? New Socio-economic Partnerships in the Outer Islands of Indonesia", in *Asia Reconstructed: Proceedings of the 16th Biennial Conference of the ASAA, 2006*, ed. A. Vickers and M. Hanlon (Canberra: ASAA and RSPAS, Australian National University, 2006), <http://coombs.anu.edu.au/SpecialProj/ASAA/biennial-conference/2006/proceedings.html>.
2. See J. C. Y. Liow, *The Politics of Indonesia-Malaysia Relations: One Kin, Two Nations* (London: RoutledgeCurzon, 2004) for an analysis of Malay identity in the bilateral relations between Indonesia and Malaysia.
3. See C. Faucher, "Popular Discourse on Identity Politics and Decentralisation in Tanjung Pinang Public Schools", *Asia Viewpoint* 47, 2 (2006): 273–85.
4. See T. P. Barnard, ed., *Contesting Malayness: Malay Identity across Boundaries* (Singapore: Singapore University Press, 2004).
5. A. Rew and J. R. Campbell. "The Political Economy of Identity and Affect", in *Identity and Affect: Experiences of Identity in a Globalising World*, ed. J. R. Campbell and A. Rew (London: Pluto Press, 1999), pp. 1–36.
6. I have been observing Malayu identity politics and related events since 2001 in Sumatran provincial towns (Medan, Padang, Pekanbaru, Pangkal Pinang, Palembang) and in Melaka in Malaysia by attending some key events. The data also draws on my interviews with local leaders.
7. See A. L. Abu Bakar, *"Kesatuan dan Perpaduan" Dunia Melayu Dunia Islam* (Batu Berendam: Institut Kajian Sejarah dan Patriotisme Malaysia, 2001), pp. 17–35.
8. Interview, 17 Feb. 2001, Melaka.
9. A similar message was delivered by Malaysia's Deputy Prime Minister, Datuk Seri Najib Tun Razak at the opening ceremony of the Malay and Islamic World Convention in 2005. See "Dunia Melayu Dunia Islam Elakkan Pergaduhan—Najib", *Melaka Hari Ini*, 1 Sept. 2005. The Indonesian delegates I talked to after his speech were highly motivated to unite the Malay world.

10. Tenas Effendi, a Malay cultural leader from Riau, who is a key intellectual working to revive Malayness, also expressed a similar view. Interview, Sept. 2005, Melaka.
11. See the DMDI website, <http://www.melayuislam.com> [accessed 14 Aug. 2008] for more details.
12. At the 2005 annual convention, Bangka-Belitung Province showed an elaborate presentation to promote investment opportunities within the region.
13. For example, at the time of the 6th workshop in Pontianak, the West Kalimantan governor, Usman Jafar expressed the government's commitment to DMDI activities, stating that he believed that they would become an important source of capital for West Kalimantan through collaborations between the DMDI members. See "DMDI Pacu Kemajuan Kalbar", *Equator*, 5 July 2006.
14. See T. P. Daniels, "Imagining Selves and Inventing Festival Sriwijaya", *Journal of Southeast Asian Studies* 30, 1 (1999): 38–53.
15. Until its recent renovation, the Grand Mosque of Palembang was surrounded by bustling shopping malls, shops and houses, was not an eye-catching building. During the renovation, surrounding buildings were demolished, which made the mosque visible from the main streets of Palembang.
16. Interview with Djohan Hanafiah in Palembang, Dec. 2004.
17. "Pesertanya Didominasi Sumsel", *Suara Karya*, 29 Nov. 2001.
18. Interview, Dec. 2004 in Palembang.
19. I attended this workshop.
20. Three more luxury hotels (Novotel, Aston and Horison) were built before PON and are now used by the government to hold events.
21. In 2000, Palembang authorised Pelangi Air to fly between Melaka and Palembang to facilitate communication between the two cities. However, the business did not last for long. At the time of writing in April 2008, Air Asia flies to Palembang from Kuala Lumpur and Silk Air flies to Palembang from Singapore.
22. "Festival Seni Tari Melayu Upaya Mempertahankan Kesenian Melayu", *Kompas*, 8 Sept. 2006.
23. For further details of the activities, see the official website, <http://www.visitmusi2008.com/sumsel.php?a=dis>.
24. Interest in reviving Sultanates increased dramatically in various parts of the Indonesian archipelago after the fall of Suharto. For a summary of the revival movements linked to the Sultanates, see G. van Klinken, "Return of the Sultans: Local Community and the Rejection of Modernity after Suharto", in *The Revival of Tradition in Indonesian Politics: The Deployment of Adat from Colonialism to Indigenism*, ed. J. Davidson and D. Henley (London: Routledge, 2007), pp. 149–69.
25. "Silsilah SMB III Dapat Dipertanggungjawabkan", *Sriwijaya Post*, 28 Mar. 2003.
26. The conference proceedings were published as *Menelusuri Jejak Melayu-Minangkabau*, ed. S. Y. Bakry and M. S. Kasih (Padang: Yayasan Citra Budaya, 2002).

27. Interview, Apr. 2002
28. Interview, Apr. 2002.
29. I attended this conference in person.
30. See A. Reid, *The Blood of the People: Revolution and the End of Traditional Rule in Northern Sumatra* (Kuala Lumpur: Oxford University Press, 1979).
31. An interview with O. K. Saidin, July 2004 in Medan.
32. N. Fau, "Reviving Serumpun Identity across the Straits of Malacca", a paper presented at the International Symposium "Thinking Malayness", 19–21 June 2004, University of Foreign Studies, Tokyo.
33. After completing his first term (1998–2003), Tengku Rizal Nurdin was elected for a second term.
34. Tengku Rizal Nurdin also supported the development of an Islamic economy and sponsored the inaugural meeting of the Ikatan Ahli Ekonomi Islam (Association of Islamic Economists) in 2005.
35. "Masyarakat Melayu Sumut Kian Terpinggirkan", *Kompas*, 13 June 2000.
36. Interview, July 2004, Medan.
37. V. Wee, "Ethno-nationalism in Process: Ethnicity, Atavism and Indigenism in Riau, Indonesia", *Pacific Review* 15, 4 (2002): 502.
38. Ibid.
39. A. F. Saifuddin and Z. Hidayah, "Etnisitas dan Proses Politik: Rekonstruksi Kemelayuan di Riau", in *Laporan Penelitian: Kebijakan Kebudayaan di Masa Orde Baru*, ed. Pusat Penelitian dan Pengembangan Kemasyarakatan dan Kebudayaan (LIPI) with the Ford Foundation (Jakarta: LIPI, 2001), pp. 557–86.
40. M. Ford, "Who are the Orang Riau? Negotiating Identity across Geographic and Ethnic Divides", in *Local Power and Politics in Indonesia: Decentralisation and Democratisation*, ed. E. Aspinall and G. Fealy (Singapore: ISEAS, 2003), p. 137.
41. See W. Derks, "Malay Identity Work: Riau in Transition", *Bijdragen tot de Taal-, Land- en Volkenkunde* (Special Issue: Riau in Transition) 153, 4 (1997): 702–6.
42. Ibid.
43. The first Riau People's Congress was held to demand the separation of Riau Province from Central Sumatra Province in the 1950s.
44. See T. Rab, *Menuju Riau Berdaulat: Pilihan Kongres Rakyat Riau II* (Pekanbaru: Riau Culture Institute and UNRI Press, 2002), which cites historical, economic, political and cultural arguments for the independence of Riau from Indonesia.
45. Ibid., pp. 151 and 253.
46. A similar case of territorial division took place in South Sumatra Province which lost territory to the newly created Bangka-Belitung Province. See M. Sakai, "Resisting the Mainland: The Formation of the Province of Bangka Belitung (Babel)", in *Autonomy and Disintegration in Indonesia*, ed. D. Kingsbury and H. Aveling (London: Routledge, 2003), pp. 189–200.

47. Wee, "Ethno-nationalism in Process".
48. S. Napitupulu and F. Jaswir, "Kepulauan Riau: Melayu Punya Susu Jakarta yang Enak", *Gamma* 2, 5 (2000): 36.
49. See Provinsi Kepulauan Riau (Kepulauan Riau Province), <http://kepriprov.go.id/id/index.php?option=com_content&task=view&id=55&Itemid=91> [accessed 15 Aug. 2008].
50. Some symposia on the theme of inclusive Malayness were held in the 1990s, for example, in July 1994 in Pekanbaru. See Derks, "Malay Identity Work", p. 711.
51. See Suryadi, "Identity, Media and the Margins: Radio in Pekanbaru, Riau (Indonesia)", *Journal of Southeast Asian Studies* 36, 1 (2005): 141.
52. This vision was initially stipulated in a provincial by-law (36/2001) regarding the foundation of regional economic development for 2001–5.
53. See Sakai and Morrell, "Reconfiguring Regions".
54. In practice, the company is run by the provincial government and was not customer-oriented. For example, when I flew in January 2007, it was difficult to buy a ticket. The planes were old and the in-flight service was not appealing. However, the airfare was competitive.
55. I attended this conference in person. Riau delegates initially wanted to propose Bahasa Melayu as one of the official languages at the United Nations. They did not feel that the term Bahasa Indonesia had to be used. However, in trying to write a recommendation, committee members from Jakarta and Sulawesi insisted that, for the United Nations, the language should be called not only Bahasa Melayu, but also Bahasa Indonesia. The discussions clearly showed that Melayuness was not easily accepted beyond the boundaries of Malay Sumatrans.
56. Wee, "Ethno-nationalism in Process", p. 513.
57. K. Widen, "The Resurgence of Dayak Identities: The Symbols of their Struggle for Regional Autonomy are Self-Evident", in *Beyond Jakarta: Regional Autonomy and Local Societies in Indonesia*, ed. M. Sakai (Adelaide: Crawford, 2002), pp. 102–20; G. van Klinken, "Indonesia's New Ethnic Elites", in *Indonesia: In Search of Transition*, ed. H. Schulte Nordholt and I. Abdullah (Yogyakarta: Pustaka Pelajar, 2002), pp. 67–106.
58. For recent accounts of Islamic publications in Indonesia, see C. W. Watson, "Islamic Books and Their Publishers: Notes on the Contemporary Indonesian Scene", *Journal of Islamic Studies* 16, 2 (2005): 177–210.
59. M. Charras, "The Reshaping of the Indonesian Archipelago after 50 Years of Regional Imbalance", in *Regionalism in post-Suharto Indonesia*, ed. M. Erb, P. Sulistiyanto and C. Faucher (London: RoutledgeCurzon, 2005), pp. 87–108.

CHAPTER 4

Indonesia, Aceh and the Modern Nation-State

Anthony Reid

Models of Nationalism and the Nation-State

Much of the recent literature on the rise of ethno-nationalism in Central and Eastern Europe points to certain socio-economic factors—industrialisation, urbanisation, mobility within certain borders, mass education, print capitalism—which transformed Europe in the late nineteenth and early twentieth centuries.[1] The same factors have been transforming Southeast Asia almost a century later, as its population shifts from a predominantly rural and agrarian to a largely urban, industrial and educated one. As the lid of authoritarian regimes such as Suharto's Indonesia is lifted and populist politics flourish, should we expect new forms of ethno-nationalism to begin redrawing the boundaries of Southeast Asia? Do we gain more insight into the likely path of a country like Indonesia by contemplating France in the late nineteenth century, when a post-revolutionary centralising state turned "peasants into Frenchmen" through education and mass communications,[2] or the Hapsburg and

Turkish empires of the same period, increasingly rent by populist nationalist movements, each demanding a separate nation-state?

If the latter were the model, the twenty-first century might see a repeat in Asia of the ghastly history of twentieth-century Central Europe, in which a new order of ethnically homogeneous nation-states struggled into being at a terrible cost in warfare and the persecution of minorities. The fate of Marxist, post-revolutionary regimes in Moscow and Belgrade, which for a half-century or more prolonged imperial boundaries at the expense of ethno-nationalist claims, could suggest similar outcomes for post-revolutionary Indonesia and Burma, or eventually China.

Twentieth-century Asian nationalisms were on the whole designed to bring about European-style nation-states, because these had proved "the sure and attested way of attaining power and wealth", as William McNeill has put it.[3] But ethnic homogeneity was not part of the original agenda of most of these Asian nationalisms,[4] and even democracy was relatively low on that agenda in comparison to anti-colonialism, modernisation, Western-style education and Marxist economics. Now that democracy and mass politics *are* central parts of the agenda, will ethnic homogeneity prove a necessary accompaniment? Must Asians undergo similar traumas before emerging with the kind of nation-states that western Europeans had by 1945? If so, they are in for a very rough century, and Indonesia (along with countries such as Burma, India and Pakistan) will be as doomed as the Austro-Hungarian empire. This possibility seemed very real to Indonesians and others as they contemplated the upheavals in the Balkans and experienced their own painful democratisation in the 1990s. Many Indonesianists began to think about this previously unthinkable future for Indonesia.

On the other hand, international conditions have changed greatly in the past century, and chiefly in the direction of a post-nationalist globalised order. In this new world, might national sovereignty have so little meaning that people will no longer die for it? Rather, from Palestine to Chechnya and Ayodhya, is twenty-first century political violence motivated rather by newly imagined global communities and in reaction to globally demonised enemies?

Southeast Asia is an important place to ponder these questions, because like Europe it represents one of the crumpled extremities of the Eurasian land-mass where empires failed to unify and pluralisms remain intense. So far, the borders of its states, however, are those created by foreign imperialisms, and not by the kind of mass politics, ethnic competition and warfare which created the nation-states of Europe. Nor do Southeast Asian borders have any of the antiquity of those between China and its former tributaries in Korea and Vietnam, where more than a thousand years of bureaucratic government have built the most stable (though far from peaceful) borders in the world. The rest of pre-colonial Southeast Asia is a world where we can speak historically of cultural cores, or mandalas of influence, but not of borders. Let me now turn to the particular case of Indonesia.

Indonesia and the Nation-State

I have argued elsewhere that the political genius of the archipelago in the long term has been the way complex cultural communities were formed and sustained by something other than central military/bureaucratic power—be it kinship networks, market cycles, charismatic kings, sacred sites or the "theatre" of ritual. The intense pluralities and mutualities of such systems may have allowed for much low-level violence and contestation, or in places even required it. Yet, the attractions of flexibility and freedom in such a system seemed to outweigh the disadvantages of instability. It was not because Indonesians were unaware of bureaucratic states that they persevered with their looser systems, since they had interacted with the mother of all bureaucracies, China, since at least the thirteenth century. In the sixteenth century, Chinese chroniclers still spoke of these southern barbarians (*man* and *yi*) as inherently antithetic to states—"Like the birds and beasts, without human morality."[5] Malay texts of the same period seem to acknowledge the power of Chinese bureaucracy but to rejoice in the proverbial agility of weak-state southerners in outmanoeuvring the great behemoth through sheer trickery.[6]

For at least the past decade, one of the thrusts of new history-writing about pre-colonial Indonesia has been to explore the fascinating absence of states in our modern sense of military and police power, law and bureaucracy. If I may quote myself:

> In Indonesia the state has always been essentially coastal and sustained by foreign resources, while the highlands have been miracles of statelessness, tenuously held together by kinship systems and ritual obligations rather than bureaucracy.... So persistently has each step towards stronger states in the archipelago arisen from trading ports, with external aid and inspiration, that one is inclined to seek the indigenous political dynamic in a genius for managing without states.[7]

David Henley took me to task in a recent publication, for implying that this semi-statelessness was a preferred condition, whereas his evidence, especially from northern Sulawesi before 1900, appeared to show an eagerness to escape from the uncertainties of statelessness once a Dutch presence provided an alternative.[8] He may be onto something here. There were certainly Indonesian societies which behaved this way, even including the Balinese, who fought dramatically to the point of ritual suicide against the new Dutch order, and yet appeared to accept peacefully the notion of a Dutch referee for their conflicts once the war was lost. The low state or magical state phenomena we keep finding in Indonesia may be imposed as much by environmental factors as by cultural preference. Port rulers who *could* generate bureaucratic power from the wealth of maritime trade, of whom the Dutch were the most important, were often seen as a necessary evil or perhaps even a good. I will return to this issue in the case of the successor Indonesian state.

The kind of description of pre-colonial society which set historians off in this direction is well reflected by Stamford Raffles' description of the Sumatran societies he encountered from his base in Bencoolen:

> Sumatra is, in a great measure, peopled by innumerable petty tribes, subject to no general government.... At present the people are as wandering in their habits as the birds of the air, and until they are congregated and organised under something like authority, nothing can be done with them.[9]

Lest this seem an extreme "stateless" example, one might explore the internal workings of polities generally taken by the outside world to be hierarchic monarchies, such as those of the Bugis in South Sulawesi. In fact these were wonderfully complex contractual alliances between lineages, where at the enthroning of each new king (in Wajo) the constituting lineage chiefs would ritually declare, "I will conduct my own affairs, I will preserve my manners, I will maintain my custom, only if I need it will I appeal to your advice."[10]

Older writers sometimes consigned to a little-understood Weberian "charisma" this curiously different Southeast Asian understanding of how power worked. Indonesianists of my generation have been particularly indebted, however, to their two most influential gurus—Benedict Anderson and Clifford Geertz—who began to look at the phenomenon more carefully in the 1970s and 1980s, initially cooperatively.[11] Anderson's influential 1972 essay famously contrasted a Javanese idea of power, "that intangible, mysterious and divine energy which animates the universe", to a more abstract understanding in the modern West.[12]

Subsequently, Geertz published *Negara* in 1980, perhaps his most influential book among historians at large, though irritating to Bali-scholars. On the largely historical evidence of nineteenth-century Bali (supplemented of course by his fieldwork in the 1960s) he developed the paradigm of the "theatre state",

> In which the kings and princes were the impresarios, the priests the directors, and the peasants the supporting cast, stage crew and audience.... Court ceremonialism was the driving force of the court politics; and mass ritual was not a device to shore up the state, but rather the state, even in its final gasp, was a device for the enactment of mass ritual. Power served pomp, not pomp power.[13]

As happens all too often, the historians then began to elaborate the trail blazed by a political scientist and an anthropologist. If Geertz had found the key to what pre-colonial Indonesian politics were about in theatrical state ritual, Wolters found it in the way Southeast Asian "men of prowess" appropriated Hindu concepts of the sacred.[14] Anthony Milner found in Malay texts evidence that the purchase of "ceremonial rulers" around the Strait of Melaka was modest but real.[15] Writing in the 1990s, Jane Drakard (for Minangkabau) explained kingly power in terms of the charismatic power of the written word; Luc Nagtegal (for Java) and Henk Schulte Nordholt (for Bali) in terms of unstable competing networks of kinship and ritual; Merle Ricklefs (for Java) and Margaret Wiener (for Bali) in magical ritual means of weaving, or at least asserting, coherence and unity. Finally, Leonard Andaya argued for Maluku that its political system required carefully balanced dualities and quadripartite division, which warred with each other even while recognising each other's indispensability to the system.[16]

While all these writers used the abundant Dutch evidence of the seventeenth to nineteenth centuries to document Indonesian political styles, others were in a parallel way demolishing the myth that the ancient states of which less was known had been powerful "empires" before the modern period of decline. Indonesian nationalism had, of course, been particularly excited by the European discovery in the period 1890–1920 of the Javanese kingdom of Majapahit (which flourished in the fourteenth century) and the Sumatran one of Sriwijaya (more amorphously potent from seventh to twelfth centuries). But Jan Christie has systematically shown how decentred Majapahit and all other Javanese "kingdoms" were.

"Political ties and tax rights in Java tended, over time, to devolve into somewhat unstable and territorially unfocussed chains of patron-client ties, as tax-collecting authority, like everything else, tended to subdivide rather than accumulate."[17] Wolters, Manguin and others similarly laboured to make sense of the relative absence of temple remains at what was believed to be the heart of Sriwijaya, preferring a loose model of shifting trade centres and sacred or magical sites.[18]

Riding as I have on these many attempts to grapple with the elusive "otherness" of statehood in Southeast Asia, Tony Day has produced the first attempt to synthesise and interpret the new work on a Southeast Asian scale—though the scheme works best for Indonesia (and not at all for Singapore and Vietnam). His *Fluid Iron* helpfully rejects any traditional/modern or indigenous/external dichotomies of state. Rather, he categorises the different theories about how power was managed and society made to cohere in terms of four themes, all of which survive in contemporary Indonesia. The first is kinship, encompassing both familiar kinship ties and the gendered and hierarchic imagery of family, love and paternalism. The second is the role of knowledge, particularly outside knowledge, in cosmological sources of power, which he insists, "continue to exist until this very day, even in Marxist writings".[19] Bureaucracy qualifies as Day's third category, even though he takes the rather strong position that "Even in its most authoritarian and totalitarian forms, the Southeast Asian state is closer to anarchy than to statehood in a Weberian sense."[20] Yet "bureaucratic polity" arguments remain prominent in the literature of colonial and post-colonial polities. What is it, Day asks, "that looks like a bureaucracy, in early as well as contemporary times, but is not one, according to a Weberian definition".[21] The missing glue the first three categories fail to provide is to be found in Day's fourth category, state violence and terror, still "the primary 'sanctioning capacity' of the modern Southeast Asian nation-state".[22]

The debate continues. While appreciating Day's emphasis on hybridities and subtle interactions over time between his four themes, I continue to see foreign-ness as essential to the purchase enjoyed by both his second and third categories.[23] In pre-colonial, inland and upland Indonesia, processes of fragmentation and balance prevented economic power from accumulating, while maintaining socio-cultural interactions of various kinds that maintained the high culture. More bureaucratically or militarily powerful states always drew their wealth, power and legitimation from the outside through trade, like the Muslim gunpowder empires of Aceh,

Makasar and Banten. By far the greatest such concentration of power was the Dutch East India Company (VOC), which in many areas made such a mark that its successor, the Dutch colonial state of the nineteenth and twentieth centuries, continued to be known as the *kumpeni*. Before 1900 the great majority of Indonesians experienced the modern bureaucratic state as an external and alien phenomenon to be negotiated around, even if it was sometimes useful.

The modern sense of state, as an entity monopolising the legal use of force within fixed boundaries, came unusually late to the Indonesian archipelago. It came, moreover, at Dutch hands. Only in the few years before and after 1900 did the Dutch abandon the elaborate process of signing hundreds of diverse treaties with local rulers through whom they would attempt to rule, in favour of short, sharp declarations (*korte verklaring*) that:

> territory X forms a part of Netherlands India and thereby stands under the sovereignty of the Netherlands.... And I will follow all commands that are or shall be given to me by or on behalf of the Governor-General or His representative.[24]

From the point when Van Heutsz, Idenburg and Colijn imposed this declaration throughout the archipelago in the first decade of the twentieth century, all Indonesians encountered some elements of the modern nation-state—a monopoly of force, single currency and unified market, uniform bureaucratic and military structures and the beginning of a unitary education system. But of course other key elements of the nation state were *not* encouraged by the colonial system, including mass education, political mobilisation and the welding of common consciousness through symbolic representation. Given the extent of indirect rule through myriad rajas and sultans, the Netherlands Indies in several respects never reached even the degree of common consciousness of the absolutist states of seventeenth-century Europe, or perhaps China of the Ming and Qing dynasties. This imagining of community was of course the task of nationalism. Under the Japanese occupation and during the revolution, in the hands of Sukarno, nationalism did achieve an astonishing if unstable invention of national consciousness. Finally, under Suharto's 33-year regime it did really appear to many observers that this consciousness was creating stable roots through sustained manipulation of education, indoctrination classes (P4) and the controlled media.[25]

Nevertheless the Indonesian state remained a successor of the alien and imposed colonial one, and constantly resorted to force and censorship to impose itself. Some, including Anderson in the 1980s, tended to see it as an artificial and necessarily authoritarian successor of Netherlands India, with little indigenous life in it.[26] I too had been questioning, before Suharto's fall and Timor's independence, whether true mass nationalism was in the past or the future of states like Indonesia.[27] I thought we should be looking carefully at potential ethno-nationalisms in Indonesia and elsewhere to see whether any of these were likely to tear the fabric of the post-colonial plural autocracies under new conditions of popular democracy. However, the lectures I gave in 1996 and 1997, largely based on fieldwork in northern Sumatra in 1995, took the view that conditions were unfavourable for the breakup of Indonesia into populist ethno-nationalist states. The reasons were essentially twofold:

- Internally, Indonesia was urbanising into inherently plural, "Indonesian" cities, leaving very few large cities which could serve as hothouses for ethnonationalism (as Budapest, Prague or Zagreb did in the Austrian empire). I was astonished, for example, at the high proportions (over 90 per cent) of my student sample in Medan who said that they spoke Indonesian not only to each other but to their parents. At the same time, my surveys showed exceptionally high rates of education and outmigration from three rural Batak villages. Although I spent only a few days in Aceh during that fieldwork, this experience did not dissuade me from the conclusion that nineteenth-century France was a better parallel for contemporary Indonesia than Austro-Hungary.
- Externally, the world is now so integrated economically and in communications that much of the point of independence struggles is removed, and the international community has become less tolerant of them, while the need for internal cultural homogeneity is lessened.

Since Suharto's fall in May 1998, the pressures of democratisation at a time of drastic economic downturn have of course been extremely destabilising, and pressure to break up Indonesia into smaller and possibly more homogeneous units grew much faster than anyone could have imagined. After the radical shift in opinion in Aceh during 1999, I paid two more brief visits there (January 2000 and January 2003), which required severe rethinking of these earlier conclusions. But for most of Indonesia I want to modify rather than abandon them. Indigenous society's very resistance to rational/bureaucratic states in the past has made the externally-imposed colonial/Indonesian state more necessary today. The long-term pattern is still for the Indonesian state and mass media to turn the archipelago's peoples into Indonesians, similar enough in their educated and popular use of the Indonesian language to create a moral community. Democratisation, however, entails an overdue lowering of expectations about how the myths and emotions of Indonesian unity are translated as political uniformity and loyalty. Increasingly in a globalised world, "Indonesia" becomes the frame or window through which global forces are embraced, rather than the wall to keep it out.

In short, most Indonesians outside Java experienced "state" in its modern sense only in the form of an alien imposition, the *kumpeni*, through the last century. This was liberating for some, oppressive for others. Within a generation of its imposition, however, this concept of state became firmly associated with modernity, progress and power. Nationalism sought to invent an "Indonesian" face for it. Within a single decade of the 1940s, the magic was effected of making this appear the only valid concept of state, endowed with a great deal of passion and rhetoric. Unfortunately, but not surprisingly, it proved impossible to maintain this novel and once-alien concept except with increasing levels of force. Nevertheless, the archipelago has maintained, better than most contemporary places, viable non-state systems of cultural coherence. It seems likely both that many of them will remain, and that the only modern state positioned above them as a mediator of international forces will continue to be something like the Indonesian state, the descendant of the *kumpeni*.

Aceh's Anomalous Position

What then is the particular problem of Aceh and Papua? Historically, the reasons are as opposite as their locations in the archipelago. In terms of my theme, the central anomaly of Aceh is the way it was defined by a state; while the central anomaly of Papua is that it experienced neither a state, until the very late (1920s) Dutch conquest, nor a common culture of the type that united stateless societies like the Batak and Minangkabau. While this difference makes Acehnese more likely than Papuans to relate effectively to their own state, there are of course international factors which lean much more in Papua's direction. Let me focus henceforth on Aceh.

I mentioned above that the more bureaucratically powerful states were always sustained and legitimated by outside forces, such as trade, technology and religion. At least three of Indonesia's modern ethnicities,

Aceh, Makasar and Banten, were in fact created by gunpowder empires of the same name in the "age of commerce". The Makasar and Banten states, however, were conquered and demoralised by the Dutch in 1669 and 1684, respectively. In Banten's case, a client sultan survived into the nineteenth century, and enough memory of state remained to motivate the successful 1998 movement for a separate Banten Province. The misfortune of the Makasarese in these terms was that their capital became the centre of Dutch and later Indonesian power in Sulawesi, and hence other ethnicities came to dominate it. Aceh is virtually alone as an identity explicitly formed by a state over four centuries, the memory of which was still vigorous in the twentieth. For Acehnese, it was the Dutch/Indonesian state that appeared the more artificial, with only a century of heavily contested occupancy of the territory.

Besides this central relation to the state, there are some other historically distinctive features of Aceh, which may be summarised as follows.

Firstly, until the Dutch conquest in the late nineteenth century, Aceh's diplomatic and economic linkages were to the Indian Ocean and the Malayan Peninsula, not to the Java Sea world dominated by first Java and then the Dutch. It was part of the Indian Ocean Islamic œcumene ever since Pasai was visited and described by Ibn Battuta in the fourteenth century. Aceh's "tribute" to Ottoman Turkey in the period 1538–68[28] was as natural in this connection as was that of Java to Ming China in the fifteenth century.

Secondly, Aceh's pepper production, first in the sixteenth and seventeenth centuries, and again in the period 1800–70, when the sultanate provided half the world's supply, gave it strong trade links to Turkey, India, England, the United States, France and Italy, all of which were appealed to diplomatically at some time. From about 1850 trade was reorganised through entrepôts on the regular steamer route, so that Penang became for Aceh "the gateway to the world; yes, the world itself", according to Snouck Hurgronje in 1893. "Exclusively on the experience of Acehnese in Penang rests the general conviction in Aceh that the rule of the English would be infinitely preferable to ours."[29]

The sultanate was particularly active internationally in the period 1868–74, as Dutch determination to round out its claims to Sumatra became increasingly clear. Britain had signed a treaty of protection and alliance with Aceh in 1819 (through Stamford Raffles), and in handing over its rights to Sumatra to the Dutch in 1824 had consequently required that

Aceh's independence be respected. This guarantee was waived by Britain in 1871 in return for Dutch concessions in West Africa, and the Dutch immediately thereafter began to bully Aceh into recognition of Dutch sovereignty. In consequence, Aceh renewed an active policy of seeking alliances with Turkey, France, Britain, Italy and the United States. It was Acehnese contacts with the US consul, in particular, that gave the Dutch war party the opportunity to propel Holland into a war for which it was astonishingly ill-prepared.

Acehnese pride in this distinct past took shape in the extremely bitter resistance to the Dutch of 1873–1914, the last part of which was focused in the Gayo area, ethnically distinct but sufficiently associated with the sultanate to resist heroically in its name. In total about 100,000 people died through war and attendant disruption on the Acehnese side, as against about 16,000 on the Dutch side.[30] Even at the most peaceful moment of the Dutch occupation, the 1930s, the Dutch governor could warn that every Acehnese nourished "a fanatical love of freedom, reinforced by a powerful sense of race, with a consequent contempt for foreigners and hatred for the infidel intruder", so that a constant display of superior force was the only thing which kept Dutch rule intact there.[31] One should never underestimate the readiness of Acehnese to sacrifice for this national pride.

Rebellions have been a constant theme, in every decade of the twentieth century. The periodic anti-Dutch rebellions of the 1920s and 1930s culminated in early 1942, as a Japanese invasion became imminent. An uprising forced the Dutch to abandon Aceh before any Japanese had landed—the only place where this happened. And although the insurgent Acehnese then welcomed the Japanese, by 1944 there was another rebellion, among the bloodiest in wartime Indonesia, against the Japanese military. The rebellions against Jakarta's control under Teungku Daud Beureu'eh (who had been the most influential ulama and revolutionary leader of 1945–50) in 1953–62, and the then little-known Hasan Tiro since 1976, left relatively short periods of the twentieth century during which Aceh was not disturbed by rebellion against Jakarta.

The specific idea of an Acehnese state was never far from the minds of those opposing the Jakarta status quo in Aceh. Until his submission to the Dutch in 1903, the "pretender sultan", Tuanku Muhammad Daud, had been at the heart of resistance for forty years. In 1938–40 the groups most dissatisfied with the power of the *ulèëbalang* aristocracy in Aceh, notably including many reformist ulama, rallied behind the idea of a restored sultanate.³² During the anti-Dutch revolution of 1945–49 these same groups shifted to supporting the Indonesian Republic and seized the opportunity to eliminate their *ulèëbalang* rivals, a few of whom were pro-Dutch. Aceh was a model of resistance to all ideas emanating from the Dutch in this contested period, including federalism, though in practice Acehnese had no need of federal safeguards since they were fully in control of Aceh. Daud Beureu'eh's 1953 rebellion was overtly to support not an independent Aceh, but an Indonesian Islamic state (NII) for which he believed Aceh had fought in the revolution. Nevertheless, two years later, a separate Negara Bahagian Aceh (Aceh federal state) was established by the rebels through the Batee Kureng Declaration of 23 September 1955, under a powerful *Wali Negara* or head of state (Daud Beureu'eh himself), a prime minister and a cabinet.³³

The different way in which Acehnese have experienced being part of a state in the past does not in itself mean they cannot live within the bounds of an Indonesian state. Aceh has had two important elites in the past century, the Islamic-educated and the state-educated. In 1945 enough of both elites, including the young Hasan Tiro himself, enthusiastically supported the Indonesian Republic to carry the day against some of the Dutch-educated *ulèëbalang* who wanted to defend the established order. The new history developed by Hasan Tiro in the 1970s, and becoming popular after 1998, is wide of the mark in claiming that, after the Japanese surrender, Aceh "was turned over by the Dutch to the Javanese—their mercenaries—by hasty fiat of colonial powers", and that Acehnese had no part in this transition.³⁴ It may be true that the rural majority of Aceh's population had not been effectively socialised as Indonesians by the 1940s, but Tiro's generation of educated youth threw themselves enthusiastically onto the Indonesian side, taking their mentors like Daud Beureu'eh with them.

Indeed, Aceh has a particularly central historical relationship to two factors—Islam and the Malay/Indonesian language—which help to make Indonesia coherent. A Malay-language, Southeast Asian variant of Islam was first developed in Pasai (near modern Lhokseumawe) in the fourteenth and fifteenth centuries, and was given literary substance in Aceh in the sixteenth and seventeenth centuries through such writers as Hamzah Fansuri, Nuruddin ar-Raniry, and Abdurra'uf of Singkel or Syiah Kuala (the last two being celebrated in the names of Aceh's two universities).

Acehnese appear to have written in Malay as far back as they were able to write, and all the early Acehnese texts are in that language or

Arabic. Only in the late seventeenth century does there begin to be evidence of writing in Acehnese, which remained for the most part a language of speech and recitation. The Aceh linguist Mark Durie has described the Acehnese texts which were written in the nineteenth and twentieth centuries as being "framed" in a context of Malay and Arabic, whereby the beginning and end of texts were in Malay, with an Arabic exordium.[35] Durie believes there has never been "an established tradition of instruction in reading and writing Acehnese"—those who could recite Acehnese texts to an audience had already learned to read through Malay and Arabic.[36] Despite the considerable effort since 1999 to publish Acehnese dictionaries and writings and to press for its use in schools, Acehnese are wedded to Malay/Indonesian in a fundamental way.

On the other hand, Hasan Tiro exposed a vulnerable nerve when he attacked the viability of the Indonesian state concept.

> Indonesia' is merely a new label, in a totally foreign nomenclature ... to replace the despicable 'Dutch East Indies' in an attempt to unite the administration of their ill-gotten far-flung colonies.... If Dutch colonialism was wrong, then Javanese colonialism which was squarely based on it cannot be right.[37]

The emotional and moral capital invested in the Republik Indonesia concept in the period 1945–98 created expectations of conformity that the colonial state had never imagined and the independent one could only appear to deliver through violence and often terror.

A more matter-of-fact acceptance of the state as a necessary and convenient window to the modern world can live more comfortably with diversity, anomalies and even rivals. The Indonesian government's acceptance of the Helsinki Memorandum of Understanding of 15 August 2005 was a remarkable step towards pragmatism on this front. The agreement itself departed radically from the centralised unitary state so dear to both Sukarno and Suharto, by allowing for the position of *Wali Nanggroe* (a head of state by another name), "regional symbols including a flag, a crest and a hymn", and full self-government in all areas not reserved to Jakarta, i.e. "foreign affairs, external defence, national security, monetary and fiscal matters, justice and freedom of religion".[38] In principle this was a completely new departure towards pragmatically asymmetric government, in which one constituent of the Republic has considerably more legal autonomy than others. Such arrangements are familiar in federal Malaysia and Canada, and long accepted in the United Kingdom, but go against the grain in post-revolutionary centralised republics such as

Indonesia.[39] Nationalists within the Indonesian parliament and military, as well as conservatives within its bureaucracy, have means to negate the agreement which ended the long-festering rebellion. Nevertheless, at the time of writing, a year after the first locally elected governor of Aceh took office in February 2007, there was reason for optimism. A democratic Indonesia has made giant steps towards accepting a more realistic sense of what the imperial successor state can do.

Notes

1. The most influential arguments for such factors being decisive in the rise of nationalism were B. Anderson, *Imagined Communities: Reflections on the Origin and Spread of Nationalism* (London: Verso, 1991 [1983]); and E. Gellner, *Nations and Nationalism* (Oxford: Blackwell, 1983). The debate has subsequently expanded, and finally included work of more direct relevance to Asia, such as *Asian Forms of the Nation*, ed. S. Tønnesson and H. Antlöv (Richmond: Curzon, 1996).
2. E. Weber, *Peasants into Frenchmen: The Modernization of Rural France, 1870–1914* (Stanford: Stanford University Press, 1976).
3. W. H. McNeill, *Poly-ethnicity and National Unity in World History: The Donald G. Creighton Lectures* (Toronto: University of Toronto Press, 1985), p. 56.
4. A major exception was the first, anti-Manchu, stage of Chinese nationalism, while Malay and Khmer nationalist thought also had clear strains of ethnonationalism.
5. Emperor Shi-zong, 1536, cited in G. Wade, "The Ming Shi-lu (Veritable Records of the Ming Dynasty) as a Source for Southeast Asian History: Fourteenth to Seventeenth Centuries", doctoral dissertation, University of Hong Kong, 1994, vol. I, p. 61. I am indebted to Geoffrey Wade for access to this rich source.
6. Archipelago stories about the Chinese presence in the fifteenth century are reviewed in *Sojourners and Settlers: Histories of Southeast Asia and the Chinese*, ed. A. Reid (Sydney: Asian Studies Association of Australia with Allen & Unwin, 1996), pp. 23–5. Particularly revealing are the China stories in "Sejarah Melayu or Malay Annals", trans. C. C. Brown, *JMBRAS* 25, 2–3 (1952): 89–91, and *Hikayat Hang Tuah*, ed. K. Ahmad (Kuala Lumpur: Dewan Bahasa dan Pustaka, 1966), pp. 359–72. Vietnamese literature about China is of a completely different order, sharing the concerns of anti-colonial and post-colonial nationalism in the twentieth century to emulate the superpower in order to seek equality with it. See notably O. W. Wolters, "What Else May Ngo Si Lien Mean? A Matter of Distinctions in the Fifteenth Century", in *Sojourners and Settlers*, pp. 94–114; and Insun Yu, "Le Van Huu and Ngo Si Lien: Their Perception of Vietnamese History", in *Viet Nam: Borderless*

Histories, ed. N. Tran and A. Reid (Madison: University of Wisconsin Press, 2004), pp. 45–71.
7. The quote is from A. Reid, "Inside-Out: The Colonial Displacement of Sumatra's Population", in *Paper Landscapes: Essays in the Environmental History of Indonesia*, ed. P. Boomgaard *et al.* (Leiden: KITLV Press, 1998), pp. 61–89, though the argument was made a little differently in A. Reid, "Kings, Kadis and Charisma in the 17th Century Archipelago", in *The Making of an Islamic Political Discourse in Southeast Asia*, ed. A. Reid (Clayton: Centre of Southeast Asian Studies, Monash University, 1993), pp. 90–6; and became the central argument of A. Reid, "Political 'Tradition' in Indonesia: The One and the Many", *Asian Studies Review* 22, 1 (1998): 23–38.
8. D. Henley, *Jealousy and Justice: The Indigenous Roots of Colonial Rule in Northern Sulawesi* (Amsterdam: VU University Press, 2002), p. 1: "Indigenous leaders, far from possessing 'a genius for managing without states', possessed a near-Hobbesian awareness of the inevitability of conflict in tribal life and the desirablility of a certain amount of state intervention to alleviate this problem. At the same time, their mutual jealousy and distrust made it easier for them to accept outsiders (whose lack of local blood ties was supposed to help guarantee their impartiality) in the role of arbitrators, judges, and enforcers of the peace than it was to create indigenous institutions with the same functions. In tandem with the role of foreigners as traders, and hence as distributors of valuable and prestigious foreign goods, this logic of jealousy and justice probably goes a long way toward explaining the importance of 'stranger-kings' (Indonesian as well as European) in the history of eastern Indonesia."
9. Cited in S. Raffles, *Memoir of the Life and Public Services of Sir Thomas Stamford Raffles* (London: J. Duncan, 1835), p. 142.
10. Cited in C. Pelras, "Hiérarchie et Pouvoir Traditionnel en Pays Wajo", *Archipel* 1 (1971): 173.
11. In writing "The Idea of Power in Javanese Culture", Anderson was explicitly influenced by Geertz's call for a "scientific phenomonology of culture". Reprinted in B. Anderson, ed., *Language and Power: Exploring Political Cultures in Indonesia* (Ithaca: Cornell University Press, 1990), p. 18, n. 4.
12. Ibid., p. 22.
13. C. Geertz, *Negara: The Theatre State in Nineteenth Century Bali* (Princeton: Princeton University Press, 1980), p. 11.
14. O. W. Wolters, *History, Culture and Region in Southeast Asian Perspectives*, rev. ed. (Singapore: ISEAS, 1999).
15. A. Milner, *Kerajaan: Malay Political Culture on the Eve of Colonial Rule* (Tucson: University of Arizona Press for AAS, 1982).
16. J. Drakard, *A Kingdom of Words: Language and Power in Sumatra* (Kuala Lumpur: Oxford University Press, 1999); L. Nagtegal, *Riding the Dutch Tiger: The Dutch East Indies Company and the Northeast Coast of Java* (Leiden: KITLV

Press, 1996); M. C. Ricklefs, "Unity and Disunity in Javanese Political and Religious Thought of the Eighteenth Century", in *Looking in Odd Mirrors: The Java Sea*, ed. V. J. H. Houben *et al.* (Leiden: Vakgroep Talen en Culturen van Zuidoost-Azië en Oceanië, Rijksuniversiteit te Leiden, 1992), pp. 60–75; M. C. Ricklefs, *The Seen and Unseen Worlds in Java, 1726–1749: History, Literature and Islam in the Court of Pakubuwana II* (Sydney: ASAA with Allen & Unwin and University of Hawai'i Press, 1998); H. Schulte Nordholt, "Leadership and the Limits of Political Control: A Balinese 'response' to Clifford Geertz", *Social Anthropology* 1, 3 (1993); M. Wiener, *Visible and Invisible Realms: Power, Magic and Conquest in Bali* (Chicago: University of Chicago Press, 1995); L. Andaya, *The World of Maluku: Eastern Indonesia in the Early Modern Period* (Honolulu: University of Hawai'i Press, 1993).
17. J. W. Christie, "States without Cities: Demographic Trends in Early Java", *Indonesia* 52 (Oct. 1991), p. 40.
18. P.-Y. Manguin, "Etudes Sumatranaises 1: Palembang et Sriwijaya: Anciennes Hypothèses, Recherches Nouvelles", *Bulletin de L'Ecole française d'Etrême-Orient* 76 (1987): 337–402; Wolters, *History, Culture and Region in Southeast Asian Perspectives*, pp. 32–3 and 119–20.
19. T. Day, *Fluid Iron: State Formation in Southeast Asia* (Honolulu: University of Hawai'i Press, 2002), p. 288.
20. Ibid., p. 282.
21. Ibid., p. 288.
22. Ibid., p. 283.
23. As he indeed concedes: "I cannot think of a single example of a Southeast Asian state form that is essentially, purely authentic. Foreignness haunts the formation of Southeast Asian states." Ibid., p. 292.
24. J. M. Somer, *De Korte Verklaring* (Breda: Corona, 1934). The text of the uniform *korte verklaring* is reproduced, in Malay and Dutch, at pp. 362–3.
25. See, for example, D. Ramage, *Politics in Indonesia: Democracy, Islam and the Ideology of Tolerance* (London: Routledge, 1995).
26. B. Anderson, "Old State, New Society: Indonesia's New Order in Comparative Historical Perspective", in Anderson, *Language and Power*, pp. 94–120.
27. A. Reid, "National and Ethnic Identities in a Democratic Age", in *Religion, Ethnicity and Modernity in Southeast Asia*, ed. O. Myung-Seok *et al.* (Seoul: Seoul National University Press, 1998), pp. 11–43.
28. A. Reid, "Sixteenth Century Turkish Influence in Western Indonesia", *Journal of Southeast Asian History* 10, 3 (1999): 395–414; slightly revised in A. Reid, *An Indonesian Frontier: Acehnese and Other Histories of Sumatra* (Singapore: Singapore University Press, 2004), pp. 69–93.
29. "Atjeh Verslag of C. Snouck Hurgronje, 1893", as translated in A. Reid, *The Contest for North Sumatra: Atjeh, the Netherlands and Britain, 1858–1898* (London: Oxford University Press, 1969), p. 269.

30. Reid, *The Contest for North Sumatra*, p. 296.
31. Governor Goedhart, cited in A. Reid, *The Blood of the People: Revolution and the End of Traditional Rule in Northern Sumatra* (Kuala Lumpur: Oxford University Press, 1979), p. 19.
32. A. J. Piekaar, *Atjeh en de Oorlog met Japan* (Bandung: W. Van Hoeve, 1949), pp. 14–6; Reid, *The Blood of the People*, pp. 28–9.
33. The Piagam Batee Kureng is reproduced in S. M. Amin, *Sekitar Peristiwa Berdarah di Atjeh* (Jakarta: Soeroengan, 1956), pp. 293–5.
34. "Redeclaration of Independence of Acheh, Sumatra, 4 December 1976", in Tengku H. M. di Tiro, *The Price of Freedom: The Unfinished Diary of Tengku Hasan di Tiro* (Norsborg: Information Dept., National Liberation Front Acheh Sumatra, 1984), p. 16.
35. M. Durie, "Framing the Acehnese Text: Language Choice and Discourse Structures in Aceh", *Oceanic Linguistics* 35, 1 (1996): 113.
36. Ibid.: 116.
37. di Tiro, *The Price of Freedom*, p. 17.
38. The text of the Memorandum is given in full in D. Kingsbury, *Peace in Aceh: A Personal Account of the Peace Process* (Jakarta: Equinox, 2006), pp. 199–208, and available on various websites. *Wali Nanggroe* is an Acehnese rendering of Indonesian *Wali Negara*, the term used for the heads of constituent states in the Federal Republic of Indonesia established at Indonesian independence in January 1950, though suppressed within six months by the unitary Indonesian Republic. This office has not been filled in practice in Aceh.
39. This issue is discussed in M. Keating, *Plurinational Democracy: Stateless Nations in a Post-Sovereignty Era* (Oxford: Oxford University Press, 2001), and B. He, B. Galligan and T. Inoguchi, eds., *Federalism in Asia* (Cheltenham: Edward Elgar, 2007).

CHAPTER 5

Problems of Integration: West Sumatra's Place in Indonesia

Audrey R. Kahin

Introduction

Despite the many centrifugal challenges confronting independent Indonesia, for its first 50 years of existence the Republic's governments successfully maintained the country's unity. Only after Suharto's fall were serious questions raised as to whether the disparate group of peoples and land that made up the Indonesian nation could continue to exist within a single state and what the form of that state should be.

The character of the Indonesian polity was determined over a half century ago when the newly independent federal Republic of Indonesia was transformed into a unitary Republic. This change encountered opposition from the outset, with the outbreak of the Republik Maluku Selatan (RMS, Republic of South Maluku) rebellion in Ambon and east Indonesia, and the ensuing bloody conflict and exodus of several thousand dissidents to the Netherlands at the end of 1950.[1] Throughout the 1950s, Jakarta faced regional dissidence both from the Darul Islam movement in West Java,

Aceh and South Sulawesi and the Pemerintah Revolusioner Republik Indonesia (PRRI)/Perjuangan Semesta (Permesta) rebels in Sumatra and Sulawesi.[2] Although the primary goal of the Darul Islam was an Islamic state and that of the PRRI/Permesta a more equitable distribution of power and resources between the centre and the regions, both sought to change the Republic's unitary form of government. Once Jakarta had crushed these movements, the country's unity was enforced primarily through the sheer weight of military power and repression exercised from the centre. However, throughout Indonesia's independent existence its disparate societies were also held together by the idea of a unified (if not unitary) Indonesia embracing the entire archipelago—an idea that was deeply embedded within the consciousness of many of its peoples even prior to the Declaration of Independence.

How the concept of an Indonesian nation became such a potent force throughout the Netherlands East Indies during the final decades of Dutch colonial rule is a necessary background to understanding the success of Indonesia's post-independence governments in maintaining a unitary state and also to assessing whether the country will remain viable if control from the centre continues to be relaxed in accordance with the 1999 decentralisation law. Equally important in gauging the country's viability is the nature of the allegiance felt by its many diverse peoples toward the Indonesian state.

In considering these questions, this chapter will focus on one region of Indonesia, West Sumatra. It will look briefly at the region's political history from the late colonial period up to the present, and the process by which it was integrated into the Indonesian state. I recognise that West Sumatra is not typical of other areas outside Java in that it was the birthplace of a disproportionate number of the national political leaders who emerged in Indonesia in the decades immediately before and after independence.[3] On the other hand, it does share with many Indonesian societies, especially in the coastal regions of the archipelago, such characteristics as the strength of modernist Islam in organising its educational and social institutions and the importance of trading communities in all aspects of its life.

To a remarkable degree, the Minangkabau people of West Sumatra on the one hand, and the Javanese on the other, in their idealised view of power relationships, exemplify the two contradictory concepts of state government that have struggled for dominance in post-independence Indonesia. The traditional Javanese belief is that the well-being of the state depends on the strength of the ruler at the centre. As Ben Anderson has characterised it in his perceptive analysis of traditional Javanese political conceptions and their influence on the post-colonial state, "The welfare of the collectivity does not depend on the activities of its individual components but on the concentrated energy of the center. The center's fundamental obligation is to itself. If this obligation is fulfilled, popular welfare will necessarily be assured."[4]

This perception dominated Indonesian government at least after the late 1950s, and resulted in a centralised authoritarian state, which brought prosperity but little democracy to much of the archipelago in the 1970s and 1980s.

In contrast, in the traditional Minangkabau view, the welfare of the polity depends on the harmony and agreement amongst its components—in the case of West Sumatra, the extended villages or *nagari*, which were the "highest order of human settlement acknowledged by the adat".[5] These *nagari* (often described as village republics),[6] exercised their own consensus democracy, a form of government very distant from that of the Javanese ideal.

Thus, during the nationalist struggle, the Javanese perceived a post-independence Indonesia as necessarily requiring strong central control, but the Minangkabau always assumed that Indonesia would emerge as a democratic egalitarian state, with its component provinces enjoying a considerable degree of local autonomy. The clash between the two concepts heavily affected developments not only during Sukarno's presidency but particularly under Suharto's New Order and up to the present day, and it largely determined West Sumatra's place within post-independence Indonesia. In the half century following the transfer of sovereignty in 1949, the centralised authoritarian ideal of the Javanese always emerged triumphant. But the dissident strands of the Minangkabau vision, looking to create both a more egalitarian and a more decentralised form of government, have provided a balance and dynamic tension that are still visible today and, since the overthrow of the Suharto regime, undergird many of the ideas for ultimately reordering the society in a form less determined by the hierarchical unitary structure that characterised pre-colonial Java, the colonial state and the postcolonial Republic of Indonesia.

In looking at the history of the clash between these concepts, this chapter divides the past three-quarters of a century into four distinct periods: first, the late colonial years; second, the 1940s, which saw both the Japanese Occupation and the Indonesian Revolution against the Dutch; third, the period of the Sukarno regime, from 1950 to its violent overthrow in 1965; and finally the years of Suharto's New Order. I will deal very briefly with each of these periods.

The Nationalist Struggle

Basic to nationalist activity in West Sumatra in the late colonial period were the political movements based in the private (non-Western, non-government) schools, a majority of which were largely independent of Dutch control and developed as a counterweight to what the local leaders saw as Dutch efforts to use Western education as the sole path to advancement within the Netherlands East Indies. Most of these schools—extending from the Sumatra Thawalib and Diniyyah schools of modernist Islam[7] to the vocational school (known as the INS) founded by Mohammad Sjafei[8]—refused Dutch subsidies, used Indonesian or Arabic as the language of instruction, and emphasised a wide range of educational subjects, in addition to religious teaching. Through their training in these schools thousands of young people in West Sumatra were able to perceive themselves as part of an Indonesian-speaking society whose ties with the Islamic and Malay world were stronger than those with the Dutch-dominated colonial order. The independent schools and youth organisations were supported financially by local entrepreneurs, and many of their classes were taught by local Islamic scholars. Frequently, the teachers in the schools were also traders. The cooperation and interdependence among religious, trading and educational groups formed the basis of the most potent opposition movement against the Dutch in West Sumatra, and provided the fulcrum for developing the concept of an Indonesian nation there.

It was from this background that a majority of the political and nationalist figures leading the struggle in West Sumatra emerged, in strong contrast to those Minangkabau political leaders heading the nationalist movement on Java, nearly all of whom had received advanced Western schooling in Dutch educational institutions.

Events in West Sumatra during the two decades leading up to World War II do much to contradict the frequent contention, particularly in Western scholarship, that the Indonesian nationalist movement was restricted to a narrow Dutch-educated urban elite on Java, sparking little interest or genuine support among the rural masses on that island and elsewhere, a view typified in John Ingleson's assertion that "the nationalist movement was essentially a Java movement, the product of a western-educated elite who, whatever their ethnic origins, made their careers in Batavia or in one of the other major Javanese cities".[9]

Ideological currents penetrating from Java and Europe did have a strong influence on West Sumatra's politics but they were always balanced by those from the Islamic world. As they were absorbed into the society, both types of influences assumed overwhelming Minangkabau characteristics. This is evident across the ideological spectrum. In the 1920s, the Communist movement's Sarikat Rakyat (People's League) adapted to the religious climate in the region and continued to exist in open defiance of the orders coming from the central committee of the Partai Komunis Indonesia (PKI, Indonesian Communist Party) in Java.[10] Similarly, the Muhammadiah and the Partai Sarekat Islam Indonesia (PSII, Indonesian Islamic Union Party) in West Sumatra assumed completely different and more political, nationalist and radical characteristics than their parent organisations in Java. The strongest political organisations in West Sumatra were either indigenous to the area, such as Persatuan Muslimin Indonesia (Permi, Union of Indonesian Muslims), or gained their strength from the loyalty of their followers to a party leader who was from the region and enjoyed high prestige as a native son—for example, Tan Malaka's Partai Rakyat Indonesia (Pari) and Hatta's Pendidikan Nasional Indonesia (Indonesian National Education, PNI Baru or New PNI).[11]

There is some truth to the contention that the cooperative wing of the nationalist movement in the mid to late 1930s was drawn in large part from the Dutch-educated elite. But the mainstream of the nationalist movements which were forced out of the political arena in the early 1930s was deeply embedded in Indonesian society. In West Sumatra the strongest of these movements was the Permi party, whose leaders all came from the groups of teachers, religious scholars and traders, and which was based on an adherence to both religion and nationalism. Even a majority of the local leaders and members of the non-religious nationalist parties headed by Mohammad Hatta and Tan Malaka (PNI Baru and Pari) were drawn principally from these entrepreneurial and religious groups.

The calm political atmosphere in West Sumatra in the final years leading up to World War II was, then, largely a result of political repression— the nationalists had tried armed opposition against the Dutch in the Communist uprisings of 1926/27 and democratic political party methods in the early 1930s. The Dutch responded by repressing non-violent political activity as harshly as they had armed opposition. Local nationalists had of necessity to limit any further action to underground activities or within the narrow parameters sanctioned by the colonial power. Reluctance to challenge the Dutch was exacerbated by the harsh economic conditions that battered the region sporadically after the onset of the Depression at the end of 1929.

Achievement of Independence

During the Japanese Occupation and the independence struggle of the 1940s, the autonomous character of the nationalist movement in West Sumatra became even stronger than in the pre-war period. Under the Japanese, Indonesia was divided into three separate administrations; and even on Sumatra, which was administered by the Japanese 25th Army, the provinces were largely autonomous of one another. In isolating West Sumatra from the rest of the island, as well as from Java, the Japanese encouraged development of organisations whose strength was rooted in their local region. Their isolation from other parts of Indonesia, particularly from the heartland of Java, does not, however, appear to have loosened the psychological ties and loyalty felt by West Sumatrans both to the Indonesian nationalist leaders on Java, particularly to those of Minangkabau origin, and to the goal of an independent Indonesia. The humiliating Dutch defeat at the hands of the Japanese and the fact that the Japanese provided basic military training to a large group of Minangkabau young men in the volunteer militia, Gyu gun, meant that West Sumatrans no longer viewed colonial rule as an inevitable fact of life. From their Japanese instructors they gained self confidence and pride in being Asian, while their West Sumatran officers and political leaders made sure that these feelings were directed toward attaining the goal of Indonesian independence.

During the first two years after Sukarno and Hatta declared Indonesia's independence in August 1945, the revolution within West Sumatra continued along a path that was largely independent of outside control. The local military and civilian leaders, although loyal and generally obedient to the Republican government in Yogyakarta, were able to observe their own priorities, carrying out their own interpretations of the government's orders at their own pace. At the same time, they remained steadfastly loyal to the Indonesian Republic as they themselves perceived it, in part because their isolation from the Republican capital in Yogyakarta meant that little pressure could be exerted from the centre. This situation changed between mid-1947 and the end of 1948, when Mohammad Hatta, as vice president and later also prime minister of the Republic, attempted to impose the centre's priorities on the West Sumatran civilian and military administration. These attempts led to friction and dissatisfaction in large parts of Minangkabau society which reached their peak when military headquarters on Java replaced the local Sumatran army commanders with officers from West Java's Siliwangi division immediately before the second Dutch "police action" of 19 December 1948.[12]

The centre's attempts to manipulate the situation in West Sumatra resulted in complete chaos and disarray within the region's military forces in the immediate aftermath of the Dutch attack. In subsequent weeks, however, the local authorities reasserted their control and were able to organise a remarkably effective guerrilla war and underground administration to which the vast majority of the Minangkabau people remained loyal.

It was in West Sumatra that the Pemerintah Darurat Republik Indonesia (PDRI, Republic's Emergency Government) was established after the Dutch arrested Sukarno, Hatta and the rest of the Republic's cabinet in Yogyakarta.[13] Traditional trading routes were reestablished between Singapore and small ports on Sumatra's east coast, with a fleet of small boats successfully evading Dutch efforts at a blockade.[14] And the fact that Minangkabau government traditionally rested on the basis of autonomous villages (*nagari*), rather than being dependent upon an administrative hierarchy, meant that the shock and disarray of the early weeks after the Dutch advance did not long cripple the functioning of the Republican administration. So long as the province-level authorities were able to issue general guidelines, the method of their implementation could effectively be left to the local governments.

The transfer of sovereignty from the Dutch in December 1949 ended the anti-colonial movement that had done much to define West Sumatra's political landscape since the end of World War I. Throughout the 1920s and 1930s the colonial authorities had faced a turbulent and uneasy situation in the region. In bolstering their position they had relied on a traditional system of local administration that they had manipulated and distorted to serve their own ends, and by so doing had undermined the customary leaders who cooperated with them. The revolutionary years had proved the Dutch wrong in believing that these *adat* leaders were their natural allies and that the traditional system of governance was as rigid as the colonial government had tried to make it. The Minangkabau people embraced religious movements, political parties and an electoral system, in large part because these represented the most potent opposition to a continuance of colonial rule. Similarly, the Dutch had been proven wrong in believing that local Minangkabau nationalism could be used to combat Indonesian nationalism, and that anti-Javanese sentiments could be played on to undermine the people's loyalty to the Republic of Indonesia. The Dutch failure was in large part due to the fact that during the pre-war period a nationalism embracing the whole of the archipelago had sunk deep roots in Minangkabau society. This nationalism was strengthened not only by the struggle against a clearly perceived Dutch enemy but also by the fact that, for the most part, the central Republican government had been too weak to impose its wishes on the local scene, and regional political leaders were able to define the characteristics of the Indonesian nation in their own terms. Confidence in this perception was tied, of course, also to the presence of so many Minangkabau leaders in the Republic's government on Java.

Rebellion in the 1950s

During the early 1950s, West Sumatra's hopes that an Indonesian state and nation could be created conforming to the earlier concepts that guided the local nationalist movement were crushed. Even before the transfer of sovereignty from the Dutch, West Sumatra's Banteng division was dissolved and subordinated to military commands in northern and southern Sumatra. The resulting disillusionment within the local armed forces was matched among civilian groups by dissatisfaction at the centralised character of the new Indonesia, at Jakarta's heavy-handed policies in removing elements of regional autonomy, and at Java's political and economic domination of the Republic. Growing regional disaffection led to the formation of the Banteng Council at the end of 1956 and the establishment the following year of similar councils in other parts of Sumatra and Sulawesi which joined with the dissatisfied Minangkabau elements in defying the central government. After the outbreak of the PRRI/Permesta rebellion in February 1958, the rebels' strategy in West Sumatra was to carry out a guerrilla war against Java's invading forces similar to the one they had waged against the Dutch during the revolution. At the same time, the PRRI civilian administration continued to function down to the village level, competing with that of the Javanese occupying authorities in the major towns and villages.

Despite the many similarities between the PRRI rebellion and the independence revolution a decade earlier, the contrast between the struggle against the Dutch and the one against the Sukarno government soon became evident. By far the most important difference was that in 1949 the goal had been clear: achieving an independent Indonesia free from foreign occupation. In the PRRI rebellion, the lack of any consensus as to the precise goal of their struggle eventually led to growing dissension among the rebel leaders, particularly between the military and civilians.

In addition, the divisions within West Sumatra society were now much deeper. During the revolutionary war, the Dutch had believed that the traditional order of Minangkabau society would stand with them in opposition to the growing power of political parties and the future threat of Javanese domination of an independent Indonesia. They had been very wrong: over the previous 30 years, Indonesian nationalism had penetrated deeply into the society, and the vast majority of traditional, religious and radical forces within it united in support of their leaders on Java.

The situation was very different during the PRRI rebellion, when the rebel leaders in West Sumatra were overwhelmingly from the majority religious stream. Their movement focused on isolating and opposing Communist and other radical elements both on Java and within West Sumatra itself. At the same time, they derived much of their support from playing on some of the same anti-Javanese sentiments that the Dutch had unsuccessfully attempted to use during their efforts to combat Indonesian nationalism. The rebels met with a similar failure. For, however loyal the mass of the people were to the Banteng Council's struggles for autonomy, it was difficult for them to support a rebel government which, while accepting military assistance from outside powers such as the United States, at the same time opposed the national government in Jakarta headed by Sukarno and other long-time nationalist figures who had led their country to independence. The fact that so many of the Minangkabaus' most respected representatives at the centre, most notably Mohammad Hatta, refused to approve the rebellion further undermined the rebels' cohesion.

Long before the rebels finally surrendered in 1961, Javanese forces had occupied much of West Sumatra, humiliating its people. Many of those who had participated in the rebellion fled the area, and wherever they found a haven were often ashamed even to acknowledge their Minangkabau identity. West Sumatra itself was like an occupied territory, governed, as the American embassy reported, by "the horde of Javanese officials and soldiery which poured in during and immediately after the rebellion...."[15]

Nor did the harshness of this occupation relax after the rebellion was completely defeated and the rebels surrendered.

Centralisation under Suharto

In the immediate aftermath of the 1965 coup in Jakarta, West Sumatra's relationship to the centre underwent little change. General Suharto's ascent to power in 1965/66 did not mean an end to the Javanese military occupation of West Sumatra, for the Javanese-officered 17 August Command continued to control the region, albeit increasingly headed by anti-Communists. Nor was there any immediate rehabilitation of the soldiers and civilians who had participated in the PRRI rebellion, nor of the strongest political party in West Sumatra, the still-banned Masyumi (Majelis Syuro Muslimin Indonesia, Consultative Council of Indonesian Muslims). The military officers who now held supreme power at the centre still portrayed the regional rebellion as having posed one of the greatest internal threats to independent Indonesia, second only to the attempted coup of 1965. Thus, despite the change in regime, the people of West Sumatra still felt themselves to be despised inhabitants of an occupied territory.

Local leaders, most notably the new Minangkabau governor Harun Zain who took office in early 1966, attempted to restore a level of self-confidence to the people of the region after the trauma of the previous decade during which they had experienced rebellion, defeat and occupation by Javanese troops. But, conscious of West Sumatra's inherent political weakness, Zain felt the only way for the society to survive was by accommodation with Jakarta. The governor and his successors essentially struck a bargain with the centre under which they received economic development resources in return for political acquiescence.

Suharto's New Order government took steps to destroy the political parties throughout Indonesia, in particular removing ideology and religion from the political scene. Its law making the national state ideology (the Pancasila or 5 principles) the sole basis for all social and political organisations in Indonesia, in particular, undercut the political legitimacy of the Islamic Partai Persatuan Pembangunan (PPP, United Development Party) and other Muslim organisations.[16] At the same time, the government attempted to remove regional differences by introducing legislation, notably the 1979 Village Law, aimed at creating a uniform system of administration (with common norms) at the village level throughout Indonesia. This led in West Sumatra to the replacement of the *nagari* by smaller and weaker *desa* units.[17]

The Indonesian state became ever more centralised and authoritarian during the decades of Suharto's regime. Although a superficial harmony was established between the West Sumatra region and the centre during these years, this was only achieved by the Minangkabau people accepting West Sumatra's place as merely one of many provinces within Indonesia, rather than as an influential arbiter of the character of the post-revolutionary state.[18] The degree of prosperity the region enjoyed under Suharto's rule was within the context of accepting the Javanese view of a centralised authoritarian state. Only those officials who were prepared to play that game were successful in achieving and maintaining a significant role within the local administrative hierarchy from governor down to village head. And, as in other parts of Indonesia, administrative positions became sources of profit as well as influence, and increasingly were given to the highest bidder. Even before Suharto's fall, revulsion against this state of affairs had led to months of protest demonstrations in West Sumatra, as in many other parts of the country.

Changes in the *Reformasi* Era

After the president's forced resignation in favour of his vice president B. J. Habibie in May 1998, it was striking how rapidly the people in West Sumatra embraced the new freedoms and took into their own hands responsibility for removing vestiges of the previous regime and instituting a more democratic order. Political parties and newspapers proliferated, as did their criticisms of all aspects of government. Dissidents and former participants in the PRRI rebellion, who, as one said to me, "have had (a) toothache for the past 35 years" now felt free to express not only their criticisms of those in power, but also their visions for a country more in accord with their earlier ideals. They seemed determined not to let this opportunity be lost as they believed previous ones had been.

As the hopes raised immediately after Suharto's fall paralleled those of the period following the transfer of sovereignty from the Dutch in 1949, many of the basic problems that the country now confronted also paralleled those of the past. As in the early days of independence, the rapid reversal of power in 1998 revealed that members of the Indonesian elite, both those who headed the government and those who opposed it, underestimated the strength of the people's desire for a political order that was equitable and responsible and their willingness to act independently to remove the corruption they saw undermining the state and society.

Subsequent years have demonstrated the almost insurmountable difficulties involved in dismantling the well-entrenched centralised state structure built up over the previous 40 years. The lack of autonomy and decision-making powers in the regions over such a long period had tended to draw the most qualified people to Jakarta, while the standards for a regional official to achieve success had lain in his ability to interpret the wishes of the central government, with the result that a culture of subservience permeated even the previously most independent-minded regions. This, together with the pervasive corruption at all levels of the administration, hampered efforts at change.

Frequently heard warnings that the devolution of power envisaged in the decentralisation law introduced by the Habibie government in 1999 would lead to Indonesia's disintegration, however, seem to have been proved wrong. Such views tended to underestimate the depth of the loyalty to the ideal or "dream" of the Indonesian nation—nourished in large part by memories and legends of the national struggle and the independence war—that still existed in many parts of the archipelago, though it had been seriously undermined by the repression and injustices exercised from the centre under both Sukarno and Suharto. When the regions rebelled in the late 1950s, their goal had not been to secede from the state but rather to change its character, correct the central government's policies, and establish a just balance between central and local government power. It was only when their pleas were rebuffed that the dissidents moved to consider even a federal system, let alone secession. That situation had many parallels in post-Suharto Indonesia though much of the nationalist idealism still alive in the earlier period had turned to cynicism. The pressures for separatism still sprang from bitter resentment at a government that had been oppressive and too centralised, exercising its power with little concern for the needs and desires of the nation's component elements.

These pressures did increase in the early post-Suharto years especially in Aceh and Papua, both of which were still subjected to military repression despite being officially granted special autonomy status in 2001. In Aceh secessionist pressures were to a considerable degree alleviated with the peace agreement that the government of Susilo Bambang Yudhoyono (SBY) reached with the former Gerakan Aceh Merdeka (GAM, Free Aceh Movement) rebels in the aftermath of the December 2004 tsunami. Under this agreement local parties and candidates were allowed to run in the province's December 2006 elections, and the government permitted the winners to assume power, even though they had led opposition to Jakarta and were strong critics of the central government. The situation in Papua was less clear, though there, too, the central government gained credibility by allowing a transparent electoral process through which its critics succeeded in coming to power. In both Papua and Aceh these elections revealed internal frictions within the societies, which lessened the likelihood that the various forces would coalesce against Jakarta in support of secession.[19]

Developments since the overthrow of Suharto and Indonesia's tentative moves toward a democratic decentralised state, then, have given some hope of reversing the previous trend of the country's post-independence history. Despite the bloodshed and disorder that characterised developments in several parts of Indonesia in the aftermath of Suharto's fall, the country also registered considerable achievements in its conduct of relatively honest elections in both 1999 and 2004. Despite the bewildering way in which Abdurrahman Wahid (Gus Dur), who came to power in 1999, exercised his authority, he and his supporters largely pursued policies that, while weakening the military, also emphasised inter-faith dialogue and tolerance among competing groups, and gradually transferred decision-making authority to the country's component regions. These policies were to some degree reversed under Megawati Sukarnoputri. Her strong ties to the military and her response to international pressures to wage a "war on terrorism" targeting Islamic groups within Indonesia tended to undermine an already fragile and uncertain effort at implementing democracy. The election of SBY to the presidency in 2004, however, demonstrated that the people rejected the types of policies Megawati's government had pursued.

The imprecision of Decentralisation Law 22/99, as well as the continuation in office of most of the officials who had held positions in the Suharto period despite the proliferation of new political parties, did initially hamper many positive results emerging from the weakening of central control of the regions. To a large extent, it appeared that the rampant corruption that had characterised the late Suharto period had merely spread from central to local office-holders, many of whom were now businessmen rather than bureaucrats or traditional leaders, with the people in the regions experiencing none of the benefits that might be expected from local control.[20] However, in contrast to the Suharto period, the electorate was now able to demand a degree of accountability. As

Daniel Slater has written, "society at large was more restless than its ostensible representatives" in parliament, forcing constitutional reform and the holding of direct elections in 2004 when voters threw out many of the parties and officials who had abused their positions.[21] In West Sumatra, for example, even before the elections, 43 members of the Dewan Perwakilan Rakyat Daerah (DPRD, Regional People's Representative Council) were convicted of corruption and sentenced to jail, a case that had repercussions in 30 other provinces. And throughout Indonesia in the 2004 elections the voters registered their discontent with political trends under Suharto's successors "by giving all five major parties a lower vote share than they had received in 1999".[22]

But these positive signs were to some degree vitiated by the introduction, also in 2004, of new decentralisation laws (No. 32/2004 and No. 25/2004), which specified that the regional councils and governments had to consult with the central government (through the governor) concerning every local policy they drafted before it could be approved as a definite policy. Clearly, by taking back some of the regional governments' authority, Jakarta was attempting to ensure that "the dynamics of local politics in the post 2004 elections era would be fully under the control of the central government".[23]

At the present moment the degree to which the balance of power is again shifting back to the centre remains unclear. Nor is it certain whether local officials and political party leaders will in fact begin to respond to their electorate's demands rather than merely enriching themselves at the people's expense. It still seems possible that the central government could react to the failings of many of the local governments, as well as the pressures brought to bear from the international community for a crackdown on dissident groups, by bringing an end to the tentative steps taken in the early years of *Reformasi* toward a more democratic and representative order. But, at the same time, the honesty and transparency of the elections held thus far do give hope that a new decentralised Indonesia might still emerge through a more healthy accommodation amongst the country's regional components and that a more equitable and democratic state might finally take shape.

Notes

1. See R. Chauvel, *Nationalists, Soldiers and Separatists: The Ambonese Islands from Colonialism to Revolt* (Leiden: KITLV Press, 1990).

2. On the Darul Islam, see C. van Dijk, *Rebellion under the Banner of Islam: The Darul Islam in Indonesia* (The Hague: Nijhoff, 1981); on the regional rebellions, see B. S. Harvey, *Permesta: Half a Rebellion* (Ithaca: Cornell Modern Indonesia Project, 1977); R. Z. Leirissa, *PRRI Permesta* (Jakarta: Grafiti, 1997); A. Kahin and G. Kahin, *Subversion as Foreign Policy* (New York: New Press, 1995).
3. These included vice president Mohammad Hatta and the Republic's first prime minister, Sutan Sjahrir, as well as Tan Malaka, Mohammad Natsir, Muhammad Yamin, Assaat and many others.
4. B. Anderson, "The Idea of Power in Javanese Culture", in *Culture and Politics in Indonesia*, ed. C. Holt *et al*. (Ithaca: Cornell University Press, 1972), p. 52.
5. T. Kato, *Matriliny and Migration: Evolving Minangkabau Traditions in Indonesia* (Ithaca: Cornell University Press, 1982), pp. 41–2.
6. Traditionally the *nagari* had clear geographical limits, and met certain specific criteria, including possessing a council hall (*balai*), mosque, road, public bathing place, and open field. The *nagari* followed a matrilineal system of inheritance and were governed by a council made up of the traditional heads (*penghulu andiko*) of the component groups or clans (*kaum* or *suku*).
7. The best history in English of these schools is still T. Abdullah, *Schools and Politics: The Kaum Muda Movements in West Sumatra, 1927–1933* (Ithaca: Cornell Modern Indonesia Project, 1971). See also A. Kahin, *Rebellion to Integration: West Sumatra and the Indonesian Polity* (Amsterdam: University of Amsterdam Press, 1999), especially chapters 1–3.
8. The school, which is still in existence, has always been known by these initials, which first denoted "Indonesische Nederlandsch School". During the Japanese occupation the name was changed to "Indonesian Nippon School", then following Independence, "Indonesian National School", or even according to some, "Institut Nasional Sjafei". See *Haluan* (Padang), 13 Nov. 1976.
9. J. Ingleson, *Road to Exile: The Indonesian Nationalist Movement 1927–1934* (Singapore: Heinemann Educational Books Asia, 1979), p. 230.
10. See R. T. McVey, *The Rise of Indonesian Communism* (Ithaca: Cornell University Press, 1965) and Kahin, *Rebellion to Integration*, pp. 45–6.
11. Ibrahim gelar Datuk Tan Malaka came from West Sumatra, was trained as a teacher in Holland, and was chairman of the Indonesian Communist Party (PKI) from 1921 until he was exiled by the Dutch in 1922. He was Comintern agent for Southeast Asia from 1923, but broke with the PKI over the 1926/27 rebellion. He founded the Pari in Bangkok in 1927 with Djamaluddin Tamin and Subakat. See H. Poeze, *Tan Malaka, Strijder voor Indonesia's Vrijheid: Levensloop van 1897 tot 1945* (Leiden: KITLV Press, 1976). The New PNI (PNI Baru) or Pendidikan Nasional Indonesia was founded in 1931 by Mohammad Hatta and Sutan Sjahrir, to compete with Sartono's Partindo as a successor to the Indonesian Nationalist Party (PNI). See Ingleson, *Road to Exile*, pp. 152–5.

12. See Kahin, *Rebellion to Integration*, pp. 131–3.
13. See M. Zed, *Somewhere in the Jungle: Pemerintah Darurat Republik Indonesia: Sebuah Mata Rantai Sejarah yang Terlupakan* (Jakarta: Grafiti, 1997).
14. For an informative account of this trade, see Twang P. Y., *The Chinese Business Elite in Indonesia and the Transition to Independence 1940–1950* (Kuala Lumpur: Oxford University Press, 1998).
15. "The West Sumatran Political Scene", Airgram to Department of State from Floyd L. Whittington, Counselor of Embassy for Political Affairs, No. A-69, 19 July 1963, available from National Archives, College Park, Maryland.
16. The PPP had been formed in 1973 as a forced merger of the four existing legal Muslim parties.
17. The fullest discussion of the changes involved in the replacement of the *nagari* by *desa* appears in *Nagari, Desa dan Pembangunan Pedesaan di Sumatera Barat*, ed. M. Hasbi, M. Naim and D. D. B. Sampono (Padang: Yayasan Genta Budaya, 1990). See also *Perubahan Sosial di Minangkabau*, ed. M. Zed, A. Miko and E. Chatra (Padang: Universitas Andalas, 1992) and Kahin, *Rebellion to Integration*, pp. 257–61.
18. Or, as Ichlasul Amal expresses it, "[accepting] West Sumatra as 'just one region' rather than as an 'alternative centre' or a region with a special calling to lead the Outer Islands or the forces of Islam". See I. Amal, *Regional and Central Government in Indonesian Politics* (Yogyakarta: Gadjah Mada University Press, 1992), p. 193.
19. On the situations in these two autonomous provinces, see M. Mietzner, "Local Elections and Autonomy in Papua and Aceh", *Indonesia* 84 (Oct. 2007): 1–40.
20. It is noteworthy in West Sumatra that the number of businessmen in the DPRD increased as a result of the 2004 elections, usually at the expense of ulama and teachers. See A. Sanit, "Political Parties, Society, and DPRD: The Case of Padang, Agam and Padang Pariaman", in *Political Parties' Performance at Local Parliament in Indonesia*, ed. S. Nuryanti (Jakarta: LIPI, 2007), p. 188.
21. D. Slater, "Indonesia's Accountability Trap: Party Cartels and Presidential Power after Democratic Transition", *Indonesia* 79 (Oct. 2004): 84.
22. Slater, "Indonesia's Accountability Trap", p. 64.
23. Nuryanti, *Political Parties' Performance*, p. 13.

CHAPTER 6

Beyond Economic Imperatives: Resources, Identity and Conflict in the Asia-Pacific

Glenn Banks

Introduction: Resources and Conflict in the Asia-Pacific

Many of the pressures connected with regionalism and counter-centre movements in Indonesia occur in its resource-rich peripheral provinces. There are parallel situations elsewhere in the Asia-Pacific, including the Philippines, Malaysia, Thailand and Papua New Guinea. In the case of Papua New Guinea, the most overt example is Bougainville, where a civil war erupted in the late 1980s in response to grievances over the environmental impact of, and revenue distribution from, a large-scale mine. Indeed, across the region, resource-rich margins frequently rebel or resist centralising tendencies, indicating a relationship between the presence of natural resources and the development of these strong counter-centre movements and conflicts.

This chapter investigates the ways in which natural resources may contribute toward local or provincial pressures for greater autonomy or self-determination across the Indonesian archipelago. It specifically examines whether natural resources lead to regional conflicts, and if so, what mechanisms are involved? I explore the extent to which a desire for greater control over local resources is at the heart of the development, articulation and deployment of regional identities and political movements. I will argue that existing frameworks and analysis of civil conflicts and resources lack the recognition that local places, people and identities are intimately linked with control and conflicts over natural resources. When national actors or institutions usurp this control over local resources, and local actors lose control over decisions relating to these resources without adequate balancing benefits, tension and conflict are likely. Such outcomes are being accentuated by global processes that provide access to international audiences, resources and discourses.

The chapter begins by reviewing existing research linking resources with local and regional conflict. An elaboration of this existing framework is then proposed, centred around notions of identity and globalisation. Although both identity and globalisation suffer from porous definitions, if used judiciously, they can add significantly to the analysis and understanding of the relationship between conflict and resources. To illustrate, a number of case studies will be drawn on, predominantly from Melanesia's mining sector. I conclude with a call to place questions of identity, discourse and resource control at the centre of debates around resources and conflict across Indonesia.

Existing Frameworks

The evidence of links between natural resources and conflict has its origins in studies by economists from the 1980s that identified a statistically robust relationship between an economic dependence on natural resources and slower than average growth.[1] This "resource curse" thesis[2] has generated debate about the extent of the problem, the measurement of resource dependence, and whether a reliance on hard-rock minerals produces a different outcome to oil, or timber or agriculture. Different data sets and statistical treatments have also produced complex and often contradictory findings. Nevertheless, there is strong evidence that the more an economy is dependent on natural resources, the generally slower its subsequent growth. For instance, Michael Ross[3] cites a World Bank study on the economic performance of countries with large mining sectors over the period 1990–99 which shows that the larger the dependence on mineral exports, the poorer the economic growth. Likewise, Jeffrey Sachs and Andrew Warner highlight a strong relationship between the extent of a country's exports of natural resources in 1970 (as a percentage of GDP) and real GDP growth per capita over the subsequent 20 years.[4]

From these, and many other empirically and statistically sophisticated examples, the same pattern occurs: natural resources are not the blessing they appear to be for a country. We will return to reasons for this below, but it is worth noting here that they include: the effects of a reliance on natural resources on the competitiveness of other economic sectors (linked in the literature with the notion of a "Dutch disease"), and the apparent debilitating effects of resource rents on state institutions. Ross has summarised a range of other "effects" of natural resource dependence.[5] These include links between resource dependence and increased rates of poverty, dependence on oil or minerals and higher child mortality rates, and more generalised findings that link resource-dependent economies and lower-than-average investment in education. In addition, "oil- and mineral-rich governments generally spend unusually large sums on their military forces",[6] in some instances leading to well-documented human rights abuses.

Resources and Conflict

Since the late 1990s, a more explicit link has been made between natural resources and civil conflict. At the forefront of this work are Paul Collier and Anke Hoeffler, from the World Bank's Development Research Group. Using a largely econometric perspective, they carried out a creative statistical analysis of the causes of 47 civil wars in the period 1965–99. At the core of their analysis is a comparison between what they label "grievance" and "greed" models of rebellion—are civil conflicts about legitimate grievances or simply contests over economic resources? Natural resources assume a central role in their analysis because, as Collier points out, they are often the "most lootable" of all economic activities.[7]

Two of his findings are particularly pertinent here. First, is the finding that "the most powerful risk factor is that countries which have a substantial share of their GDP coming from the export of primary commodities are radically more at risk of conflict".[8] In other words, the possession and development of natural resources is more likely to lead to civil conflict. Second, they dismiss, through the use of their model and analysis, the effects of religious and ethnic diversity on civil conflict, arguing that ethnic and religious fractionalisation actually makes a society *safer* and less prone to civil conflict. The one social element that is influential in their analysis is the role of a large diaspora, with these able to garner international support (financial and/or political) for the rebel parties. Collier and Hoeffler argue that although religious and ethnic factors, and other measures of grievance such as inequalities, are unlikely to start a civil war, once initiated, the conflict can fuel powerful grievances through human rights abuses which will extend the conflict.[9]

If we were to apply this model to the risk of civil conflict within Indonesia, for example, the combination of ongoing human rights abuses and significant natural resources would lead to Aceh, Papua and East Kalimantan exhibiting a relatively high risk of sparking civil conflict. This is hardly a surprise, however, it does show that internally Indonesia largely fits the profile of "at-risk" countries in this analysis because of the dependence on primary commodity exports, rather than because of ethnic or religious differences.[10] Aceh does indeed rate a mention in Collier's work, but not in the form that we might expect. Noting that Aceh has a per capita income three times the national average and that rebellion generally seems to be "the rage of the rich", Collier sees Aceh as an example of a resource-rich area fighting a political cause. This cause is, in his analysis, "the grievance of a rich minority at paying taxes to the poor majority"![11]

Despite the statistical evidence on which it is built and the attraction of its simplicity, there are several reasons to be cautious in applying this literature to the current situation in Indonesia and its margins. First, the econometric and statistical analysis on which the resource conflict literature is built is underpinned fundamentally by the notion of spatial association—that is, because two phenomena (in this case, conflict and natural resources) occur together in one place, there must be some relationship between them. This concept has an obvious weakness in that there may be a range of other factors that give rise to the co-presence of the two phenomena such that they give the *appearance* of having a direct relationship. In this case, a resources-conflict relationship courts a degree of environmental determinism that cannot withstand historical or contemporary scrutiny. Following from this, the notion of a generalised relationship between resources and civil conflict ignores the specificities of each case. The "extremities" of Indonesia—Aceh and Papua—are a case in point, with diametrically opposed cultural, political and developmental histories. The conflicts in these two provinces only hold up to the most cursory of direct comparisons. Finally, the resources–conflict literature, while establishing a statistical pattern, is relatively weak in terms of causation. How exactly do resources bring about civil conflicts? Accounts from Africa which describe rebel movements securing sources of mineral wealth (predominantly diamonds) hold no relevance to Aceh, Papua or other provinces in Indonesia. Here the resources are oil, copper, gold and timber, and the state (rather than any "rebel movement") has tight control over these.

The question of natural resources and conflict was also addressed recently by the Mining, Minerals and Sustainable Development (MMSD) project, a global assessment of the role that minerals can play in sustainable development. In a report commissioned by the MMSD project, Jason Switzer notes that "mineral production can reduce the likelihood of conflict through economic development". However, he goes on to say that "large-scale mining may contribute to conflict by creating grievances—inequitable distribution of impacts and benefits—that contribute to violent uprising. Moreover, it may provide a source of funds to sustain oppression, fuel corruption, or to attract armed bandits seeking easy riches".[12] Again Indonesia, or at least parts of Indonesia, clearly fits the former argument: the massive wealth generated by PT Freeport Indonesia (Freeport), for example, has sparked tension and conflict over the distribution of this revenue as it provides an economic focus for the political aspirations of many Papuans.

Environmental Security and Conflict

A second literature that deserves mention is the so-called "new security paradigm" with its emphasis on "environmental security". This also links the issues of natural resources and environmental damage with conflict. Ironically, the bulk of this literature is concerned with resource *scarcity* and the effects on the internal stability and external relations of countries. Here, the argument (with links to Malthus) is that as natural resources (such as land, water and forests) come under increasing pressure from population, utilisation and competition, then community tensions will rise, leading potentially to conflict. While a simple population pressure-conflict link has long been debunked, the rise of new forms of pressure on, for example, the forests (see Dawkins, this volume) or fisheries (see Adhuri, this volume) of the region through increasing incursions from state and corporate interests or migrants to the area is leading to new forms of tension and conflict.

Conceptually, such disputes are at the opposite end of the spectrum from the notion of conflicts generated by the abundance, or excess, of resources discussed above. This suggests that the issue is not simply the absence or presence of resources, as either appears capable of generating conflict, but rather that it is the socio-political construction of resources and the control over and ownership of these resources.[13] Here the recent work in political ecology[14] offers an important antidote to the often apolitical environmental security literature by arguing that "environmental problems" (be they drought, famine, denudation or deforestation) are at their essence a reflection of power relations within a society, and particularly the power to control access to and the use (or abuse) of natural resources.

Though rights to, and control over, land and resources are not central concerns in the environmental security literature, the above argument suggests that they are themes that can link it with the resource conflict literature, particularly if the fundamental premise of political ecology is incorporated. Resource control, and hence livelihoods, can be an important component of environmental security in this sense.

Resources, Nations and Indigenous Peoples

A final relevant approach to resources and conflict comes from Richard Howitt, John Connell and Philip Hirsch who note that "local groups with a cultural identity distinct from the national culture of the nation state (e.g. Bougainvilleans within Papua New Guinea; Karen within Burma; Melanesian West Papuans within Indonesia) link claims of independence to arguments about resource sovereignty".[15] Here we have the confluence of notions of indigeneity, identity, resources and conflict. The process that is driving this conjuncture is the expanding resource frontier in the Asia-Pacific—the relentless drive for natural resources outwards from the regional population centres—that is impacting increasingly on the last remaining territories of the region's indigenous peoples. It is precisely because of the previously marginal nature of these regions that indigenous populations have remained, in practice if not always in theory, largely in control of them. In this approach, it is the co-presence of natural resources and identities that are regarded as different to the ethnic majority that provides the conditions for conflict.

While this conjunction of specific places and people may account for some of the resource conflicts in the region, there are others where it does not. For one, the notion of an "indigenous" category of citizen in Indonesia (or its neighbours, Malaysia and Papua New Guinea) is problematic, given the appeals to unity and equality that have underpinned nation-building in each of these countries. Such an analysis can also reify the category of "indigenous" in ways that disempower particular communities. Li, for one, cautions against a simple, static view of "indigenous" peoples, and argues that

> a group's self-identification as tribal or indigenous is not natural or inevitable, but neither is it simply invented, adopted, or imposed. It is, rather, a *positioning* which draws upon historically sedimented practices, landscapes, and repertoires of meaning, and emerges through particular patterns of engagement and struggle. The conjunctures at which (some) people come to identify themselves as indigenous, realigning the ways they connect to the nation, the government, and their own, unique tribal place, are the contingent products of agency and the cultural and political work of *articulation*.[16]

This approach offers a way of thinking about counter-centre movements from resource-rich regions in a way that begins to account for local histories, places and identities, in contrast to both the resources-conflict and environmental security frameworks. This is the basis for the approach I wish to develop in the following section.

Globalisation and Local Identity

Stepping back from the focus on resources and conflict for a moment, it is useful to introduce recent arguments concerning globalisation and its effects on culture and, particularly, identity. There is a huge and burgeoning literature on these terms and the links between them. Until recently, much of the literature treated globalisation as a homogenising influence. There are many laments, for example, on the decline or loss of local cultures in the face of a proliferating universal global (read American) culture.[17] There is also, though, growing recognition that the evidence does not support this. Certainly, many of the accounts of local change by anthropologists and geographers from Indonesia and elsewhere around the Asia-Pacific region point towards a much more complex process.[18]

In place of the notion of flattening or homogenising, the notion of "hybridity" gained traction,[19] with the concept of an insidious "global" culture and economy producing multiple local and national "hybrids", with different elements being adapted, adopted and incorporated into different societies. In other cases, "counter-global" trends have been identified, built around the construction, revitalisation or reinvention of local cultures and identities. These processes underline the point that globalisation is not muting or dissolving difference, rather difference is creatively emerging from encounters with it. Local identities are being shaped and forged in response to global and national influences, and by changes in local circumstances. The often opportunistic, sometimes strategic "positioning" (to adopt Tania Li's terminology from above) that communities and individuals adopt in response to the intrusion of new pressures on local resources itself then becomes the context within which "conflict" can arise—internally, and with interests or parties from outside the community. It is also particularly important to underline, as Li does, that this process of identity politics—positioning—in each context is contingent on the conjuncture of a specific and particular array of external factors (including global corporations, demand for particular resources, state initiatives and agendas, and forms of governance over natural resources) and yet is also strongly place-based—custom, tradition, environments, cosmology and social relationships drive local interpretations and responses by local communities.

Identity, Resources and Conflict: Melanesian Examples

In this section two different examples are used to illustrate how identity becomes a critical axis for understanding the development of conflict around major resource projects. The first is the massive in-migration that accompanies large-scale mining in the region. This has in most cases promoted an intense discourse around localism and "indigeneity": it has in a sense created the indigenous communities.[20] This is certainly the case at the massive Freeport mine in Papua, Indonesia.[21] Within the mine's Contract of Work (CoW) area as a whole, the extent of in-migration is truly enormous. From a base population of around 2,500 people (overwhelmingly indigenous Amungme and Kamoro) within the CoW area at the start of the mine in 1970, in the the early 1990s it was estimated to be some 50,000 people. About 17,000 of these were Freeport employees, and most in the area were directly or indirectly connected with the mine operation. By the late 1990s the CoW population estimates ranged from 75,000 to 100,000 and a 2002 estimate was that more than 120,000 resided in the CoW area.[22] Within this population two trends are evident—the total PT Freeport workforce as fallen (although mine contractor numbers have increased), and the proportion of the residents who belong to the two indigenous communities, the Amungme and the Kamoro has fallen, to the point where they now represent less than 15 per cent of the total population.

Migration into the CoW area is incredibly complex. Groups represented include mine employees and their families, contractors and support services, police and every branch of the Indonesian military (a few years ago the area was described as one of the most militarised in Indonesia), government-sponsored transmigrants from other parts of Indonesia (including Papua), state and company sponsored "local transmigrants", so-called "spontaneous migrants" (people who have moved to the area without company or government support), and the movement along kinship and ethnic lines of Amungme and Kamoro from areas outside the CoW area. The sheer magnitude and variety of migrants into this area, and indeed movements within its populations (for instance, there is a sizeable highlands Amungme community now established within the lowlands population), has created a complex cosmopolitan mosaic of local and non-local, corporate or state sponsored, or "spontaneous" communities across the CoW area, leading to a range of local conflicts over resources, power and identity.

In this context the very issue of indigeneity has been muddied. Following disturbances around the mine and the lowlands town in 1996, the state recognised a set of so-called "seven *suku*" (tribe) as the indigenous peoples of the area who should be (equally) a particular focus of the cash, infrastructure and development flowing from the mine operation. While both the Kamoro and the Amungme were included, so too were five other groups from outside the CoW, all of whom came from other parts of the highlands (including the Dani), and all of whom had an established community of migrants in the area by 1996. The officially acknowledged "indigenous" at Freeport, then, are a state creation—a politically motivated, convenient response to growing ethnic tensions and pressures occurring within the CoW. This deployment of the term indigenous effectively undermined the Amungme and Kamoro position as the original inhabitants of the CoW. To Freeport's credit, it has followed this up (from 2001) with a more formal program of *rekognisi* that is intended to retrospectively compensate the Kamoro and Amungme for the "release" of their land for the mine development, but these groups continue to exist in a political arena where their indigenous status is compromised.

Identity is also confounded for local communities by migration through another process. As at mining sites in Papua New Guinea,[23] local communities have found themselves host to Amungme and Kamoro kin from outside the CoW area who move to access the infrastructure and benefits that are available to the indigenous communities within the CoW. In a series of surveys carried out in the late 1990s, it was found that these migrants had, on average, higher rates of employment at Freeport and subsequently higher household incomes and a more "modern" lifestyle than that of Amungme and Kamoro from within the CoW area.[24] Critically, the pre-existing nature of regional relationships between locals and migrants was a central element in facilitating the movement of these migrants into the mine area, with ethnically-related Dani able to exploit the regional connections between themselves and the Amungme, filtered through early Damal migrants, to access the CoW area, while better educated Kamoro from outside the CoW area could also establish themselves on part of the Kamoro CoW territory through their shared ethnic identity. At Freeport, as at the mines in Papua New Guinea,[25] this complicated any simple identification of "true" landowners, and led to tensions within the indigenous groups over access to employment and other economic benefits. Again, though, this is an issue that transcends simple economic motives in the Melanesian context, where identity is forged from within morally encoded social relationships and behaviour. The rapidly changing social world for communities around the large-scale resource projects that flows from migration makes the assertion of local identity at once increasingly necessary and yet also subject to a range of constraints and competing local, national and global influences.

For many of the resource frontier communities in the region, identity is also closely tied to local resources. This is in many senses obvious—local people depend on local environments for many of their basic necessities, and their lives and identity are intimately linked with their local environments and resources. This rhetoric though can lead into a romantic portrayal of local people in harmony with nature, which in fact glosses important development imperatives in these communities.[26] Local resentments often arise not because pristine environments are being threatened, but because control over resources or revenue from these resources is lost to local communities. In a number of regional contexts across Indonesia (and elsewhere in the region), the military and powerful political forces have been behind this excision of local rights and control, and it has often been accompanied by resistance, conflict and human rights abuses. Freeport's history of financial and logistical support for resident military forces[27] left it exposed to charges of, at the minimum, providing material support for abuses against Amungme and Kamoro and others in and around the CoW area. The loss of control over resources and environments, combined with victimisation and abuse by predatory and commercially-driven members of the armed forces, can make communities particularly vulnerable, and promotes parochial localism and the development of new forms of local identity "positioning".

One example, at a regional scale, of the importance of resources to identity politics (or positioning) from Papua New Guinea comes from the Huli people of the Southern Highlands Province. Here, a people who believe that they inherently have a central role in national and even international affairs have found themselves literally surrounded by large resource projects on the territories of what they consider to be inferior people. To the south there is the large Kutubu, Gobe and Moran oil and gas projects, to the north Mt. Kare and Porgera gold projects, and a little further west, the Ok Tedi copper/gold mine (the smallish Hides gas project is on the southern extremity of their territory). Despite this central position, Huli are not the identified owners of the land of any of the major projects, and only receive indirect, marginal benefits from them. There is also a long history of perceptions of government neglect, and of active discrimination and violence by the more centrally located Mendi who have reaped the bulk of the benefits from the oil projects in the province.[28]

In a response that exemplifies the argument, the Huli have been responsible for the promotion of a separate "Hela" Province in the Highlands, one that ties together the descendants of a group of mythical original brothers who spread from the Huli heartland and settled in the neighbouring areas that, perhaps not coincidentally, are now home to these global resource projects. While few in the resource-rich areas lend the notion much support, the Huli have been busy pushing the concept at the national level, and the Hela "people/tribe" and even "district" or "province" are regularly reported on in the media.[29] The Huli here are attempting to reshape their role in the regional geopolitical balance, and seeking to maintain their self-perceived dominant position as the central people in the region by drawing on a common, mythical regional identity that will provide them with greater control over the natural resource bounty of their "nation". Both migration and tensions over local resource control have at their core, then, the reshaping—the forging—of identities for communities and individuals, usually configured around heightened notions of difference and positioned in relation to new opportunities and constraints afforded by national and global influences.

Fundamental to these processes is scale: resource developments and the tensions they engender are both intensely local but, as Anna Tsing reminds us, also intimately global.[30] They are global in two senses: first, as discussed, national and global influences are promoting a stronger identification with the local, and second, these processes are now played out on a global stage. Conflicts over local resource control or ownership often become entangled or intersect with international environmental rhetoric. Both the Freeport and Ok Tedi (Papua New Guinea) mines are good examples of critical issues of local resource control and decision-making becoming international "environmental issues" in such a way that the dynamics of local societies, cultures and economies are totally obscured.[31]

To come back to Freeport, the core international concerns expressed by non-governmental organizations (NGOs) and academics have been around human rights and environmental concerns. These have dominated high profile campaigns and attacks on the behemoth with good reason, given first the sustained history of abuses on communities by government and security forces and, second, the highly visible[32] nature of the environmental impact of the enormous mine and its wastes. At the same time, the focus on these issues has subjected other, differing aspirations of Amungme and Kamoro (for recognition and various forms of development, for example) to these international agendas. Indeed, given the high profile of the Amungme in these anti-Freeport campaigns, the Kamoro have, in the discursive sense at least, virtually disappeared.[33]

The environment in this sense has become as Krista Harper puts it, "a quintessentially global narrative"[34] that is deployed and refigured in particular local political and cultural settings. Local resource concerns intersect with global narratives of environmental issues, and indigenous and human rights, with global actors—large multinational mining, oil or forestry companies, and international NGOs. The "fragments"[35] or moments in the life of resource developments generated by these global connections are then delicately contingent on an array of actors, markets and states. As Tsing writes, "...space and scale both enable capitalist proliferation and embroil it in moments of chaos".[36]

Scale is central to this alternative conceptualisation. This is not, however, a simple hierarchy of global-national-local actors and arenas. Rather, we see continuous transgressions across scales by actors. Key local actors at Freeport exemplify this. Two Amungme, for example, achieved international recognition and profiles for their work on human rights and environmental issues at Freeport. The first, Thom Beanal, gained repute in the mid-1990s through leading litigation in the United States against Freeport for cultural and environmental destruction.[37] He was awarded an international Tides Foundation award in 1997, and then co-opted as a Commissioner onto the Board of Freeport. From 2002 to 2007 he chaired the Papuan Customary Council and continues to chair the highly influential Papuan Presidium Council (PDP). The second, Mama Yosepha Alomang, like Beanal, was a litigant in action against Freeport in 1998 that attracted the support of international environmental and human rights NGOs. For her activism, she was awarded the prestigious Goldman Environmental Prize in 2001 and used the proceeds from this to fund her local Amungme Yamahak Women's Rights Group in Timika, Papua. Today, in the chaotic politics typical of large-scale resource developments, Yamahak now receives funding support from Freeport. Both Thom and Yosepa continue to travel internationally and occupy complex positions straddling local concerns and representations, and global audiences. Scale here, as with the resource multinationals themselves, is also self-consciously socially constructed and utilised. The local is identified as global, and the global as local, when circumstances permit and when it is seen as being of value. Contests over local resource control in the context of globalisation, then, are intimately related to this telescoping of scale, and the complex ways in which "local" identities are constructed and deployed.

Resources in Context

To return to the question posed in the introduction. Do natural resources cause conflict, and if so, how? Existing frameworks offer several valuable pointers towards resolving this question. Clearly, the presence of natural resources provides several mechanisms that can heighten the prospects for centre–periphery conflict. Collier's work certainly underlines the centrality of natural resources to counter-centre movements in the region. But there are also clear dangers in translating the complexities of civil conflicts into raw and processed numbers. I am not at all convinced, for example, by Collier's argument that local grievances in civil conflicts are simply rationalisations for local greed. Rather, we need to recognise that the resources at stake are themselves socially constructed, and the discourses around them even more so. This is not to argue that resources are *simply* social constructs—having stood at the top of the open pit at Freeport's Grasberg mine I can certainly attest to the physicality and materiality of large-scale mines. As Karen Bakker and Gavin Bridge note, the material matters in these resource conflicts because of its diversity—each mine, each forest, each setting, is different and this "heterogeneity differentially enables, constrains and/or disrupts the social practices through which resource regulation is achieved".[38] This diversity provides the initial ground whereby, to use Tsing's analogy, global 'universals' (global capital, environmentalism, etc.) find purchase and are articulated differentially on the varied grounds of the "local".[39] And while this is certainly evident from the diversity of outcomes apparent around resource developments in the region, I would argue that it is not the materiality of these resources that is the most critical element in terms of the development of local or regional conflicts, but rather the coming together of these "physical" resources with the processes involved in identity politics that provides the fertile ground for the development of tensions and conflict.

The role of resources in generating conflict in Indonesia and elsewhere is clearly contingent on a range of other factors.[40] In particular, examples of conflicts over resources from contemporary Indonesia illustrate that struggles over resources (local–state or local–migrant) are fundamentally entwined with issues of local resource control and identity.[41] The economic motives ascribed by Collier and others in such conflicts are simply one component, and the one most readily seized upon, absorbed and applied by external observers, of what are essentially *moral* conflicts about the right to access, control and utilise resources for many communities in Indonesia and beyond, especially those at the geographic and/or political margins.

This chapter has sought to use a grounded approach to questions of resources and conflict, drawing on local and regional scale examples and "working up". The argument is that, *contra* the resource conflict and environmental security approaches, that the specifics of the local are important: we can learn more about the nature and causes of resource conflicts from an understanding of the particulars than we can from generalising across data sets. Having said this, resource extraction is no longer simply a local event, if indeed it ever was. National and global actors and discourses impact centrally on the way in which local tensions surrounding resources are worked through. What is significant is the way the discursive construction of these resources, and especially discourses of control, loss and lack of benefits, intersect and become entangled with global narratives about the environment or about human rights, for example, and the subsequent construction of the "local". Like Tsing,[42] I see the notion of a universal "resource conflict" framework being undermined by the need to appreciate the particularism of the "chaos" of local resource conflicts, and the conditional positioning and framing of such conflicts by local, regional and global actors and influences. These concepts and processes, derived from understandings of globalisation and identity, are the ones I believe we need to engage with if we are to fully understand the dynamics of resource conflicts and regionalism in the Indonesian archipelago and beyond.

Notes

1. M. Ross, "The Political Economy of the Resource Curse", *World Politics* 51, 2 (1999): 297–322.
2. R. Auty, *Sustaining Development in the Mineral Economies: The Resource Curse Thesis* (London: Routledge, 1993).
3. M. Ross, "The Natural Resource Curse: How Wealth Can Make You Poor", in *Natural Resources and Violent Conflict: Options and Actions*, ed. I. Bannon and P. Collier (Washington, D. C.: World Bank, 2003), pp. 17–42.
4. J. Sachs and A. Warner, "The Curse of Natural Resources", *European Economic Review* 45 (2001): 827–38.
5. Ross, "The Natural Resource Curse".
6. Ibid., p. 25.
7. P. Collier, "Economic Causes of Civil Conflict and their Implications for Policy", in *Leashing the Dogs of War: Conflict Management in a Divided World*, ed. C. A. Crocker, F. O. Hampson and P. Aall (Washington, D. C.: US Institute of Peace, 2007), p. 9.
8. Ibid., p. 6.
9. P. Collier and A. Hoeffler, "Greed and Grievance in Civil War", *Oxford Economic Papers* 56, 4 (2004): 563–95.
10. The issue of scale is glossed here, but it is clearly problematic to apply national level data and analysis to advance arguments concerning internal, provincial conflicts.
11. Collier, "Economic Causes of Civil Conflict", p. 11.
12. J. Switzer, "Armed Conflict and Natural Resources: The Case of the Minerals Sector", MMSD Report no. 12 (London: International Institute for Environment and Development, July 2001), p. 9.
13. C. Timura, "'Environmental Conflict' and the Social Life of Environmental Discourse", *Anthropological Quarterly* 74, 3 (2001): 104–13 makes a similar argument.
14. See, for example, P. Walker, "Political Ecology: Where is the Ecology?", *Progress in Human Geography* 2, 1 (2006): 73–82.
15. R. Howitt, J. Connell and P. Hirsch, "Resources, Nations and Indigenous Peoples", in *Resources, Nations and Indigenous Peoples: Case Studies from*

Australasia, Melanesia and Southeast Asia, ed. R. Howitt, J. Connell and P. Hirsch (Melbourne: Oxford University Press, 1996), p. 1.
16. T. M. Li, "Articulating Indigenous Identity in Indonesia: Resource Politics and the Tribal Slot", *Comparative Study of Society and History* 42, 1 (2000): 151.
17. For a recent example, see D. Korten, "From Empire to Earth Community", *Development* 49 (2006): 76–81.
18. Two exemplary recent examples of this are: A. L. Tsing, *Friction: An Ethnography of Global Connection* (Princeton: Princeton University Press, 2005); and J. F. McCarthy, *The Fourth Circle: A Political Ecology of Sumatra's Rainforest Frontier* (Stanford: Stanford University Press, 2006).
19. For a review and comment on this literature, see K. Bakker and G. Bridge, "Material Worlds? Resource Geographies and the 'Matter of Nature'", *Progress in Human Geography* 30, 1 (2006): 5–27.
20. See also Li, "Articulating Indigenous Identity in Indonesia", for a similar argument.
21. For background on Freeport, see D. Leith, *The Politics of Power: Freeport in Suharto's Indonesia* (Honolulu: University of Hawai'i Press, 2003); C. Ballard and G. Banks, "Between a Rock and Hard Place: Corporate Strategy at the Freeport Mine in Papua, 2001–2006", in *Development and Environment in Eastern Indonesia*, ed. B. Resosudarmo and F. Jotzo (in press).
22. C. Ballard, "The Denial of Traditional Land Rights in West Papua", *Cultural Survival Quarterly* 26, 3 (2002): 39–43.
23. See G. Banks, "Globalization, Poverty, and Hyperdevelopment in Papua New Guinea's Mining Sector", *Focaal: European Journal of Anthropology* 46 (2006): 128–43.
24. See G. Banks, "'Faces We do not Know': Mining and Migration in the Melanesian Context", in *Mining Frontiers: Comparative Perspectives on Property Relations: Social Conflicts, and Cultural Change in Boom Region*, ed. T. Grätz and K. Werthmann (University of Nevada Press, forthcoming).
25. D. Jorgensen, "Who and What is a Landowner? Mythology and Marking the Ground in a Papua New Guinea Mining Project", *Anthropological Forum* 7, 4 (1997): 599–627.
26. In the context of mining, see G. Banks, "Mining and Environment in Melanesia: Contemporary Debates Reviewed", *Contemporary Pacific* 14, 1 (2002): 39–67.
27. J. Perlez and R. Bonner, "Below a Mountain of Wealth, a River of Waste", *New York Times*, 27 Dec. 2005.
28. N. Haley and R. May, *Conflict and Resource Development in the Southern Highlands of Papua New Guinea* (Canberra: State, Society and Governance in Melanesia Program, The Australian National University [ANU], 2007).
29. H. Wayne, "Give Services or Forget Pipeline: Hela", *The National*, 22 July 2002; A. Kaiabe, "Why a Hela Province!", *Post-Courier*, 14 Nov. 2006.

30. Tsing, *Friction*.
31. See Banks, "Mining and Environment in Melanesia"; and *The Ok Tedi Settlement: Issues, Outcomes and Implications*, ed. G. Banks and C. Ballard (Canberra: National Centre for Development Studies, ANU, 1997).
32. D. Paull et al., "Monitoring the Environmental Impact of Mining in Remote Locations through Remotely Sensed Data", *GeoCarto International* 21, 1 (2006) 1–9.
33. T. S. Harple, "Controlling the Dragon: An Ethno-Historical Analysis of Social Engagement among the Kamoro of South-West New Guinea (Indonesian Papua/Irian Jaya)", doctoral dissertation, ANU, Canberra, 2002.
34. K. Harper, "Introduction. The Environment as Master Narrative: Discourse and Identity in Environmental Problems", *Anthropological Quarterly* 74, 3 (2001): 101.
35. Tsing, *Friction*.
36. Ibid., p. 12.
37. E. Jessup, "Beanal v. Freeport-McMoran, Inc.: Anatomy of an International Environmental Tort Case", *New England International and Comparative Law Annual* 5 (1999), <http://www.nesl.edu/intljournal/VOL5/jessup.htm>.
38. Bakker and Bridge, "Material worlds?", p. 21.
39. Tsing, *Friction*, pp. 8–10.
40. See G. Banks, "Linking Resources and Conflict the Melanesian Way", *Pacific Economic Bulletin* 20, 1 (2005): 117–23; L. Horowitz, "Daily, Immediate Conflicts: An Analysis of Villager's Arguments about a Multinational Nickel Mining Project in New Caledonia", *Oceania* 73 (2002): 35–55.
41. See Adhuri, this volume, and L. Visser, "Remaining Poor on Natural Riches? The Fallacy of Community Development in Irian Jaya/Papua", *Asia Pacific Journal of Anthropology* 2, 2 (2001): 68–88.
42. Tsing, *Friction*.

CHAPTER 7

Social Identity and Access to Natural Resources: Ethnicity and Regionalism from a Maritime Perspective

Dedi S. Adhuri

Introduction: The Sea, the Imagined Bridge

The political ideology of the sea in Indonesia is embedded in the concept of *Wawasan Nusantara* (the archipelagic principle). The essence of Wawasan Nusantara is the "oneness" of Indonesia in terms of territory (*wilayah*), nationhood (*bangsa*), goal and spirit of struggle (*tujuan dan tekad perjuangan*), the law (*hukum*), socio-cultural attributes (*sosial-budaya*), the economy (*ekonomi*), and defense and security (Hankam).[1] The territorial "oneness" of Indonesia assumes that the many islands (land), sea (water) and the atmosphere (air) are a single integrated entity.[2] Thus, the sea is not considered as dividing the islands of Indonesia; on the contrary, the sea is believed to unite all the Indonesian islands and the people living on them. In Indonesia, this ideology is commonly expressed by the proverbs that *"laut adalah perekat kepulauan Indonesia"* (the sea is the substance that binds the Indonesian archipelago) and *"laut adalah jembatan yang menghubungkan pulau dan penduduk yang menempatinya di seluruh Indonesia*" (the sea is a bridge connecting all the islands and people of Indonesia).

If we look at marine fishery policies in Indonesia, it appears that these concepts have been adopted literally; as a bridge for all Indonesians, the sea is "free for all people" to use. In doing so, the government detaches the sea from all, or any individual, social groups in Indonesia. The Indonesian Constitution of 1945, Article 33 (3),[3] states that "*Bumi, air, angkasa, dan kekayaan alam yang tekandung di dalamnya dikuasai oleh negara dan dipergunakan untuk sebesar-besarnya kemakmuran rakyat*" (the land, water, air and the natural wealth therein are under state control and to be used for the betterment of peoples' welfare). As a result, unlike other resources such as forests and minerals—where the government splits the resource rights into units and distributes them to people or institutions—the sea is treated as indivisable. Again, unlike the rights to manage forests in Indonesia (*Hak Pengusahaan Hutan*), which are given to a particular institution (company or cooperative) to the exclusion of other institutions for a particular area, many fishermen or fishing companies may hold the licence to fish for the same resource in the same zone. In short, this means that those who live in the western limits of Indonesia's territorial boundaries may fish anywhere, including in the waters of the eastern edge of the archipelago alongside people from different places and cultural backgrounds.

There are, of course, taxes to be paid and procedures to follow but these are only based on the fishing technology used. The Ministry of Agriculture Decree No. 32/1999, for example, stipulates that those who use "traditional" technology are free to fish wherever they like but they are given exclusive rights in Zone I (minimum low tide up to six miles); those who use middle-range technology can only fish in Zone II (outside Zone I, up to 12 miles); and those who use high-tech or modern technology are only allowed to fish outside both zones (see Table 7.1).

Is this ideology, and the marine resource management practices which derive from it, adhered to by the fishermen themselves? Do local people perceive the sea in the same way as the Indonesian government? What do fishermen think when they enter fishing zones, extract resources or prohibit others from doing so? In the following sections, I will discuss cases of conflicts over fishing grounds, which will shed some light on these issues.

TABLE 7.1
Ministry of Agriculture Decree No. 392/1999 on Marine Zoning for Fisheries

Zone	Sub-zone	Allowed Fishing Boat and Gear
Zone I Minimum low tide (− 6 miles)	Minimum low tide −3 miles	Stationary fishing gear Non-modified non-stationary fishing gear Un-motorised boat with max. 10 m length
	>3–6 miles	Modified non-stationary gear Un-motorised or outboard engine, max. 10 m long Outboard or inboard engine with max. 12 m long or less than 5 GT (gross tons) Purse seine max. 150 m Drift gill net max. 1,000 m lon
Zone II Outside Zone I (−12 miles)	No sub-division	Vessel of maximum 60 GT Vessel with purse seine max. 600 m operated from single vessel or max. 100 m operated by two vessels Tuna long line max. 1,200 hooks Drift gill net max. 2,500 m long
Zone III Outside Zone II (to the outer line of EEZ)	No sub-division	Indonesian vessels max. 200 GT, with the exception of all vessels using purse seine for large pelagic fisheries that are forbidden to operate in Teluk Tomini Bay, Maluku Sea, Seram Sea, Banda Sea, Flores Sea and Sawu Sea. Indonesian EEZ in Strait of Melaka is open for maximum 200 GT Indonesian vessels, with exception of minimum 60 GT boat using fish net EEZ outside of Strait of Melaka is open for: Indonesian or foreign vessels of max. 350 GT of all gear types; Vessels >350–800 GT using purse seine are only allowed to operate beyond 100 miles from Indonesian coastal line; Purse seines operating in group are only allowed to operate beyond 100 miles from the outer coastline of Indonesia archipelago

FIGURE 7.1
The Kei Islands

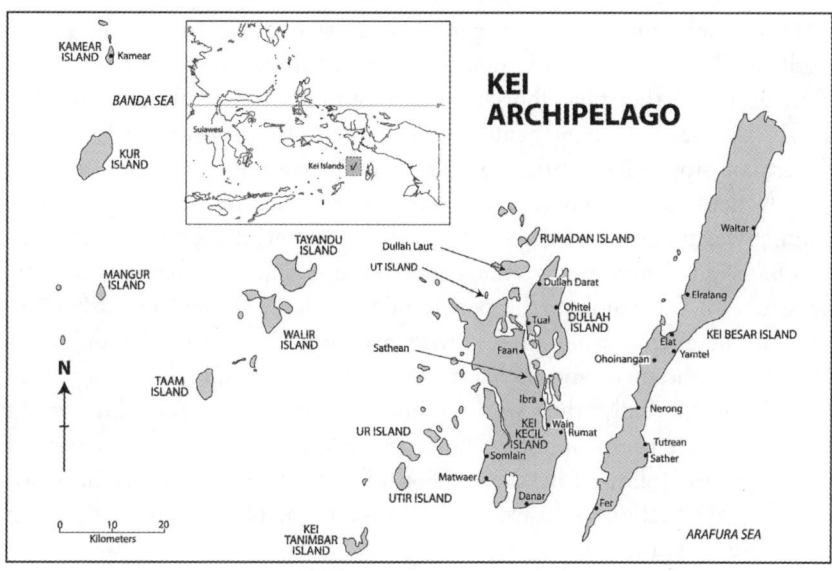

Ethnicity and Access to Fishing Grounds

Conflicts over fishing grounds in the Kei Islands, southeastern Maluku, as in other parts of Indonesia, are not a new phenomenon. Local people remember conflicts over sea boundaries and resources taking place since the 1930s. The causes and the consequences of these conflicts are various. The cases that I am going to discuss are recent examples of conflicts that demonstrate the role of ethnicity in access to fishing grounds.

The first incident was a fisheries conflict in the village of Sathean on Kei Kecil Island (see Figure 7.1). This village consists of two hamlets (*ohoi*) called Ohoisaran and Ohoislam. Ohoisaran is twice as big as Ohoislam: in 1993 when the combined population of Sathean was around 1,500, almost 1,000 lived at Ohoisaran. As well as being unequal in size, there were important differences between the two hamlets: those in Ohoisaran were Christian, while the people in Ohoislam were all Muslim. In Ohoisaran, most people were farmers; a few occasionally went fishing for subsistence purposes. In contrast, the majority of Ohoislam's adult males spent most of their time fishing and only farmed in their spare time. Some adult females in Ohoislam also sold the fish caught by their husbands, brothers or relatives in the village or at the market.

Conflict between the people of these two hamlets occurred in 1964 when a Ohoislam fisherman began using a lift-net in Sathean's shared sea territory. Those from Ohoisaran, subsistence fishers who used lines or gill nets, protested that the Ohoislam fisherman's lift-net would give him the unfair advantage of a bigger catch. In response to the protests, the Ohoislam fisherman stopped operating his lift-net, thus avoiding further conflict.

A new conflict broke out twenty years later, in 1984. Again, this conflict was triggered by the adoption of lift-net technology by a fisherman at Ohoislam. Interestingly, the conflict was resolved differently on this occasion. In this conflict, the people of Ohoisaran allowed the fisherman to continue operating his lift-net with two conditions. First, he and other Ohoislam fishermen who used lift-nets had to pay a special tax (*ngasi*) to the village. Secondly, they were prohibited from setting their lift-nets in the area where the people of Ohoisaran traditionally fished.[4] The second condition was followed by the division of Sathean's sea territory into two sections: one section exclusively for Ohoisaran people and another section accessible to both.

In terms of traditional sea ownership, the people of Ohoisaran, who formed the majority in Sathean, considered the fishermen of Ohoislam to be a minority of "outsiders" who were not allowed to fish in the village territory without their consent. To put it differently, the people of Ohoisaran thought that the people of Ohoislam did not have the same rights over the village's traditional sea territory and resources. Their claims were based on the village's origin myth, which narrates that Sathean was established by the ancestors of the people of Ohoisaran. Thus, the Ohoisaran villagers considered themselves to be the founders of Sathean, and used this as a source of legitimacy to lay claim to ownership of the land and the surrounding sea. On the other hand, the people of Ohoislam were said to be the descendants of a Buginese man who had married a Sathean woman. Since the local kinship system is patrilineal, they were not considered to be part of the original social group. In fact, the people of Ohoisaran identified the population of Ohoislam as "Buginese". However, since the people of Ohoislam had adopted the family name of an origin kin group, the Yamlean, which indicated their willingness to be associated with the founder kin-group of the village, they were also considered *Yamlean Tempel* (attached to the Yamlean). As such, they were not considered complete outsiders.

It is clear from an assessment of this conflict that it was not only technology which constrained the people of Ohoislam from accessing the sea territory of the village, it was their "otherness", from the perspective of the Ohoisaran people. Furthermore, the parameter of this otherness was not locality or biological connections but it was a cultural parameter, namely ethnicity. In terms of locality, the people of Ohoislam had lived in the village for generations. Biologically, they also shared the same blood with the people of Ohoisaran through a Sathean woman. Yet, in terms of ethnicity, they were, as people of Ohoisaran address them, "Buginese". This is the reason that they were excluded from accessing marine resources. It was only with permission from the origin group, which was bought by paying the *ngasi*, that these "outsiders" were allowed to enter and make use of the village's sea territory.

The second conflict occurred between Dullah Laut villagers and Butonese fishermen in the second half of 1997. Again, the conflict was triggered by a fisherman who was using a lift-net, this time in Dullah Laut's sea territory (see Figure 7.1). Dullah Laut villagers knew that the owner of the lift-net must have been an "outsider" because none of them were using this technology. After some investigation, they discovered that the owner was a Butonese man who was married to a woman from Ut Island in the Kei archipelago (Figure 7.1). Initially, although he had entered their sea territory without requesting permission, Dullah Laut villagers did not take harsh measures against the lift-net fisherman because he was associated with the people of Ut Island, whom they respected. Dullah Laut villagers recount that the ancestors of the Ut islanders had once assisted their ancestors in a time of war. This respect was expressed by allowing them to do some fishing in Dullah Laut's sea territory. However, when an increasing number of lift-net fishermen—most of whom had nothing to do with the Ut islanders but were Butonese compatriots of the first operator—entered their fishing ground, Dullah Laut villagers reacted firmly. They raided the lift-net fishing boats, forcing them out of the Dullah Laut fishing grounds; the Butonese fishermen did not return.

A third case concerns a conflict between Madurese and local fishermen in Perigi, on the south coast of East Java. The conflict, which took place in 2000, was provoked by the use of kerosene lamps (*petromaks*) by the Madurese fishermen while they were fishing. This was considered to be a threat to the catch of local fishermen because, although they used the same fishing technology (but without the *petromaks*), the light of the lamps attracted more fish to the Madurese boats and reduced the catch of the

Perigi fishermen. For this reason, the latter protested against the use of *petromaks*, but the Madurese resisted. Locals responded by burning four of the six Madurese fishing boats, destroying the Madurese huts and driving the Madurese themselves from the area. When I did my fieldwork in early 2002, none of these Madurese fishermen had returned to Perigi.

My reading of this last conflict is as follows. Unlike in the Kei Islands where the coastal area is communally owned, in Java, normatively, the sea is "free for all". Therefore, fishermen working in the area came from different places and ethnic groups. Even so, however, non-locals were differentiated from local fishermen. The former were called *nelayan andong* (visiting fishermen). Interestingly, at least from the perspective of the locals, this category also reflects the different rights and obligations of each in relation to the sea as well as modes of conduct in daily life. In relation to the sea, the *andong* fishermen were not to use fishing technology that might disturb or disadvantage the operations of the locals. The locals also thought that, as guests of the local community, the *nelayan andong* should behave in accordance to local norms.

Unfortunately, the Madurese fishermen had breached these rules. The first mistake was their use of kerosene lamps. The second mistake was something to do with the "character" and behaviour of the Madurese. Local fishermen judged the Madurese to be violent: they were said to be easily provoked to arguments and physical violence, which often involved the traditional Madurese weapon (*clurit*). According to local people, this contrasted with the Javanese who were humble and tended to avoid conflict. The Madurese were also disliked because they were considered to be ill-mannered (*tidak sopan*). They walked from the coast to their huts—approximately 300 to 400 metres, passing through public spaces such as the market, and in front of offices and hotels—clad only in their underwear. Again, according to the local norms, this was not acceptable.

These conflicts clearly show how local people manipulate local and non-local identities in order to control maritime resources or exclude others from access to resources. In this regard, ethnicity is used to define "non-localness" or "otherness". This was obvious when the people of Ohoisaran called the Ohoislam fishermen "Buginese" or, "half Buginese"; the Dullah Laut villagers addressed the lift-net fishermen as Butonese; and the Perigi fishermen labelled those who used *petromaks* as "Madurese". These ethnic groups were defined as non-local, and were then excluded from accessing local marine resources. It is also apparent that technological differences or the use of new types of fishing gear precipitated the ethnic labelling.

Regionalism and the Politics of Exclusion

Fisheries-based disputes in Indonesia have continued during the era of decentralisation. Since 2000, many serious conflicts over fisheries have occurred across the archipelago, including in North Sumatra, Bengkulu, Lampung, Java, Madura and Pontianak in Kalimantan. These conflicts have not only caused the loss of many boats and much fishing gear but also many lives.

From the accounts of conflicts that I have compiled, it is apparent that the politics of exclusion plays an important role in fishing disputes (Table 7.2). The two grounds for exclusion involve fishing ground violations, and technological differences (that is, in fishing gear and methods and/or technology). Fishing ground violations refer to the operations of "outside" fishermen in a fishing ground claimed to be under the control of a particular local group. Unlike the three cases that I discussed in the previous section (where ethnicity was used to define otherness)—in many cases the boundaries of the fishing ground and the "otherness" now derive from official Indonesian government definitions. Thus, all the conflicts recorded in Table 7.2 relate more to the *desa* (village), *kecamatan* (sub-district), *kabupaten* (district) or *provinsi* (province) rather than ethnicity or other "traditional" boundaries. For example, the burning of four purse seines belonging to Indramayu and Cirebon fishermen in Serang (Table 7.2, no. 9), shows that the Serang fishermen used the provincial boundaries as a basis for accusing those from Indramayu and Cirebon of violating their sea boundaries. The same explanation may be applied to the conflict between Cilacap (Central Java) and Pangandaran (West Java) fishermen (no. 5), and between Bengkulu and North Sumatra and South Kalimantan fishermen (no. 10). Other cases, however, show that conflicts can be more complex. Conflicts between fishermen from the northern coast of Java and Masalembo (no. 1, 2 and 8) demonstrate that disputing parties are not always synonymous with administrative units. In these disputes, the fishermen from several different districts in the northern coast of Java acted in concert against fishermen from Masalembo, who were from a single district.

The second issue, technological violation, refers to the use of "illegal" technology in a particular fishing ground. Illegality could be defined by literal interpretation of government regulations or by perceived wrongdoing. For example, since the use of trawl fishing was banned according to a presidential decree in 1980, protests against trawler operations provide an example of a legally based dispute over technological violations

TABLE 7.2
Some Conflicts between Fishermen in Indonesia (2000–2)

No.	Incident	Issues	Location	Time	Source
1.	The burning of six boats, hostage-taking, torture of Pati and Tegal (Central Javanese) fishermen by Masalembo fishermen	Fishing ground and technological violations (the use of lamp)	Masalembo, East Java	Early 2000	*Republika*, 13 Nov. 2000
2.	The burning of one fishing boat belonging to Central Javanese fishermen by Masalembo fishermen	Fishing ground violation	Masalembo, East Java	Nov. 2000	*Rakyat Merdeka*, 17 Nov. 2000
3.	Jakarta fishermen protest against non-local trawl operation in traditional fishing zone	Trawl operation in traditional fishing zone	Jakarta	Aug. 2001	*Kompas*, 13 Aug. 2001
4.	Physical fight between fishermen from Wedung and Bonang sub-districts, Demak district	The operation of police owned mini-trawlers assisted by Bonang fishermen	Demak, Central Java	Jan. 2002	*Kompas*, 12 Jan. 2002
5.	The arrest and hostage-taking of eight Cilacap (Central Java) fishermen by Pangandaran (West Java) fishermen	Fishing ground and technological violations (the use of *payang* net)	Pangandaran, West Java	Feb. 2002	*Kompas*, 23 & 27 Feb. 2002

TABLE 7.2 (Cont'd)

No.	Incident	Issues	Location	Time	Source
6.	Confiscation of 16 mini-trawler boats owned by Panciran sub-district, Lamongan district and Paceng sub-districts, Gresik district by traditional fishermen from Ujung Pangakah sub-district	The use of mini-trawlers considered ecologically destructive and reduced the local fishermen's catch. (Note: the conflict was settled by an agreement that: 1. Operation of mini-trawler was prohibited within 30 fathoms depth. 2. Fishermen from Ujung Pangakah have the right to arrest those who violate this rule. 3. Violation is pubished by the burning of the boat.)	Gresik, East Java	Mar. 2002	*Kompas*, 12 Mar. 2002
7.	The burning of eight mini-trawl boats belonging to Sampit village (Matan Hilir Utara sub-district) fishermen by fishermen from Sukabaru village, Matanhilir Selatan sub-district	The Sampit boat owners did not pay the fine of three million rupiah to fishermen from Sukabaru as a consequence of the fishing ground violation	Pontianak, West Kalimantan	Mar. 2002	*Kompas*, 21 Mar. 2002
8.	Madurese Karimunjawa fishermen taken hostage by locals	Fishing ground violation	Brebes and Tegal, Central Java	Apr. 2002	*Kompas*, 18 Apr. 2002

(Cont'd overleaf)

TABLE 7.2 (Cont'd)

No.	Incident	Issues	Location	Time	Source
9.	The burning of four purse seine boats owned by fishermen from Indramayu and Cirebon districts (West Java), by locals	Fishing ground and technological violations	Serang, West Java	May 2002	*Kompas*, 21 May 2002
10.	The burning of a trawl boat and protest by traditional Bengkulu fishermen over the use of trawl and purse seine originating from North Sumatra and South Sulawesi	The use of trawl and purse seine in the zone for traditional fishing technologies (Note: It had been an agreement between purse seine fishermen and locals that the purse seine fishermen give 100 kg of their catch/trip to the locals. The locals contested this agreement. A new agreement was proposed that half or more fishermen working on a purse seine boat should be local fishermen.)	Bengkulu	July 2002	*Kompas*, 19 July 2002
11.	Protest by traditional fishermen in North Sumatra	Trawl operation in the zone for traditional fishing. Resistance to the government's plan to legalise trawl operations	Medan, North Sumatera	Sept. 2002	*Kompas*, 17 Sept. 2002

Sources: *Kompas*, "Nelayan Jakarta Protes Kehadiran Kapal 'Trawl'", 13 Aug. 2001; "Buntut Bentrokan Nelayan: 2.500 Nelayan Demak tidak Berani Melaut", 12 Jan. 2002; "HNSI Cilacap: Penyanderaan, Bisa Picu Konflik antar Nelayan", 23 Feb. 2002; "Buntu, Pertemuan HNSI Cilacap-Ciamis", 27 Feb. 2002; "Nelayan Ujung Pangkah Menyita 16 Perahu Pengguna 'Mini-Trawl'", 12 Mar. 2002; "Nelayan Ketapang Bakar Delapan Kapal Trawl", 21 Mar. 2002; "Kerawanan Laut Meningkat", 21 May 2002; "Konflik Nelayan di Musim Paceklik", 19 July 2002; "Nelayan Tradisional Sumut Tolak Pukat Harimau", 17 Sept. 2002. *Republika*, "Hari ini Nelayan Pantura akan Demo di Jakarta", 13 Nov. 2000.

(nos. 3, 4, 6, 7, 10). Some cases also show that such technological violations are defined by differences between local and non-local fishing technologies. The use of more advanced technologies by outsiders was often considered "illegal". Thus, in Bengkulu local fishermen protested against the use of a purse seine (no. 10). Masalembo fishermen burned six Central Javanese fishing boats because the fishermen were using lamps while fishing. The more advanced technologies was believed to unfairly increase the outsider's catch at the expense of local fishermen.

Research conducted by the Maritime Study Group[5] found that similar conflicts continue. Indrawasih, Wahyono and Adhuri reported that conflict between muro-ami fishermen versus line and nets operators broke out in Belitung in 2003–4.[6] In the same period, conflict also occurred between *gaek* (purse seine) and *payang* (bag seine) operators in Sungai Liat on Bangka Island.[7] Similarly, in Kepulauan Riau, the use of mini-trawlers in the waters around Numbing Island provoked conflict with line users.[8] The use of mini-trawlers also resulted in the burning of fishing gear and physical confrontation between some fishermen in Lembar and Sekotong Barat districts on Mataram Island, East Nusa Tenggara, in 2004.[9]

Like the earlier conflicts, those reported by the Maritime Study Group which broke out between 2003–6 involved not only the issue of fishing gear but also the identity of the fishermen. In all the above conflicts, the aggravating parties were outsiders. The resentments which led to these conflicts arose because locals considered that the outsiders had encroached their waters and maritime resources using superior technologies, hence threatening their fishing harvests and jeopardising their livelihoods, usually by flooding local markets with their catch.

Evidently, these conflicts reveal that people associate technological differences with perceptions of local and non-local. All the conflicts caused by technological violations mentioned above show that those who controlled more advanced technologies were not locals but were fishermen from somewhere else, that is, other regions. Furthermore, the proposal of fishermen in Bengkulu that the locals might allow the purse seines to operate in their territory if half or more of the operators were local (Table 7.2, no. 10), indicates that the problem relates to the issue of who has better access to, and hence control over, the resource. The proposal obviously represented the interests of locals; unless locals controlled the resources, other fishermen would not be allowed to use superior technology. This also implies that the outsiders were not supposed to harvest more fish than the locals.

All these cases indicate a high level of regional identification in the maritime world of Indonesia. Regionalism provides fishermen with the basis for strong associations with local marine resources. Such associations enable locals to prohibit fishermen from other regions from making use of particular marine resources or, at least, of restricting access to those resources.

Ethnicity, Regionalism and Marine Resource Management

The ideology that "the sea is a bridge for all Indonesians", is still actively used by the government to understand the problems facing marine fisheries. Thus, the Department of Marine Affairs and Fisheries perceives that the core issues in the above conflicts are based on differences in fishing technology or a misinterpretation of the Law of Autonomy (22/1999).[10]

Indonesian officials categorise fishermen according to the technology they use: traditional, medium scale and modern. Beyond that, in accord with state ideology, they are all Indonesians. Fisheries officials also consider the association of ethnicity or regionalism in conflicts over sea resources as a reflection of misinterpretations of the Law of Regional Autonomy by local fishermen. The law[11] stipulates that provincial territory covers land and sea as far as twelve miles from the coastline toward the open sea (Article 3); the authority to manage the first third of a province's sea territory is in the hands of the district government (Article 10). Department of Marine Affairs and Fisheries officials have argued that the Law of Regional Autonomy has been misunderstood by local fishermen as the right to exclude from their sea territory fishermen from other ethnic groups or regions.

Officials propose that maritime conflicts resulting from technological discrepancies could be resolved both by assisting fishermen using traditional methods and gear to adopt more modern technology[12] and by enforcement of zoning systems.[13] They argue that, once the government declares that only a particular type of fishing technology can be used in a zone, conflicts amongst fishermen in that area would cease. Similarly, the government could overcome misunderstandings by promoting the "proper" meaning of the Law of Regional Autonomy.

There are several problems here. First, despite a record of failure, fisheries officials are still using a legalistic and formal approach towards understanding and mitigating marine resource conflicts. The fact that some of the conflicts were triggered by the use of trawlers is clear evidence of the failure of relying on legislation to prevent conflict. The banning of trawlers in 1980[14] as well as fisheries zoning regulations passed since 1976 and 1999, have not stopped disputes from occurring.

Briefly, the failure of this regulatory approach stems from the following:

Inconsistencies in the Indonesian government's fisheries policy, such as the Marine Affairs and Fisheries Ministry's policy of allowing trawlers to operate in West Kalimantan[15] without lifting the 1980 presidential decree.

The regulations not reflecting real resource management issues on the land or at sea; for instance, they are aimed only at preventing conflicts between fishing operations of different scale but not those between users of the same small boats and traditional technology. Social identity is another issue missing in the regulations.

The inability to effectively implement or enforce these regulations; there is a lack of sufficient personnel to help implement these laws as well as a lack of coordination between the various agencies supposed to enforce the regulations.[16] I will come back shortly to this point.

The second crucial issue is that the current approach ignores the perceptions of those actually involved in the disputes. Since the perspective of the government is different from that of the fishermen, the government has no option other than to use its "powers" to make the people comply. Yet, it has little ability to do so. It was widespread distrust of the government that contributed to the collapse of the Suharto regime in 1998. Despite hopes of a more trustworthy government replacing the authoritarian New Order, I do not think that perceptions about the capacity of those in power to act in the interests of the people have much improved. Indeed, within the last eight years, there have been many examples of individuals taking the law into their own hands.

Third, the current approach shows that the central government still considers itself the only legitimate agency for issuing fisheries policy; it still advocates a centralised marine resource management system. Yet, many studies have shown that such centralised resource management suffers from several weaknesses, including: the state's limited ability to provide the human and financial resources needed to collect and analyse data on the condition of the resource; limited capacity to develop effective policies and regulations and to monitor and enforce them; subordination of environmental concerns to particular state economic and political interests; and resistance from resource users due to a lack of trust between local communities and state authorities.[17] These shortcomings make it difficult to believe that governments, particularly those in many Third World countries, can be expected to develop sustainable, effective and socially just resource management systems.

In saying that, I do not mean either that the current use of "ethno-claims" or regional identity during fisheries disputes is appropriate. Almost all such fisheries conflicts have ended in violence. We might also question whether the politics of exclusion as practiced by locals using either "ethno-claims" or regionalism was driven by an awareness of the sustainability of marine resources. It appears instead that economic reasons stimulated locals to exclude others from extracting marine resources from their sea territory. Such disagreements can occur even where the fishery is controlled by the local community, under a community-based marine resource management system.

Analysis of the conflicts presented in this chapter suggest that there are three important issues to be considered in terms of moving towards a sustainable and socially just marine resource management system in Indonesia. The first issue is the presence of various vague or confusing claims over the sea and marine resources. Clearly defined tenure is an essential element of good resource management. Although there is no consensus on which property rights regime can universally achieve sustainable and socially just management, it is believed that resources that do not belong to *anybody* (or, do not clearly belong to any particular group) are doomed to be overexploited.[18] Thus, the existence of clear tenure over a particular resource area is a prerequisite for better management of that resource.[19]

The second issue is that these conflicts also involved legitimate concerns of social justice and the distribution of resources.[20] I believe that these two issues are enough reason for the Indonesian government to take into account local capacity and interest in crafting and implementing marine resource management regimes that are sustainable and fair. This does not mean, however, that we should totally abolish the ideology that the sea is a "bridge" for all Indonesians but, since a particular sea territory is closer to a particular community, it might be better to promote local agency in maintaining that "bridge". In return, their interest in relation to making use of that "bridge" could be given priority.

Some fisheries conflicts have given rise to co-management practices, where resource users and government share some rights and responsibility to manage the resources.[21] Co-management is considered an improvement

Social Identity and Access to Natural Resources   **149**

on centralised management. The conflict and subsequent mitigation processes in Sungai Liat on Bangka Island is a case in point. The dispute was triggered by the operation of a *gaek* (purse seine supplemented with powerful lights) by outsiders in Sungai Liat's waters. This was opposed by locals, who fished with *payang* (a bag seine net supplemented with a *rumpon*, a floating fish-aggregating device), in the same territory. The latter believed that the *gaek*'s powerful lights attracted fish away from their *rumpon*, causing a significant decrease in their catch. In addition, the sales of the *gaek* fishermen's catch in the local market caused an oversupply, and hence a lowering of fish prices, which further diminished local fishermen's income. On the verge of a violent confrontation, the leaders and representatives of both groups met and negotiated a settlement. They agreed to divide the fishing ground into several zones: two zones for the exclusive operation of each group, one zone for both and a no-fishing zone. They also defined sanctions for violations of these fishing zones and appointed arbiters to make judgements and apply sanctions as required.[22] These regulations were made known to both groups and acknowledged by the district fisheries office. Thus, these community-initiated solutions were given formal weight as the local government was invited to be involved in supervising the implementation of the ensuing agreement.

The way in which the conflict in Sungai Liat was handled offers a possible alternative to Indonesia's highly centralised marine resource management system. The mismatch between regulations, and between the regulations and reality, coupled with the inability of fisheries authorities to implement these regulations, were overcome in the Sungai Liat case because:

> the regulations were developed in response to an actual crisis or problem;
> all parties involved were represented in the drafting of the regulations; and
> all parties appointed, and hence trusted, their own arbiters to monitor the implementation of the final agreement.

Conclusion

Throughout this chapter, I have tried to demonstrate that the ideology of "Wawasan Nusantara", although politically laudable, is problematic if it is used as a basis for marine resource management. This is because this ideology is not one that is shared in reality by the resource users on land or at sea. Wawasan Nusantara, which was translated through various laws and regulations, has resulted in the sea becoming a "free for all" site of conflict. Those using superior fishing gear and technology have fared much better than less fortunate fishermen who cannot afford to compete. Hence, when conflicts between fishermen occurred, local people—usually at a disadvantage due to their use of traditional fishing gear and methods—resorted to arguments such as tradition, ethnicity and regionalism to lay claim, often violently, over local resources. Thus, they opposed those who, often supported by government policies, used more advanced fishing technology to encroach upon their resources. Of course, such exclusivist local claims were in turn considered illegal by fishermen who used more sophisticated technology as well as by government officials, setting the stage for conflict.

However, a closer look at these incidents revealed that they were not only caused by local opposition to outsider incursions but also by confusion caused by inconsistent policies, which were not adapted to actual conditions. In addition, government agencies tended to lack the resources, ability and power to implement these policies effectively. Thus, fishermen had to operate in an open and effectively unregulated competition over marine resources. I have also shown how, in one case, a fisheries conflict was resolved by the setting up of a self-governing marine resource management agreement between the opposing parties. Such a community-based or collaborative (co-)management system seems to be effective in the peaceful and just resolution of disputes. Indeed, this approach may be better not only as a means for resolving local conflicts but also for future marine resource management as a whole throughout Indonesia.

Notes

1. H. Habib, "Wawasan Nusantara dan Hubungannya dengan Ketahanan Nasional", in *Bunga Rampai Wawasan Nusantara I*, ed. Lembaga Ketahanan Nasional (Jakarta: Fa. Skala Indah, 1981), p. 27.
2. D. Anwar, "Indonesia's Strategic Culture: Ketahanan Nasional, Wawasan Nusantara and Hankamrata" (Griffith: Centre for the Study of Australia-Asia Relations, 1996), p. 10.
3. The Indonesian Constitution of 1945 has been amended four times since the fall of the New Order regime in 1998. There have been some additions but Article 33 (3) itself remains unchanged.

4. Traditionally, the people of Kei claim communal ownership over adjacent sea territory called *petuanan laut* (sea estate). The social unit claiming ownership to a particular sea territory ranges from a kin group, an *ohoi*, a village, a *ratschap* (traditional "kingdom"), a moiety or an ethnic group (the whole Kei people). This claim makes it possible for a particular social group to exclude others (or outsiders) from making use of their sea territory particularly for commercial purposes. The sea territory of the Sathean was part of their *petuanan laut* under the control of a *ratschap* named Ibra. They shared the ownership of a bigger sea territory with two other villages—Ngabub and Ibra—under the control of a *rat* ("king") who lived in the village of Ibra (the village and the *ratschap* share the same name). In practice, however, each village controlled their own sea territory and developed relatively autonomous regulations to access the territory as conflicts in Sathean reflect. See D. S. Adhuri, "Hak Ulayat Laut dan Dinamika Masyarakat Nelayan di Indonesia Bagian Timur: Studi Kasus di P. Bebalang, Desa Sathean dan Demta", *Masyarakat Indonesia* 20, 1 (1993): 143–63; and "Selling the Sea, Fishing for Power: A Study of Conflict over Marine Tenure in the Kei Islands, Eastern Indonesia", doctoral dissertation, the Australian National University, Canberra, 2002 for more detailed discussion on traditional marine tenure in Kei Islands.
5. The Maritime Study Group is a unit that conducts research on socio-cultural aspects of fisheries in Indonesia. The group was established by Prof. Adrian B. Lapian in the early 1990s and is part of the Research Center for Society and Culture, Indonesian Institute of Sciences (LIPI), in Jakarta.
6. R. Indrawasih, A. Wahyono and D. Adhuri, "Pengelolaan Sumberdaya Laut di Kabupaten Belitung, Provinsi Bangka Belitung", in *Pengelolaan Sumber Daya Alam Secara Terpadu: Co-Management Sumberdaya Alam Pelajaran dari Praktek Pengelolaan Sumberdaya Laut di Bangka-Belitung, Jawa Tengah, dan Jawa Timur serta Pengelolaan Taman Nasional Lore Lindu di Sulawesi Tengah*, ed. D. S. Adhuri (Jakarta: PMB-LIPI, 2003), pp. 20–87.
7. D. S. Adhuri and A. Wahyono, "Konflik-konflik Kenelayanan di Bangka-Belitung", in *Konflik-konflik Kenelayanan: Distribusi, Pola, Akar Masalah dan Resolusinya*, ed. D. S. Adhuri et al. (Jakarta: PMB-LIPI, 2004), pp. 83–117.
8. A. Wahyono, "Konflik-konflik Kenelayanan di Riau Kepulauan", in *Konflik-konflik Kenelayanan: Distribusi, Pola, Akar Masalah dan Resolusinya*, ed. R. Indrawasih (Jakarta: PMB-LIPI, 2006), pp. 55–69.
9. Sudiyono and J. Haba, "Konflik-konflik Perikanan di Mataram", in *Konflik-konflik Kenelayanan: Distribusi, Pola, Akar Masalah dan Resolusinya*, ed. D. S. Adhuri et al. (Jakarta: PMB-LIPI, 2004), pp. 11–55.
10. See *Kompas*, "Siapa Bilang Otonomi Mengkapling Laut?", 26 Feb. 2000, p. 1, and "Tak ada Perompak, Kekerasan di Laut Ekses Otonomi Daerah", 18 Apr. 2002, p. 19.
11. The law was replaced by a new law (No. 32/2004). However, the new law still maintains the authority of the provincial government over the management

of marine territory up to 12 miles and the first one-third of the territory to the district or municipality (Article 18).
12. The former Minister of Marine Affairs and Fisheries, Prof. Rokhmin Dahuri, suggested that, in order to reduce pressure in the over-exploited—and conflict-ridden—waters of the north coast of Java, fishermen should fish in the relatively unexploited Exclusive Economic Zone. *Kompas*, "Pukat Harimau akan Diizinkan Beroperasi", 14 Aug. 2002, p. 19. Of course, fishing in the EEZ can only be carried out if fishermen adopt more modern technology.
13. A. Sularso, A. Supardan, A. Rokhman, P. Mulyono, M. Hermawan and A. A. Zaelany, "Konflik antar Nelayan di Indonesia", paper presented in 2002 at the doctoral programme at Bogor Agriculture Institute, Bogor (<http://tumoutou.net/702_05123/group_d_123.htm> [accessed 12 Aug. 2008]).
14. See C. Bailey, "The Political Economy of Marine Fisheries Development in Indonesia", *Indonesia* 46 (1988): 25–38, and S. Matthew, *Fishing Legislation and Gear Conflicts in Asian Countries: A Case Study of Selected Asian Countries* (Brussel: International Collective for the Support for Fisherworkers, 1990).
15. D. S. Adhuri and L. Visser, "Fishing in, Fishing out: Transboundary Issues and the Territorialization of Blue Space", *Asia Pacific Forum* 36 (2007): 112–45.
16. See J.-M. Baland, and J.-P. Platteau, *Halting Degradation of Natural Resources: Is there a Role for Rural Communities?* (New York: Oxford University Press, 1996), and C. Bailey and C. Zerner, "Community-based Fisheries Management Institutions in Indonesia", *Maritime Anthropological Studies* 5, 2 (1992): 1–17.
17. Ibid.
18. G. Hardin, "The Tragedy of the Commons", *Science* 162, 3859 (1968): 1243–8.
19. See, for example, R. E. Johannes, "Traditional Marine Conservation Methods in Oceania and their Demise", *Annual Review of Ecology and Systematics* 9 (1978): 249–364; B. J. McCay and J. M. Acheson, eds., *The Question of the Commons: The Culture and Ecology of Communal Resources* (Tucson: University of Arizona Press, 1987); and K. Ruddle and T. Akimichi, eds., *Maritime Institutions in the Western Pacific* (Osaka: National Museum of Ethnology, 1984).
20. Distribution is one concern in the discourse of resource tenure. For example, some argue that communal property rights assure a fair distribution of the resource for the community which owns it. See F. Berkes, ed., *Common Property Resources: Ecology and Community-based Sustainable Development* (London: Belhaven Press, 1989).
21. See R. Pomeroy R. and F. Berkes, "Two to Tango: The Role of Government in Co-management", *Marine Policy* 21, 5 (1997): 465–80, and S. Jentoft, "Fisheries Co-management: Delegating Government Responsibility to Fishermen's Organizations", *Marine Policy* 13 (1989): 137–54.
22. J. J. Fox, D. S. Adhuri and I. A. P. Resosudarmo, "Unfinished Edifice or Pandora's Box? Decentralisation and Resource Management in Indonesia", in *The Politics and Economics of Indonesia's Natural Resources*, ed. B. P. Resosudarmo (Singapore: ISEAS, 2005), pp. 92–108.

CHAPTER 8

Violence and the Construction of Identity: Conflict between the Dayak and Madurese in Kalimantan, Indonesia

Mary Hawkins

In the early evening of 6 December 1996, groups of mainly young people from the towns and villages of the Singkawang region, northwestern Kalimantan, gathered in the town of Ledo for a *dangdut* concert. *Dangdut* as a musical style represents a fusion of Arabic, Malay and contemporary pop rhythms and melodies, and is immensely popular throughout Indonesia, where it is associated with Muslim celebrations. On this evening, a teenage boy took hold of a teenage girl's hand: she resisted him. The teenage boy, Bakrie, son of a Dayak or indigenous mother and a non-indigenous father who had left Madura, off the coast of Java, to work as a trader in Kalimantan, retaliated with insults. The girl's friends, who, like her, were local Dayak and identified Bakrie as Madurese, taunted Bakrie, calling him rough and uncouth (this loses much in translation: it is worth noting that "rough" and "uncouth" are synonyms for the Madurese, at least within an Indonesian discourse of popular ethnic stereotypes). Bakrie and a friend started a fistfight with Yukundus, the most vocal of the local Dayak, which they lost.

Some three weeks later, the boys met again by chance at another dangdut concert in the same district. This time Bakrie was in the company of nine friends. The ten Madurese boys set upon Yukundus and his brother, stabbing the pair in the back and stomach. The brothers managed to escape and ran to the local police station, from where they were taken to hospital. Although neither were badly hurt, and both were discharged that same night, rumours spread that they were dead.

The next morning the local police chief, concerned that the incident might provoke a violent response, called a meeting between Madurese and Dayak community leaders, and the parents of the Dayak brothers. In the midst of discussion, a crowd of some 100 Dayak youths arrived at the meeting, demanding retaliation, compensation and the removal of all Madurese from Kalimantan. Despite efforts by both Madurese and Dayak leaders to achieve peace, by evening a large crowd of Dayak youths had gathered and were on their way to the Madurese villages. Thus began a month of violence which would result in the destruction of more than 1,000 Madurese homes and countless livestock, in the burning of crops, in the terrified departure of Madurese for the provincial capital, Pontianak, and in the death of anywhere between five and fifty individuals, Dayak and Madurese.

Most Madurese are Muslim, while the Dayak include Muslims, Christians and followers of indigenous belief systems such as Kaharingan, (mis)recognised by Indonesia's Ministry of Religion as a variety of Hinduism.[1] In January 1997 the Madurese were fasting as part of the month of Ramadan. With the end of the fast in early February, they mounted revenge attacks, to which the Dayak responded. This time, the focus was Sanggau, an area dominated by plantations and transmigration areas. While transmigration—the government-sponsored resettlement of Javanese, Balinese and Madurese to, in particular, Sumatra, Kalimantan and Irian Jaya—has seen markedly more Javanese resettled than any other ethnic group, Sanggau was populated primarily by Madurese, both transmigrants and self-financed or "spontaneous" migrants. The end result of these attacks was devastation of crops, livestock and housing, the evacuation of some 25,000 Madurese, and the death of some 2000 individuals, most of whom were Madurese. By early May 1997, no one had appeared in court over the violence, although hundreds were in military detention.[2]

About two weeks later, on 23 May, in Banjarmasin, the provincial capital of South Kalimantan, local members of the dominant political party

Golkar (Partai Golongan Karya, Functional Groups, prime supporters of then president Suharto) were preparing for the coming national election, just six days away, with campaign marches through the city. A march past a popular mosque at the time of the Friday prayers was interpreted by some of the faithful as an insult. Indeed, insofar as it is common practice in Banjarmasin for those attending prayers to occupy the road outside the mosque as well as its interior, it is likely that Golkar supporters literally walked through those praying. Once prayers were over, a group gathered outside the Golkar office, where they burned six campaign vehicles. This was the first act in an afternoon and evening of rioting, arson and looting, which would see homes destroyed, churches burnt, shops, cars, schools, hotels and government buildings set on fire, and over 120 people die. Christians and Chinese were the rioters' main targets, but so too were government agencies and the homes and offices of South Kalimantan's timber barons. Speculation in the local press at the time connected the events of 23 May to the upcoming general election. Interesting, but difficult to credit, are later reports that identify the dead as Madurese, and portray the riots as the result of a coalition between local Malays and Dayak against newcomers. Government officials, on the other hand, were concerned to dissociate the riots from any ethnic or religious conflict interpretation: on 27 May 1997, the Indonesian national newsagency Antara quoted South Kalimantan's chief of police as saying that all the dead were criminals.

Following years have brought all-too-similar days, weeks and months of violence. In early 1999, what began as a dispute over bus fare between a Madurese driver and his Dayak passenger in Singkawang, the location of the 1997 unrest, erupted into two weeks of violence that left anywhere between 100 and 500 dead and prompted the evacuation of some 20,000 Madurese.[3] In December 2000, in Central Kalimantan, a brawl over a gambling debt saw one Dayak killed by a number of Madurese. The incident quickly escalated: on 17 February 2001 relatives of the murdered Dayak attacked and killed a number of Madurese whom they believed were responsible for their relative's death. The Madurese response, on the following day, was to burn Dayak homes and kill the inhabitants. On 19 February, armed Madurese took over the Central Kalimantan town of Sampit, and urban Dayak, using logging radios, sent messages to rural Dayak calling on them to help in "protection of the homeland".[4] It is more than likely that rural Dayak had already begun preparations for retaliation, because armed upriver Dayak began to invade Sampit from the early hours of 20 February. Claire Smith, who spent several months in 2002 and 2003 conducting individual and group interviews with Dayak and Madurese in Central Kalimantan and East Java as part of a World Bank-sponsored effort to understand the causes of the conflict, describes the invaders as "a highly organized recruitment of warrior candidates"[5] and portrays the invasion, from the point of view of a Javanese *imam*, with these words:

> On the night of February 20, 2001, a Javanese *Imam* sat on guard on his porch opposite the small white mosque of which he was the head. The call to morning prayers was still many hours away, but the *Imam* could not sleep. He feared for the safety of his neighborhood, a Javanese area of the city of Sampit, Central Kalimantan. In the distance, the *Imam* could hear the shouts of Madurese men in trucks and on motorbikes, driving around the town.... The *Imam* heard a boat docking at the small jetty behind his house, but there was no sound of an engine. He thought it strange to hear a boat so late at night, and without an engine. He then heard heavy footsteps—dozens of half-naked men were marching across the jetty and gathering in the small street between his porch and the mosque. Without street lamps, only the glow of cigarettes lit the group.
>
> The men wore headbands, with dark painted streaks over their faces. Each carried a heavy traditional sword, *mandau*, in a waistband. Each man also wore a red armband—the traditional symbol of war. They were breathing heavily. The *Imam* knew then these were not Dayak men from the city, they had come from far upstream, from the forests in the north of the province.
>
> "Brothers", said the Imam, "Where are you going so late? Stop with me for a while. We are all Javanese here, this is my hamlet and I know everyone here. I promise you that we are at peace with the Dayak people—we are brothers".
>
> "Bapak [father], we are not looking for you. You are safe. This is not a religious war. We have come only for our enemies".[6]

The enemies of the Dayak were not all migrants, Malay, Banjarese or Javanese, and not even all Madurese, but simply and solely recently arrived urban Madurese. The ensuing violence spread as far east as Palangkaraya, the capital of Central Kalimantan province. The Madurese fled, and Dayak moved in to torch their houses and crops. In April 2001, following an attack on police officers in Sampit, fighting between Madurese and Dayak again broke out, and spread to Kuala Kapuas. Estimates of the numbers dead in Sampit and Kuala Kapuas range from 1,000 to 5,000 people. In the same month a Dayak leader called on all Madurese to leave all four of Kalimantan's provinces, stating that the next area to be targeted would be Pangkalangbun.[7] In summary, in the five years between 1996 and 2001, over 60,000 Madurese either left Kalimantan for good, or fled to refugee camps in the provincial capitals, particularly Pontianak. Thousands of Dayak and Madurese died, and crop and livestock losses were enormous. To date, very few Madurese have returned, not least because the Dayak "conditions" for their return are stringent:

> We have three conditions for the return of the Madurese to this province. The community is so afraid of them coming back—there needs to be some sort of guarantee. First, they must be from a mixed family with Dayak. Second, they must have lived in Central Kalimantan for more than 20 years. Third, their return must be guaranteed by their neighbors that they are good Madurese people. If there is no guarantee, they should not come back. I made a statement to the provincial parliament on this. If these conditions are not met, and the Madurese come back, there will be another conflict. The Dayak will not wait for the police or army to protect them, they will fight for themselves.
>
> Dayak Elder, Palangkaraya, Central Kalimantan[8]

The violence in Kalimantan attracted disturbingly sensationalist reporting, from both the foreign and the Indonesian press. Be it the *New York Times* or the *Banjarmasin Post* (South Kalimantan's leading Indonesian language daily), newspaper reports depicted the conflict as causally connected to ethnic and religious difference, as if it is impossible for Dayak and Madurese to live together in peace. Hence, *Time International* wrote of a "cannabalistic rampage",[9] and the *Boston Globe* of a "race war",[10] while in the same month the *Banjarmasin Post* suggested that conflict was due to the aggressive nature of the Madurese.[11] Coming from an island variously described as desiccated, dry, barren and well known in Indonesia as a place to leave,[12] the Madurese have been depicted as being like their land— hostile, aggressive and dangerous. The Dayak, on the other hand, have been represented as savage head-hunters, heirs to, and enactors of, a tradition of violence. To provide some examples: an article in the *Australian*, following the Singkawang killings of 1997, wrote of Madurese being "decapitated in accordance with traditional Dayak rituals and their hearts and livers being cut out and eaten".[13] *Newsweek International* describes the Dayak as "an indigenous people whose ancestors were animists and cannibals".[14] They "beheaded Madurese and ripped open chests to tear out and eat still beating hearts". Another *Newsweek* article wrote at length of hearts being ripped from corpses, and children beheaded.[15] *Time International* referred in March to the Sampit conflict as "a coordinated spree of ethnic murder

... as tribal blood sport" and opined that "concepts like rule of law seemed completely irrelevant when the Dayaks, following their traditional custom, began eating the body parts of their victims".[16] Even the usually reserved *Economist* (2001) wrote of "savage traditions" and claimed that Dayak are drawing on "Borneo's past as a land of headhunters in a perpetual state of war with one another".[17]

Besides representing the contemporary killings within a framework of cultural continuity—the culture here being one of savagery—many reports mention the revival of Dayak war traditions. These traditions supposedly include the wearing of red headbands, the emergence of warrior chiefs (apparently a charismatic gift that comes over a few individuals at times of crisis), and the ritual of "the red bowl": a porcelain or clay bowl containing rice, leaves and water coloured by chicken blood which is passed from village to village as a call to arms. One report, from Human Rights Watch Asia, quotes military and local Dayak sources as saying that, by late February, the bowl was being passed from one community to another throughout the four provinces of Kalimantan. The same report viewed this as "tribal war, declared against outsiders".[18] That these "outsiders" were a subset of all outsiders—urban recently arrived Madurese and not longer settled rural Madurese or migrants from other provinces of Indonesia— passed without comment. Rather, the concern was to essentialise, to pit murderous primitive Dayak against marauding rough Madurese.

We might conclude that savagery, incessant war and a tendency to separate heads from torsos is not just characteristic of the Dayak past, but equally fundamental to the Dayak present. The identity of the Dayak, in this interpretation, is constructed around a core of violence, exemplified by the practice of headhunting. This seems fundamentally mistaken, for several reasons. In the first place, not all Dayak groups practised headhunting, and of those Dayak involved in the 1996–2001 conflict, none came from groups with a headhunting tradition.[19] Secondly, headhunting as a traditional practice is radically different in meaning from acts of decapitation as have occurred in recent years in Central and West Kalimantan. Nineteenth-century literature by travellers, such as the Norwegian naturalist Carl Bock, who went to Kalimantan to find "the missing link", or men with tails, and described in detail (though he had not witnessed any) the headhunting practices of various Dayak groups in *The Headhunters of Borneo*,[20] as well as by missionaries or government officials such as Owen Rutter, whose *Pagan Tribes of Borneo* is one of the most informative English language sources on headhunting,[21] suggests that headhunting was not simply to kill: rather, it was to capture, not just heads, but also slaves. It was furtive, stealthy and selective: Rutter wrote in the late 1920s that "natives" would eschew the easy mark, such as a sick man found alone in a jungle shelter, in favour of a cunning raid on a well-fortified longhouse. Nor, it seems, did headhunting involve mass slaughter: a dispute that had occupied three generations of Dayak in then British North Borneo had resulted in the capture of just 23 heads on one side, and 30 on the other, according to the British official who attempted to effect a resolution. Indeed, a local British official recorded in his diary in 1882 that headhunting was "cowardly and treacherous", and declared that "it ought to be called head stealing, not headhunting. They wait in the bush watching the house all day, and about three o'clock in the morning when everyone is asleep, they enter the house, take as many heads as possible, and decamp at full speed".[22]

The meaning, then, of headhunting, if it is at all possible to reconstruct it at this historical remove, seems to centre on risk-taking as a display of masculinity (hence the scorn of the easy target); on the amassing of both spirit and living slaves (souls of those whose heads had been taken became spirit slaves to the headhunter in the afterlife); and on the deployment of the captured head within ceremonies related to community prosperity. Because of this, it is likely that a 1870s Dayak would find the depiction of headhunting as savage killing sprees somewhat inexplicable. Kalimantan Dayak were more likely to see the colonial practices of the Dutch as indicative of violence and savagery. Indeed, Bock reports that the chief of a village near contemporary Teweh was confounded by the Dutch horror of headhunting. The Dutch, this chief said, "have been killing the Dayaks and Malays on the Teweh river by the hundreds because they want to take our country ... we do not know why they should come into our country at all".[23] Headhunting, for this man, is not about taking a country, nor can it be simplistically represented as "killing the enemy". In the everyday world of the nineteenth-century Dayak, at least according to those who documented it at the time, crimes of violence were largely unknown, as was cannibalism, or any eating of hearts, livers and brains. Headhunting was not part of the mundane world. Rather, it was more akin to a daring excursion, a risky venture, by which the link between the afterlife and the here-and-now was made and maintained.

The suggestion that this depiction of the historical meaning of headhunting provides any insight into the contemporary violence seems at the very least questionable. Indeed, local Dayak scholars themselves refute any explanation that relies on a historical continuity of the headhunting tradition.[24] Rather, the slaughter of recent years appears to be precisely that, slaughter, accompanied by the creation and maintenance of fear and terror. If rumours of secret ceremonies involving heads, and reports of roads to villages being lined with heads stuck on the end of poles circulate, they may or may not be true, but they have a real consequence: fear. Fear, slaughter and terror have a very definite purpose, and a purpose that is connected more to territory than to either religion or ethnicity: the departure of the Madurese, and for Central Kalimantan, the departure of the urban Madurese in particular.

The Madurese were perhaps singled out due to a coincidence in time and place rather than because of anything inherent in either Madurese culture or individual Madurese. During the late colonial period and following independence, as more land was lost to plantations and logging concessions, many Dayak were forced to move downriver, to towns like Sampit. Their movement coincided with the arrival of increasing numbers of migrants, from Java and Madura as well as from other provinces of Kalimantan. Between 1980 and 2000 the population of Central Kalimantan doubled,[25] primarily as a result of this migration. Since about 1995, however, a new sort of migrant emerged. These were Madurese traders who based themselves in both Sampit and Sampang (Madura), who came to dominate Sampit markets and transport, and who largely controlled trade between Sampit and, via Sampang, East Java.[26] Although the Dayak had cause to resent all migrants, it was this new Madurese group who came to symbolise all the problems faced by the Dayak during the years of transmigration and spontaneous migration to the region.[27] Moreover, when the Suharto regime fell in 1998 and the Indonesian government endeavoured, between 1999 and 2001, to decentralise and delegate many formerly central powers to the districts, it was this new group who suddenly appeared vulnerable. Unlike other migrants, the urban "trans-provincial" Madurese were not and had not sought to be connected by kin and neighbourhood to Dayak groups. They had profited under the New Order, but by 2001 the New Order was gone, and power was passing into local hands. The transfer of power may have been more apparent than real, but there was a new emphasis on the local, and it was this which at least in part empowered the Dayak, and identified trans-provincial Madurese as their enemy.

The outbreak of violence in Kalimantan left many foreign ethnographers of Borneo uncomfortable, and at a loss for explanations. According to Dove, this is an example of what Sherry Ortner has termed "ethnographic refusal",[28] or the tendency to privilege economic and political explanations over and above cultural concerns, and to ignore, at least as far as is possible, acts that the ethnographers find distasteful, such as acts of violence. A refusal to engage with the Dayak actors' own explanation—that they experienced the Madurese as offensive and wanted to be rid of them—provoked explanations for the conflict that positioned the state as the "real" target of Dayak anger; "the true blame for Dayak marginality and anger lay with the state.... I explicitly blamed the Suharto regime for the conflict and exonerated the Dayak and the Madurese themselves."[29] The problem, as Dove writes, is that the Dayak did not exonerate themselves.

This is not to argue that the state, its policies and practices, has no place in any explanation of the violence: the Madurese presence in Kalimantan is, after all, primarily due to state policies. In the next section, I will consider two broad areas, the ethnographies of Kalimantan, and Kalimantan's regional political economy. That they may be considered separately is itself telling. The ethnographic tradition of Kalimantan has for the most part engaged with a particular sort of anthropological discourse that is frequently ahistorical, that focuses on small units of social organisation and avoids discussion of regions, and is more concerned with relations within than between groups. Such an ethnographic disposition means that there has been scant critical examination of, for example, the relationship between agents and activities of the Indonesian state on the one hand, and the constitution of group and ethnic identities in Kalimantan on the other. As a result, ethnographers have not been well placed to discern and describe the emergence of a pan-Kalimantan Dayak identity, other than to dismiss it as a colonial imposition. Yet such considerations are vital, insofar as the conflicts of 1997–2001, while each having their own local trigger, seem to be truly regional events, within which the actors identify themselves as Dayak.

The Ethnographies of Kalimantan

The four provinces of Kalimantan occupy the greater part of the island of Borneo. Borneo itself is divided between three states: Malaysia, which administers Sabah (formerly British North Borneo) as well as Sarawak, which was until 1946 the personal fiefdom of the Brooke dynasty; Brunei, for a period a British protectorate but now an independent sultanate, which had controlled Sarawak until 1841 when the sultan of Brunei, in gratitude for assistance in war, ceded the territory of Sarawak to James Brooke; and Indonesia, of which Kalimantan is a part. Each state, whether colonial or independent, has pursued markedly different policies towards resource management and population, yet, curiously, the actions of states, and the interactions between states and local peoples, has figured little in the ethnographies of the island. There are notable exceptions. For example, Michael Dove has consistently sought to locate the Dayak Kantu of West Kalimantan within a national as well as a local context, and has written extensively of the ways in which Indonesian development policies have transformed Kantu lives.[30] Anna Tsing's work on the Meratus Dayak of South Kalimantan has also been concerned with Meratus imaginings of and relations with the Indonesian state.[31] Doug Miles' earlier work with Ngadju Dayak was also concerned with social transformation and indigenous—state relations.[32] However, Miles, Dove and Tsing are exceptions. A more typical approach is that of Victor King.

Over the past three decades, Victor King has been a major contributor to the ethnography of Kalimantan, particularly that of West Kalimantan. His 1985 ethnography, *The Maloh of West Kalimantan*, based on fieldwork conducted in the Putussibau region in the 1970s, reveals his preoccupations.[33] Following a preliminary consideration of fieldwork methodology, King moves immediately to a discussion of "who are the Maloh?", wherein he argues for the term Maloh as most "real", Dayak being an externally imposed rather than a local name. The origin of the name is not in dispute. Dayak is indeed the name given by colonial administrators, Dutch and British, to refer to the indigenous inhabitants of Borneo and to distinguish them from the Muslim Malays of the Borneo coast. With the problem of names settled, King introduces a lengthy section entitled "Historical Perspectives". Having asserted in his introduction that the "Maloh have been affected to a marked degree by outside influences",[34] King then confines his consideration of these outside influences primarily to the period before and during Dutch colonisation. Twenty pages are devoted to a discussion of Maloh-Malay and Maloh-Dutch relations: a scant two paragraphs are concerned with the Maloh and the Indonesian state. This prepares the way for the bulk of the ethnography, which is a detailed description of rank and hierarchy among the Maloh. Here King engages with the distinction between supposedly egalitarian Borneo societies, such as the Iban of northwest Kalimantan and Sarawak, and so-called hierarchical societies, such as those of the Kayan and Kenyah of Kalimantan and Sarawak, in order to argue that the Maloh too are stratified, and that they themselves identify four ranks, that of aristocrat, middle rank, commoners and slaves. These ranks are simultaneously status markers and social categories that determine differential access to land and labour.

In a paper published in 2001, King returns to the question of names, driving his analysis to a deeper level of detail. He commences with the statement, "One of the major preoccupations of the anthropological literature on Southeast Asia in general and the island of Borneo in particular is that of the problem of defining and naming ethnic categories ... and ethnic groups."[35] Much of the discussion that follows consists of a defence of his work, particularly his choice of the name Maloh, against the challenges posed by the work of younger indigenous scholars, such as Thambun Anyang. Thambun Anyang claims that the Maloh should not be called Maloh, because Maloh themselves use much more local, usually river-based, names. If a general name is to be used, it should be Dayak. Here, Anyang is in agreement with other local scholars, themselves Maloh, such as Irene A. Muslim and Samagat Yuliana Anna. Further, again according to Anyang, "real" Maloh society was relatively egalitarian: hierarchy came later, with the arrival of Muslim Malays. King responds to this twofold challenge by dismissing the latter as speculative history, and according the problem of names a lengthy examination. He admits that,

> a major problem which I faced during my fieldwork among the "Maloh" was that of deciding what to call the people of the Upper Kapuas region... [D]uring my fieldwork I probably underestimated the degree and range of internal cultural and other distinctions among "Maloh" communities... [R]ather than choose one or the other internal name, I employed the term "Maloh", a general name used by the neighbouring Iban to refer to distinctive Dayak people in the upper Kapuas who are widely known for their skills in fashioning metal.[36]

However, King goes on to explain, "Maloh"—by now he is using inverted commas—no longer practice metalwork, and itinerant Maloh artisans have all but disappeared. "Maloh" has become less acceptable and, as King comments, "its fate was sealed very decisively when several 'Maloh' scholars entered the fray and took exception to what was an externally imposed label and one which seemed to them to deny their ethnic integrity and sense of self identity".[37]

It is perhaps the rather recent emergence of nation-states, the creation of national identities, and the political deployment of these identities as fixed, meaningful and significant ways of ordering the world, which has caused us to overlook the fact that names are always set in relation to other names, and that historically the changing of names, as well as the use, by a people, of a multiplicity of names (the choice of which to use being determined by context), is common practice. The choice of which name to use, and when, is not random, or simply convenient, as Kalimantan river-based names appear to be. Rather, in Kalimantan as elsewhere, there is a politics of naming, particularly the naming of groups that are then recognised as "ethnic" groups, which deserves greater attention. Under what circumstances, and due to what factors, do people choose particular identities and why do certain identities become more popular than others? Rather than "Who are the Maloh, who are the Dayak?", it may be more fruitful to ask "Why Maloh, why Dayak?". "Why Dayak?" is precisely the question I wish to now pose.

The association of the name Dayak with headhunting has certainly provided a ready-made, if essentially mistaken, starting point for attempts by journalists to understand what has been happening in Kalimantan in recent years. On the other hand, the ethnographic preoccupation with "real" names, the authenticity of a name appearing to depend on the size of the group to which it refers, the smaller the more authentic, has largely precluded any exploration of regional identities. However, it is surely significant that local ethnographers, at least those of the Maloh, have suggested Dayak, that they have suggested this only recently, and that Dayak is a collective, regional, term. Why, then, Dayak? I want to turn now to a consideration of the political economy of Kalimantan. In so doing, my intention is to suggest that Dayak has been appropriated as an overarching category of identification for groups who, despite language and cultural differences, sense that they share an increasingly common life experience, and view themselves as sharing an increasingly common fate. This argument is not dissimilar to one that I have previously made in reference to the Banjar, a Malay group of southern Kalimantan.[38] Here, I suggested that the name Banjar, for a people rather than for an historical state, is of relatively recent origin, emerging in the 1930s as a term of ethnic identification not only for the loosely Malay population of southern Kalimantan, but also for individuals of Dayak origin who, having settled in towns and converted to Islam, appropriated the identification Banjar in order to declare their allegiance to the Malay-Javanese cultural mix that was becoming known as Banjar culture. As the Banjar sociologist Hasan Basri comments, this is the only possible explanation for the increase in the Banjar population, from 49,378 in 1920 to an astonishing 814,661 in the 1930s.[39] Basri makes the additional point that, prior to the 1930s, the Malay-speaking peoples of southern Kalimantan referred to themselves as people of a particular area, rather than as Banjar. In regional and national contexts, they are far more likely to identify themselves as Banjar. Banjar denotes in this context both ethnic affiliation, and adherence to Islam: Tsing has commented that Banjar see their religion as supporting their claims to citizenship and regional status within the Indonesian state.[40] In a similar vein, Dayak is now being appropriated by, rather than imposed upon, peoples who are coming to recognise commonalities, not of savage headhunting traditions in the past, but of experiences in the present, including their experience of the Indonesian state. Dayak, then, is the name they have chosen to use in regional and national contexts. As an example, in March 2001 the Indonesian government organised a reconciliation meeting between Dayak and Madurese leaders, which took place in West Java. A local Kalimantan newspaper reported that several Dayak leaders were disappointed that they had not been invited, quoting one as saying, "we too are Dayak, all the Dayak should be involved".[41] By 2005, Dayak leaders were proposing that regional conflict be mediated via Dayak *adat*:

> Everyone in the Dayak community obeys and appreciates adat (traditional law). No one can escape it; it is our tradition, our heritage. If we revitalize adat to solve conflicts—from simple fights, to murder, to land conflicts—we can find a solution to tensions in the community. Other ethnic groups can and should follow Dayak adat too. Village leaders will inform migrants that Dayak adat law applies and if they accept it, then the migrant can stay. Dayak adat will bind the whole community together.
>
> Dayak community leader, Palangkaraya, Central Kalimantan[42]

The Political Economy of Kalimantan: Timber and Transmigration

The forests of Kalimantan have long provided a source of subsistence and income for its indigenous peoples. Besides clearing forests for swidden gardens, forests provide leafy greens for everyday consumption, as well as rattan, resin and other trade products. Wet forests, or swamps, in South and Central Kalimantan are valuable sources of fish, prawns and shellfish of all kinds, as well as plants that are used for housing thatch, and for the construction of temporary shelters. However, from the 1970s onwards, local peoples have gradually lost access to timber, non-timber forest products, and land available for shifting cultivation and fishing. The regulations on timber concessions clearly limit access for local communities. For example, the 1967 Basic Forestry Law declares that "the enjoyment of *adat* (customary law) rights, whether individual or communal, to exploit forest resources directly or indirectly, may not be allowed to disturb the attainment of the purposes of this Law".

A 1970 elaboration of the Basic Law further weakened the ability of local peoples to use the forests and its products for their livelihood. It states:

1. The rights of the adat community and its members to harvest forest products ... shall be organised in such a manner that they do not disturb forest production.
2. Implementation of the above provision is [delegated to the Company] which is to accomplish it through concensus with the adat community, with supervision from the Forest Service.
3. In the interests of public safety, adat rights to harvest forest products in a particular area shall be frozen while forest production activities are underway.[43]

Over the last 30 years, the implementation of this Act, through timber companies who have gained their concessions from the Ministry of Forestry in Jakarta, has meant that local peoples have been effectively locked out of their forests. In East Kalimantan alone during the 1970s, over 100 forest logging leases, totalling 9.8 million hectares of coastal and interior forest and representing over 50 per cent of the province were granted.[44] A University of Toronto research team has commented on the Act as a program of enclosure, and a less-than-profitable one at that. For example, local peoples denied access to their forests should have been compensated through the development of infrastructure and the expansion of other sorts of employment opportunities, financed by land rents payable to the Indonesian government. In practice, the government has received very little in royalties, just 47 per cent of local rents, as compared to the 85 per cent of total rents captured in the oil industry, and has returned insignificant amounts to Kalimantan's provinces.[45] The primary reason lies in the political deployment, at least up until 1998, of forestry concessions by the Indonesian government. There is no doubt that the Suharto government gave concessions in return for political support: just five or six corporate groups dominate the sector. These groups have tended to import labour for their logging activities from Java and Madura. Javanese and Madurese transmigrants are also employed in the timber industry.

Somewhat belatedly, in 1998 the Government of Indonesia acknowledged that the Act had resulted in the dispossession and marginalisation of local peoples. In the Sixth (and last) Five Year Development Plan of Suharto's rule, the government acknowledged that:

> Forest exploitation by concession holders is often to the detriment of the needs for forest resources of communities living in and adjacent to the forests. The cause of this is the limits on their access to forest resources [in the concessions]. [These communities] are also largely unable to benefit from employment opportunities arising from these forestry enterprises, with the result that the gap in economic status between local people and outsiders increases.[46]

This recognition came too late, and it did not prompt any action. In May 2001, well after the fall of Suharto, Jakarta announced, as part of its programme of devolving responsibilities and rights from the centre to the provinces, that henceforth provinces would be responsible for the issuing of forestry concession leases. By this time, however, displacement and forced resettlement was already a common experience for many Dayak peoples—a World Bank report from as early as 1988 estimated that across Kalimantan over two million people had been displaced or resettled due to logging activities.[47] For these people, timber companies and government were all but indistinguishable—both spoke of funds and projects that rarely materialised—and timber workers, in Dayak experience, invariably wore a Madurese face.

The operations of timber companies in Kalimantan are similar to those in the Malaysian states of Sarawak and Sabah, minus the presence of the Madurese. Transmigration, however, is an Indonesian phenomenon, and has a long history. It began in 1905, when the colonial government moved Javanese peoples to north Sumatra, where they worked as labourers on Dutch and British-owned plantations. Following Indonesian independence, the Sukarno government sought to alleviate population pressure in Java, Bali and Madura by resettling poor, landless farmers in the outer islands, first in Sumatra, and then in Kalimantan. The numbers moved during the Sukarno years were not great, and relations between transmigrants and locals were often benign, even mutually beneficial. An example of this early form of transmigration is the village where I first conducted fieldwork in the mid-1980s, Gunung Gundul,[48] near the coast on the southeastern tip of the island.[49]

Gunung Gundul was settled in 1953 by some 500 families from Central and East Java. Each family was allotted a hectare of land for food crops, another half hectare of wet land for rice, and all received food assistance for the first three years. About 200 or so hectares had already been cleared by bulldozer at the time of their arrival, and the transmigrants were expected to clear the remainder, plant it with the seeds supplied, and build their houses themselves. Local Banjar peoples were doubtless intrigued by the arrival of the Javanese, but as fisherfolk and traders they did not make their living from the land, and there are no records or stories of any land disputes in this early period. For the transmigrants, there were frequent crop failures, and they were plagued by monkeys, which repeatedly ate or carried off anything else they could find. By the early 1960s, about half of the original transmigrants had left.

If the transmigrants had remained dependent on food crops, it is likely the settlement would have failed altogether. However, early experiments with tree crops, or at least those the monkeys rejected, had demonstrated that the land could support a variety of such crops, with clove trees the most successful. By 1985, the village was relatively prosperous, and relations between the Javanese and local Banjar relatively harmonious.

There are several reasons for Gunung Gundul's success. In the realm of religion and ritual, both Banjar and Javanese practised the *slametan* tradition, famously analysed by Clifford Geertz[50] (but see also Andrew Beatty for a more recent account[51]), and most Gunung Gundul villagers observed Islam. Of perhaps greater importance is that the transmigrants were not at any time in competition with local peoples for access to or control over resources. A fairly amiable division of labour developed between farming transmigrants and fishing and trading locals, and it has persisted to this day. The same cannot be said of the transmigration programme initiated by the Suharto government.

From about 1975 onwards, the Suharto government sought to expand transmigration, and to make it serve various, largely political, ends. Javanese, Balinese, and Madurese were moved to Irian Jaya and Timor as part of state security endeavours; to Sumatra to convert swamplands to paddy fields as part of the government's plan for self-sufficiency in rice; and to Sumatra, Sulawesi and Kalimantan to develop rubber, sugar, coffee, coconut and oil palm plantations. It is this latter move that would, in the words of a World Bank evaluation report published in 2001, "have a major negative and probably irreversible impact on indigenous peoples".[52]

Plantations have been a feature of Kalimantan's economy for more than a century, and smallholder tree cropping, particularly of rubber, has been practised by Dayak and Malays since the 1880s. Over the past 30 years, however, a new form of plantation has been developed in Kalimantan. Known as the Nucleus Estate/Smallholder Scheme (NFS) and financed by both government and international donor agencies such as the World Bank, these plantations were on a much larger scale than previously, and incorporated transmigrants as smallholders, as well as a nucleus estate operated by one of Indonesia's plantation companies. To give an idea of the scale, one such rubber project I visited in West Kalimantan, near the scene of the 1997 killings, included 4,000 transmigrant families, primarily Madurese, each with a rubber allotment of 5 hectares, and a nucleus of some 10,000 hectares. Between the West Kalimantan capital of Pontianak and Sintang to the west are seven such projects.

Local peoples have described the projects as "eating the land", for obvious reasons. It is equally obvious that neither the Dayak nor the Malays have received little in the way of compensation, be it cash for land, or employment opportunities. In 1996, a new transmigration project was announced. It was to include 2.7 million hectares, basically the entire area between the Kahayan, Kapuas and Barito Rivers south to the Java Sea, and incorporate 65,000 transmigrants. The aim of the "mega project", as it was called, was to convert peat swamp to rice cultivation. Sixty-three thousand people had arrived on the site before the Minister for Housing and Development, in a broadcast in late 2000 from a Dayak village in the project area, promised that development would stop.[53] Meanwhile, however, local people had lost their land, and had not received compensation. There is surely no coincidence that the mega project area is precisely where violence erupted in 2001.

Conclusion

For Dayak peoples of Kalimantan, from all four provinces, the past decades have seen their access to forests all but disappear, their access to rivers and wetlands recede, and their opportunities to earn income from other sources shrink. In every instance, the people who appear to stand in their way are migrants, and frequently Madurese migrants. Further, Madurese are active in small town trade, in transport in Kalimantan's cities, they are the local face of the timber industry, and in regional towns like Sampit, Madurese had established their own communities and did not mingle with locals. In 1997 this group was targeted by the Dayak. "Dayak" may have begun as an imposed name but by 1997 it had come to mean a pan-Kalimantan indigenous identity. "Dayak" now denotes indigenous status and it is employed to invoke a notion of indigenous rights to resources, rights that the Dayak see as having been usurped by some recent migrants, including Madurese, as well as by the activities of timber companies. Ongoing marginalisation in their own land, coupled with the local empowerment seemingly promised by decentralisation, served to justify attacks on Madurese as defensive acts, in protection of "the homeland". Such acts further reinforced the "new" Dayak identity. Dayak can no longer be rejected as a colonial imposition, rather, it demands investigation as a regional Kalimantan identity.

Notes

An earlier version of this article was published in *Australian Religion Studies Review* 18, 2 (2005): 179–95.

1. A. Schiller, "An 'Old' Religion in 'New Order' Indonesia: Notes on Ethnicity and Religious Affiliation", *Sociology of Religion* 57, 4 (1996): 409–17.
2. Human Rights Watch Asia, Report Excerpt, *Inside Indonesia* 51, July–September 1997.
3. *Newsweek International*, "Rule of the Headhunters", 5 Apr. 1999.
4. C. Q. Smith, *The Roots of Violence and Prospects for Reconciliation: A Case Study of Ethnic Conflict in Central Kalimantan, Indonesia*. Social Development Papers no. 23, Conflict Prevention and Reconstruction Unit (Washington, D. C.: World Bank, 2005), p. 5.
5. Ibid., p. 5.
6. Ibid., p. 2.
7. Antara, "Violence in Central Kalimantan to be Stopped in Three Days", 22 May 2001; Antara, "District Heads to be Authorized to Issue HPHs", 27 May 2001.
8. Smith, *Roots of Violence*, p. 18.
9. *Time International*, "The Darkest Season", 12 Mar. 2001.
10. *Boston Globe*, "Beheadings on Borneo Linked to Clash over Land", 9 Mar. 2001.
11. *Banjarmasin Post*, "Dayak Bakumpai Kecewa: Tak Dilibatkan Rekonsiliasi", 19 Mar. 2001.
12. The *Economist* described Madura as "famous throughout Indonesia as a place to leave" and "a one-way ticket to poverty" ("Bloodshed in Borneo", 21 Apr. 2001).
13. Reprinted in *World Press Review*, "Headhunting Again in Borneo", 44 (5), 1997 (orig. in *The Australian*).
14. *Newsweek International*, "Indonesia's Island Fever", 12 Mar. 2001.
15. *Newsweek International*, "The Bloody Birth of a 'Messy State'", 12 Mar. 2001.
16. *Time International*, "The Darkest Season".
17. *The Economist*, "Bloodshed in Borneo".

18. Human Rights Watch Asia Report Excerpt; See also Bernama (Malaysian national newsagency), "Dayak-Madurese Conflict: Settling Age Old Scores", 6 Mar. 2001; Bernama, "Indigenous Dayaks Oppose Return of Madurese to Central Kalimantan", 7 Mar. 2001.
19. M. Dove, "'New Barbarism' or Old Agency among the Dayak: Reflections on Post-Suharto Ethnic Violence in Kalimantan", *Social Analysis* 50, 1 (2006): 193.
20. C. Bock, *The Headhunters of Borneo*, rep. (Singapore: Oxford University Press, 1985 [1881]).
21. O. Rutter, *The Pagans of North Borneo*, rep. (Singapore: Oxford University Press, 1985 [1929]).
22. Ibid., p. 187.
23. Bock, *The Headhunters of Borneo*, p. 216.
24. Dove, "New Barbarism", p. 195.
25. International Crisis Group (ICG), *Communal Violence in Indonesia: Lessons from Kalimantan*, ICG Asia Report no. 18, 2001.
26. Smith, *Roots of Violence*, p. 10.
27. Ibid., p. 11.
28. Dove, "New Barbarism", p. 196; S. Ortner, "Resistance and the Problem of Ethnographic Refusal", *Comparative Studies in Society and History* 37, 1 (1995): 173–93.
29. Dove, "New Barbarism", p. 194.
30. M. Dove, *Swidden Agriculture in Indonesia: The Subsistence Strategies of the Kalimantan Kantu* (Berlin: Mouton, 1985); and *The Real and Imagined Role of Culture in Development: Case Studies from Indonesia*, ed. M. Dove (Honolulu: University of Hawai'i Press, 1988).
31. A. L. Tsing, *In the Realm of the Diamond Queen: Marginality in an Out-of-the-Way Place* (Princeton: Princeton University Press, 1993).
32. D. Miles, *Cutlass and Crescent Moon: A Case Study of Social and Political Change* (Sydney: Centre for Asian Studies, University of Sydney, 1976).
33. V. T. King, *The Maloh of West Kalimantan: An Ethnographic Study of Social Inequality and Social Change among an Indonesian Borneo People* (Dordrecht: Foris Publications, 1985).
34. Ibid., p. 3.
35. V. T. King, "A Question of Identity: Names, Societies and Ethnic Groups in Interior Kalimantan and Brunei Darussalam, *Sojourn: Journal of Social Issues in Southeast Asia* 16, 1 (2001): 1.
36. Ibid., pp. 10–1.
37. Ibid., p. 8.
38. M. Hawkins, "Becoming Banjar: Identity and Ethnicity in South Kalimantan, Indonesia", *Asia Pacific Journal of Anthropology* 1, 1 (2000).
39. H. Basri, "Perpindahan Orang Banjar ke Surakarta: Kasus Migrasi Inter Etnis di Indonesia", *Prisma* 3 (1988): 46.

40. Tsing, *In the Realm of the Diamond Queen*.
41. *Banjarmasin Post*, "Dayak Bakumpai Kecewa".
42. Smith, *Roots of Violence*, p. 21.
43. Reproduced from C. V. Barber, "Forest Resource Scarcity and Social Conflict in Indonesia", *Environment* 40, 4 (1998): 10.
44. M. Poffenberger, "Rethinking Indonesian Forest Policy: Beyond the Timber Barons", *Asian Survey* 37, 5 (1997): 460.
45. Barber, "Forest Resource Scarcity and Social Conflict in Indonesia", p. 11.
46. Ibid., p. 11.
47. Poffenberger, "Rethinking Indonesian Forest Policy", p. 456.
48. Not the village's official name.
49. M. Hawkins, "Market People, Mountain People: Identity in a South Kalimantan Transmigration Village", Ph.D. dissertation, University of Sydney, 1989.
50. C. Geertz, *The Religion of Java* (Glencoe, Ill.: Free Press, 1960).
51. A. Beatty, *Varieties of Javanese Religion: An Anthropological Account* (Cambridge: Cambridge University Press, 1999).
52. World Bank Group, Operations Evaluation Department, *Transmigration in Indonesia* (Washington, D. C.: World Bank, 2001), p. 2.
53. Down to Earth, International Campaign for Ecological Justice in Indonesia, "New Kalimantan Mega-Project will not Proceed", *Down to Earth newsletter*, no. 45, May 2000.

CHAPTER 9

National Legitimacy through a Regional Prism: Local Pilgrimage and Indonesia's Javanese Presidents

George Quinn

Pilgrimage and the Quest for Power

Two weeks before they were elected president and vice president of Indonesia in October 1999, in the midst of the manoeuvring and campaigning preceding a special session of the People's Consultative Assembly (MPR), Abdurrahman Wahid (popularly known as Gus Dur) and Megawati Sukarnoputri made a joint pilgrimage to the tombs of their respective fathers. They went first to the tomb of Megawati's father, Indonesia's first president, Sukarno, whose mausoleum is in the small town of Blitar in East Java. The following day they paid their respects to Gus Dur's father, Kiai Haji Wahid Hasyim, and his grandfather, Kiai Haji Hasyim Asy'ari, both of whom are buried in the complex of the Tebuireng Islamic Centre in Jombang, East Java. Hasyim Asy'ari was a founder of Indonesia's biggest Islamic organisation, Nahdlatul Ulama (NU). His son Wahid Hashim was for a time Indonesia's Minister of Religion in the early years of the Republic, and in the 1940s and 1950s a key NU leader.

The joint pilgrimage was widely covered in the Indonesian media,[1] though Abdurrahman Wahid and Megawati Sukarnoputri denied it had any special significance. Abdurrahman told reporters that the visit did not mean there was any power-sharing or political agreement between him and Megawati. It was purely a ritual act, he said. It was the kind of thing anyone might do to pay respects to their deceased parents. Megawati, too, was guarded. "We simply prayed that the Special Session of the MPR goes smoothly," she said. "For the sake of the nation it is important that it do so."[2]

Journalists and the general public did not take these protestations at face value. The respected newsmagazine *Tempo* described the pilgrimage as "pregnant with meaning". It noted that although Hasyim Asy'ari and Sukarno had been active in different eras of Indonesia's modern history, their combined blessing (*restu*) was "so important" for Abdurrahman and Megawati.[3] Another journalist wrote: "In my view [the joint pilgrimage] was a visual symbol of a return to the era of the *dwi-tunggal* which, it is to be hoped, will give substance to a cool, secure and peaceful atmosphere in the future life of our state and nation."[4]

Dwi-tunggal, or "two acting as one", is a reference to the decade from 1945 to 1955 when the republic was headed by president Sukarno and vice-president Hatta. Hatta was popularly seen as representing pragmatic Islam and Sukarno idealistic, secular nationalism. In popular perception the joint pilgrimage signalled that, more than 40 years on, Indonesia was about to reconnect with its history (or at least with a very rose-tinted version of it). The return to the old amalgam of forces seemed, in the eyes of some, to have been given a stamp of legitimacy by the joint pilgrimage.

Equally important was the familial aspect of the pilgrimage. By expressing thanksgiving to their own and each other's forebears, Abdurrahman Wahid and Megawati seemed to be giving expression to the comforting notion of a return to family continuity—a powerful notion after the turbulence of the *krisis moneter* (financial crisis), Suharto's fall and the presidency of Habibie.[5]

Prior to the joint pilgrimage, indeed since childhood, Abdurrahman Wahid had been a regular visitor, normally several times a year, to the tombs of his father and grandfather. Megawati too had also regularly visited her father's tomb, especially at the time of the *haul Bung Karno*, the anniversary of Sukarno's death every June 20th. It is worth adding that Abdurrahman Wahid and Megawati had made at least one previous joint pilgrimage to Sukarno's tomb, in January 1999.[6] In fact it would appear that Abdurrahman Wahid was a fairly regular visitor to Sukarno's tomb. Early in

1997, for example, with Suharto still firmly in power and the economic crisis still six months in the future, he was reported to have made a pilgrimage to Sukarno's tomb, praying and scattering flowers on the late president's grave. Eyewitnesses described the experience as "moving" with pilgrims shedding tears and Abdurrahman himself "unable to control his feelings".[7]

Pilgrimage to sacred sites, especially gravesites, plays an important role in the religious and social life of the Javanese.[8] When Abdurrahman Wahid and Megawati visited the tombs of their parents, apparently as part of a campaign to oust president Habibie from office, they were participating in a powerful, age-old practice. From distant times, opponents of established authority in Javanese society have launched their rebellions from a platform of moral and political legitimacy provided by sacred sites. Through serial pilgrimage, often called *lelanabrata* (meditative wandering), they have acquired the authority to make credible critiques of the prevailing order and have been able to convince followers that, thanks to alliances with the powerful dead, their campaigns for political power have the imprimatur of history and must be successful.

In 1976 a certain Sawito Kartowibowo was arrested on suspicion of planning to topple Suharto. His sensational trial revealed that he had undertaken *lelanabrata* visits to several sacred sites in Java, among them Mount Tidar, Borobudur, Parangtritis, the tomb of Sunan Kalijaga, Mount Muria and Ketonggo Forest. This gave him the authority and confidence to approach a number of high profile public figures and convince them to put their signatures to a letter making a mild critique of the New Order government. Apparently unnerved by Sawito's supernaturally acquired credentials, the government charged him with subversion and in 1978 he was sent to prison for eight years.[9]

At the beginning of 1997 nationalist activist and founder of the Socialist Party of Indonesia (PSI, Partai Sosialis Indonesia) Subadio Sastrosatomo published a pamphlet *Era Baru, Pemimpin Baru* (New Era, New Leader) attacking the New Order government for its moral bankruptcy. The government banned the pamphlet. Apparently reluctant to prosecute an old man with an impeccable revolutionary record, the government turned its anger on his personal secretary, charging him with insulting the president. Subadio was summoned as a witness in the trial but refused to attend, retreating instead to the slopes of the mystically charged Mount Lawu in Central Java. There he undertook meditation as, he said, an expression of concern at the continuing deterioration of the social and political situation.[10]

Early in 1998 he published another pamphlet *Politik Dosomuko Rezim Orde Baru: Rapuh dan Sengsarakan Rakyat* (The New Order Regime's Dasamuka Politics: Morally Bankrupt and Oppressive) which the government also instantly banned.[11] A little more than a month after the banning, Suharto resigned and Subadio descended from the mountain, celebrating his vindication with a big eightieth birthday party.[12]

Clearly, the tradition of political pilgrimage has remained significant, even into the twenty-first century. As I sketch below, all four of Indonesia's Javanese presidents have engaged in meditative and petitionary pilgrimage that has had political functions. Yet until recently, despite a number of largely speculative studies about "mysticism" in Indonesia's political life, this feature of politics hasn't been much noticed, let alone studied.[13]

Two recent biographies of Indonesian presidents, Bob Elson's *Suharto: A Political Biography* and Greg Barton's *Abdurrahman Wahid: Muslim Democrat, Indonesian President* make virtually no reference to the practice.[14] Indeed Bob Elson goes out of his way to reject the view that Javanese-style magical-mystical leanings may have played a significant role in Suharto's presidency.[15] Given that Abdurrahman Wahid's incessant pilgrimages to local tombs were a prominent, fairly well reported and controversial feature of his presidency, it is strange indeed that Greg Barton's otherwise brilliant biography passes over it in silence. Wimar Witoelar's memoir, *No Regrets: Reflections of a Presidential Spokesman*, supposedly a behind-the-scenes view of Aburrahman's presidency, is likewise silent on the president's obsession with saints and tombs.[16]

Pilgrimage in Java and Madura is wrapped in an aura of local culture and history, and this is probably the main reason why it has been relatively overlooked. It cannot easily be penetrated from a purely "national" point of view. A command of local languages (Javanese, Sundanese and Madurese) and knowledge of the intricacies of local history help enormously (and in some cases are absolutely essential) in understanding the significance of a pilgrimage event. Indonesia's current process of decentralisation with its attendant resurgence of regional cultures, are showing us more and more how fragile an understanding of Indonesia's social and political dynamics can be if they are approached *only* through the national language, Bahasa Indonesia, only through national institutions, or only through national culture and history.

However, I would be the first to admit that reliable information about political pilgrimage is difficult to come by. Popular magazines, pilgrims at sacred sites, and site custodians themselves (*juru kunci* or *kuncen*), often claim that one or other of Indonesia's presidents has visited a site, but it is difficult to know with certainty whether this is literally true or not. Visits by high-ranking personages are proof that a site is powerful enough attract those who are themselves already powerful, so there is a strong incentive for wishful thinking or rumour about such visits to become "fact". Naturally such "facts" should be treated with caution, but not disparaged or rejected altogether. As Marcel Bonneff puts it: "rumour must itself be seen as a political phenomenon".[17]

All this notwithstanding, there are reasonably reliable reports regarding pilgrimage or *ziarah* visits undertaken before and during their terms of office by presidents Sukarno, Suharto, Abdurrahman Wahid and Megawati Sukarnoputri. Even the phlegmatic Susilo Bambang Yudhoyono has made what appear to be politically motivated visits to gravesites.[18]

President Sukarno and Jayabaya

Prior to assuming office in 1945, President Sukarno is reliably reported to have made three pilgrimage visits to the Vanishing Place of King Jayabaya (Pamuksan Sri Aji Jayabaya) in the village of Menang, not far from Kediri in East Java. This is the place where King Jayabaya of Kediri, who probably ruled from 1135 to 1157, is believed to have lifted himself off the face of the earth and disappeared into the sky.

Sukarno made his last visit there shortly before proclaiming the independence of Indonesia in August 1945. In an interview with *Kompas* journalist Sindhunata, the retired village head of Menang, Lasi Suroharjo, claimed that on this occasion Sukarno spoke in Javanese to the members of his party. "I have come here to petition [King Jayabaya] for his royal blessing (*wahyu*)", he said. "I would like you all to help me." He then remained silent at the site for seven minutes, after which he said: "It has been granted. Now we can go."[19]

Jayabaya is popularly recognised as the ancestor of all Java's kings, the founder of the Javanese polity. (This, of course, is not literally or historically the case, but it is popularly believed to be so.) The village head of Menang claimed that Sukarno petitioned Jayabaya rather than the founder of Mataram, Panembahan Senapati, because Jayabaya represented an older, and therefore more authentic and powerful, tradition than that of Mataram. He also remarked that Sukarno, as an East Javanese, probably felt closer (*lebih akrab*) to the East Javanese king Jayabaya than to the Central Javanese Senapati.

In his commentary on the interview, Sindhunata makes the interesting claim that Sukarno was more attracted to an eastern Javanese tradition than the later "western Javanese tradition" represented by Mataram, because the Mataram tradition was derivative (taking its cultural inspiration from East Java), was establishment oriented (rather than populist), was isolationist rather than cosmopolitan (as the eastern tradition was perceived to be), and had been compromised by its entanglements with the Dutch. Sindhunata concludes:

> For this reason it would appear that he (Sukarno) felt impelled to seek a cultural tradition that could appropriately legitimise his political vision. And it was the critical, cosmopolitan and populist <u>eastern</u> tradition rather than that of the reactionary, centrist, hegemonic western tradition that he found most suitable. These factors, I would argue, support the various other speculations as to why he sought the royal *wahyu* at Jayabaya's vanishing place.[20]

Sukarno is also reliably reported to have made pilgrimage visits to the tomb of Raden Ngabei Ranggawarsita in the village of Palar, about 17 km southeast of Klaten in Central Java.[21] Although Ranggawarsita authored a diverse body of poetic and prose works in the Javanese language, he is best remembered today for his prophetic writings. Probably the most famous of these is a short poem titled "Kalatidha" (A Time of Darkness), fragments of which must be known to almost all Javanese.[22] The poem describes an age of madness (*jaman edan*) in which all the certainties of law, government and morality have been overturned. Today, this cry from the heart continues to strike a deeply resonating chord in Javanese society, confirming the view that Ranggawarsita was able to see into the future of his society and fuelling a fierce nostalgia for the (no doubt mythic) order of the past.

Among Ranggawarsita's other prophetic poems is a reworking of the *Jangka Jayabaya* (The Prophecies of Jayabaya). These prophecies are a diverse body of traditions and texts. Most people are familiar with them only through a few famous fragments, the so-called *pralambang Jayabaya*.[23] Although they are popularly believed to have been authored by Jayabaya it is unlikely that in fact the king had a hand in writing them.[24] What is more likely is that later authors created or recycled the prophecies, appropriating the king's name. One of those authors was Raden Ngabei Ranggawarsita.

There are two verses in Ranggawarsita's version of the *Jangka Jayabaya* that are particularly well known.

I have two predictions to make
About what will happen in the land of Java.
A yellow monarch will rule,
His soldiers will be very small
In fact his soldiers will be dwarfish in size.
They will come from the northeast
And the king's name will be King Jamus.
King Jamus will fall asleep
And will be overtaken by great turmoil.
He will stay only for the life span of a corn plant.

He will be replaced by Garuda Ngwangga
Whose mother will be a Balinese princess.
He will rule in the land of Java,
With an army of demons and devils.
King Jamus will come again,
But will immediately have to withdraw.
The (new) king will establish his kingdom
Eru Cakra Esmu Kingkin will be his name
And he will endure for one quarter of an age.[25]

The first verse is widely interpreted as predicting the occupation of Indonesia by the Japanese during World War II. The occupation lasted for three and a half years, this relatively short period of time being expressed in the phrase "the life span of a corn plant". The second verse refers to the rise of independent Indonesia after the war. "Garuda" is seen as symbolising the Republic of Indonesia. Indonesia's coat of arms takes the form of a garuda eagle with the symbols of the state philosophy of Pancasila emblazoned on a shield around its neck. Ngwangga is taken to refer to Sukarno. Ngwangga is one of the alternative names of the *wayang* (shadow puppet) hero more commonly known as Karno after whom the president was named. Sukarno's mother came from Bali. The "army of devils and demons" refers to Indonesia's rag-tag guerrilla army that waged a fierce and successful struggle for the country's independence between 1945 and 1949. For true believers, the clincher is in the last line. President Sukarno died in 1970, almost exactly 25 years, or "one quarter of an age" after declaring Indonesia's independence in 1945.[26]

There is good reason to believe that Sukarno was very familiar with Ranggawarsita's version of the *Jangka Jayabaya*. For example, in his famous defense speech before a Dutch colonial court in 1930, known today under the title *Indonesia Menggugat* (Indonesia Accuses), Sukarno made impassioned references to Jayabaya's prophecies.

Your Honours, please think about why the people continue to believe in a Just King, and always await his coming. Why is it that, right up to the present, King Jayabaya still inspires hope in the hearts of our people. The reason is clear. It is because in the weeping hearts of the people, ceaselessly and continuously they hope for, and they wait for, the coming of help, just as people who are living in darkness, every hour, every minute, every second wait and hope: asking when ... when will the sun rise?[27]

Sukarno seems to have discovered his own name in Jayabaya's prophecies. He also may have had prophetic pretensions himself—certainly he is popularly perceived to have been a seer. In short, there is at least a plausible case that Sukarno saw his own destiny in the prophetic writings of Jayabaya and Ranggawarsita. In the 1950s, in collaboration with historian Muhammad Yamin, he personally planned and financed the construction of the mausoleum in Palar that houses Ranggawarsita's grave. In making pilgrimage visits to this site, and possibly to others associated with Jayabaya, he sought confirmation of his destiny and legitimation of his struggle.[28]

President Suharto, the Confluence of Rivers and the Clown-God Semar

Suharto, Indonesia's second president, is also rumoured to have made pilgrimages to sacred places before and during his term of office. Again, it is not easy to come by independently verifiable evidence for all of the many pilgrimage visits attributed to him. But a variety of sources, mostly oral, claim that he made visits to at least two places: the confluence of two rivers in Semarang, Central Java, and to two *padhepokan* or meditation sanctuaries on Mount Selok near Cilacap on the south coast of Central Java.

Traditionally, and to some extent even today, many Javanese have believed that the place where two rivers come together, called a *tempuran* in Javanese, has symbolic and sacred significance.[29] One such place is the confluence of Kali Garang and Kali Sadeng, two small rivers in the village of Bendan Duwur, Gajahmungkur, in the western suburbs of Semarang. From distant times and still today, this has been a sacred place for ordinary Javanese. This is especially the case on the eve of the Javanese New Year (1 Sura or 1 Muharram), when thousands of people flock to the site. Some of them, a few women as well as men, go half naked into the river to perform what is the special ritual of the site, *tapa kungkum* or immersion meditation.³⁰ It is believed that doing this on the eve of the New Year will "wash away" the ill fortune (*siyal*) of the previous year and help you fulfil your wishes or ambitions in the coming year.

Persistent anecdotal reports have claimed that, between 1956 and 1960 when he was commander of the Diponegoro Division headquartered in Semarang, Suharto made meditative pilgrimages to this site and undertook *tapa kungkum* there together with his spiritual mentor, a certain Rama Sudiyat.³¹ Indeed, some local people believe that on the night of 30 September 1965 he was at this place when the attempted coup broke out in Jakarta (personal communication by local villager 15 July 1997). Suharto himself denied that he was in Semarang on the night of the coup.

Some time in the late 1960s, after Suharto's ascension to the presidency, his spiritual mentor Rama Sudiyat built a monument overlooking the confluence of the two rivers. Called the Tugu Suharto (the Suharto Monument) it takes the form of a pencil-like concrete obelisk about eight metres high standing on a solid, pear-shaped pedestal made of stones and concrete. There is a small plaque set into the pedestal reading *Djumat Legi 30-9-65 1-10-65 S.S.S.* The three "S" letters are in Javanese script. The day and the dates are those of the night on which the attempted coup was launched. The three "S" letters are reputed to stand for the Javanese words *sing salah seleh*, which freely translated means "whoever is in the wrong should relinquish office". In July 1997 local people told me that this is a reference to Sukarno, who, having made the mistake of tolerating, even encouraging, communism, should have (and ultimately did) leave office to be replaced by Suharto. In the eyes of the local community and pilgrims who go there, the monument confirms the view that Suharto was at the site on the night of the coup, and that it was thanks to the power of this site that Suharto was able to crush the coup so quickly and comprehensively.

Rama Sudiyat (or Rama Diyat) and another of Suharto's spiritual advisers, Sudjono Humardhani, are reported to have regularly travelled (often by VIP aircraft belonging to the air arm of the Angkatan Darat, the Penerbad) to various parts of Indonesia on "spiritual missions" in order to, as they put it, shore up or "fence" and consolidate the New Order (*membentengi/memageri dan memperkuat*). These journeys are described in what, on the face of it, looks like an authentic and honest interview dated January 2001 with retired TNI Colonel Sudjai, one of the pilots who regularly flew Suharto and other VIPs in Penerbad aircraft to various parts of Indonesia. The interview describes, for example, a trip to Cilacap to obtain a specimen of the sacred flower of life, the Wijayakusuma flower, which it is believed grows only on the island of Nusakambangan, and which traditionally was a royal heirloom with the power to confer long life and legitimacy on a king.[32]

Rama Sudiyat also had a hand in the building of a *padhepokan* or *pasanggrahan*, a place of retreat and meditation, on Mount Selok. Mount Selok is on the south coast of Java about 6 km from the small town of Adipala, which in turn is about 25 km east of Cilacap. Mount Selok is adjacent to, in fact within walking distance of, the renowned pilgrimage site of Gunung Srandil.

The construction of the *padhepokan*, called Padhepokan Jambe Pitu, was evidently begun in the 1950s by Ali Sadikin, later to become governor of Jakarta. The work was completed by Rama Diyat and inaugurated in July 1958. The site is dedicated to Mbah Lengkung Kusuma, whose altar is at the upper end of a tiled terrace, and Eyang Lengkung Saweri, whose altar is at the lower end of the terrace. These two figures are said to have been followers of Dipanagara. Eyang Lengkung Saweri is represented in the form of a small statue with the appearance of a bearded ascetic or hermit.

Not far from the Padhepokan Jambe Pitu lies the older Padhepokan Jambe Lima. The building is a well maintained, attractive structure.[33] A flight of steps leads up to a small terrace in front of the double doors leading into the building. Above the door there is a sign in Javanese script reading *Puri Giri Sagara* (Temple of Mountain and Sea). Inside the entrance there is an antechamber with doors leading to an inner chamber. To the left and right of these doors, in the antechamber, there are two grave-like structures on the floor with incense ash and flower offerings scattered around them. The one on the left is the "tomb" of Pak Cilik Cakrawangsa (another name for the *wayang* clown figure Nalagareng) and the one on the right that of Pak Cilik Cari Sukmayarengga (another name for the *wayang* clown figure Petruk).

The main chamber beyond the antechamber takes the form of an airy octagonal space with a high ceiling. On the back wall panel is a larger-than-life painting of the *wayang* clown Semar flanked to the left and right by his sons Nalagareng and Petruk. On the floor in front of the portrait of Nalagareng is a grave-like structure labelled Pak Cilik Cakrawangsa and in front of the portrait of Petruk is a similar structure labelled Pak Cilik Cari Sukmayarengga. These appear to be "twins" or duplicate "graves" of the same structures in the antechamber. In the middle between these two grave-like structures and at the foot of the painting of Semar there is a low, square, tiled, altar-like podium, where offerings evidently are placed.

Suharto frequented both Jambe Pitu and Jambe Lima, though it is not clear exactly when, and how often, he came there.[34] When I visited the two *padhepokan* in 1997 the custodian of Jambe Lima told me that before Suharto became president he often "used to sleep at Jambe Lima". Suharto also spent time at the adjacent Padhepokan Jambe Pitu with his spiritual mentor Rama Diyat. (This must have been before Jambe Pitu was constructed in its present form.) Rumour has it that Suharto continued to patronise the sites after becoming president, but when pressed on this the site custodian denied it. Suharto had not personally returned to the sites after becoming president, he said, but he had "sent emissaries" (*ngirim utusan*).

The Jambe Lima retreat is dedicated to Semar, the clown-god of classical wayang. I do not know what motivated Suharto to stay overnight and meditate at Semar's shrine. Perhaps he saw himself as a Semar-like figure. Certainly, in the minds of many Indonesians, especially Javanese, Suharto was associated with Semar. In his exercise of great power and in his peasant origins, Suharto embodied something of the god-like and earthy qualities of Semar. On 11 March 1966 Suharto was the recipient of the Decree of March the Eleventh (*Surat Perintah Sebelas Maret*) mandating him to rule Indonesia. During the subsequent years of New Order rule, this key document was universally known by its suggestive abbreviation *Supersemar*. Perhaps Suharto saw Semar as a symbol of the ordinary people of Indonesia in whom he sought inspiration and to whom he wished to dedicate himself. Or, did he see Semar as a guardian figure with whom he (Suharto), as a military man, sought an alliance?[35] I think it is possible to argue (though not yet possible to say with certainty) that if Sukarno saw the roots of his legitimacy in the prophecies of Jayabaya, Suharto may have found legitimacy and a sense of personal empowerment in Semar and in the ancient autochthonous powers of certain hallowed places.

President Abdurrahman Wahid and the Saintly Dead of Islam

Throughout his presidency Abdurrahman Wahid was a frequent visitor to the innumerable tombs of Muslim saints and revered clerics that lie scattered across Java and Madura. These visits usually took place at night and often occurred on the spur of the moment. Observers noted that pilgrimages appeared to recharge the president. Early in his term of office, for example, in the midst of one of the incessant crises that marked his presidency, Gus Dur told journalists that he had recently visited the tomb of the great saint Sunan Kalijaga at Kadilangu on the outskirts of Demak, Central Java. Alone in Sunan Kalijaga's burial chamber Gus Dur said he heard the saint speak words of comfort to him from the tomb, exhorting him to have no fear and reciting the Quranic verse "How oft, by Allah's will, hath a small force vanquished a big one?" (Al-Baqarah 249). The saint, Gus Dur said, gave him a special, powerful sentence from the Holy Qur'an which he was told recite every day. "O ye who believe, stand out firmly for justice as witnesses to Allah, even against yourselves!" (An-Nisa' 135).[36]

Visiting tombs seemed to be one weapon Gus Dur used to garner public support or sympathy. On 28–29 July 1999, prior to the MPR session at which he was elected president, he participated in a *ruwatan* (exorcism or purification) ritual at Parangkusumo. Parangkusumo is the place where Panembahan Senapati, king of Mataram in the latter part of the sixteenth century, met with the spirit Queen of the South Seas, forging an alliance with her that ensured his ascent to power. According to Sjafri Sairin, Head of Gadjah Mada University's Centre for the Study of Culture and Social Change, by taking part in the *ruwatan* ritual at Parangkusumo, Gus Dur was seeking to position himself as a man of the people, because, said Sjafri, from the point of view of culture, Gus Dur's participation in a *ruwatan* could be seen as an effort to allay public unease. He added that by his estimation almost 30 per cent of the public still believed very strongly in the efficacy of *klenik* or mystical ritual.[37] According to Dr Simuh of Universitas Islam Negeri (IAIN) Sunan Kalijaga Yogyakarta—a respected commentator on mysticism (*tasawuf*) in contemporary Javanese society, and on "Javanised" variants of Islam—the public will have more veneration (*merasa segan*) for a person who has undergone a *ruwatan* purification ritual. "And the individual himself", Simuh added, "will feel more self confident, more decisive, if he has been through a *ruwatan* ritual."[38]

Just days after his election to the presidency Gus Dur made a pilgrimage to the tomb of Kiai Haji Ahmad Mutamakin in the village of Kajen, Margoyoso, on the eastern side of Mount Muria. Kiai Haji Mutamakin is believed to have lived in the late seventeenth and early eighteenth centuries and to have been a practitioner of Sufi-tinged Islam that attracted the wrath of Susuhunan Pakubuwana II, regent of Surakarta. Rumours flew that shortly before the presidential election, Gus Dur had met with Mutamakin in a dream. The saint had urged him to persevere in his campaign for election to the presidency and promised to help him. At the tomb Gus Dur expressed thanks for successfully achieving a goal that *Mbah* (grandfather) Mutamakin had also fought for. "Mbah Mutamakin rebelled against an evil system", said Gus Dur. "He brought justice to the people, and hopefully it won't be too long before I do the same."[39]

But there appears to have been another rationale for the visit. Many people, including Gus Dur himself, believe that he is a direct descendant of Mutamakin.[40] By at least one authoritative genealogy, Mutamakin in turn was a descendant of Jaka Tingkir, later known as Sultan Adiwijaya, ruler of Pajang in Central Java in the second half of the sixteenth century. Today Jaka Tingkir is one of Java's great culture heroes.

It came as a big surprise to many when Gus Dur persuaded the Indonesian Parliament to elect him to the presidency. Most people attributed his success to his unwavering belief in himself, his superb negotiating skills and the sheer effrontery he brought to his campaign for the office. Some said he had inherited these qualities from his distant ancestor, Jaka Tingkir. Like Jaka Tingkir, Gus Dur was a newcomer from the Javanese countryside with a somewhat gauche country manner. Like Jaka Tingkir he had an impressive, though little known, pedigree. He brought with him a huge reputation for esoteric learning and mystical power. With minimal party backing he elbowed his way into the ruling elite and ultimately into the top job, as Jaka Tingkir had done. Gus Dur's visit to Mutamakin's tomb, then, was as much as anything an exercise in connecting with the powerful dead and publicly confirming a lineage that would consolidate his legitimacy as the new president.[41]

It seems beyond doubt that Abdurrahman sometimes communed with dead saints or clerics to help him reach critical decisions or to fortify him in times of exceptional stress. In April 2000, for example, while mulling over the possible sacking of cabinet ministers Laksamana Sukardi and Jusuf Kalla, the president visited the East Java city of Surabaya. According to a report in the usually reliable *Tempo*, someone told the president that Kiai As'ad Syamsul Arifin, a cleric who had died in 1990, had appeared to him in a dream complaining that the president had never visited his tomb. Before his death, the cleric had been an acquaintance of Abdurrahman Wahid and a legendary NU stalwart. Gus Dur instantly mobilised three helicopters and headed 200 km east to the sleepy town of Situbondo where the tomb is located.

According to *Tempo*, Abdurrahman paid his respects at the tomb and emerged not only spiritually refreshed but with renewed resolve. Without further hesitation, and without consulting his vice-president or anyone else, he ejected the two ministers from office. At a later press conference he bumbled his way through a rationalisation of the sackings. When journalists questioned his staff, one of them commented: "Don't waste your time trying to see logic in President Abdurrahman Wahid's cabinet changes. You can put forward a million clever explanations, but the president's controversial decisions 'come from the sky' and that is the bottom line."[42]

Gus Dur's respect for the power of tombs is dramatically apparent in the bizarre story of his supernatural (and short-lived) solution for the conflict in Aceh. According to Hasballah M. Saad, an Acehnese who for a time was Gus Dur's Minister of State for Human Rights, Gus Dur once proposed to him that the tomb of Acehnese national hero Cut Nya' Dien be removed from its present site in Sumedang, West Java, and returned to Aceh. There it would be "reunited" with the tomb of Teuku Umar Djohan, Cut Nya' Dien's husband, at Mugo south of Meulaboh, West Aceh. "If the two tombs can be united", said Gus Dur, quoted by Hasballah, "the Aceh problem can be solved".[43] But what Gus Dur no doubt saw as a conciliatory gesture was seen very differently by the Gerakan Aceh Merdeka (GAM, Free Aceh Movement). Spokesman Abu Sofyan Daud welcomed the idea, but added that it merely demonstrated that Aceh and Java were two different things. "Whatever is distinctively Acehnese should be returned to Aceh", he is reported to have said, "and likewise whatever is Javanese, and still in Aceh, should be sent back to Java."[44]

Pilgrimage was also part of Gus Dur's armoury of political manoeuvres. For example in May 2001, in the last months of his presidency, under enormous pressure, and increasingly concerned about the prospect of being deposed by forces sympathetic to his vice-president, Gus Dur decided to visit the tomb of Haji Muhammad Barokah, a revered figure in the Muslim community around the small town of Kroya in Central Java. His decision to do this was unexpected. Just a day or two previously, he had suddenly called a Cabinet meeting, summoning vice-president Megawati back to Jakarta from a working visit she was making to East Java. Megawati's visit had included plans to make a pilgrimage to her father's tomb in Blitar—a pilgrimage that apparently she had to abandon in order to return to Jakarta for the Cabinet meeting. On the day of the meeting Gus Dur suddenly abandoned his ministers, leaving the exasperated Megawati, at no notice at all, to chair the meeting.[45]

He left Jakarta by private train in the middle of the day, arriving in Kroya just after nightfall. He made his way immediately to Haji Barokah's tomb where he spent just 15 minutes at the graveside. He prayed for the repose of the Haji's soul and, according to reports, also made a silent plea for the salvation of the Indonesian nation. By nine o'clock he was back in his train heading home to Jakarta where he arrived at three in the morning.

Some interpreted this incident as an example of Gus Dur's erratic, perhaps irrational, behaviour. He couldn't face the problems and pressures of Cabinet and simply sought "escape" or refuge in a world much more familiar and congenial to him. But it is equally possible that, disturbed by growing support for Megawati, Gus Dur wanted to wrong-foot her by suddenly thrusting her unexpectedly into the chairing of a Cabinet meeting.

Gus Dur's staff, and his many critics in the public of Indonesia, were worried about what appeared to be a deep need on Gus Dur's part to consult a "higher authority" for guidance on policy matters, even (as we have seen) pleading for enlightenment to help him make particular decisions. When asked once why he took his problems to the tombs of Muslim saints and revered clerics, Gus Dur answered. "Look, it's better to take these problems to them, because at least deceased people don't have ulterior motives or interests."[46]

Commenting on the president's early pilgrimage to the tomb of Kiai Haji Ahmad Mutamakin, Azyumardi Azra argued that there was a "parallelism" between the two figures. Both Gus Dur and Mutamakin were critics of legalism in Islam and emphasised devotional substance over form. Many NU members believed that Gus Dur, like Mutamakin, had saintly qualities, so that contemporary popular veneration of Gus Dur was paralleled by Gus Dur's veneration of Mutamakin. This, said Azyumardi, gave rise to a contradiction, for while Gus Dur may have been venerated in much the same way as he himself venerated Mutamakin, he was also dedicated to the modern ideals of democracy, openness, respect for pluralism, tolerance, and egalitarianism, which seem remote from the world of esoteric religious devotion.[47]

Indeed Gus Dur's pilgrimage practices bewildered many and generated downright hostility in some. In June 2001, a month before Gus Dur was removed from office, the exasperated head of a *pesantren* school and prominent NU figure, Attabik Ali, bluntly told him that he should take more account of realities in making decisions about political, security and economic matters. After meeting with the president, Attabik complained to reporters: "... frankly, there is an impression among the public that the President spends more time visiting the tombs of old figures than living people".[48]

One of the president's younger brothers, Kiai Haji Salahuddin Wahid, discussing Gus Dur's pilgrimage habits, expressed disbelief that a dead person could provide blessings or benefits (*berkah*) to the living. He said that he had debated this issue with his elder brother. Gus Dur had been entirely unswayed by his younger brother's criticism, and had held fast to his view that certain deceased holy men could confer *berkah* on petitioners.[49]

Megawati and her Father, Indonesia's Founding President

It is an almost universal custom for Muslims in Indonesia to regularly pay their respects to their deceased parents. This may happen at any time (for example on the anniversary of the death of the parent), but it is a particularly widespread custom for people to go to the graves of their immediately deceased forebears at, or approaching, Idul Fitri (also called Lebaran), the celebration at the end of the fasting month. Megawati Sukarnoputri's regular visits to her father's tomb, then, are not necessarily different from what many millions of ordinary Indonesians do. But as I have already suggested, Megawati (and other members of her family) appear also to have made political use of their father's tomb.

When Sukarno died on 21 June 1970 he was buried in a simple grave in a public cemetery in Blitar, East Java, not far from the family home in the town where he had spent much of his youth. His grave quickly became a pilgrimage site. By custom in Java it is not appropriate to place a tombstone over a deceased person's grave until 1,000 days after the person's death (i.e. almost three years). In the early years after Sukarno's death people came in large numbers to his grave, often taking away with them a handful of earth from the open gravesite.[50] This aroused concern on the part of the New Order authorities, not only because the New Order government had demonised Sukarno and regarded veneration of him as a sign of opposition, but also because, so I was told during a visit there in 1997, on some occasions the earth on Sukarno's grave threatened to disappear entirely.

The government took action to regulate access to Sukarno's grave and in 1978 decided to build a mausoleum on the site.[51] The building was quickly completed and formally opened by Suharto on the ninth anniversary of Sukarno's death on 21 June 1979.[52] The construction of the elaborate mausoleum was represented to the Indonesian public as an act of respect by the government for the *proklamator*, the proclaimer of Indonesia's independence. (Under the New Order, Sukarno's role in the modern history of Indonesia had been largely reduced to that of "proclaimer of independence".) But the new mausoleum was probably intended to function as a more intimidating context in which to regulate the use of the site. Moreover, although the government claimed that the mausoleum had been built with the approval of Sukarno's family,[53] in fact its construction seemed intended, at least in part, to stymie complaints from some members of the family that Sukarno had not wanted to be buried in the small, remote town of Blitar at all, but had explicitly asked to be buried in Bogor, just south of Jakarta.[54] Clearly, it was not in the interests of the New Order government to approve the removal of Sukarno's grave to Bogor, where, in all likelihood, it would have become a much more potent rallying point for anti-Suharto and anti-New Order forces.

Nevertheless, through the years of the New Order government, Sukarno's mausoleum in Blitar was a modest symbol of dissent. This dissent congealed around the *haul* or commemoration of Sukarno's death held during the day and into the evening of 20 June each year. The New Order government made it clear that political activities in the precincts of the mausoleum were strictly forbidden. Indeed the perimeter of the burial chamber was glassed in to keep visitors at a distance from the grave. But the government could not prohibit members of the family from entering to pay their respects to a deceased parent. In a delicate tug-of-war, it was possible for Megawati and her family to make the *haul* a subtle, necessarily low-key, but nevertheless pointed, annual focal point of dissent that was always reported on in the mass media. The number of people attending the *haul* steadily increased through the 1990s reaching, according to one report, more than 10,000 people in 1995.[55]

This number jumped in June 1998, one month after the fall of Suharto, and in June 2001, a month before Megawati assumed the presidency, around 25,000 people a day were visiting the site. The *haul* commemoration of 20 June 2001 is estimated by some to have jammed the otherwise sleepy little town with as many as a quarter of a million people. Certainly Blitar's town square was unable to accommodate the hundreds of thousands who attended the commemorative mass prayer.[56] Today, the annual *haul* has continued to be a major event in Blitar, and daily visitor numbers at the mausoleum are never less than a thousand.

This has become a dilemma for Megawati and the Sukarno family. On the one hand the family feel they should comply with their father's wishes. There are also compelling symbolic-political reasons for making the move. Clearly, Megawati would boost her legitimacy as leader of Partai Demokrasi Indonesia-Perjuangan (PDI-P, Indonesian Democratic Party of Struggle) and chances of re-election to the presidency if the tomb were close to the capital. In the pronouncements of some, this political rationale can assume a "mystical" guise.

> From the viewpoint of the supernatural, if Bung Karno's tomb were shifted to Bogor it would rescue the nation and state from its current turmoil. This at least is the opinion of a public figure from Banten, KH Tubagus Ali Imran. His reasoning is, if Bung Karno's tomb were in Bogor it would be more accessible to admirers of the nation's founding father. Tubagus Ali believes that Suharto chose Blitar as Bung Karno's resting place because he feared the continuing influence of the mystical powers that Bung Karno possessed during his lifetime. As we know, Bung Karno was a man of great insight, spiritually and physically. He was someone who was accepted in two worlds: the real world and the world of the supernatural. If Bung Karno's tomb had been in Bogor, there is no doubt that the spirits that had done his bidding when he was alive would have influenced the Soeharto government. And if that had happened Soeharto might not have been able to rule for 32 years.[57]

But since Megawati's loss in the presidential election of 2004 her family's initial determination to move the tomb to Bogor has been put on hold. I think there are two reasons for this. First, the tomb in Blitar has acquired iconic status. It is now an historic site, the focal point in a political struggle that achieved its immediate goal when Megawati acceded to the presidency in 2001. It is a New Order-built edifice that was appropriated by opponents of the New Order and turned against it. Second, the town of Blitar has come to rely economically on Sukarno's tomb. Local people have even set up a committee to resist any attempt to move the tomb and there have been demonstrations against the idea.[58] Its removal would be a commercial disaster for the otherwise poorly endowed locality, and would also be, at the very least, problematic in public relations terms, for Megawati and the Sukarno family.

Right from the beginning of Megawati's presidency, the view emerged in the nation's media that pilgrimages to her father's tomb were components in her decision-making technique.

> Straight after her inauguration Megawati made a brief statement to the press, then, without any interviews, whoosh … off she went to Mount Geulis, Bogor. After spending time there on her own she headed for Blitar to scatter flowers on the tomb of her father, Bung Karno, the first president of the Republic of Indonesia. Up until last Wednesday she was still incommunicado: even her inner circle in the PDI-P couldn't contact her. "This is a tactic of Megawati's", said one official high up in the PDI-P, "to avoid getting confused by all the names that are being thrust at her for positions in the Cabinet".[59]

In the course of her presidency (2001–4) Megawati visited her father's tomb at least two or three times a year. In July 2002, for example, one year after becoming president, she made a pilgrimage there. The complex was cleared of other visitors and she entered the burial chamber alone. She remained at her father's graveside praying for one hour.[60] As her term proceeded observers noted that Megawati's stays at her father's graveside seemed to be getting longer and longer. Between April and October 2004, during the six months of incessant electioneering that accompanied the two rounds of presidential elections, she made pilgrimage visits to the tomb of her father no fewer than seven times. Twice she took her vice-presidential running mate Hasyim Muzadi and on one occasion was accompanied on a late-night visit by ex-president Abdurrahman Wahid. She paid a final visit to her father's tomb three weeks after her defeat in the second round of the election.[61]

National Legitimacy and Local Practice

Political legitimacy is what persuades people that a ruler, a government or a state has the right—without using coercion or terror—to regulate their lives, to demand their obedience, perhaps even to command their respect and devotion.

The sources of political legitimacy in Indonesia are difficult to describe and even more difficult to compare and quantify.[62] Since independence in 1945 the state, its governments and its leaders, have wrought legitimacy in constantly shifting ways. Commentaries on legitimacy have tended to focus on political economy, on democratic institutions, and on the creation or appropriation of key national symbols.

The argument from political economy is that national leaders, their governments, even the state itself, engineer legitimacy through stability, security and good economic policy producing rising living standards. The New Order government's legitimacy was usually argued in these terms. Despite the manifold abuses that were an integral part of the New Order, it was legitimate, or at the very least "tolerable", because of the perception that it was successful in managing the economy.

The governments of Abdurrahman Wahid and Megawati Sukarnoputri, on the other hand, despite their mostly appalling record of economic management, claimed legitimacy through the institutions of democracy—voter support underpinned by credible electoral and legislative processes. The word "credible" is important here, because previous governments have also felt it necessary to claim democratic credentials, but unlike Abdurrahman Wahid and Megawati they declined to implement free, open electoral and legislative processes. Suharto's "Pancasila Democracy" was little more than a *sembah* (sign of obeisance) in the direction of democracy, while Sukarno made an ultimately pathetic attempt to hide the authoritarianism of his rule behind the bankrupt rhetoric of "Guided Democracy".

Legitimacy through the creation, appropriation and management of national symbols has meant mainly the mythologisation of certain historical events such as the anti-colonial struggle, the 1945–49 revolution, the crushing of the Communist "threat" in 1965–66, and the forging and defence of Indonesia's unity. It has also meant the creation, the "rescue" and the institutional or personal appropriation of national symbols like the Pancasila, the Constitution of 1945 and Nasakom (Nasionalis, Agama, Komunis; Nationalism, Religion, Communism).

All these mechanisms for engineering legitimacy are important and powerful. But the national political practices of Indonesia, its national institutions, even (perhaps *especially*) its national history, are not strongly rooted. History in Indonesia stretches far back into the pre-nationalist era. This history is what, in the context of the modern Republic, is called, sometimes dismissively, "local history". It is not easy to claim legitimacy through appeals to a single national history in a country that, until recently did not *have* a national history. Indonesia's Javanese presidents have all sought legitimacy in the powerful legitimating criteria of the modern state, but very clearly they have felt that there is something lacking in this. The pull of local history and local practice has drawn them to the places *traditionally* regarded as sources of political legitimacy. One of the most important of these practices, at least for ordinary Javanese people, has been the practice of local pilgrimage—a practice that is wholly outside the country's national culture.

Local pilgrimage jumped dramatically in profile under the presidencies of Abdurrahman Wahid and Megawati (though, as I have shown, the practice was also important but less visible in the times of Sukarno and Suharto). In part this was due to a dramatic decline in the status of some of the New Order's main legitimating mechanisms. Indonesia's economic success story fell to pieces in the closing year of the New Order, and subsequent governments—even that of Susilo Bambang Yudhoyono—have failed to fully revive it. Pancasila, through its recruitment to the parochial interests of the New Order elite, became collateral damage in the New Order's demise. The previously untouchable Constitution of 1945 has been briskly dismantled and renovated. In addition, post-Suharto openness directed a spotlight of harsh revisionism on the revolution and the coup of 1965, wounding the symbolic sanctity of these key events.

Perhaps most important, the mechanisms and institutions of democracy put in place since the fall of Suharto, have not erased disillusionment with democratic reform. Stability, security and living standards are still widely seen as fragile and nostalgia for the certainties of the Suharto era remains strong. Regionalism is again a powerful force and is likely to re-invigorate what used to be called "primordialism". In other words, the decline we might have expected in the viability of local, "traditional" or "pre-modern" legitimating practices will be countered by decentralisation, the renewed authority of regional cultures and disillusionment with "modern" democracy.

The most spectacular recent example of the continuing relevance of tombs and local pilgrimage in Indonesia's political life was the funeral of ex-president Suharto following his death on 27 January 2008. He was laid to rest beside his wife Siti Hartinah (informally called Ibu Tien, who died in 1996) in Giribangun, the lavish family mausoleum adjacent to the Mangadeg burial ground of Solo's Mangkunegaran royal family on the slopes of Mount Lawu in Central Java. His final illness, dramatic death and funeral generated huge public interest that seems to have triggered renewed enthusiasm for pilgrimage to his mausoleum. Many thousands of visitors—many of them district officials and public servants—crowded the mausoleum in the weeks after the funeral, and the spike in visitor numbers looks set to continue at least until the presidential and parliamentary elections in 2009.[63]

Java now has two formidably prestigious pilgrimage sites representing the rival dynasties that have dominated post-independence Indonesian politics: Sukarno's mausoleum in Blitar, and the Suharto family mausoleum on Mount Lawu. As the presidential and parliamentary elections of 2009 approach, the two sites will become increasingly important as symbols in the contest for the votes of ethnic Javanese. This does not mean that we have to translate all the processes of political legitimisation among Javanese into the symbolism of *ziarah*, *makam* and *berkah*, not to mention *wahyu*, *wayang*, *kraton*[64] or any of a host of other exotic notions conventionally traced back to Javanese pseudo-mystical practices. It is, after all, Javanese who have been among the most hard-nosed activists for the institutionalisation of political legitimacy based on openness and credible, modern electoral processes.

I suppose what I am arguing for is a more nuanced vision of what constitutes political legitimacy in Indonesia—one in which the economy, national political institutions and national symbols are not the only components. Indonesia is not a 'new' country, but rather one with powerful age-old local practices that will not lie down and die. In the discussion of legitimacy at the national level and in the regions these need to be factored in as a matter of course and not treated as afterthoughts or as mere examples of exotica.

Notes

1. See, for example, *Suara Pembaruan*, "Mega dan Gus Dur Ziarah Bersama", 9 Oct. 1999; *Media Indonesia*, "Gus Dur, Megawati Berdoa Khusyuk di Makam Bung Karno", 9 Oct. 1999; *Tempo*, "Menunggu Kata Putus Para Kiai Waskita", 27, 11–17 Oct. 1999; *Gatra*, "Kartu di Tangan Senior Brother", 16 Oct. 1999.
2. *Media Indonesia*, "Gus Dur, Megawati ..."; *Suara Pembaruan*, "Mega dan Gus Dur. ...".
3. *Tempo*, "Menunggu Kata Putus...".
4. W. Wibowo, "Gus Dur: Mega Sebagai 'Simbol'", *Suara Pembaruan*, 11 Nov. 1999.
5. Within days of their respective elections to the presidency, Abdurrahman on 20 Oct. 1999 and Megawati on 23 July 2001, both Abdurrahman and Megawati made pilgrimages of thanksgiving to the tombs of their respective fathers. See *Suara Pembaruan*, "Gus Dur Ziarah ke Makam Kakek dan Ayahnya", 23 Oct. 1999 and *Suara Merdeka*, "Nyekar ke Makam Ayah", 26 July 2001.
6. *Bali Post*, "Mega-Gus Dur Ziarah ke Makam BK", 14 Jan. 1999.
7. *Media Indonesia*, "Yapeta Urung Buat Pernyataan Politik", 24 Feb. 1997.
8. The phenomenon has been little studied. In the early years of the twentieth century there were scattered studies of sacred sites and local pilgrimage by Dutch scholars, most notably by D. A. Rinkes whose seminal series of articles on Javanese saints in the *Tijdschrift voor Indische Taal, Land- en Volkenkunde*

(1910–13) has been published in English translation as *The Nine Saints of Java*, trans. H. M. Froger (Kuala Lumpur: Malaysian Sociological Research Institute, 1996). Local pilgrimage is mainly observed in numerous articles of a popular nature in Javanese-language and Indonesian-language newspapers and magazines. In his renowned study, *The Religion of Java* (Glencoe, Ill.: Free Press, 1960), Clifford Geertz failed to notice it. Recent valuable contributions to the field include J. Pemberton, *On the Subject of "Java"* (Ithaca: Cornell University Press, 1994); H. Chambert-Loir and C. Guillot, eds., *Le Culte des Saints dans le Monde Musulman* (Paris: École française d'Extrême-Orient, 1995); Abdul Ghofur Muhaimin, *The Islamic Traditions of Cirebon* (Canberra: ANU E-Press, 2006); and H. Chambert-Loire and A. Reid, eds., *The Potent Dead: Ancestors, Saints, and Heroes in Contemporary Indonesia* (Crows Nest: Allen & Unwin, 2002).

9. D. Bourchier, *Dynamics of Dissent in Indonesia: Sawito and the Phantom Coup* (Ithaca: Cornell Modern Indonesia Project, Cornell University, 1984).
10. *Kompas Online*, "Soebadio Bertapa di Gunung Lawu", 5 Dec. 1997; *Kompas Online*, "Soebadio Tetap Bertapa di Gunung Lawu", 17 Dec. 1997.
11. See *Kompas Online*, "Buku 'Politik Dosomuko' Karya Soebadio Dilarang", 8 May 1998. Dasamuka, also called Rawana, is the rapacious ogre king of Ngalengka in the Ramayana.
12. *Suara Merdeka*, "Paku Buwono Hadiri Peringatan HUT Tokoh PSI", 28 May 1998. It has to be said that although Subadio made a hermit-like retreat to Mount Lawu, in fact he appears to have lived in a house in Tawangmangu rather than climbing right to the hallowed but icy-cold summit. As a very elderly gentleman, perhaps he can be excused this concession to comfort.
13. An outstanding exception is Marcel Bonneff's study "Semar révélé: La crise indonesienne et l'imaginaire politique javanais", *Archipel* 64 (2002): 3–37, which presents a wealth of fresh sources and insights on political pilgrimage, and which cries out for translation into English and Indonesian. I have published a study on the role of a burial ground and its saint-like occupant in the legitimation of the bupati of Banyumas, see G. Quinn, "The Role of a Javanese Burial Ground in Local Government", in Chambert-Loir and Reid, *The Potent Dead*.
14. R. E. Elson, *Suharto: A Political Biography* (Cambridge: Cambridge University Press, 2001); G. Barton, *Abdurrahman Wahid—Muslim Democrat, Indonesian President: A View from Inside* (Honolulu: University of Hawai'i Press, 2002).
15. Elson, *Suharto*, pp. 301–2.
16. W. Witoelar, *No Regrets: Reflections of a Presidential Spokesman* (Jakarta: Equinox, 2002).
17. M. Bonneff, "Semar révélé", p. 8.
18. President Habibie, born in Pare-Pare, South Sulawesi, was not known for undertaking local pilgrimages. But in May, 1999, he paid a visit to the tomb of his forebears on his mother's side who are buried in the village of Baledono

in the district of Purworejo, Central Java. *Republika*, "Habibie Ziarahi Makam Moyangnya di Geger Menjangan", 29 May 1999.
19. Sindhunata, *Bayang-Bayang Ratu Adil* (Jakarta: Gramedia Pustaka Utama, 1999), p. 22.
20. Ibid., p. 24. Emphasis in the original.
21. Personal communication by the tomb custodian (*juru kunci*), 18 May 1997.
22. There are many popular editions of Ranggawarsita's prophetic writings, a relatively recent one being R. N. Ranggawarsita, *Zaman Edan* (Yogyakarta: Bentang Budaya, 1998).
23. Depending on context, *pralambang* means "symbol", "omen" or "portent".
24. The prophecies as we know them show no signs of having been written in twelfth-century Javanese: they are all in modern Javanese. And they display the very strong influence of Islamic traditions: a feature that is unlikely to have been inherited from the predominantly Hindu-Buddhist culture of the twelfth century.
25. M. H. Soewarno, *Ramalan Jayabaya Versi Sabda Palon* (Jakarta: Yudha Gama, n.d.), translation by author.
26. Ibid., p. 54.
27. Soekarno, *Indonesia Menggugat: Pidato Pembelaan Bung Karno di Muka Hakim Kolonial* (Jakarta: S. K. Seno, 1960), p. 75.
28. Labrousse summarises the contents of several popular works about Sukarno, noting that the president was widely believed to possess prophetic powers. See P. Labrousse, "The Second Life of Bung Karno: Analysis of the Myth (1978–1981)", *Indonesia* 57 (April 1994): 175–96. K. Lelono, in his hugely successful *Satrio Piningit: 25 Sandhi Gaib Mengenai Pemimpin Bangsa, Para Tokoh dan Situasi Politik Indonesia* (Jakarta: Gramedia, 1999), notes in his introduction that Sukarno made use of the prophecies of Jayabaya to galvanise support for the nationalist struggle.
29. Probably the biggest surviving ritual involving the confluence of rivers is the well known Rebo Wekasan (Last Wednesday) ceremony held annually on the last Wednesday in the month of Sapar at the confluence of the Opak and Gajah Wong rivers just south of Yogyakarta.
30. See, for example, *Suara Merdeka*, "Meriah, Peringatan Malam 1 Sura", 16 Mar. 2002.
31. Ibid.
32. *DeTAK*, "Misi Klenik Orde Baru", 24 Jan. 2001. Bonneff gives other, perhaps less well documented, instances of Suharto's interest in collecting *pusaka*, magically charged artefacts ("Semar révélé", p. 17).
33. During the New Order, Jambe Lima and Jambe Pitu stood in a picturesque forest setting with wild monkeys racing through the trees. But when I went there in 1999 most of the trees around the retreats had been chopped down in the tragic assault on Java's forests that happened after the fall of Suharto.

34. See, for example, *MWeb*, "Srandil: Sejenak Menuju Nirvana", available from <http://www.mweb.co.id> [accessed 9 Aug. 2002]; *Satulelaki*, "Jambe Pitu, Tempat Bertapa Mantan Presiden Soeharto", available from <http://www.satulelaki.com> [accessed 9 Aug. 2002].
35. Semar is widely regarded as the spiritual guardian of Java. In this role his simple grave is to be found at the summit of Mount Tidar in the southern suburbs of Magelang. Mount Tidar is believed to be the head of the great nail driven through Java by the gods to hold the island steady on the face of the earth. Mount Tidar is immediately adjacent to the Indonesian armed forces cadet training school the Military Academy (Akademi Militer or AKMIL).
36. *Jawa Pos*, "Gus Dur Ziarah ke Makam Syeh Damanhuri", 25 July 2000.
37. *Gatra*, "Meruwat Wahyu Presiden", 12 Aug. 2000.
38. *Gatra*, "Tahlilan Kehilangan Sesajen", 12 Aug. 2000.
39. A. Azra, "Mistifikasi Politik Indonesia di Awal Milenium Baru: Gus Dur dan KH Ahmad Mutamakin", *Kompas*, 31 Dec. 1999.
40. A. Wahid, "Islam: Apakah Bentuk Perlawanannya?" *Kompas*, 7 June 2002.
41. When Gus Dur's government fell apart and he was hounded from office in 2001, parallels with Jaka Tingkir again appeared. In the *Babad Tanah Jawi* our last glimpse of Jaka Tingkir is as an old man making a pathetic sally against the growing might of his former vassal, the state of Mataram. He tries to enlist the help of a dead saint, as Gus Dur repeatedly did, but finds the door of the holy tomb closed against him. He takes a tumble from the back of an elephant, somehow presaging the slapstick incompetence of Gus Dur's attempts to save his government. He eventually expires as a sea of foes camp at the gates of his palace, just as Gus Dur's government expired with its leader holed up in Jakarta's presidential palace and under siege in Parliament.
42. *Tempo*, "Di Balik Pencopotan itu", 29, 1–7 May 2000.
43. *Kontras*, "Solusi Gaib untuk Aceh", 146, 11–17 July 2001.
44. *Kontras*, "Maunya Jangan Cuma Kubur yang Dipulangkan", 146, 11–17 July 2001.
45. *Kompas*, "Presiden Ziarah ke Makam H. Mohammad Barokah", 21 May 2001; *Bali Post*, "Mega Jengkel Gus Dur Pilih Ziarah", 21 May 2001.
46. *Gatra*, "Meruwat Wahyu".
47. Azra, "Mistifikasi Politik Indonesia di Awal Milenium Baru".
48. *Jakarta Post*, "Gus Dur Told to Prove his Competence", 15 June 2001.
49. *Kompas*, "KH Salahuddin Wahid: Presiden Menganggap Enteng Megawati!", 6 June 2001.
50. Pierre Labrousse claims that in a period of one year beginning 1 June 1980, almost one and a half million visitors went to the newly completed mausoleum. "The Second Life of Bung Karno", p. 177.
51. Ibid., pp. 175–6.
52. See T. C. Lindsey, "Concrete Ideology: Taste, Tradition, and the Javanese Past

in New Order Public Space", in *Culture and Society in New Order Indonesia*, ed. V. M. Hooker (Kuala Lumpur: Oxford University Press, 1995), pp. 167–8, for a detailed description and evaluation of the mausoleum.

53. *Makam Bung Karno: Proklamator Kemerdekaan dan Presiden Pertama Republik Indonesia*, Panitia Pemugaran Makam Proklamator Kemerdekaan R.I., Bung Karno, (n.d.), p. 7.
54. According to family members, in his will of 1962, Sukarno asked to be buried somewhere in the precincts of his home at Batu Tulis, Bogor, "under a shady tree on the banks of a stream with the sound of water trickling" (*Suara Merdeka*, "Dibahas, Rencana Pemindahan Makam", 21 June 1998). A certain air of sanctity envelopes Batu Tulis. Right opposite Sukarno's home is a tiny museum housing a stone inscribed in Old Sundanese dating from 1533. Pilgrims come to the site to pray for good fortune. This is also the place where Megawati's Minister of Religion, Said Agil Al-Munawar, on the advice of a seer, initiated an infamous dig for buried treasure. See *Tempo*, "Akibat Pergaulan Gaib", 31, 26 Aug.–1 Sept. 2002.
55. *Media Indonesia Minggu*, "Haul: Antara Zikir dan Politik", 25 June 1995.
56. *Suara Merdeka*, "Bung Karno Milik Kita Semua...", 21 June 2001.
57. *Majalah Misteri*, "Kaul Harlah Bung Karno?", <http://www.paranormal.or.id/article.php?sid=17>.
58. *Surabaya Post*, "Soal Rencana Pemindahan Makam BK: Warga Bentuk Paguyuban", 28 July 1998. On 17 July 2001, RCTI television's *Nuansa Pagi* program carried a report on a demonstration in Blitar involving thousands of people. The demonstrators demanded the rejection of rumoured plans to shift Sukarno's tomb to Batu Tulis, saying that the tomb "has become one with the people of Blitar" and "we feel that we would lose half of ourselves" if the tomb were taken away.
59. *Kontan*, "Tinggal Membagi Kue", 30 July 2001, <http://www.kontan-online.com/05/44/politik/pol1.htm>.
60. *Suara Merdeka*, "Satu Jam Mega di Makam Bung Karno", 7 June 2002.
61. Among the many news reports of these visits, see, for example, *Detikcom*, "Mega Ziarah ke Makam Bung Karno", 3 Apr. 2004; *Media Indonesia*, "Mega Hasyim Ziarah Lagi ke Blitar", 5 Sept. 2004. Although President Susilo Bambang Yudhoyono is not as fixated on pilgrimage as his two predecessors, it is worth adding that, at least twice during the presidential campaign of 2004, he visited the tomb of his father in Pacitan, East Java, and twice paid his respects to Sarwo Edhie Wibowo, his late father-in-law and one-time senior general in the Indonesian armed forces who lies buried in Purworejo, Central Java. Two weeks after his election victory he made a thanksgiving pilgrimage to President Sukarno's tomb in Blitar, paying his respects just four days before Megawati's final visit. See *Website Resmi Pemerintah Kabupaten Pacitan*, "SBY Melakukan Ziarah ke Makam Orang Tuanya", 7 Oct. 2004,

<http://www.pacitan.go.id/berita.php?id=111>; *Republika*, "SBY Ziarah ke Makam Mertuanya", 18 June 2004; *Republika*, "Yudhoyono, Nilai Ziarah dan Rekonsiliasi", 7 Oct. 2004.

62. One of the few attempts to concentrate explicitly on the question of legitimacy is that of M. Pabottinggi, "Indonesia: Historicizing the New Order's Legitimacy Dilemma", in *Political Legitimacy in Southeast Asia: Quest for Moral Authority*, ed. M. Alagappa (Stanford: Stanford University Press, 1995), pp. 224–56.

63. In part, the spike in visitor numbers has ridden on a mini-wave of new books and mass media articles about the role that mystical practices are thought to have played in Suharto's presidency. See, for example, K. J. Bangunjiwo, *Misteri Pusaka-Pusaka Soeharto* (Yogyakarta: Galangpress, 2007), and the bestseller by A. T. Artha, *Dunia Spiritual Soeharto: Menelusuri Laku Ritual, Tempat-Tempat dan Guru Spiritualnya* (Yogyakarta: Galangpress, 2007). Also, *Suara Merdeka*, "Senantiasa Diselimuti Dunia Mistik", 12 Jan. 2008; *Misteri*, "Misteri Kehidupan Semu Soeharto", 5–19 Feb. 2008; and many more.

64. These phrases can be glossed as "pilgrimage, tomb and divinely bestowed personal favour" and "supernatural insight or revelation, Javanese shadow puppetry and the Javanese palace/court".

CHAPTER **10**

Papuan Nationalism: Christianity and Ethnicity

Richard Chauvel

To mark the 57th anniversary of Indonesian Independence in 2002, *Tifa Papua*, the Jayapura weekly, published an article entitled "Papuan nationalism is stronger on the anniversary of Indonesian Independence". It argued that the feeling for Indonesian nationalism was becoming less important for Papuan society, while the sense of Papuan nationalism has strengthened during the Reformasi era. Papuans do not feel that there is anything particularly special about 17 August.[1] The article reminds us that Papuan identity has evolved with reference to and, for the most part, in opposition to Indonesian nationalism. This suggests that the relationship between a Papuan identity and an Indonesian identity is of a different order than that which prevails elsewhere in the archipelago between regional and ethnic identities and an evolving national one. With the risk of over-simplifying, being Sundanese, Balinese or Batak has come to complement and enrich being Indonesian. The accommodation of regional and national identities has taken time and has been the subject of much debate and political struggle, but to varying degrees, accommodations have been reached.

Papuan identity has more in common with its Indonesian rival than it does with its regional counterparts. Papuans do not have the assurance of a shared common community and historical experience that a Minangkabau or a Buginese can have. A Papuan identity is in itself being created by peoples from diverse societies whose contact with each other has been mixed, often limited and recent.

The notion of Papuan and Indonesian nationalisms being alternatives to each other is symbolised in Imbi Square in Jayapura, where in 1961 the Papuan *Bintang Kejora* (Morning Star Flag) was raised for the first time and was acknowledged as one of the national symbols of the territory then renamed West Papua. In 1999 and 2000 the political changes generated by Reformasi enabled flag-raising ceremonies to commemorate that of 1 December 1961. The Papuans witnessing the flag-raising ceremony in 2000 had their backs turned on a memorial built on the other side of the square to those Indonesian servicemen, including the deputy commander of the Indonesian navy, who died in a naval clash with the Dutch in January 1962. Commodore Yos Soedarso and his men died implementing Sukarno's *Trikora* commands, the first of which was the destruction of the Dutch-created puppet state of West Papua—the state that many Papuans believe was proclaimed with the first raising of the *Bintang Kejora* in 1961.

The events commemorated in Imbi Square took place just 46 years ago. In 1961 Indonesia had been independent for 16 years. The ideal of an Indonesian state had been the object of political struggle for about half a century; the ideal of a Papuan state was still being formulated. In the months before the first flag raising, while Indonesia and the Netherlands were fighting about who had sovereignty over the land of Papua, the first generation of Papuan nationalists were debating what it meant to be Papuan and whether they wanted to establish a Papuan state. Those who formed the Komite Nasional and proposed that the *Bintang Kejora* should be the national flag did assert the right of the Papuan people to obtain their own place like other free peoples amongst the nations of the world.[2] These politicians were among the first generation who began to think of themselves as Papuans.

Most of the members of the Komite Nasional were also members of Dewan Papua (*Nieuw Guinea Raad,* New Guinea Council) and as such were the elected representatives of the Papuan people. However, their world, life experience and political awareness were very different from many of the communities they represented. At the time of the first flag-raising ceremony in Hollandia, similar ceremonies were held throughout the territory. The Dutch *controleur* of Mimika, in the residency of Fakfak on Papua's southwest coast, reported that the flag-raising ceremony had attracted some interest but little understanding among the local population. The people had only a vague idea of what the word "Papuan" meant. People still thought in local and regional terms. Being part of Mimika had meaning.[3] At the centre of administration in Fakfak, the responses to the Komite Nasional's activities, the raising of the *Bintang Kejora* and president Sukarno's speech on 19 December 1961 indicated that there were opposing groups of Papuans, some supporting the emerging nationalist position of the Komite Nasional while others wanting integration with Indonesia. The substantial Indonesian community in Fakfak also favoured integration with Indonesia.[4] Fakfak was remote from Hollandia, but a few of the Papuan leaders from Fakfak were members of the emerging nationalist elite. The Raja of Rumbati, for example, was associated with the Komite Nasional. The issues of debate were not dissimilar from those in Hollandia. Being so close to the Indonesian islands of central Maluku, Fakfak was on the frontline for Indonesian infiltrations. The naval encounter in which Yos Soedarso and his men died was along the coast from Fakfak. Two of the casualties in Soedarso's boat came from Fakfak.[5]

The emergence of a Papuan identity with reference to and in opposition to Indonesian nationalism had its roots in the structures of the Netherlands colonial administration in Papua. In various configurations, prior to the Pacific War, Papua was governed as part of administrations based in the neighbouring Maluku Islands. There was a curious dual colonialism, quite different from indirect rule structures employed elsewhere in the archipelago in that the Dutch ruled through Indonesians rather than indigenous Papuan elites. Dutch officials occupied a handful of the most senior positions, while the middle and lower positions in the civil administration and police as well as those in the schools and missions were held by people from eastern Indonesia, mainly Ambonese, Menadonese and Keiese.[6] These mainly Christian Indonesians were at the frontline of colonialism. Netherlands New Guinea had a form of colonialism perhaps more Indonesian than it was Dutch in that Papuans had more contact with the east Indonesians than with the Dutch. Indonesian nationalists, in making their claim that Papua was part of Indonesia, cited the contribution made by Indonesians to the development of Papua. It was missionaries, however, not the government, the east Indonesians or the Dutch who contributed largely to the development of Papua. In education, it was asserted that there was not a single Dutch person teaching Papuan students, rather

Indonesian teachers from elsewhere in the archipelago brought civilisation to the Papuans (*de beschaving van de inheemse Irianese te bevorderen*).[7]

In the years after the Pacific War the dynamics in the relations between Indonesians and Papuans began to change, partly in response to developments in Dutch policy. The first post-war resident of New Guinea, J. P. K. van Eechoud, established colleges to train the Papuan graduates of mission schools as officials and police. The students were deliberately drawn from various regions in Papua so as to broaden local identification into a pan-Papuan one. As Papuans graduated from van Eechoud's colleges, they developed a keen sense of rivalry with the east Indonesians. The latter occupied the positions the educated Papuans thought they should have.[8] Papuan nationalism has some of its roots in the personal experiences of this first generation of "Papuans".

Papuans resented the mistreatment and discrimination they suffered at the hands of Indonesian officials. Many felt they had been treated as animals (*binatang*), as being dumb and not able to speak good Malay (Indonesian) by their Indonesian teachers. Those Papuans who had obtained positions in the administration felt that they were kept in the lower positions by Indonesian officials, who regarded them as incapable of being anything else. The Dutch officials were regarded as bearers of development—of education, Christianity and material progress. The Indonesians were not only the source of discrimination and prejudice, but were suspected as working against the progress offered by the Dutch. As young educated Papuans contemplated independence in the early 1960s, they were uncertain about the future role, if any, of the east Indonesian officials, teachers and missionaries. Some thought that they should be permitted to remain, but not without conditions.[9]

The graduates of van Eechoud's training colleges were prominent among the members of the New Guinea Council and Komite Nasional, who were responsible for the first formulations of Papuan national aspirations. They acknowledged van Eechoud's influence on their ideals. During the New Guinea Council debates about the recognition of the *Bintang Kejora* as the national flag, one of the Papuan members proposed that, if the flag was raised, a flower should be placed on van Eechoud's grave as he was the one who had planned all that they were now about to achieve.[10] About the same time Markus Kaisiepo recalled a discussion with "Father" van Eechoud in 1945. Van Eechoud told the students that they had to study diligently because they were the new Papuans for a new New Guinea. "This is what I have been trying to do ever since. Not only me; all of us."[11]

This strand of nationalism, based on rivalry with Indonesians, remains strong among some of the most successful Papuans in the administration. Indonesian domination of key positions in the provincial government is a strong motivating factor in Papuan nationalism among the educated elite. Michael Menufandu, a senior Papuan civil servant and a former mayor of Jayapura, complained of the intellectual arrogance of officials who believed that policy could only be made in Jakarta, when it is the local people who know the region and its problems best.[12] Another cause of resentment among Papuan officials is that, while they have to compete with Indonesians for senior positions in Papua, they are themselves rarely appointed to positions in other provinces.[13]

A Christian Core of Papuan Nationalism?

There are complexities and tensions within Papuan nationalism. It is been argued that Papuan nationalism grew out of the tensions, rivalries and conflicts with the Indonesian officials, missionaries and teachers who served in Papua as servants of the Dutch regime. They were also the people who brought Christianity to Papua.

In the August 2002 edition of *Tifa Papua* noted earlier, there was an article entitled "Independence according to Papuans". It began with the arrival of the first German missionaries, Carl W. Ottow and J. G. Geissler, and finished with the Special Autonomy Law of 2001. It related that Ottow and Geissler were emissaries of God sent to liberate Papuans from the world of the Devil. It was the work of the Holy Spirit for this land and its inhabitants. Since then, stated the article, Papuans have understood and accepted change from outside, especially, they have known and accepted the Gospel of Jesus Christ.[14] The article reminds us that Christianity is a core element in Papuan identity and the churches are key institutions in Papuan society. The anniversary of the landing of Ottow and Geissler on 5 February 1855 near Manokwari has become a major celebration of Papuan identity and liberation, especially since 2000 when any public celebration of "independence day", 1 December, has been prohibited. The anniversary of the arrival of Ottow and Geissler has been used by church leaders to address the most critical issues confronting Papuan society. In 2007 the leaders of the major Christian denominations together with their colleagues from other religions, supported by the Governor, committed themselves to support the campaign against HIV/AIDS.[15] In 2006 the theme of the anniversary was the establishment of Papua as a "land of peace", a political ideal first advocated by the post-Suharto independence movement.[16] The slogan is a code for a reduction in, if not elimination of, the Indonesian military presence and the violence associated with the security forces. In his address to the public meeting during the 2006 anniversary, the Rev. Socratez Sofyan Yoman, the head of the Baptist Church in Papua, argued:

> From the presence of the Gospel of Jesus Christ in the land of Papua, through the mediation of the two missionaries (Ottow and Geissler), their commitment and objective can be clearly seen: that is to gather the spirit of the Papuan people to become the flock of the Lord. Because of this, the churches in the land of Papua, as the protector of the community, very appropriately have a commitment and a central role to nurture, guard and protect God's flock from intimidation, detention, abduction, torture, imprisonment, rape and murder together with the stigmatisation as separatists, traitors and members of the Organisasi Papua Merdeka (OPM, Free Papua Movement).[17]

Often missionaries were the first contact Papuan societies had with the world outside. Many Papuan societies were introduced to the "modern" world by the churches. Missionaries brought education, training, health services and a new understanding of the world Papuans lived in. Government and business followed the churches.[18] The Papuan theologian and intellectual, Dr Benny Giay, has argued that Papuans have come to regard the churches as "liberating institutions" and as a "bearer of new hope for a society shackled by the cold ideology of development that the New Order Government taught".[19]

Papuan Christians thus celebrate the arrival of the first missionaries in 1855. The history of missionary activity and conversion is complex and diverse, involving several Christian denominations of different national backgrounds over more than a century. Christianity in Papua is generally of much more recent origins, especially in the isolated but densely populated central highlands. The first missionaries, who were Americans, arrived in the Baliem Valley in 1954. Obed Komba, church leader and member of the Team of 100 Papuans who met president Habibie in February 1999 and demanded independence, recalled that he met the Americans first in 1957 as a 12-year-old. "When I first saw them, I thought, "This is very strange. This is something new. We would run away and then go back to see them again. Back and forth. We would look from afar because we were very scared."[20] Missionaries had reached Paniai some years earlier than the Baliem. Benny Giay relates how his parents were among the first of his people, the Me of Paniai, to become Christians. Zacheus Pakage was the missionary who brought the gospel to the Me. Benny Giay wrote his doctoral thesis on Zacheus Pakage at the Free University in Amsterdam.[21]

Contemporary Papua expressions of Papuan identity *vis-à-vis* other groups, particularly Indonesians, are made in very clear terms: "we" Papuans and "you" Indonesians. The differences with Indonesians are expressed in simple, physiological, cultural and ethnic terms. Sometimes they are given a religious legitimacy:

> ...God created people to be different. Papuans are different to Javanese, and different to other people too. God gave Papua to Papuans as a home, so they could eat sago and sweet potatoes there. God gave them a penis gourd (koteka) and loincloth (cawat) for clothes. God gave them curly hair and black skin. Papuans are Papuans. They can never be turned into Javanese or Sumatrans, nor vice versa. The Javanese were given Java. Tahu (soya bean curd) and tempe (soya bean cake) is their food. Their skin is light and their hair straight.[22]

Papuan identity is an ethnic identity. In its political expression, it is an ethnic nationalism. The leading pro-independence organisation, the Presidium Dewan Papua (PDP, Papuan Presidium Council), is a Papuan ethnic organisation. At the anniversary of "independence" on 1 December 2000 in Jayapura there were a few settlers observing from the periphery, but otherwise the only Indonesians present were the police and military surrounding a couple of thousand Papuans. The author observed a number of Presidium meetings where the only Indonesians present were the wives of some senior independence leaders.

Papuans distinguish their own from Indonesian values by emphasising and linking together their Christianity, Melanesian cultural values and respect for human rights. Overtly political aspirations are often framed with reference to these three factors. When the Evangelical Christian Church (GKI, Gereja Kristen Injil) was confronted at its 2000 Synod meeting with the task of negotiating its way between the demands of its own congregations for *merdeka* (independence), on one side, and the government's offer of "special autonomy", on the other. It resolved to assess special autonomy on the basis of how, and to what extent, it would facilitate the implementation of Melanesian cultural values, the teachings of the gospels and the prevention of further human rights abuses.[23] Beyond the overtly political, the association of these values reflects the way in which Christianity has been assimilated into Papuan culture and

Melanesian cultural values retained in Papuan Christian belief and practice. The fusion of Christian messianic ideas and Papuan cargo cult traditions is an element in this accommodation.

One of the banners that adorned the old building of the Dutch-created New Guinea Council in central Jayapura, where, until 1 December 2000, the Papuan flag was flown read: "The *Bintang Kejora* flag will always be flown. Whoever pulls the flag down by force will be damned by God." The evocation of God's support for the cause of Papuan independence is expressed in numerous ways. At the ceremony to mark the anniversary of independence, a number of impassioned sermons were given and prayers said.[24] The Presidium meetings observed by the author, including ones led by the Muslim secretary-general, Thaha Al Hamid, began and ended with prayers, usually with the specific inclusion of Muslim Papuans. God's support was evoked to emphasise the inevitability of independence, but there was also implied recognition that the timing and manner of independence was in God's hands—an acknowledgement of the power relationship with Indonesia.

Since 1962 church leaders in Papua have been confronted with a significant portion of their congregations and some of their colleagues being opposed to the government of Indonesia and Papua's incorporation into Indonesia. This is argued in reference to Romans 13, which begins:

> Every person must submit to the supreme authorities. There is no authority but by act of God, and the existing authorities are instituted by him; consequently anyone who rebels against authority is resisting a divine institution, and those who so resist have themselves to thank for the punishment they will receive.[25]

Willem Rumsawir, a former head of the GKI, argued that it has been his task to monitor whether the government is performing God's command. "If the government does not fulfill their duties, then I reject them as a government. Can a government, as God's servant, kill people, like here in Papua. God's servants don't kill people."[26] Benny Giay has been critical of the churches' attitude towards the Indonesian government. The churches have continued to pray that God will bless the government, while the government has killed thousands of civilians. Giay argued that the churches should change their prayers. They should pray not only that God bless the government, but also that God transform the government and make them repent. "In fact the church here must confess its sins for supporting the government by reading Romans 13 in the past."[27]

Benny Giay has argued that senior churchmen became agents, mediators and peacemakers for the government. He cites the examples of a pastoral letter by GKI's Moderator, Rev. Rumainum, written in support of the Indonesian conduct of the Act of Free Choice in 1969 and the role of leaders of the Tabernacle Bible Church of Indonesia (GKII, Gereja Kemah Injil Indonesia, Kingmi) in negotiating settlements to the 1977 revolts in the Baliem Valley and of the Me in Paniai.[28] In personnel and institutional terms, the churches and Papuan politics are intertwined. In the last years of Suharto's New Order, it was the Catholic Bishop of Jayapura, Mgr H. F. M. Munninghof, OFM, who produced a report detailing the Indonesian security forces' abuses of human rights around the Freeport Mine in 1994-95.[29] The Catholic Church had the stature inside Papua and Indonesia as well as internationally to attract national and world attention to the nature of Indonesian governance in Papua. The report was a turning point in Papuan politics in that it established human rights, the role of the security forces, and the activities of the Freeport Mine as issues that would dominate Papuan politics and Papua's relations with Jakarta in the post-Suharto era. It also made the church leaders key political actors. Benny Giay recalled that some of the people killed by the military were ministers of his own church. "One pastor was shot dead on December 25, on Christmas Day, while he was preaching. I thought this was something we in the church should address. I thought we had to talk about this. It was a pastoral concern." However, Giay recognised that his own church, despite the murder of its own workers and ministers, had remained silent. He started to work with the Catholics and Elsham (Lembaga Studi dan Advokasi Hak Asasi Manusia, Institute for Human Rights Study and Advocacy).[30] Elsham was established and funded by a number of Papuan churches. In the immediate post-Suharto years it was the foremost human rights organisation in Papua and one in which church figures, like Benny Giay, were key leaders. In more recent years, the Catholic Church's Secretariat for Justice and Peace (SKP, Sekretariat Keadilan dan Perdamaian) has become more prominent.

Christian leaders are prominent in the pro-independence movement. The Rev. Herman Awom is a moderator of the Presidium and, until November 2000, Dr Benny Giay was a member, as was Beatrix Koibur. In the regional organisation of the Presidium Dewan Papua, the Panels, there are many church ministers. At the height of the tension leading up to "independence" day in 2000, it was the leaders of the major churches who appealed to the security authorities and the OPM alike for restraint.[31]

Likewise, the leaders of the Catholic and the Evangelical Christian churches have publicly defended the leading human rights organisation, Elsham, against harassment from the security authorities.[32]

The politics of the independence struggle is reflected in all its complexity within the churches themselves. The churches are among the most important institutions in Papuan society and as such mirror the spectrum of political opinion of the society as a whole. The independence issue and the church's attitude towards it dominated GKI's General Assembly in October 2000, both inside and outside the formal sessions.[33] It was the first such gathering held since the fall of Suharto and the first occasion during which the Assembly was able to discuss explicitly political issues. Ministers and lay members attending represented congregations from all over the province; all were members of the educated Papuan elite. They represented dispersed and often isolated communities of which they were the leaders; levels of political understanding varied considerably from the most sophisticated and experienced to the relatively straightforward and passionately held.

There were two bodies of opinion in the GKI. Many of its members were supporters of independence, actively or otherwise. The then deputy Moderator, Herman Awom, a member of the Presidium, was the best known figure. He was one of the Presidium leaders who had been imprisoned and tried for treason. In contrast, Herman Saud, then Moderator of the Synod, was a much more cautious man and very cognisant of the dangers for the church and its members of any confrontation with the Indonesian authorities. Herman Saud's views are reflective of those Papuans who have to deal with the reality of Indonesian control of the province and have responsibility for the moral and physical welfare of their fellow Papuans. For such people, the best way of doing that is to minimise political involvement. In Saud's view, it is not the role of the church to express views on the various political options confronting Papuans—independence, autonomy or federations. Rather, it is the church's role to discuss the core issues that motivate Papuans to demand separation from Indonesia. "Thus, the church will discuss human rights, injustice and untruthfulness in the revision of the facts of history. This is the responsibility of the church to discuss the roots of the problems." Herman Saud sees *merdeka* in broader terms than just the political. It is about community development and welfare. He is aware of the difficulties confronting separatist movements and argues, in part from the East Timor experience, that Papua will need the agreement of Indonesia if it is to become an independent country.[34]

Saud and Awom were re-elected to their respective positions with support that suggested that the openly pro-independence supporters and the more cautious delegates were finely balanced. The re-election of leaders with such different positions reflected a desire to maintain the unity of the church by insuring that both bodies of opinion were represented. The resolutions of the assembly show the same desire to steer a middle course. There were two key resolutions:

> The GKI's 14th Synod recognises and supports the desire for independence (*aspirasi merdeka*) that has to be reflected in real development, respect for human rights, and a national and international dialogue in the context of special autonomy.
>
> The GKI's 14th Synod strongly supports the granting of special autonomy, with conditions, not as an alternative but as part of the struggle of the Papuan people for independence through legal, formal and democratic processes.[35]

The assembly was the Papuan elite in microcosm. Delegates from all over the land of Papua reflected the strong support for independence among their own congregations. The congregations hoped that the church would clearly state its position on independence. The church leaders tempered that support, so that rather than reject the government's offer of special autonomy, the church sought to use autonomy as a phase of transition to independence.

Since the detention of the Presidium leaders at the end of 2000 and the curtailment of political activity, often it has been the church leaders who have (re)emerged as the *de facto* leaders of Papuan society. In June 2001 the leaders of Papua's churches and the Muslim community issued an appeal for the establishment of "a culture of peace and dialogue", so that Papua could become "a zone of peace". They observed that over the previous six months a pattern of violence had emerged, with one act of violence being followed by another to the extent that violence was becoming the only way by which problems are handled.[36] The atmosphere of open and vigorous debate that had developed since the fall of Suharto in 1998 had given way to the domineering presence of the security forces. The feeling that the people's aspirations were being listened to had gone and people did not know what to expect.[37]

The churches have been involved in various ways in the various conflicts between Papuans and the security forces that have led to the mass displacement of Papuans in Wasior in 2001 and the central highlands since 2004. The churches have congregations in the most remote regions of

Papua. In contrast to the more "secular" political leaders, the church leaders have an organisational and communications infrastructure that links them to village society. In Wasior it was the GKI that attempted to establish a pastoral team to look after its congregations in the area, but was prevented from doing so by the local police.[38] In the central highlands which has been a focus of conflict between the security forces and Papuans since the fall of Suharto, church leaders have been involved as victims of security force violence, negotiators, providers of humanitarian aid and chroniclers of the conflict. Most of the Papuan accounts of the conflicts outside the major urban centres and mining operations were from the churches and church-linked human rights organisations. The churches have been nearly the sole channel of communication through which news of these conflicts and displacements have reached Jayapura and the world outside Papua. In these circumstances it is not surprising that the churches and the OPM have been linked in the minds of some Indonesian government officials.[39] This suspicion is not restricted to these recent conflicts in the central highlands, but is part of the general perception shared by both church leaders and government officials. For example, Willem Rumsarwir, one of the most politically experienced of the Papuan Church leaders, observed that "The military views the pastors with suspicion because the pastors support aspirations to political independence. The military suspects that the funds that the church receives from the international community are used to support the OPM".[40]

Demographic Transformation and Papuan Nationalism

Papuan nationalism is both driven and constrained by the ethnic and religious demography of Papua. The demographic transformation in Papua had been considerable by any standards. In 1960 the "Asian" population, mainly eastern Indonesians, Javanese and Chinese, numbered just 18,600 out of an estimated population of 736,700 or 2.5 per cent.[41]

The 2000 Census was the first one under Indonesian administration to collect data on self-identified ethnic affiliation. It asked people to identify their tribe (*suku*) membership. Some 312 Papuan *suku* were identified, with 117 having fewer than 100 members. The number of non-Papuans resident in the province was 772,684 or 35 per cent, while the Papuans numbered 1,460,846 or 65 per cent.[42] In 1998 Moslems constituted 21.14 per cent of the province's population,[43] an increase from 11 per cent in 1982.[44] The settler communities are most evident in the urban areas of Papua. In the capital Jayapura, the settler communities constitute about 68 per cent of the population, as they do in Sorong and Fakfak.[45]

However, in contrast to the sharp ethnic distinction Papuans make between themselves and Indonesians, there is not always a coincidence of ethnic and religious difference. There are Papuan Muslim populations in some western coastal areas of the province around Fakfak, Sorong and the Raja Ampat Islands. These Papuan Muslim communities have strong cultural, religious and family relationships with the neighbouring Muslim communities in north and central Maluku, which long predate the establishment of a Dutch administrative presence in Papua and the beginning of Christian missionary activity. In the last years of the Dutch administration, Papuan Muslim leaders from Fakfak were involved in the first flowering of Papuan nationalism and the creation of a pan-Papuan identity. However, in Fakfak and other Papuan Muslim communities along the west coast, there were alternatives. Indonesia, as a focus of political loyalty, through the family, cultural and religious networks in Maluku, had a strong appeal. To what extent did they feel themselves Papuans? To what extent, through their religious, cultural and family networks in Maluku, did they feel Indonesian? When the open expression of Papuan nationalism briefly re-emerged after the fall of President Suharto, the politics of the Papuan Muslim communities along the west coast suggests that there is no simple correlation between religious belief and political orientation. The PDP endeavoured to be inclusive of Papuan Moslems. One of its most influential leaders and secretary general, Thaha Al Hamid, was a Papuan Muslim.[46]

Serui, on the island of Japen, was one of the early areas of conversion to Christianity. It became one of the centres of Christian education and training. Like the people from the neighbouring island of Biak, Seruiese were prominent among the first "Papuans", the mission school and Dutch-educated, who became officials, police, teachers, paramedics and politicians. From the late 1940s to the end of the Dutch regime, Christian Serui was the principal base of pro-Indonesia sentiment and the home of the most substantial and best-sustained pro-Indonesia political party. That pro-Indonesia sentiment has not been maintained in Serui since 1963 suggests that deeply rooted *alirans* have not been established.[47]

Many of the Indonesian settlers are Christians from Maluku and North Sulawesi. Christians from eastern Indonesia were a significant presence in Papua during the Dutch administration as missionaries, teachers, officials, police and military. Papuan Christians celebrate the arrival of Christianity with the landing of two German missionaries in 1855. Yet, east Indonesian missionaries greatly outnumbered foreign ones in Papua. The Ambonese and Menadonese presence in the leadership of the GKI is a testament to this history. Many of the GKI's congregations, especially in urban areas, are multi-ethnic, including the descendants of the east Indonesian missionaries and more recent settlers from Maluku and Sulawesi.

If one of the factors in the emergence of Papuan nationalism was the sense of rivalry with Indonesian officials, missionaries and teachers employed by the Dutch, as well as the discrimination and ill-treatment experienced by the first generation of Papuans, then the vastly greater numbers of Indonesian settlers since 1963 has produced a feeling much more broadly in society that Papuans are being displaced in their own land. The massive demographic change—the influx of Indonesian settlers—has facilitated the spread of an identification as being Papuan beyond the confines of a small Dutch-educated elite to most sections of a society that now calls itself Papuan.

From the earliest years of the Indonesian administration, there has been a concern amongst Papuans that it was Indonesia's intention to promote Islam. Reflecting the religious composition of Indonesia's population, a majority of the post-1963 Indonesian settlers in Papua are Moslems. This impression was bolstered by Sukarno's decision to build a large mosque in predominantly "Christian" Biak, the Papuan belief that Indonesian authorities were more supportive of Muslim than Christian organisations and activities, and Indonesian suspicion of the influence and activities of foreign missionaries.

The conversion of some Dani Christians (in the central highlands) to Islam has been a source of disquiet, reflecting broader anxieties about mass migration and suspicions about the Indonesian government's intentions to "Islamise" Papua. Some conversion to Islam in the highlands occurred as Indonesian Muslim government officials married Dani women. In the mid-1970s, a time of conflict with the Indonesian security forces in the highlands, larger-scale conversions occurred in the Dani villages of Walesi and Kimbin. In Christian circles, conversion to Islam caused resentment for two reasons. First, conversion was related to the receipt of material benefits and privileged access to government resources. Second, during the 1977 Dani struggle against the Indonesian security forces, some Christians assert that the Muslim converts assisted the Indonesians. There is also the suggestion that the Dani converts to Islam were permitted to consume pork.⁴⁸ The resentment and concern about conversion to Islam remains strong among highland Christian leaders. The Rev. Obed Komba asked, rhetorically: "Why are Papuan Christians becoming Muslim? Because Papuans have children who want to go to school. The children say, 'we have no money, Muslims have money. Lets go with them'".⁴⁹

Conclusion

Papuan society is Christian in the same sense and with some of the same complexity as Indonesia is predominantly Muslim. As Benny Giay has argued, the churches have been "liberating institutions" in Papua and Christianity is the "bearer of new hope for a society...."⁵⁰ and has introduced Papuans to the modern world. With the emergence of Papuan nationalism and identity as a rival and an alternative to Indonesian nationalism, rather than another regional identity that complements and enriches Indonesia, it was nearly inevitable that Christianity and the church leaders have been central. It is significant that the churches are the only Papuan institutions that have organisations stretching from the administrative centre of Jayapura to most remote villages. The churches' infrastructure is only equalled by that of the Indonesian administration and security forces, but the church leaders enjoy a greater level of trust among indigenous Papuans. Church leaders are also amongst the best educated members of the Papuan elite. Through the churches' respective international networks, the leaders have links into the international community, which many secular politicians do not. That church leaders have also been political leaders should not be a surprise. Several church leaders have been prominent in the leadership of the independence movement that developed after the fall of Suharto. However, the relative importance of church leaders as political leaders has been greater at times when freedom of expression and political organisation has been curtailed, such as during the New Order and since the detention of the PDP leaders at the end of 2000. Through the churches' status and international links, politically active church leaders have enjoyed an element of protection.

Despite or perhaps because of the centrality of the churches in Papuan society, since 1963 church leaders have had to manage a most difficult relationship with the Indonesian government. They have been caught between the pro-independence political sympathies of many in their congregations and the Indonesian government's offer of Special Autonomy. They have to negotiate a balance between their advocacy of

Papuan interests, values and aspirations, on one hand, and obligation to protect their flock, on the other. The churches share with Papuan society as a whole great concern about the continuing influx of "spontaneous" migrants. Indonesian settlement in Papua is one of the most sensitive issues in Papuan politics and fuels the sense of being disadvantaged and marginalised. When two of Papua's senior religious leaders addressed the provincial parliament (DPRD) in June 2005, they asked rhetorically:

Are you sending the migrants from outside because this is the only way to build our land? What is the purpose of sending the six white ships (Indonesian Royal Passenger Ship [paid for out of Special Autonomy funds] who every week bring thousands of migrants from Java, Sumatra, Kalimantan, Sulawesi and Ambon to Papua? Is this what you call building Papua?[51]

The churches have a particular concern about the conversion of Papuan Christians to Islam. The churches' support of the declaration of Manokwari, not far from where the first missionaries landed in 1855, as the *Kota Injil* (City of the Gospel), indicates the churches' support for the preservation of Papuan identity and religious beliefs.

Notes

1. C. Mano, "Nasionalisme Papua Lebih Kuat di HUT RI", *Tifa Papua* (Jayapura), 2nd week of August, 2002, p. 3.
2. *Hollandia*, "Manifest Politik" (Political Manifesto), 19 Oct. 1961; *Pengantara: Het Nieuwsblad voor Nederlands-Nieuw-Guinea* (*Pengantara*: The Newspaper for Netherlands New Guinea), 21 Oct. 1961; *Hollandia*, "Politiek Leven over Oktober 1961" (*Hollandia*: Political Developments during October 1961); Nieuw Guinea Archief, Dossier G 16725, ARA, 28 Nov. 1961.
3. J. W. van Eek, "Bestuursverslag van de Afdeeling Fak Fak over de Maand December 1961" (Administration Report of the Fakfak Residency for Dec. 1961), Resident of Fakfak, Nieuw Guinea Archief, Dossier G 16721, ARA, 14 Feb. 1962.
4. J. W. van Eek, "Politiek Overzicht van de Afdeeling Fak Fak over de Maand December 1961" (Political Report of the Fakfak Residency for Dec. 1961) Nieuw Guinea Archief, Dossier G 16721, ARA, 5 Jan. 1962.
5. J. W. van Eek, "Politiek Overzicht van de Afdeeling Fak Fak over de Maand Januari 1962" (Political Report of the Fakfak Residency for Jan. 1962), Nieuw Guinea Archief, Dossier G 16721, ARA, 8 Feb. 1962.
6. In 1940 there were 15 European officials and 72 Indonesians in the civil administration. K. W. Galis, "Geschiedenis" (History), in *Nieuw Guinea: de Ontwikkeling of Economisch Social en Cultureel Gebied, in Nederlands en Australisch*

Nieuw Guinea (New Guinea: Socio-economic and Cultural Development in Netherlands and Australian New Guinea), ed. I. W. G. Klein ('s-Gravenhage: Stadtsdrukkerij, 1953), vol. 1, p. 30.

7. *Rapport van de Commissie Nieuw-Guinea (Irian) 1950*, 3e Stuk (Report of the New Guinea [Irian] Commission 1950, vol. III) (The Hague: De Nederlands-Indonesische Unie, 1950), pp. 81, 112.
8. A 1949 report of the administration in Papua identifies an educated group of Papuans of some 1,700 in the territory—village schoolmasters, government officials, para-medics, agricultural officials, police and tradesmen—most of whom have had some secondary education. They follow political developments in Indonesia through radio and newspapers. "Report on Activities, Reactions and Aims of the Autochthonic Population of Neth. New-Guinea Concerning the Future Political Status of their Country in Connection with the Dutch-Indonesian Round-Table-Talks", *Hollandia*, Sept. 1949.
9. "Papoea Elite en Politieke Partijen" (Papuan Elite and Political Parties), Rapport van de Wetenschappelijk Ambtenaar G. W. Grootenhuis in NNG, Ministerie van Kolonien, ARA, Dossier 11575, 1961, Deel I, pp. 16, 106.
10. "Nieuw Guinea Raad, Handelingen Eerst Buitengewone Zitting" (New Guinea Council, Minutes of the First Extraordinary Sitting), 30 Oct. 1961, p. 33.
11. "Vraaggesprek met Kaisiepo and Jouwe" (Interview with Kaisiepo and Jouwe), Kabinet van de Gouverneur van Nederlands Nieuw Guinea, Dossier 35, ARA, 13 Oct. 1961.
12. *Tokoh*, "Michael Menufandu, Senior Advisor Masalah Otonomi Daerah untuk Irian Jaya", Denpasar, 20–26 Dec. 1999, p. 26.
13. *Papua Post*, "Papuanisasi Jurus Jitu dan Sederhana", Jayapura, 25 Nov. 2000.
14. D. Bleskadit, "'Merdeka' Menurut Orang Papua", *Tifa Papua*, 2nd week of Aug. 2002, p. 3.
15. The author attended the celebrations in Jayapura. Papua has the highest level of HIV/AIDS infections in Indonesia.
16. "Papua Butuh Pejabat dan Birokrat yang Takut Tuhan: Dari Perayaan HUT 151 Injil Masuk ke Papua", *Cenderawasih Pos*, 6 Feb. 2006, <http://www.cenderawasihpos.com/Utama/h.2.html>.
17. Socratez Sofyan Yoman, Pesan-Pesan Moral dengan Tema: Hak Asasi Manusia dan Pemasalahan di Tanah Papua dalam Rangka Hari Ulang Tahun Penjinjilan di Tanah Papua Tanggal 5 Februari 2006, Jayapura, Gedung Olah Raga, email, 8 Feb. 2006.
18. B. Giay, "Church and Society: The Church Leaders of Irian Jaya in the Midst of Change and Conflict", paper presented at the Eukumindo meeting, De Tiltenburg, the Netherlands, 18–19 Apr. 1996, p. 1.
19. B. Giay, "'Towards a New Papua': When They Hear the Sacred Texts of the Church, Papuans See a Better Future", in *Memoria Passionis di Papua*, ed. T. P. A. van den Broek *et al.* (Jakarta: LSPP, 2001).

20. C. E. Farhadian, ed. *The Testimony Project PAPUA: A Collection of Personal Histories in West Papua* (Sentani: Penerbit Deiyai, 2007), p. 51.
21. *The Testimony Project PAPUA*, p. 20.
22. Ibid.
23. *Keputusan dan Ketetapan, Sidang Sinode XIV GKI di Tanah Papua, Tahun 2000* (Sorong: Panitia Sidang Sinode XIV GKI di Tanah Papua, 2000), p. 68; *Tempo Interaktif*, "Gus Dur Minta Theys Dibebaskan", 7 Dec. 2000.
24. It is important to note that a Muslim Papuan *ulama* also gave a sermon.
25. *The New English Bible: New Testament* (London: Oxford University Press, Cambridge University Press, 1961), pp. 273–4.
26. *The Testimony Project PAPUA*, p. 42.
27. *The Testimony Project PAPUA*, p. 35.
28. B. Giay, "Gereja dan Politik di Papua Barat", unpublished paper, Jayapura, Jan. 2000; Benny Giay, "Church and Society", p. 2.
29. Mgr. H. F. M. Munninghof, OFM, Violations of Human Rights in the Timika Area of Irian Jaya, Indonesia: A report by the Catholic Church of Jayapura, Aug. 1995, <http://www.hamline.edu/apakabar/basisdata/1995/08/31/0004.html>.
30. *The Testimony Project PAPUA*, pp. 29–30.
31. *Astaga.com*, "Gereja di Irja Serukan Aparat dan OPM tahan diri", 30 Nov. 2000.
32. L. L. Ladjar and H. Saud 2000, "Letter, 157/TB/00/7.2 re The Situation in Irian Jaya, Bishop Mgr. Leo Laba Ladjar OFM and Moderator, Rev. Herman Saud MTh to the Director, Indonesian National Commission for Human Rights", available at <http://www.kabar-irian.com> [accessed 16 Dec. 2000].
33. The GKI is the largest and oldest of the Protestant churches in Papua. The other major denominations are the Catholic Church and the Tabernacle Bible Church of Indonesia (GKII, Kingmi).
34. *Suara Papua*, "Sidang Sinode GKI XIV Membahas Akar Permasalahan Aspirasi M", (Sorong), 25 Oct.–1 Nov. 2000, p. 9.
35. *Keputusan dan Ketetapan, Sidang Sinode XIV GKI di Tanah Papua, Tahun 2000*, p. 101.
36. "Appeal for a Cessation of Violence in Papua", Jayapura, 14 June 2001, <http://www.kabar-irian.com>. The appeal was signed by the leaders of the Islamic Council of Indonesia (MUI), the Catholic Church and the major Protestant churches.
37. Office for Justice and Peace, "Recent Developments in Papua: Papua Congress II, 29 May–4 June 2000, and the Situation Pasca-Congress", Office for Justice and Peace, Diocese of Jayapura, Jan. 2001.
38. "West Papua: Brimob Violence Engulfs Manokwari", *Tapol: The Indonesia Human Rights Campaign Bulletin Online* 162, Aug. 2001, <http://tapol.gn.apc.org/bulletin/2001/bull162.htm>.

39. Letter, Ramli Sa'ud, Minister Counsellor, Embassy of the Republic of Indonesia, London, to the Rt Revd. R. D. Harries, Lord Bishop of Oxford, No. 47/IV/07/LON/05, 30 June 2005, available at <http://www.kabar-irian.com>. For a more detailed discussion of conflict and displacement in Papua, see Richard Chauvel, "Refuge, Displacement and Dispossession: Responses to Indonesian Rule and Conflict in Papua", in *Dynamics of Conflict and Displacement in Papua, Indonesia*, ed. Eva-Lotta Hedman, RSC Working Paper no. 42, Oxford University, Sept. 2007, <http://www.rsc.ox.ac.uk>.
40. *The Testimony Project PAPUA*, p. 43.
41. Government of the Netherlands, *Netherlands Government Annual Report to the United Nations on Netherlands New Guinea* (The Hague: Government Publishing House), pp. 6–7.
42. *Tifa Papua*, 3rd week of May, 2002, p. 5.
43. *Irian Jaya dalam Angka 1998* (Jayapura: BPS Propinsi Irian Jaya, 1998), p. 193.
44. J. R. Djopari, *Pemberontakan Organisasi Papua Merdeka* (Jakarta: Gramedia, 1993), p. 81.
45. *Tifa Papua*, 3rd week of May, 2002, p. 5.
46. For a more detailed discussion of the history and politics of Fakfak, see R. Chauvel, *Constructing Papuan Nationalism: History, Ethnicity and Adaptation*, Policy Studies no. 14 (Washington, D. C.: East-West Center, 2005), p. 63.
47. "Papoea Elite en Politieke Partijen", Part II, see n. 9 above.
48. C. E. Farhadian, *Christianity, Islam, and Nationalism in Indonesia* (New York: Routledge, 2005), pp. 81–4.
49. *The Testimony Project PAPUA*, p. 54.
50. Giay, "Towards a New Papua".
51. Rev. Herman Saud and Rev. Socratez Sofyan Yoman, "Joint Statement on Regional Elections, Special Autonomy and the MRP (Papua People's Assembly)", at DPRD, Jayapura, 9 June 2005, available at <http://www.westpapua.ca/?q=en/node/398>.

CHAPTER 11

Indonesian *Adat* Communities: Promises and Challenges of Democracy and Globalisation

Leena Avonius

While doing fieldwork in North Lombok, I spent an entire morning in April 2000 waiting in a Mataram-based non-governmental organisation's office for a village teacher. We were to make a trip to Bali where a meeting of Aliansi Masyarakat Adat Nusantara (AMAN, the Alliance of the Indigenous Peoples of the Indonesian Archipelago), was to take place. The village teacher—a man in his forties who also was the chairman of the *adat* (customary law) council in his village—had never been to Bali before and was somewhat nervous about the trip. After some delays we finally boarded a ferry that would take us from Lembar to Padangbai. An old and sluggish ferry took us to our destination; we passed the time watching *dangdut* music videos.[1] When we finally arrived in Padangbai the sun was already setting. We still had a long way ahead of us, all the way up the mountains to Kintamani where the meeting was to be held at a remote hotel by Lake Batur, a beautiful crater lake. Since there was no public transport running at that hour, we had to find a car and a driver to take us to Kintamani. As it was already late the drivers who usually only took tourists to nearby destinations were not eager to bargain with us, but finally two young men agreed to take us there.

Put simply—the trip that followed was scary: our driver was apparently inexperienced in the art of driving along those curving, narrow hill-roads, and the thickening fog and occasional rain made it even worse. After several hours of frightened shrieks and sighs of relief we arrived in Kintamani, only to find out that the hotel was still several kilometres away, and our driver refused to take us there. So, there we were, abandoned after dark in a village with no accommodation. Luckily, we met a man who knew a man with a car who was willing to take us to Lake Batur. So down we went in the pitch-dark night, not knowing exactly where we were headed but slightly more hopeful about reaching our destination. And great was our relief when we finally arrived. The hotel was teeming with activity as young activists who had come to take part in the meeting were rushing in and out of the rooms greeting each other. We checked in, got our rooms and enjoyed a late dinner. After a good night's sleep and a rich Indonesian breakfast in a restaurant overlooking the magnificent Lake Batur, we were ready to start the three-day discussions on the position of *adat* and indigenous peoples in contemporary Indonesia.

My recollection of this trip symbolises, in some respects, the transformation many Indonesian villagers are undergoing in the process of moving from Suharto's New Order Indonesia to the regionalism of the post-Suharto era that has become known as Reformasi. Since the late 1990s, villagers in Lombok and elsewhere in Indonesia have been willing to take such a journey towards a still unknown future—symbolised by a trip from Lombok to the mountains of Bali—encouraged by the promises of better opportunities under regionalism. The importance of being the master of one's own destiny, even though the journey may not always be a pleasant one, cannot be exaggerated in a situation where most Indonesians have been born and raised under a strict state-controlled system that discouraged any individual ambitions and initiatives. Such journeys were unnecessary under the New Order: the state provided the villages with everything that it considered essential and longing for anything extra or different was not encouraged.

But there is another aspect to the transformation. The village teacher had to count on me—a foreign, young female anthropologist—to fund and organise the trip to Kintamani. I am not saying that he would not have been able to get there by himself, but that my presence made the trip faster, as hired cars with drivers were beyond the financial means available to most Lombok villagers during that time. My presence made the journey easier. The transformation of villages from recipients of development programs to communities actively seeking funding and making decisions about their own future can be made faster with access to external funding, often foreign funding, mostly from non-governmental and international organisations. It needs to be asked, however, what limits outside funding place on the agency of Indonesian villages under regionalism.

At the meeting, the village teacher, who, through his profession as a civil servant had been accustomed to the modernisation schemes promoted by the New Order government, had to confront another feature of the Western world—namely the world of NGOs, international activism and globalised discussions on the rights of indigenous peoples. To be sure, I was the only foreigner at the meeting and my Western/foreign presence was even criticised by some participants. Yet, the conventions of working and also the language used at the meeting were much closer to those of Western workshops or business meetings than to any 'indigenous Indonesian' gatherings. As such, they seemed unfamiliar to many representatives of *masyarakat adat* (adat communities or indigenous peoples). This issue was certainly raised during the meeting, participants claiming repeatedly that they had difficulties understanding the half-English-half-Indonesian spoken by NGO activists (most of whom were from Jakarta). It is these problems of the reorganisation of the relations between Indonesia's national centre and the regions through such organisations as AMAN that I wish to consider here below. My focus in this chapter is on the emergence and early years of the indigenous peoples' movement in Indonesia.

From Isolated Communities to Global Rights-Based Network

While the rise of *masyarakat adat* after the fall of Suharto regime in 1998 is essentially related to the domestic processes of decentralisation in Indonesia, it is also well connected with the indigenous peoples' movement elsewhere in the world. Through the national indigenous peoples' organisation, AMAN, and its network with domestic and international NGOs, Indonesian adat communities are now linked to such international forums as the International Working Group on Indigenous Affairs (IWGIA), the Asian Indigenous Peoples Pact (AIPP) and the United Nations Working Group on Indigenous Populations (UNWGIP). Mainly through NGO networks, Indonesian indigenous groups have become part of a global struggle for the recognition of indigenous peoples' rights that has gained momentum within the last two decades. The global indigenous peoples' movement has been particularly empowered by the developments in Latin American countries where indigenous groups have united forces with environmental activists since the 1980s.

However, as Tania Li[2] has pointed out, the rise of the concept of *masyarakat adat* in Indonesian public discourse in the Reformasi era cannot simply be seen as a repetition of the emergence of the indigenous peoples' movement in Latin America. It would be unwise to assume that there has merely been a shift of attention from one geographic region to another among the institutions and organisations that busy themselves with indigenous affairs. Rather, the issues and concerns over democratisation and regional autonomy that have been major topics for the Indonesian post-Suharto era are similar to the demands made in Latin American countries in the 1980s and other regions where indigenous peoples' rights have become important. Thus, when exploring why the issue of *masyarakat adat* emerged so powerfully in Indonesian public discourse in 1999, it is equally important to look for similarities and differences the Indonesian case has in relation to developments elsewhere.

AMAN was established in May 1999 at the first conference of Indonesian indigenous peoples in Jakarta. The conference was organised by thirteen NGOs which had paid attention to the environmental problems and the human rights issues of isolated communities (*masyarakat terasing*) in Suharto's New Order Indonesia since the early 1990s.[3] But it was only one year after the fall of Suharto's regime that the organisations considered the atmosphere liberal enough to introduce indigenity into public debate. Until then, Indonesia's official position was that the concept "indigenous peoples" would be meaningless as the whole nation was predominantly indigenous.[4] The NGOs behind the conference wanted to argue otherwise. They contacted some 200 representatives from the Indonesian regions whom they saw as indigenous, inviting them as well as some civil society activists from national and international NGOs to join together and discuss the problems that indigenous peoples have in Indonesia and the ambitions and wishes these communities might have for the future. The conference in Jakarta was held around the time when president Habibie's interim government signed and published the Law on Regional Autonomy (22/1999) that came into force at the beginning of 2001. This law, and its successor law (34/2004), have become major reference points for the rights of *masyarakat adat* in Indonesia.

Since 1999, AMAN has grown rapidly and its network covers the whole archipelago, from Sumatra to West Papua. A comparison between the data on organisations linked to AMAN in 2002 and 2007 shows that, in addition to increasing numbers, some organisations have either dropped out or changed names, indicating the ongoing dynamics of a movement in formation. The total number of organisations involved in AMAN has more than tripled in five years. In its third national congress AMAN passed its statutes and formalised a hierarchical structure that divides the organisations according to how wide an area they cover: *pusat* refers to the national-level umbrella organisation; *wilayah* to organisations that cover at least three *kabupaten* (administrative districts), towns or islands; and *daerah* to organisations that cover one *kabupaten*. Although organisations are not AMAN's members, the adat communities these organisations represent are. AMAN states that its membership consists of 776 adat communities and that some 50 to 70 million Indonesians should be included in the category of *masyarakat adat*, which is between one-quarter and one-third of the whole Indonesian population.[5] AMAN does not say how this estimate is made, but, as Li[6] has noted, AMAN's definition of indigenous people is very broad and access to the organisation is open to most who wish to enter.

AMAN and its member organisations receive funding from Indonesian and international donors.[7] Despite all their efforts, AMAN and its regional member organisations have stated that they have had difficulties in becoming economically self-supporting, a fact that makes them dependent on the policies of donor organisations and international aid trends. A national adat congress has now been organised three times: 1999 in Jakarta, 2003 in Lombok and 2007 in West Kalimantan. If the first congress managed to attract some 200 participants, their number had risen to 1,000 by the second congress in Lombok. AMAN's Jakarta office also runs working meetings with regional representatives and supporting NGOs, during which information on regional activities is exchanged and new strategies are developed. Thus, AMAN's major activities take place in the regional organisations that in turn consist of adat communities, the size of which varies from village communities to entire ethnic groups.[8] Although NGOs do not hold an official position in AMAN, their influence is apparent through funding and is visible in the management of the organisation, as well as in its agenda. It is through NGOs that AMAN is linked to the global indigenous peoples' movement. It is also noteworthy that many of the NGOs working closely with AMAN are environmental organisations, which may influence the issues the organisation focuses on in its work.[9]

Through its organisational structures AMAN actually appears extremely "Indonesian": it has internalised the country's regional administrative divisions and it acknowledges the existence of a state bureaucracy. Despite the radical statement, "if the state will not recognise *masyarakat adat* then the *masyarakat adat* will not recognise the state", which was uttered during AMAN's founding conference, the movement has not attacked the foundations of the nation-state; instead, it advocates reforms strictly within the given framework of Indonesia, also recognising Pancasila, the Indonesian state ideology, as a part of its organisational basis in the statutes. Similarly to the indigenous peoples' movement globally, the aim is not to advocate the cause of separate statehood, but rather that of more autonomy.[10] AMAN's acceptance of the Indonesian nation-state can, for example, be seen in the organisation's willingness to collaborate with state officials rather than challenge their authority. This, however, varies from region to region, as some of AMAN's regional organisations have employed oppositional strategies to advance their claims for the recognition of adat.[11]

When AMAN prepares suggestions for legislators, it does not question the Indonesian legal system or the position of adat law within it. One should also point out here that Indonesian law actually acknowledges legal pluralism, and through that, the position of local adat laws in the legal system. Thus, AMAN does not need to struggle in order to introduce adat law to Indonesian national law. However, throughout Indonesia's first 50 years of independence, and particularly during Suharto's New Order era, adat laws were in practice ignored as dying traditions, and court cases were solved on the basis of national law instead of adat law, and it is this disregard for adat that adat organisations wish to change.[12] The situation has indeed changed in the post-Suharto era, and adat has again received more recognition as a legal source, though it is often still sidelined in legal practice and considered most suitable for the purposes of local dispute settlement.[13]

Initially AMAN defined *masyarakat adat* as "a group of people located in a geographically specific place that has become its property as an inheritance from its ancestors. The group has its own normative system, ideology, economy, political system, culture and social system."[14] As has been pointed out by Greg Acciaioli, the definition has been revised since this early form and has received, for example, an addition that asserts sovereignty over land and natural resources.[15] Thus, in the current statutes that were accepted in the third national congress, *masyarakat adat* is defined as a

> population group that lives on the basis of their hereditary ancestral origins in a specific geographical region; that possesses value system, society and culture of their own; that possesses sovereignty over their land and natural resources; and that orders and manages their social life through customary law and institutions.[16]

AMAN's definition is similar to international definitions of indigenous peoples, and emphasises socio-economic, legal and political conditions as distinctive characteristics. A clear difference between the Indonesian and international definition, for example, the one by the International Labour Organisation (ILO),[17] is that the Indonesian definition does not make any reference to colonialism. This is characteristic of many other Asian indigenous peoples' movements, such as those of tribal peoples in India, and due to the fact that in Asia the colonial rulers did not stay in the region after the countries gained independence. The ethnic and religious complexity of most Asian societies further complicates efforts to provide a good global definition for indigenous peoples.

A solution that has been offered to the problem of definition, both internationally and within AMAN, has been to stress the self-identification of the groups of people as indigenous. The United Nations Declaration on the Rights of Indigenous Peoples, which was adopted with an overwhelming majority by the UN General Assembly in September 2007 after two decades had been spent on drafting it, stresses that it is the right of indigenous communities to decide over their identity and membership.[18] While self-identification is without a doubt a better option than such derogatory labels attached to people as *masyarakat terasing*, it still does not solve the problems multicultural communities encounter in everyday life. Making indigenity the main criteria and allocating national and international agencies' funding, educational opportunities, and positions of power to the groups of people who identify themselves as *masyarakat adat* in their region may lead to exclusion of other groups who are possibly just as needy but cannot identify with the existing demarcation. Despite AMAN's openness to new groups, the introduction of yet another distinction to the communities may also lead to new and strengthened boundaries at the local level.[19] For example, in North Lombok, *masyarakat adat* is nowadays identified with Wetu Telu, a group from the ethnically Sasak population which previously followed, and to some extent still follows, a syncretic form of Islam that combines Islamic dogma with ancestral beliefs and local traditions. As *masyarakat adat* has come to refer to Islamic Sasak culture, North Lombok's Buddhist Sasaks, who are similarly indigenous to the region, have had difficulties gaining access to adat projects in the villages and the whole region.

What has AMAN accomplished during its first decade of existence? It has understandably busied itself with building its network and institutional structures. AMAN's regional organisations have been established, often with the help of local NGOs that have facilitated the meetings and offered both financial and professional support for the new organisations. AMAN has also widened its association with international institutions by joining IWGIA and AIPP, and sending representatives to international meetings such as the World Social Forum. The issues that were taken up during the first AMAN congress as its future fields of interest were the following: the right of *masyarakat adat* to land and communal landownership; the right to use natural resources and the problems caused by their exploitation; the social and cultural rights of *masyarakat adat*; the particular problems caused by mining, forest plantations, industrial fishing and the tourist industry; the issues concerning the then forthcoming regional autonomy; and the particular problems of indigenous women.[20] In the second national congress, the importance of accelerating law enforcement that would equate indigenous peoples' rights with human rights, democratisation and natural resources conservation were stressed, as well as the need to build up strong alliances with other "pro-democracy and progressive reform organisations at the national and the international level".[21] In practice, much work has focused on land reform and the territorial rights of adat communities, which is not surprising considering the complexities of land laws and practices and the widespread exploitation of land and natural resources by the state and state-linked conglomerates during the Suharto era.[22] Efforts to make claims on forest land by declaring it to be *tanah adat*, communally owned adat land, have received a variety of reactions from regional authorities. To cite two examples, indigenous groups in Central Sulawesi have repeatedly clashed, sometimes violently, with state authorities over forest use in and around the Lore Lindu National Park. In contrast to this, in North Lombok a village managed to chase away a commercial logging company from their alleged adat land.[23]

Villages and North Lombok's Regional Aspiration

The North Lombok village referred to above is the same one where our village teacher comes from. Why is it that he and his fellow villagers, and more generally people in North Lombok, became so enthusiastic about the indigenous peoples' movement in the late 1990s? I think that the answer is not too difficult to find—the reasons lie to a large extent in poverty and previously suffered injustices that carry the signs of cultural and religious discrimination.[24] To take poverty first: the province of West Nusa Tenggara is among the poorest in Indonesia. There are no remarkable natural resources and there is no manufacturing industry with the exception of some small-scale handicraft production. The two sources of livelihood in Lombok are agriculture and tourism. Yet, the former does not produce enough food for the people of Lombok and the latter provides jobs only for the fortunate few. Lombok's climate is much drier than in the western parts of the archipelago and droughts appear almost every year. Famines occur from time to time, and according to health organisations working on the island, the children of Lombok are malnourished. Despite the official New Order statistics that showed otherwise, the educational level is very low and the illiteracy rate is high, particularly among women; the age of marriage is the lowest in the whole country;[25] and the infant mortality rate is high. One could go on with this list for much longer, but the diagnosis would be the same: people in Lombok are suffering from the typical effects of poverty. The hardships of villagers have been further increased by the New Order officials and businessmen who have taken scarce land for building luxury tourist resorts, golf courses, or for establishing their own farming enterprises.

Lombok villagers have suffered culturally from unjust rulers, the latest of which was Suharto's New Order. In its ruthless project of unifying the country's various cultures into one—an Indonesian one—the New Order showed little respect for local social systems or customs. Many Lombok villages that adhered to Wetu Telu, a localised form of Islam, were forced to leave their old social and belief systems behind and to show their adherence to what was considered orthodox Islam. During the New Order, Wetu Telu customs were rejected, even forbidden, by the state. In the late 1960s and early 1970s, a person who was found organising a Wetu Telu ritual, for example a purification ritual that usually included animal sacrifice and ancestral worship, could be caught by the police and publicly beaten up as a punishment. Being Wetu Telu was synonymous with being backward, possibly communist and potentially subversive. In 1968, when the New Order state forced all Indonesians to convert into one of the five officially recognised world religions, many Wetu Telu villages were attacked by the military and so-called *Waktu Lima Muslims*,[26] and the ancestral shrines and other symbols of Wetu Telu were destroyed. Later on, the open violence stopped, but during the New Order's developmentalist and modernising moves in the 1980s, North Lombok's Wetu Telu, and particularly its cultural centre Bayan, was labelled as *masyarakat terasing*, that is, an isolated community. Claims over Bayan's socio-economic backwardness were awkward as its social development was in no way different from that of the rest of Lombok. It seems that the condemnation had more to do with continuing Wetu Telu customs in the region than with the level of socio-economic development, which was the announced criterion for the *masyarakat terasing* concept.[27] Bayan protested the labelling successfully, but Wetu Telu was generally considered and talked about as non-modern and especially religiously dubious throughout the New Order period.

Keeping this historical background in mind, it is not too surprising that when it was suggested that under Reformasi it might finally be possible to be proudly *orang daya gunung*, North Lombokese again, many listened. Importantly, the initiative came from local persons, rather than from an outside organisation, as people had grown rather suspicious of efforts by outsiders to "develop" the region. Injustices suffered under the New Order were discussed and there was a common understanding that North Lombok villages had been in a disadvantaged position in relation to other parts of the island. The last years of the New Order had also brought a logging company to the nearby mountains, and the effects of erosion had started to show in the villages that lost their rice crops due to flooding. In May 1999, this led to a protest, during which the logging company's machines were burnt and its workers chased away from the village land, and perhaps surprisingly even for the protesters, the company also stayed away.[28] The locals were very empowered to see that what they thought and how they acted did matter.

Through NGO connections a number of North Lombok villagers were given the opportunity to take part in the first indigenous peoples' conference in Jakarta in 1999. Their new enthusiastic ideas about the indigenous cause were welcomed by others back home. North Lombok became one of the regions most eager to explore the possibilities of adat for building new administrative structures under the regional autonomy law. Its 25 villages formed an adat organisation called Perekat Ombara that is a member organisation of AMAN. Perekat Ombara unites the northern Lombok villages, most of which are usually labelled in Lombok as Wetu Telu. Under Perekat Ombara, the villages drew a development plan for North Lombok that would benefit local people. With the help of a Mataram-based NGO, strengths and weaknesses, as well as the hopes and fears of villagers, were summed up and discussed, and possible solutions were sought for their problems.

The new adat organisation also encountered some difficulties during the first months of its existence. Villages differed in their skills and capacity to participate in the work of Perekat Ombara, and generally speaking, those closest to the organisation's office in the northwestern village of Tanjung were most active while the remotest villages in the east were less often present at meetings. Lacking telephone lines, there was limited communication between the villages, and even if the people in remote villages did receive information about meetings and other activities, they did not necessarily have the money for transportation costs. At the same time, the most active villages also had the best access to Mataram, both to the regional government and to NGOs there.

The vital support of NGOs in establishing organisations promoting the rights of adat communities has been pointed out by both Greg Acciaioli in his study on AMAN-related activities in Central Sulawesi and by Minako Sakai in South Sumatra.[29] NGOs have the know-how and access to information that Indonesian villages, especially the ones far away from urban or regional centres, do not possess. Through the AMAN network, North Lombok villages were able to meet adat communities from other parts of Indonesia, as well as NGOs working in various fields: land rights and mapping, environmental protection and biodiversity, legal consultation, gender issues, organisational skills and alternative education, to name a few. The lack of information as a serious hindrance to grassroots projects was often brought up in North Lombok by villagers themselves; AMAN's network opened up the villagers' access to necessary information.

However, one should not assume that the adat network became accessible to all people in North Lombok. The people active in the villages and in Perekat Ombara were mostly relatively well-educated young men. As I have mentioned above, not everyone in the region felt indigenous in the same sense. And there were many who felt that the indigenous label did not match their idea about themselves or North Lombok as a region at all. Some of these people—those previously referred to as Waktu Lima—considered themselves modernist Muslims and felt uncomfortable with the resurgence of traditional customs. The enthusiastic promotion of adat even triggered fears of a possible renewal of the old conflict between Waktu Lima and Wetu Telu Muslims. Recognising this, Perekat Ombara tended to play down the religious aspects of Wetu Telu, instead presenting it as local custom. On the other hand, they also considered it necessary to stress even more North Lombok's adherence to Islam.

Despite the problems in communication and possible inequalities between villages, Perekat Ombara has received widespread support in North Lombok. Without a doubt, the help it has offered to draw up a local development plan that is based on villagers' own judgement about their situation, as well as the spirit of collaboration it has managed to create among North Lombok villages, have been important factors behind this support. Another factor has more to do with the political aspects of regionalism. Perekat Ombara has a clear political goal for the future: their aim is the establishment of the *kabupaten* (district) of North Lombok. It wishes to separate its 25 villages from the West Lombok district that currently has its administrative centre in Mataram. The idea of a *kabupaten* of North Lombok has been around at least since the 1980s, but never before has it appeared as a realistic possibility. The New Order government, which considered North Lombok's Wetu Telu villages as possibly subversive and surely underdeveloped, would not hear about the formation of such an administrative unit. North Lombok has felt marginalised within the West Lombok district, which is led by people in or close to Mataram. During Perekat Ombara's public meetings, attended by hundreds of North Lombok village men and also guests from Mataram, including state officials and representatives of Lombok's intelligentsia, it has often been stressed that North Lombok is culturally different from the rest of the island. Thus, both its geographic location, which puts North Lombok at a disadvantage, and its cultural distinctiveness, which has been interpreted in terms of indigenousness, have been used as arguments for widening regional autonomy. Since 2000, the leading members of Perekat Ombara have lobbied for the idea of a new *kabupaten* among provincial political leaders. Though this has produced some positive and promising statements about the initiative, it remains to be seen whether promises will be fulfilled.

Demands for Democracy through Indigenity

The aspirations heard in the discussions and observable in the activities of Perekat Ombara during its first year of existence illustrate well the great optimism that characterised the indigenous peoples' movement and early Reformasi in general. The fall of the Suharto regime opened up opportunities few had even dreamt of before, and the goals and aims that were brought up seemed endless. One could present the initial aims of North Lombok's adat organisation as roughly belonging to four types: juridical, cultural, political and economic. As one of its main functions, Perekat Ombara announced it would map out and collect information and documents over local adat, particularly adat law. Some efforts were made to write down adat law in North Lombok villages, though the work has been difficult due to a lack of both financial and human resources. I will not discuss the problems of the position of adat law here, suffice to say that while the juridical aims expressed by some individuals within Perekat Ombara were quite extreme—including the bypassing of national law in an autonomous North Lombok in future—the probability that these aims would one day be reached was never very high. There is a lack of unanimity concerning these juridical aims in North Lombok, and vast changes in the Indonesian legal system would be needed to enable the resurgence of local adat courts.[30] The formation of local civil security troops under the name of adat in various North Lombok villages since 2000 could also be mentioned here, as they were supposed to partly function as a police force in the villages. The legal position of these adat guards (*lang-lang jagat adat*) remains unclear, and it seems that they were a reaction to the outbursts of collective violence in the region and more generally to the insecurity people felt during the transitional period after the fall of New Order.[31]

Perekat Ombara's cultural aims are various, and here "culture" should be taken in its broad anthropological sense and not limited to artistic adat performances as in the New Order.[32] To be sure, the revitalisation of adat rituals, the gamelan and traditional dances have been part of the adat-related activities in North Lombok during recent years, and have been welcomed enthusiastically by most villagers in the region. But in addition to these, the need to advance the teaching of local culture (*kearifan lokal*) in primary schools has been stressed in order to uphold and strengthen local customs and the Sasak language among future generations. Returning to local customs is considered to have moral value and to function as a safeguard against the demoralising effects of modern culture, often identified with a "Western" lifestyle. Remarkably, even Arab culture has also been mentioned as potentially corrosive to local culture, even though such remarks are always followed with assurance that local adat is in no sense contradictory to the Qur'an. Some of Perekat Ombara's cultural conservation work resembles the activities of Majelis Adat Sasak, which is best characterised as the Lombok representative of *pembina adat*, a semi-governmental adat body that was established in Indonesian provinces in the late New Order period.[33] One example of the latter's conservation efforts is the collecting of old palm-leaf manuscripts for the Museum of West Nusa Tenggara Province. Some of the Lombok palm-leaf manuscripts, which are usually written in Old Javanese (*jawa kuno*), have also been translated into Sasak and Indonesian, and thus made accessible to a wider audience.

A more visible part of Perekat Ombara's work in its early months was the above-mentioned efforts to advance regional development, and economic as well as political collaboration amongst the northern villages. The Perekat Ombara meetings that I personally observed in 1999–2000 focused primarily on visualising the possible paths which decentralisation could take in North Lombok. The authoritarian rule of the New Order, under which all decisions concerning the village were made outside of it, at higher administrative levels and without any consultation with the villagers, was severely criticised. Examples of the abuses by the New Order government and companies, particularly in the tourism and forest industries, were frequently brought up in the discussions. On the other hand, the laws on regional autonomy were seen as an opportunity for establishing a new kind of local government which would be more democratic and transparent (*demokratis dan transparan*). While the establishment of the district of North Lombok was seen as an ideal form of self-determination for the region, development plans acknowledge the current situation as being the framework for change.

It is the demand for more democracy that seems to lie at the core of the adat movement both in North Lombok and nationally. Demands were made in Perekat Ombara meetings that the decisions over the use of local natural resources should be exclusively in the hands of local people. The concept of *tanah adat*, adat land, was used in order to oust commercial enterprises from forest land that is seen to rightfully belong to the village community. One plan was to re-establish in North Lombok a system of adat functionaries called *pemangku* to secure local supervision of forest use, including logging, using forests as garden land, as well as for recreation and tourism. In addition to this, there were plans to establish forest cooperatives. Cooperatives did not reflect any former adat institution, but were a contemporary way to guarantee a more equitable use of land. A second demand concerned the issue of *putra daerah*, the sons of the soil: Perekat Ombara proposed that officials at all administrative levels should be chosen among locals, instead of importing state officials from other islands or other regions in Lombok. Local officials were considered to be more receptive to local needs and aspirations, and thus seen as being more democratic.[34] A further plan was to replace the village councils (LMD, Lembaga Musyawarah Desa) by adat councils, at least in some North Lombok villages, as the village administrative structures created under the New Order were considered wholly corrupt and undemocratic. For example, criticism was directed at the position of village chief, even though under the New Order this was the only position in the local government that was filled through public election: New Order village chiefs were considered to have been answerable to higher administrative levels rather than to their own villagers. During the preparatory period before the Law on Regional Autonomy (22/1999) came into force in 2001, various models on how to secure the establishment of democratic village government in the future were discussed in North Lombok villages.

The main point of these discussions and plans was how best to fulfill the promise of regional autonomy by placing power in the hands of local people in matters that concerned them and their immediate environment. The acknowledged problem was the lack of democracy and the announced aim was to attain more democracy. Adat was seen as a proper tool for reaching this goal, but it was just one part of the repertoire in use. The North Lombokese were eager to learn about models that had been used elsewhere for similar purposes. A return to adat is not the goal per se; finding the best way to create a functioning system of regional autonomy for North Lombok is.

Indigenous Peoples' Movement and Democracy

The emergence of the indigenous peoples' movement in the form of adat organisations in post-New Order Indonesia should be seen as part and parcel of a turn towards building a more open and democratic country, in which the country's socio cultural pluralism should more carefully be taken into consideration. This is not a straightforward process, and certainly not an unproblematic one. AMAN and the regional adat organisations that are part of its network are in this respect in a very similar position to indigenous peoples in other countries. Benedict Kingsbury, among others, has remarked that the discourse on the rights of indigenous peoples has gradually moved away from the debates on decolonisation with which it was closely linked in the period just after World War II. Unlike then, most indigenous groups today do not see full independence as an ultimate goal, but rather a functioning form of self-determination within the existing states. Kingsbury calls this tendency a "relational approach" to the indigenous cause, and maintains that it is a question of continuous negotiations between groups of people that view themselves as indigenous and state bureaucracies.[35] But these negotiations always inevitably affect and are influenced by the relations between indigenous peoples and other population groups.

Darren Zook has described at least three kinds of unsolved problems in the international system that recognises indigenous peoples' rights, all of which are also relevant in the case of Lombok discussed in this chapter.[36] Demands for self-determination by some groups based on their claim to an indigenous identity inevitably influences the rights of other people inhabiting the same areas, and the issue of priorness needs to be solved: if some are indigenous to a region, then others must be less so. Will their rights become limited if the rights of one group are formally recognised? Second, protecting a way of life may lead to the imposed ossification of a way of life, and persons belonging to the indigenous groups may be forced to follow their "indigenous lifestyle" which can curtail their ability to change and adopt new ideas. In Lombok, this came up in discussions during which inhabitants of villages that had retained traditional houses were pondering whether they could attach such signs of "modernity" as satellite dishes or concrete floors to their houses without losing their indigenous lifestyle in the eyes of outsiders. Zook's final point is that the current system tends to ignore the injustices that may be inherent in the cultures considered indigenous. The rights of individuals, or minority groups within an indigenous group should also be guaranteed. In North Lombok, the emergence of an indigenous peoples' movement that became identified as Sasak and Islamic soon invited scepticism not only from the region's ethnic and religious minorities, but also from modernist Muslim Sasak, as well as from women (who were often excluded from the indigenous meetings). Unless these problems are properly addressed and satisfactorily resolved, the indigenous peoples' movement's claims to building democracy will become questionable.

The emergence of the indigenous peoples' movement in Indonesia also illustrates aspects of globalisation and the related crisis of the nation-state. Constant references are made in AMAN statements to global in addition to national structures of inequality that weaken the position of adat communities in Indonesia. As Li has pointed out

> AMAN's demands, far from being narrow or sectarian, continually blur the boundaries between *rakyat* (people) and *masyarakat adat* to pose a fundamental challenge to what the state has become and argue for a comprehensive re-evaluation of the meaning of citizenship.[37]

I would add to this that AMAN also continuously blurs the national boundaries by equating the situation of Indonesian adat communities with the position of indigenous peoples in other countries. The indigenous peoples' movement in Indonesia and globally is part of a growing and strengthening group of NGOs that have brought into question the ability of current nation-states to provide services to all citizens. Indigenous people see that, even when they form the original population of certain territories, their rights and needs have not been taken into account by states. As elsewhere, in Indonesia the demands for indigenous rights have been demands for democratisation. Socio-economic inequality has not decreased despite decades of development programmes. In many of these countries, NGOs have taken over some of the duties of the inefficient state, and they have also responded to needs that have been ignored by the state. The globalisation of the world's economic structures has made the issues concerning indigenous groups extend beyond national boundaries; what is more, it has made NGOs and specific population groups—namely indigenous peoples—to push for the renegotiation of the roles of nation-states, the global market and the globalising civil society.

Notes

1. *Dangdut* is a form of Indonesian popular music with a strong Indian influence.
2. T. M. Li, "Masyarakat Adat, Difference and the Limits of Recognition in Indonesia's Forest Zone", *Modern Asian Studies* 35, 3 (2001): 649–50.
3. The relation between the concepts of *masyarakat terasing* and *masyarakat adat* is a complicated one, and I will not go into details here. *Masyarakat terasing* is a developmentalist label attached to certain population groups by the New Order government, while *masyarakat adat* has been introduced to the public discourse by *adat* organisations to challenge that label. For the term *masyarakat terasing*, see G. Persoon, "Isolated Groups or Indigenous Peoples: Indonesia

and the International Discourse", *Bijdragen tot de Taal-, Land- en Volkenkunde* 154, 2 (1998): 281–304. For *masyarakat adat*, see Li, "Masyarakat Adat"; G. Acciaioli, "Grounds of Conflict, Idioms of Harmony: Custom, Religion, and Nationalism in Violence Avoidance at the Lindu Plain, Central Sulawesi", *Indonesia* 72 (2001): 1–32; M. Sakai, "Regional Responses to Resurgence of Adat Movements in Indonesia", in *Beyond Jakarta: Regional Autonomy and Local Societies in Indonesia*, ed. Minako Sakai (Adelaide: Crawford House, 2002), pp. 245–69; and L. Avonius, "Reforming Adat: Indonesian Indigenous People in the era of Reformasi", *Asia Pacific Journal of Anthropology* 4, 1 (2003): 93–111.
4. Persoon, "Isolated Groups or Indigenous Peoples", p. 281.
5. Information from AMAN website, <http://aman.or.id/> [accessed 25 Jan. 2008].
6. Li, "Masyarakat Adat", p. 649.
7. AMAN's donors so far have included at least: Canadian International Cooperation Agency (CIDA), Court Aid, European Union, Ford Foundation, Japan International Cooperation Agency (JICA), NRM, Humanistisch Instituut voor Ontwikkelingssamenwerking (HIVOS, Humanist Institute for Cooperation with Developing Countries), Oxfam-UK and Oxfam Netherlands (NOVIB), United Kingdom Department for International Development (DFID), UNDP-Partnership Program for Local Governance, U. S. Agency for International Development (USAID), Yayasan Kemala and Yayasan Tifa.
8. G. Acciaioli, "From Customary Law to Indigenous Sovereignty: Reconceptualizing Masyarakat Adat in Contemporary Indonesia", in *The Revival of Tradition in Indonesian Politics: The Deployment of Adat from Colonialism to Indigenism*, ed. J. S. Davidson and D. Henley (Abingdon and New York: Routledge, 2007), pp.295–318.
9. Indonesian WALHI (Wahana Lingkungan Hidup Indonesia, the Indonesian Friends of Earth) and London-based Down to Earth are working most closely with AMAN.
10. D. Henley and J. S. Davidson, "Introduction: Radical Conservatism—the Protean Politics of Adat", in Davidson and Henley (eds.), *Revival of Tradition in Indonesian Politics*.
11. G. Acciaioli, "From Customary Law to Indigenous Sovereignty", pp. 302–3.
12. In March 2000, I had a discussion about the position of adat law in Indonesia with Lombok's adat law specialist, the vice dean of the Faculty of Law at the University of Mataram. According to Dr Subardi, despite the legal pluralism that acknowledges adat law and religious law alongside the national legislation, adat law would not or even should not have a position beyond village level, and even there it should be a limited one. In his view, adat law should remain in the private sphere and be used for reconciliation in minor matters in villages.

13. D. Henley and J. S. Davidson, "In the Name of Adat: Regional Perspectives on Reform, Tradition and Democracy in Indonesia", *Modern Asian Studies* 42, 4 (2008): 815–52; L. V. Aragon, "Communal Violence in Poso, Central Sulawesi: Where People Eat Fish and Fish Eat People", *Indonesia* 72 (2001): 45–79; G. Acciaioli, "Grounds of Conflict, Idioms of Harmony"; M. Sakai, ed., *Beyond Jakarta: Regional Autonomy and Local Societies in Indonesia* (Adelaide: Crawford House, 2002); and L. Avonius, "Reconciliation and Human Rights in post-Conflict Aceh", in *Reconciliation from Below: Grassroots Initiatives in Indonesia and East Timor*, ed. Birgit Bräuchler, forthcoming.
14. "*Masyarakat adat adalah kelompok masyarakat setempat yang memiliki asal usul leluhur secara turun temurun di wilayah geografis tertentu, serta memiliki sistem nilai, ideologi, ekonomi, politik, budaya, dan sosial sendiri*". Statutes of AMAN, May 1999, Article 10/2.
15. G. Acciaioli, "From Customary Law to Indigenous Sovereignty", p. 299.
16. "[*Masyarakat adat*] *adalah sekelompok penduduk yang hidup berdasarkan asal usul leluhur dalam suatu wilayah geografis tertentu, memiliki sistem nilai dan sosial budaya yang khas, berdaulat atas tanah dan kekayaan alamnya serta mengatur dan mengurus keberlanjutan kehidupannya dengan hukum dan kelembagaan adat*". Statutes of AMAN, March, 2007, Article 10/2.
17. The International Labour Organisation (ILO) is one of the most important international bodies that determine the rights of indigenous peoples. In 1957 it produced the *Indigenous and Tribal Peoples Convention* (Geneva, ILO Convention no. 107, 1957). In 1989, ILO Convention no. 169, *Indigenous and Tribal Peoples in Independent Countries*, was passed. ILO Convention no. 169 has so far been ratified by the following countries: Norway, Mexico, Bolivia, Colombia, Costa Rica, Denmark, Ecuador, Fiji, Guatemala, Honduras, the Netherlands, Paraguay and Peru.
18. "Indigenous peoples have the right to determine their own identity or membership in accordance with their customs and traditions...." and "Indigenous peoples have the right to determine the structures and to select the membership of their institutions in accordance with their own procedures". *United Nations Declaration on the Rights of Indigenous Peoples*, Article 33.
19. Indigenous identity has been used as a tool in the violent conflict between the indigenous Dayak population and Madurese migrants in West Kalimantan. See J. Davidson, "Culture and Rights in Ethnic Violence", in Davidson and Henley (eds.), *The Revival of Tradition in Indonesian Politics*, pp. 224–46. Similar problems with indigenous identity in Brazil have been discussed by B. A. Conklin, "Body Paint, Feathers, and VCRs: Aesthetics and Authenticity in Amazonian Activism", *American Ethnologist* 24, 4 (1997): 711–37.
20. S. Kartika and C. Gautama, eds., *Menggugat Posisi Masyarakat Adat terhadap Negara: Sarasehan Masyarakat Nusantara* (Yogyakarta: AMAN, 1999).
21. G. Acciaioli, "From Customary Law to Indigenous Sovereignty", p. 296.

22. See S. Moniaga, "From Bumiputera to Masyarakat Adat: A Long and Confusing Journey", in Davidson and Henley (eds.), *The Revival of Tradition in Indonesian Politics*, pp. 275–94.
23. These and other cases on indigenous and local people's rights over forest land can be read in *Down to Earth*, "Special report 'Forest, People, and Rights'" (June 2002).
24. For a more detailed analysis of North Lombok's *masyarakat adat* movement, see L. Avonius, "Reforming Wetu Telu: Islam, Adat, and the Promises of Regionalism in post-New Order Lombok", doctoral dissertation, Leiden University, 2004.
25. Gavin Jones's fieldwork in East Lombok revealed that some girls were dropping out of primary school in order to marry, and that if still unmarried at the age of 17 a girl would be considered an "old maid" in the region (p. 72). My own observations in North Lombok are very similar to his. G. Jones, "Which Indonesian Women Marry Youngest, and Why?" *Journal of Southeast Asian Studies* 32, 1 (2001): 67–78.
26. *Waktu Lima* is the name for Lombok Muslims who consider themselves religiously orthodox. In North Lombok most Waktu Lima Muslims have been migrants from East Lombok villages, and traders by profession rather than farmers. See S. Cederroth, *The Spell of Ancestors and the Power of Mekkah: A Sasak Community of Lombok* (Göteburg: Acta Universitatis Gothoburgensis, 1981).
27. Bayan was proclaimed to be *masyarakat terasing* in a book published by the Department of Education and Culture, T. Adonis, *Suku Terasing Sasak di Bayan, Daerah Propinsi Nusa Tenggara Barat* (Jakarta: Departemen Pendidikan dan Kebudayaan, 1989). For a discussion on the concept of *masyarakat terasing*, see G. Persoon, "Vluchten of Veranderen: Processen van Verandering en Ontwikkeling bij Tribale Groepen in Indonesië" (Flee or Change: Processes of Changes and Development amongst Indonesian Tribal Groups), doctoral dissertation, University of Leiden, 1994.
28. The villagers demanded that the concession of the PT Angkawijaya Raya Timber logging company should be withdrawn, and the regional government finally agreed to do that. This was regarded as a great victory in the village, and plans were made for how to use the communal forest land (*hutan kemasyarakatan*) that would be returned to villagers in the future. Since the withdrawal of the logging company, however, there has been a conflict amongst local population groups, some of whom have continued to exploit the forest while others have advocated conservation of the forest land. Perekat Ombara has tried to reconcile the two groups. "Mari kita wujudkan pengelolaan hutan secara kolaboratif dan integratif", *Lestari: Lembar Suara Antara Mitra*, 2nd ed., July–Aug. 2006, pp. 11–2.

29. G. Acciaioli, "Re-empowering the 'Art of the Elders': The Revitalisation of Adat among the To Lindu People in Central Sulawesi and throughout contemporary Indonesia", pp. 217–44, and M. Sakai, "Regional Responses to Resurgence of Adat Movements in Indonesia", in Sakai, *Beyond Jakarta*, pp. 245–69.
30. A joint report by UNDP and the Indonesian Legal Aid Bureau YLBHI on access to justice indicates that North Lombok's traditional court functioned in 2006. It comprised of government representatives, adat leaders and religious leaders of thirty-two villages. There was also a special board to hear inter-village disputes. The report vaguely formulates that "the court applies customary law norms and procedures" though it is likely that it has no legal power but rather focuses on reconciliation efforts between disputing parties. UNDP, YLBHI and the Commission on the Legal Empowerment of the Poor, *Legal Empowerment of the Poor: Lessons Learned from Indonesia*, July 2007, <http://www.undp.org/legalempowerment> [accessed 18 Feb. 2008].
31. The role of *adat* guards and other type of security groups in Reformasi Lombok is outside the scope of this article. See further, L. Avonius, "Reforming Wetu Telu".
32. G. Acciaioli, "Culture as Art: From Practice to Spectacle in Indonesia", *Canberra Anthropology* 8, nos. 1, 2 (1985): 148–72.
33. For *pembina adat* in South Sumatra, see Sakai, "Regional Responses to Resurgence of Adat Movements".
34. One should note that I am here presenting the views of the people in North Lombok on what they see as democratic in this particular context, and not making any general claims about democracy.
35. B. Kingsbury, "Reconstructing Self-determination: A Relational Approach", in *Operationalizing the Right of Indigenous Peoples to Self-determination*, ed. P. Aikio *et al.* (Turku: Institute for Human Rights, Åbo Akademi University, 2000).
36. D. Zook, "Decolonizing Law: Identity Politics, Human Rights and the United Nations, *Harvard Human Rights Journal* 19 (2006): 95–122.
37. Li, "Masyarakat Adat", p. 649.

CHAPTER 12

Chinese Indonesian Identities: Challenging Homogenising Discourses

Charles A. Coppel

In a nation comprising so many different ethnic groups (*suku bangsa* or *suku*), Indonesia's national motto *Bhinneka Tunggal Ika* (Unity in Diversity) seems apt enough. The ethnic Chinese have, generally speaking, been denied the status of a *suku*, however. They have been discursively and legally classified in a different way. They have been classified as a minority of foreign descent (*minoritas keturunan asing*).[1] At the discursive level, this "othering" of the ethnic Chinese is allegedly justified because they are said to have no region (*daerah*) of their own in Indonesia. As immigrants—or, in more recent history, descendants of immigrants in almost all cases—they have been differently treated in law as well. Colonial laws treated them not as "natives" (*Inlanders*) but as "foreign orientals" (*Vreemde Oosterlingen*). They were thus regarded as "foreign" even if they had the status of "Netherlands subjects" (*Nederlandsche Onderdanen*). This differential treatment carried over into the independent Republic of Indonesia. Although Article 27 of the 1945 Constitution provides that all Indonesian citizens (WNI, *warga negara Indonesia*) have the same legal rights and obligations in law and government, Article 26 makes a categorical distinction between "native-born (*asli*) Indonesians" and persons of other nationality (*orang-orang bangsa lain*) who are legalised by statute as being citizens. The logical consequence of this constitutional dichotomy is that the native-born are *ipso facto* Indonesian citizens, whereas persons of other nationality need to take further steps to qualify for Indonesian citizenship, steps which themselves depend on the terms of citizenship legislation passed by the Indonesian parliament.[2]

Although these Articles of the Constitution were amended on 17 August 2002, the amendments had no material effect on this point.[3] However, according to Article 26 (3) (as amended in 2002), matters relating to citizens and inhabitants are regulated by law. On 1 August 2006 a new Indonesian Citizenship Law (*Undang-Undang* 12/2006) came into effect. Section 2 of this law repeated the wording of Article 26 of the Constitution, but in its official clarification (*penjelasan*) the term "native-born (*asli*) Indonesians" was now redefined to mean "those who became Indonesian citizens at the time of their birth and have not voluntarily accepted any other citizenship". This is a crucial change as it strips the word *asli* of its original racial connotation and replaces it with a juridical one. Despite such a fundamental shift at the legal level, it must be acknowledged that the racial paradigm will probably continue to influence government officials and members of the public well into the future.

The Indonesian language, Bahasa Indonesia, has been a prominent symbol of Indonesian nationalism since the inauguration of the Youth Pledge (*Sumpah Pemuda*) on 28 October 1928, but only a minority of indigenous Indonesians use it as their home language, especially in Java where most of the population lives. Paradoxically, the ethnic Chinese are much more likely to speak the Indonesian national language at home than "indigenous" Indonesians,[4] but this has not silenced the accusation that they are "foreign" even when their roots in Indonesia go back for centuries.

The question of national identity for the ethnic Chinese has long been a thorny issue in Indonesia. Indeed, dual nationality loomed larger there than in other Southeast Asian countries. It had already arisen between the Dutch colonial government and the Chinese government in the early years of the twentieth century. The Chinese government—first the Manchus, then the Republic of China—claimed all ethnic Chinese outside China (*huaqiao*, sojourners) as their nationals. The Netherlands claimed those born in Indonesia as Netherlands subjects. Later, under the terms of the Round Table Conference Agreement between the Indonesian and Netherlands governments in 1949, ethnic Chinese who held Indonesian citizenship were given the right to renounce it within the space of two years. Many took the opportunity, and joined the China-born as sole Chinese nationals. In the early 1950s, the People's Republic of China (PRC) and the Republic of China competed for the support of the ethnic Chinese. Indonesia was one of the first Southeast Asian countries to recognise the PRC, and in 1955 Indonesia and China signed a treaty by which those ethnic Chinese who held the nationality of both countries would lose one and keep the other. The treaty itself was the subject of considerable political debate in Indonesia, and it was modified in its implementation precisely at the same time that changes to the Indonesian Citizenship Act were under consideration. Anti-communist Cold War rhetoric portrayed the ethnic Chinese as a fifth column for an expanding communist China, and this had echoes in Indonesia. The dual nationality treaty—designed to remove an irritant between the PRC and Indonesia—may, paradoxically, have contributed to the salience of the issue of nationality in Indonesia.[5]

The political debates in Indonesia of the 1950s and 1960s among and about the ethnic Chinese focused heavily on questions of national status and assimilation. Ethnic Chinese with dual nationality allegedly had divided loyalties (*loyalitas ganda*) and were compelled to make a choice between China and Indonesia. Assimilationists among those with Indonesian citizenship argued that this choice required further demonstrations of Indonesian identity, which ranged from abandoning "exclusive" Chinese organisations, to changing their names to Indonesian-sounding ones, intermarriage with indigenous Indonesians, and even conversion to Islam, the religion of a majority of Indonesians.[6] The New Order regime of president Suharto adopted this assimilation program and stigmatised Chinese culture, but its policies were shot through with contradictions. On the one hand it proclaimed that all Indonesian citizens had equal rights; on the other hand it discriminated against Indonesian citizens who were of Chinese descent.[7]

Since the fall of Suharto in May 1998, precipitated by traumatic anti-Chinese violence in Jakarta and Solo, the assimilationist pressures have eased. Ethnic Chinese have been emboldened to speak out against discrimination and to assert their Chineseness. Many have, like other Indonesians, taken advantage of the freer environment to become politically active. Although much of the discriminatory legislation is yet to be repealed,[8] the bans on the public expression of Chineseness are no longer enforced. There have been public performances of the lion (*barongsai*) and dragon (*liong*) dances even to launch mainstream Indonesian political party election campaigns, the Chinese language is now quite widely and openly taught, Chinese-language publications are freely available, Chinese is spoken on radio and television, and the celebration of the Chinese New Year (*tahun baru Imlek*) has even become an Indonesian national holiday.[9] A number of ethnic Chinese have told me that the atmosphere of this cultural opening up was "euphoric".

As well as the policies and legal stipulations of the governments of China, the Netherlands Indies and Indonesia that have made claims upon their political loyalty, for many Chinese in Indonesia, like immigrant communities anywhere, the pull of their country of origin has of course been a feature of their ethnic identity. At a political level, this can be depicted as an orientation to China, but at a personal level it is more likely to be an attachment to something much more particular, namely the ancestral village. Immigrants in general often originate from a particular town or village, having arrived through a process of chain migration. In the case of the Chinese, links to their home village in southern China have been reinforced by the practice of ancestor veneration and remittances sent back from the diaspora. These *qiaoxiang* (literally "sojourner's village") ties are attenuated for many because of the long lapse of time since their ancestors' original migration, but they retain some instrumental value as "cultural capital" by means of which the south China places of origin can attract investment and the Chinese overseas find local partners.[10] For Chinese Indonesians, these attachments (where they exist) are to particular localities, but this specificity is not so apparent to non-Chinese Indonesians who are more likely to discern in them an identification with China as a whole. Even where they recognise the specific attachment, non-Chinese Indonesians will often fail to regard it as the equivalent to their own nostalgic attachments to their own home village (*kampung halaman*) because it is located in China rather than in Indonesia.

In recent years the ethnic Chinese have been exposed to another external claim on their loyalty and identity. This is the global discourse of a Chinese diaspora. The World Huaren Federation set up a website (<www.huaren.org>) in early 1998 to mobilise ethnic Chinese worldwide in protest against anti-Chinese violence in Indonesia. Contributors to the website expressed solidarity with their persecuted *huaren* (ethnic Chinese) brothers and sisters in Indonesia. Like the earlier demands made on *huaqiao* by the Chinese state, this "transnational nationalism", as Ien Ang calls it, assumes all ethnic Chinese are essentially the same and different from non-Chinese. Unlike the *huaqiao* discourse, however, "diasporic nationalism produces an imagined community which is deterritorialised, but which is symbolically bounded nevertheless".[11]

The extension of the concept of diaspora to apply to the Chinese outside China has encountered resistance from some ethnic Chinese scholars. For example, Wang Gungwu, the doyen of historians of the Chinese overseas, has expressed his concern that the word diaspora may "be used to revive the ideas of a single body of Chinese, reminiscent of the old term the *huaqiao*...."[12] Elaine Tay has similar concerns: "The process of renaming as a diaspora may acknowledge the different histories and cultures of the various collectivities, but, in the end, these differences are obscured in favour of solidarity based upon shared Chinese 'characteristics' and 'stateless' power."[13]

To counter the homogenising tendencies of either *huaqiao* or "diaspora", Wang advocates the study of the Chinese overseas "in the context of their respective national environments".[14] While she shares Wang's insistence on difference and diversity among the Chinese, Ang criticises him for not going far enough because he fails to problematise "the use of the term 'Chinese' as such".[15] She goes on to ask at what point a "Chinese" ceases to be a "Chinese", which in turn leads her to stress processes of hybridisation which she locates in the metropolitan space of the global city.[16]

I share their common desire to stress the diversity among the ethnic Chinese in Indonesia against the homogenising discourses of either *huaqiao* or "diaspora", but I wish to explore different dimensions of their heterogeneity. Where Wang Gungwu points to the context of the "national environment", I want to draw attention to their regional diversity within the national environment of Indonesia; and where Ien Ang points to the global city as the locus of hybridisation, I want to stress the multiple adaptations that ethnic Chinese have made in the ethnically varied regions of Indonesia.

In an essay on patterns of Chinese political activity in Indonesia, I once identified an unresolved problem in the ideas of those favouring assimilation. It was unclear in their project whether they should "assimilate to the indigenous sukus first" or "assimilate in one jump to the all-Indonesian culture" which was developing in the large, ethnically heterogeneous urban centres.[17] Both processes were, of course, under way, at least at a cultural level; and they were happening naturally long before the initial campaign by the assimilationists or the later demands of the New Order government. I have already referred above to the paradox that *peranakan* (locally born) Chinese are more "Indonesian" linguistically than "indigenous" Indonesians in that they are more likely to use the national language, Bahasa Indonesia, as their home language. This can be explained as a consequence of their concentration in the larger urban centres and in the intermediary trade of the archipelago. Analysis of the data in the 1920 colonial census shows that a significant number of other *peranakan* Chinese used an Indonesian regional language other than Malay/Indonesian as their home language. This was true of much of Java, where more than one in seven of the total Chinese population used a regional language as their home language, and in some parts of the Outer Islands.[18]

In those parts of the archipelago where the *peranakan* did not predominate among the Chinese—especially those parts of Sumatra and Kalimantan closest to Singapore—the *totok* ("full-blooded") Chinese-speaking communities were also diversified and distinctive. They varied according to the prevailing Chinese speech group (Hokkien speakers in North Sumatra and the Riau Archipelago, Teochiu speakers in Pontianak, and Hakka speakers in Bangka, Belitung and the northern parts of West Kalimantan) but also in the different adaptations which their communities had made in their interaction with their diverse indigenous Indonesian neighbours.[19]

A systematic comparison of regional variations among the ethnic Chinese of Indonesia is yet to be undertaken, but Chinese Indonesians themselves are well aware of these differences. As Thung Ju-lan observes:

> Internal differentiation among the Indonesian Chinese, such as among the *Cina Medan* (Chinese of Medan), *Cina Bangka* (Chinese of Bangka) and *Cina Pontianak* (Chinese of Pontianak), indicate that local Indonesian traits have been incorporated into domestic Chinese identities. Even among the Chinese in Java, there are local variations (between the Chinese of Semarang, the Chinese of Sukabumi and the Chinese of Malang) although they also recognise their common characteristics as compared to those of the Chinese of the outer islands.[20]

In researching the origins of Confucianism as an organised religion in Java, I found that regional differentiation among the ethnic Chinese was an important variable. The West Javanese urban centres (Jakarta, Bogor, Sukabumi) were crucial to the first wave of the movement, influenced by their interaction with Dutch Protestant missionaries from the Nederlandsche Zendingsvereeniging (Dutch Missionary Union).

Central Javanese Chinese, especially in Solo, had an important role in later developments, with influences from Theosophy and Javanese *kebatinan*. Chinese associated with the Confucian temple (Boen Bio) in Jalan Kapasan in Surabaya contributed another distinctive strand, reflecting the stronger representation of *totoks* among the Chinese there.[21]

Such regional differentiation can persist long after remigration elsewhere. For example, Michael Godley and I conducted interviews in Hong Kong in early 1986 with ethnic Chinese who had been born and educated in Indonesia, then gone to mainland China, and eventually made their way to Hong Kong. We found that, despite absences of several decades from Indonesia, many still experienced Indonesia in some sense as home. "Home" was not a generalised Indonesia, however. It was their particular place of origin within Indonesia which formed the basis of their networks and identification. We attended a Chinese New Year reunion of hundreds of Chinese who originated from Medan and nearby parts of North Sumatra. Although they were speakers of Hokkien (albeit a locally-influenced dialect which some called *Medan hua*), the reunion featured Indonesian food and songs. Other reunions were more specific, limited to the alumni of a particular Chinese school (or even of a single class cohort from that school) in a single city such as Jakarta, Tegal, Semarang or Malang.[22]

Local variations of Chineseness can also persist after remigration within Indonesia. Not unlike indigenous Indonesian "spontaneous transmigrants" (as opposed to those whose transmigration was sponsored by the Indonesian government), Chinese Indonesians not uncommonly migrate from one part of the country to another. Their movement has typically been prompted either by the pull factor of economic opportunity or the push factors of discriminatory legislation or the experience of racial violence. Such Chinese Indonesian "transmigrants" are particularly evident in Jakarta which is, according to Thung Ju-lan "the place where Chinese from all over the country meet and mix with each other as well as with indigenous Indonesians of various ethnic groups",[23] and it is not unknown for Chinese from a certain locality elsewhere (e.g. Medan) to cluster in a particular Jakarta neighbourhood. According to Hugh Mabbett and his co-author Ping-Ching Mabbett (herself born in Medan) the Medan Chinese community in Jakarta numbers "tens of thousands" who have "aroused complaints among the older, Java-oriented residents, who feel that the Medanese lack delicacy and patience in their dealing with the Javanese".[24] Mary Somers Heidhues reports that so many Chinese from

West Kalimantan were moving to Jakarta in the late 1990s that observers joked that "parts of northern and western Jakarta were becoming a little Pontianak".²⁵

When Wang Gungwu urges us to study the Chinese overseas "in the context of their national environments", he is warning against the dangerous tendencies of a wider homogenisation either of *huaqiao* or diaspora. I respectfully agree, but I add my own caution against any tendency to homogenise the ethnic Chinese within a particular national environment. This has to be particularly true in a country as large, fragmented, populous and diverse as Indonesia; the more so in the post-Suharto era when demands for regional autonomy have become increasingly insistent. According to Wang:

> The single word, Chinese, will be less and less able to convey a reality that continues to become more pluralistic. We need more words, each with the necessary adjectives to qualify and identify who exactly we are describing. We need them all to capture the richness and variety of the hundreds of Chinese communities that can now be found.²⁶

This is as true of the variety of Chinese communities to be found in different parts of Indonesia as it is in countries like the United States, Canada or Australia which have recently been receiving increasing numbers of "Chinese" from many different sources.

When Ien Ang argues that our attention should be focused on the urban centres in which different "peoples" encounter one another and, through these encounters, bring about "processes of hybridisation" which blur the boundaries between them, she has in mind a modern "era of globalisation" and, perhaps, specifically those countries which, unlike Indonesia, continue to receive large-scale immigration.²⁷ In Indonesia, however, much of the hybridisation has its roots deep in the past. This is by no means confined to what Skinner calls "creolised" societies like the *peranakan* Chinese of Java which mostly developed in urban centres.²⁸ Mary Somers Heidhues has drawn attention to the urban bias in histories of the Chinese in Southeast Asia and to the relative neglect in research of rural Chinese communities.²⁹ Her own work on Bangka and West Kalimantan³⁰ has been an important corrective in supplying *rural* examples of what Ang elsewhere called "the irreducible *specificity* of diverse and heterogeneous hybridisations in dispersed temporal and spatial contexts".³¹ Even in Java there have been examples of villages in which ethnic Chinese have been almost completely assimilated into the wider community.³²

Despite the many different ways in which people of Chinese ancestry have encountered indigenous Indonesians of different ethnicities in different parts of the archipelago, they have also been pressured to conform to extralocal expectations. In addition to the claims of Chinese governments on the *huaqiao* and the demands for *huaren* diaspora solidarity with their tendency to homogenise the meaning of Chineseness worldwide, there has also been the exercise of power by the Indonesian state (and its colonial predecessor) upon the Chinese within its borders. The state's "regime of truth and power"[33] has constrained them in various ways, but Chinese Indonesians still have agency. Donald Nonini and Aihwa Ong suggest ways in which Chinese transnationalists can "seek to elude the localisations imposed on them by nation-state regimes by, above all, moving between national spaces, playing off one nation-state regime against another...."[34] Ang also emphasises agency when she argues "if I am inescapably Chinese by *descent*, I am only sometimes Chinese by *consent*. When and how is a matter of politics."[35]

The "localisations" to which Nonini and Ong refer are at the *national* level, and they are speaking of transnational moves to elude them. On the other hand, the "transnational nationalism" of *huaren* solidarity can similarly be experienced by Chinese Indonesians as something akin to a "regime of truth and power", even if the discursive pressure is not backed by the power of a state. Ang gives a poignant example of this,[36] and she confesses her own discomfort with the transnational appeals of Huaren.[37] Her answer to what she calls "the drift towards ethnic absolutism and diasporic Chinese tribalism" is a politics of hybridity.[38]

Caught in the cross-currents of these opposing "regimes of truth and power", ethnic Chinese have been divided among themselves for more than a century, arguing over what it means to be "Chinese" in Indonesia.[39] The debate was largely suppressed under Suharto's authoritarian New Order, but has resumed with vigour since May 1998.[40] Some aspire to create a united Chinese Indonesian community organisation which could strive to make Chinese Indonesians good citizens and accepted as such. Others fear that that might be counter-productive. If Indonesian politics were again to become highly polarised, such a mass organisation might meet the same fate as Baperki in 1965. In any case, a united Chinese community in Indonesia is probably an impossible goal. People have many possible identities. Ethnicity is only one of them, together with such other identities as those based on social class, gender, education, language, political ideology, and sexual orientation. The concept of "Chineseness" itself is, in Ang's words, "an open signifier, which acquires its peculiar form and content in dialectical junction with the diverse local conditions in which ethnic Chinese people, wherever they are, construct new, hybrid identities and communities".[41]

In a post-Suharto Indonesia in which regional autonomy is being asserted ever more stridently, Chinese Indonesians also need to negotiate their way through the "diverse local conditions" of the archipelago. When there are tensions between the centre and the regions, where are the ethnic Chinese in the regions to stand? Will they identify with the centre, relying on their status and rights as Indonesian citizens? Or will they identify with the region in which they live? There is no reason to assume that the answers to these questions will be the same in all localities, or that all Chinese in any locality will be of one mind.

Moreover, when and how people are "Chinese" is not always a matter of their own choice. It may be thrust upon them. A Chinese Indonesian informant in Bandung in July 2002 told me of his bemusement at being invited to meet a Chinese *imam* from China. The latter is able to speak Arabic and Chinese but not English or Indonesian; my informant can speak English and Indonesian but not Arabic or Chinese (except some scraps of Hokkien from childhood) and has little knowledge of Islam beyond the Arabic greeting *assalam alaikum* (peace be upon you). The invitation was made because of their supposedly shared Chinese ethnicity.

Zhou Fuyuan describes the May 1998 violence as "a devastating psychological blow" to the Chinese community. Among his friends,

> those most affected were the ones who had always carried their Chinese identity lightly....[Those] who had always thought of themselves as Indonesian suddenly faced the fact they were actually regarded as Chinese, and as such deserved to be alienated. They had to seriously rethink what this meant and to reorientate themselves.[42]

It is by no means always ethnic Chinese who find themselves confronted by such dilemmas. Many indigenous Indonesians are not confined to "their own *daerah*" and, like ethnic Chinese, are scattered across Indonesia living among people from other *suku bangsa*. Centuries of population movement (of Minangkabau, Buginese and Makasarese, for example) and the large scale government-sponsored transmigration of Javanese, Sundanese, Madurese and Balinese over the last century have created multiple ethnic diasporas across the archipelago.[43]

Tension between indigenous Indonesians can be just as great as between indigenous and Chinese Indonesians.[44] For example, the violence in West Kalimantan in 1997 and 1999 was largely directed at Madurese settlers, and the Chinese there were not targeted as they had been in 1967. As the peoples indigenous to the different regions of Indonesia assert their claims to autonomy, those who are perceived to be strangers in their midst may find themselves called upon to make their own local adaptations and hybridisations if they are to establish their right to belong there. In this context the position of the ethnic Chinese is not qualitatively different from that of other Indonesians.

If Indonesia as a state and Indonesians as a nation are to survive, they will need to find ways to accept the irremediable diversity of themselves as a people which is embodied in the national motto *Bhinneka Tunggal Ika* (Unity in Diversity). By this I do not mean that all *suku bangsa* are essentially separate and unable to live within the one nation. Nor do I mean that all Indonesians should be pressured into uniformity in the way in which the New Order demanded that the ethnic Chinese abandon their Chineseness. Rather, I am calling for a recognition and acceptance of the infinite variety of the processes of hybridisation which will inevitably take place. This appeal goes beyond the notion of multiculturalism. As Ang argues, "One of the merits of the concept of hybridisation is that it undermines the binary and static way of thinking about difference which is dominant in theories of cultural pluralism, which are premised on the *distinctness* of cultures and ethnicities."[45]

Such an acceptance can be promoted through the telling and celebration of the myriad stories of individual experience by way of autobiography, biography, history and literature as opposed to homogenising discourses such as triumphalist narratives of the nation, ethnic group or religion.

Notes

1. They are not alone in this. Ethnic Arabs, Indians and Europeans have also been classified in this way, but the ethnic Chinese outnumber them to such a degree that the discourse often almost seems to treat the category as peculiar to the ethnic Chinese.
2. See C. A. Coppel, "The Indonesian Chinese: 'Foreign Orientals', Netherlands Subjects, and Indonesian Citizens", in *Law and the Chinese in Southeast Asia*, ed. M. B. Hooker, pp. 131–49 (Singapore: ISEAS, 2002) for a more detailed discussion of the history of these distinctions.
3. T. Lindsey, "Reconstituting the Ethnic Chinese in Post-Soeharto Indonesia: Law, Racial Discrimination, and Reform", in *Chinese Indonesians: Remembering, Distorting, Forgetting*, ed. T. Lindsey and H. Pausacker (Singapore: ISEAS,

2005). Although the requirement in Article 6 that the president should be a native-born Indonesian (*orang Indonesia asli*) has been removed in a recent amendment by the MPR, the distinction between citizens who are native-born Indonesians and other WNI in Article 26 (1) was left unchanged by amendments to that Article.

4. C. A. Coppel, "Mapping the Peranakan Chinese in Indonesia", *Far Eastern History* 8 (Sept. 1973); P. Weldon, *Indonesian and Chinese Status Differences in Urban Java*, Singapore: University of Singapore Department of Sociology Working Paper no. 7, 1973.
5. D. E. Willmott, *The National Status of the Chinese in Indonesia 1900–1958*, rev. ed. (Ithaca: Cornell University Modern Indonesia Project, 1961); M. F. A. Somers, "Peranakan Chinese Politics in Indonesia", doctoral dissertation, Cornell University, 1965.
6. Somers, *Peranakan Chinese Politics in Indonesia*; C. A. Coppel, *Indonesian Chinese in Crisis* (Kuala Lumpur: Oxford University Press, 1983).
7. C. A. Coppel, "Chinese Indonesians in Crisis: 1960s and 1990s", and "Appendix I", in *Perspectives on the Chinese Indonesians*, ed. M. R. Godley *et al.*, pp. 20–40 and 302–29 (Adelaide: Crawford House, 2001).
8. Lindsey, "Reconstituting the Ethnic Chinese".
9. P. Allen and S. Turner, "Speaking Out: Chinese Indonesians after Suharto", *Asian Ethnicity* 4, 3 (special issue, ed. P. Allen and S. Turner) (Oct. 2003): 327–459.
10. L. Douw *et al.*, eds., *Qiaoxiang Ties: Interdisciplinary Approaches to "Cultural Capitalism" in South China* (London: Kegan Paul with IIAS, 1999).
11. I. Ang, *On Not Speaking Chinese: Living Between Asia and the West* (London and New York: Routledge, 2001), pp. 57–60 and 81–4.
12. Wang G., "A Single Chinese Diaspora? Some Historical Reflections", in *Imagining the Chinese Diaspora: Two Australian Perspectives*, ed. Wang G. and A. Shun Wah (Canberra: Centre for the Study of the Chinese Southern Diaspora, 1999), p. 2, cited by Ang, *On Not Speaking Chinese*, p. 82.
13. E. Tay, "Global Chinese Fraternity and the Indonesian Riots of May 1998: The Online Gathering of Dispersed Chinese", *Intersections* 4, Sept. 2000. <http://intersections.anu.edu.au/issue4/tay.html> [accessed 29 Feb. 2008].
14. Wang, "A Single Chinese Diaspora?", p. 1, cited by Ang, *On Not Speaking Chinese*, p. 84.
15. Ang, *On Not Speaking Chinese*, pp. 84–5.
16. Ibid., pp. 87–92.
17. C. A. Coppel, "Patterns of Chinese Political Activity in Indonesia", in *The Chinese in Indonesia: Five Essays*, ed. J. A. C. Mackie (Melbourne: Nelson with Australian Institute of International Affairs, 1976), p. 54.
18. Coppel, "Mapping the Peranakan Chinese in Indonesia".
19. M. F. S. Heidhues, *Bangka Tin and Mentok Pepper: Chinese Settlement on an Indonesian Island* (Singapore: ISEAS, 1992); M. F. S. Heidhues, "Indonesia",

in *The Encyclopedia of the Chinese Overseas*, ed. L. Pan (Cambridge, Mass.: Harvard University Press, 1998), pp. 160–2; M. F. S. Heidhues, *Golddiggers, Farmers, and Traders in the "Chinese Districts" of West Kalimantan, Indonesia* (Ithaca: Southeast Asia Program Publications, Cornell University, 2003).
20. Thung J.-L, "Identities in Flux: Young Chinese in Jakarta", doctoral dissertation, La Trobe University, 1998, pp. 61–2.
21. C. A. Coppel, "The Origins of Confucianism as an Organized Religion in Java, 1900–1923", *Journal of Southeast Asian Studies* 12 (1981): 179–96.
22. M. R. Godley and C. A. Coppel, "The Pied Piper and the Prodigal Children: A Report on the Indonesian-Chinese Students Who Went to Mao's China", *Archipel* 39 (1990): 179–98, and M. R. Godley and C. A. Coppel, "The Indonesian Chinese in Hong Kong: A Preliminary Report on a Minority Community in Transition", *Issues and Studies* 26 (1990): 94–108.
23. Thung, "Identities in Flux", p. 62.
24. H. Mabbett and P.-C. Mabbett, "The Chinese Community in Indonesia", in *The Chinese in Indonesia, the Philippines and Malaysia*, ed. C. A. Coppel, H. Mabbett and P-C. Mabbett (London: Minority Rights Group Report no. 10, 1982 [1972]), p. 13.
25. M. F. S. Heidhues, "Kalimantan Barat 1967–1999: Violence on the Periphery", in *Violence in Indonesia*, ed. I. Wessel *et al.* (Hamburg: Abera Verlag, 2001), p. 147.
26. Wang, "A Single Chinese Diaspora?", p. 16, as cited by Ang, *On Not Speaking Chinese*, p. 85.
27. Ang, *On Not Speaking Chinese*, pp. 87–92.
28. G. W. Skinner, "Creolized Chinese Societies in Southeast Asia", in *Sojourners and Settlers: Histories of Southeast Asia and the Chinese*, ed. A. Reid (St. Leonard's: ASAA with Allen & Unwin, 1996).
29. M. F. S. Heidhues, "Chinese Settlements in Rural Southeast Asia: Unwritten Histories", in Reid, *Sojourners and Settlers*.
30. Heidhues, *Bangka Tin and Mentok Pepper* and *Golddiggers, Farmers, and Traders*.
31. Ang, *On Not Speaking Chinese*, p. 36, her emphasis.
32. Go G. T., *Eenheid in Verscheidenheid in een Indonesisch Dorp* (Unity in Diversity in an Indonesian Village), Amsterdam: Sociologisch-Historisch Seminarium voor Zuidoost Azië, Universiteit van Amsterdam Publikatie no. 10, 1966.
33. D. M. Nonini, "Shifting Identities, Positioned Imaginaries: Transnational Traversals and Reversals by Malaysian Chinese", in *Ungrounded Empires: The Cultural Politics of Modern Chinese Transnationalism*, ed. A. Ong and D. M. Nonini (New York and London: Routledge, 1997).
34. D. M. Nonini and A. Ong, "Chinese Transnationalism as an Alternative Modernity", in Ong and Nonini (eds.),*Ungrounded Empires*, pp. 23–4.
35. Ang, *On Not Speaking Chinese*, p. 36, her emphasis.

36. Ibid., pp. 69–70, citing the case of "Mrk" in Bandung.
37. Ibid., pp. 57–60 and 65–70.
38. Ibid., pp. 70–4.
39. L. Suryadinata, ed., *Political Thinking of the Indonesian Chinese 1900–1995: A Sourcebook*, 2nd ed. (Singapore: Singapore University Press, 1997).
40. A. Hamzah, ed., *Kapok Jadi Nonpri: Warga Tionghoa Mencari Keadilan* (Bandung: Zaman, 1998); I. Wibowo ed., *Retrospeksi dan Rekontekstualisasi "Masalah Cina"* (Jakarta: Gramedia Pustaka Utama with Pusat Studi Cina, 1999); I. Wibowo, ed., *Harga yang Harus Dibayar: Sketsa Pergulatan Etnis Cina di Indonesia* (Jakarta: Gramedia Pustaka Utama with Pusat Studi Cina, 2000); I. Wibowo, "Exit, Voice and Loyalty: Indonesian Chinese after the Fall of Soeharto", *Sojourn* 16 (2001): 125–46; T. D. Siauw and H. D. Oey, eds., *Sumbangsih Siauw Giok Tjhan dan Baperki dalam Sejarah Indonesia* (Jakarta: Hasta Mitra, 2000); and Allen and Turner, "Speaking Out".
41. Ang, *On Not Speaking Chinese*, p. 35.
42. F. Zhou, "Where Do We Belong?" *Asian Ethnicity* 4, no. 3 (2003): 454.
43. R. Cribb, *Historical Atlas of Indonesia* (Honolulu: University of Hawai'i Press, 2000), pp. 52–7.
44. C. A. Coppel, ed., *Violent Conflicts in Indonesia: Analysis, Representation, Resolution* (London and New York: Routledge, 2006).
45. Ang, *On Not Speaking Chinese*, p. 87; emphasis in original.

CHAPTER 13

"More Indonesian than the Indonesians": A Chinese-Indonesian Identity

David Reeve

The Chinese in Indonesia have long been suspected of having an incomplete Indonesian identity. As a result, at various periods in Indonesia's turbulent history, they have been vilified, made scapegoats and brutally attacked. Yet many Chinese have themselves been ambivalent about their Indonesian identity and some inherited Dutch prejudices about Indonesians as lazy, shiftless and unreliable.

This chapter focuses on Professor Ong Hok Ham, 1933–2007, an historian who was often described as "more Indonesian than the Indonesians" and "more Javanese than the Javanese".[1] Although there is an element of extravagant Indonesian flattery (and also exclusion) here, there is no doubt that Ong Hok Ham was widely recognised in his country as a Chinese whose identity was unequivocally Indonesian. This chapter suggests, however, that although he decided early in the 1950s that he was Indonesian, that identity took another two to three decades to be inhabited with confidence and passion.

Why is Ong Hok Ham interesting? One reason is that he came from a generation that is passing, one which experienced the last years of Dutch colonialism, the Japanese Occupation, the Revolution, and all the subsequent periods of Indonesia's post-revolutionary history. Far more than that, he was an Indonesian historian in a country where few Chinese become intellectuals, let alone historians of Indonesia. He played a role as a public intellectual since 1959 and especially in the period from 1976–2000 when he wrote regular columns in the daily *Kompas* and the weekly *Tempo*, as well as lengthier articles for the academic journal *Prisma*.[2]

Scholars of Indonesia knew Ong Hok Ham for his hospitality, his humour, his broad humaneness, his liberalism, his cooking and his knowledge. He was a favourite of journalists and diplomats, asked frequently to dinners and receptions. He was a great wit, impish and mischievous, and loved to laugh and make others laugh. His best sallies were often pungent one-liners that combined a reference to the Dutch, to Indonesia's past and its present, giving listeners the gratifying feeling that they were gaining a sharp insight into the country just as they roared with laughter. He seems to have minted at least one new witticism every week, quite an achievement for a public career spanning over 40 years.

Ong Hok Ham was also an eccentric, a category welcomed and approved by Westerners, but perhaps more scandalous for Indonesians. He was not a Chinese-Indonesian synthesis, but a rebel against all three categories. For most of his life Ong was a lone wolf, an original, an annoyance, a rebel, a wanderer, a flâneur, an iconoclast, a maker of his own life, a hedonist and, as one Japanese researcher said, "a weird guy". At one stage I thought he simply did not care about others' opinion of him. When I said so he replied, "but I cared very much what other people thought. I had created my own life and I very much wanted them to approve of it". I now think that his individuality must have involved considerable strain, even though he also felt great joy in it. And he offered his individuality as a model for others to follow. It had a clear teaching function, for his friends, his students and his family.

Press articles often highlighted Ong's singular presence: the bald head, the thick spectacles, the sweating brow, the impatient retorts and the spurts of anger. He tended to be a careless dresser in a neat society, though he could look quite dashing in a good batik shirt, and striking in a tuxedo, borrowed from his good friend Siddharta. He brushed aside the conventions of a conformist society, whose narrow expectations drove him to distraction. Ong was a startling and alarming teacher, a "killer lecturer", hurling chalk, dusters and anything else to hand at his horrified students when they annoyed him. In a largely Muslim society he was an enthusiastic eater of pork, and relished a drink. In a largely religious society, he had no evident religion. In a society where middle-class men rarely go near the kitchen, he was famed as a cook.

His presciently post-modern house with three separate open-air pavilions, no windows and open-air toilet and bathroom was startling, and appeared in the serious architectural style books. In a society where almost everyone is married, he remained a bachelor in an all-male household. In a society where everyone longs for a car, he always used public transport. People said, "A professor! In a bus!" in a tone which seemed to indicate they were not quite sure whether to be amusedly scandalised or deeply shocked at the betrayal of class solidarity.

In a society particularly concerned with status, he never worried about his promotions and remained at a low level, causing his early retirement. He had a vast reservoir of knowledge, but it could be difficult to access; friends called him an encyclopaedia with no alphabetical order. In Indonesian society he was an outsider who became a living national treasure.

In early 2001, Ong's career as a public intellectual was brought to an end by a severe stroke. His mind remained active, but trapped in a crippled frame. For a man who loved to talk, joke and laugh, it was a tragedy that he could no longer speak clearly. In the evening of 30 August 2007, Ong Hok Ham was found dead in his wheelchair, just after finishing a meal. On the 100th day after his death, 8 December 2007, a book was launched containing reminiscences of Ong by 54 of his friends, colleagues and family members.[3]

In the wake of his recent death, this chapter attempts a description of the processes by which Ong Hok Ham came to inhabit an Indonesian identity. It focuses on the first four decades of his life. As mentioned above, this chapter argues that although Ong decided early in the 1950s that he was Indonesian, that identity took another two to three decades to be inhabited with confidence and passion. The chapter is divided into four sections: first, Ong's youth, 1933–55, in which his "Indonesianness" was decided; second, Ong's years at Universitas Indonesia, 1955–68, in which that identity was developed but threatened; third, the underlying theme of Ong's emotional and sexual development in those years; and fourth, the Yale University years, 1968–75, which brought him renewed strength and confidence. We leave Ong in 1975, returning from the

United States to Indonesia, about to begin that career as teacher and public intellectual that he would enjoy with such zest for the next 26 years.

Youth, 1933–55: Choosing an Identity

Ong Hok Ham was born on 1 May 1933 in Surabaya, inheriting the traditions of three lines of Chinese. On his mother's side he came from the Han line. The Hans were very successful entrepreneurs, deeply involved in the commercial development of East Java, particularly through sugar mills. This line of Hans had been in Java since around 1700, when Ong's ancestor Han Siong Kong came to Lasem in Central Java, moving later to East Java. This was a family of great wealth, style and substance and from it came leaders (captains and lieutenants) of the Chinese community in East Java, particularly in Pasuruan and Surabaya.

In the eighth generation of Han Siong Kong's descendants in Java, one Han Loen Nio married Tan Hie Sioe from a successful family of Tans involved in opium farms and other monopolies. The couple had two daughters, Tan Siang Tjia, Ong's mother, and Tan Siang Loen, both of whom married Ong's father.

Ong's father's family did not trace its origins in Indonesia nearly as far back as did the Hans. Ong's great-grandfather is thought to have been a schoolteacher in Madura, who later moved to East Java. He had a son, Ong Ik Sien, a frugal, hardworking and ambitious young man who became a cashier in a sugar mill. The cashier had two sons, Ong Thwan Hian, Ong's father, and Ong Thwan Tjiang. The Ongs were a family that embraced Dutch education as a means of social mobility and wealth and both Ong's father and his brother valued Dutch education and the Dutch lifestyle.

Ong's father, the eldest son, married Tan Siang Loen, but around 1919 she died in the influenza pandemic following World War I. Tan Siang Tjia, her elder sister, had married Liem Yoe Tik, a young man from Central Java with aristocratic connections, but he also died young. This left the family with a young widow with two children, Tan Siang Tjia, and a young widower with no children, Ong's father.

The match between them was not love at first sight. In fact it may be that they did not even like each other very much. But there was an influential elder in the family, Koppo, the "dowager empress" (Mrs Tio Tjien Tiong) who was the sister of Ong's grandfather. She decided that the young widower and the young widow should marry. So Tan Siang Tjia married her sister's widower husband, Ong Thwan Hian. This marriage produced two more children, Ong Hok Ham in 1933 and Ong Hok Hai in 1936.

So, on Ong's mother's side were the Hans, a family proud of its long tradition, social status and wealth. On Ong's father side was a family which took great pride in its upward mobility though the pursuit of Dutch education. The two families were united by a sense of status and privilege and by identification with Dutch culture. Their first language was Dutch; Ong spoke Dutch at school and at home and the family used the Dutch names they had been given at school. Ong's mother, father and uncles were Lies, Klaas, Piet and Jan. Ong and his elder brother and sister were Hans, Freddy and Olga. Olga still refers to Ong as "Hans". Only his younger brother was not given a Dutch name; by the time he started school the Dutch empire was collapsing.

Ong went to a Dutch school from 1938 to 1942. His was a tight, enclosed world, with Dutch-oriented parents and a Dutch education. At school Ong was academically precocious and a high achiever and quickly won the approval of his Dutch teachers. Ong's existence, however, suffered a rude shock in 1942 with the collapse of the Dutch empire and the beginning of the Japanese Occupation. The Chinese were particularly alarmed as they were well aware of what had been happening in Manchuria under the Japanese Occupation in the 1930s. Early in the Japanese Occupation of Indonesia, the family fled to Malang, 82 km to the south of Surabaya, where they had wealthy relatives. Later they returned to Surabaya under what turned out to be, for them, the relative calm of the Japanese invasion. The Dutch schools had been closed, however, and Ong and his brother attended a Chinese school in Surabaya.

If Ong's family had hoped that the Dutch would return after the Japanese surrendered, they were to be disappointed; on 17 August 1945 Sukarno declared Indonesia's independence and four years of armed conflict followed as the Dutch sought to regain control of their former colony. The Revolution was a time of great fear for the Chinese, with atrocities committed against Chinese all along the north coast of Java. After the Battle of Surabaya the family again fled to Malang. Surabaya was relatively quickly controlled by the returning Dutch, however, and became a Dutch town for most of the rest of the Revolution. So, after an interval in a Chinese school, Ong was able to return to Dutch schooling in Surabaya.

By 1949 the Dutch had lost the struggle, and in December Holland recognised Indonesia's independence. However in Surabaya Dutch schools remained open, and so from 1950–52 Ong was able to continue his high school education in the Dutch system. It was during this time that Ong's family, and Ong himself, made a very important and in many ways very difficult decision. Rather than leaving for Holland or some other destination, the family chose to remain in Indonesia and become Indonesian citizens. This decision was a highly serious one for Ong, and one that he would strive to live up to throughout his life.[4] For Ong, one important factor in this decision was the role of an inspiring teacher, Brother Rosario. Brother Rosario had set Ong's imagination afire in his history classes. He also deeply influenced Ong in a class on civics, urging his students to "become good citizens, whichever country you live in!"

As a result of his schooling, Ong was fluent in Dutch, English, German and French but he was not yet fluent in Indonesian, the language of the new nation which Ong's family had adopted. So from 1953–55 he was sent to an Indonesian high school in Bandung, repeating the last years of his Dutch high school but in an Indonesian environment. This was a time of liberation from family and although Ong was a serious student, he greatly enjoyed the independence of his years in Bandung. One high point was the Asia Africa Conference in Bandung in April 1955, where he worked as a student assistant-interpreter for French-speaking delegations from Vietnam and Cambodia. Foreign languages were introducing him to a wider world. In the middle of 1955 Ong finished high school. He was 22 years old.

Ong's childhood and early youth were, then, a Dutch-Chinese synthesis in which Dutch education and lifestyle were highly valued, and Chinese customs respected. It was a rich but highly confined existence, studying European classics at school, mostly in Dutch but also in German, English and French, confined at home to his extended Chinese family and therefore insulated and distanced from Indonesian natives. By 1955 Indonesian was Ong's most foreign language, although both he and his family had made the serious decision to become Indonesians.

Ong's schooling, and his experiences during these years, gave him a strong sense of the vulnerability of the Chinese community. Ong recognised that in the face of the massive social and political upheaval brought about by the fall of the Dutch Empire, the Japanese Occupation, and the Revolution, it was the insularity of the Chinese community in Indonesia that made them so vulnerable. This certainty was to influence

Ong's ideas about his own place in Indonesian society and the wider role of the Chinese in Indonesia throughout his life.

Universitas Indonesia, 1955–68: Identity Challenged

Ong's undergraduate university career was the major formative period of his life. He entered the University of Indonesia in September 1955 at the age of twenty-two as a law student. Thirteen years later, at the age of thirty-five, Ong graduated with a degree in history.

It was not unusual at that time for students to spend a long time at university. The pressure to finish quickly was not strong and "eternal students" (*mahasiswa abadi*) were common. Ong had many outside interests. This was a period of starts and stops and of experimenting with new approaches to his world. It was during this period of experimentation that Ong came closer to finding ways of living his own Indonesian identity.

This process of discovery was influenced by three phases in Ong's university career. The first phase covers the early years from 1955 to about 1961: studying law, working as a research assistant for an American scholar, forming friendships with foreign scholars, beginning his career as a writer, and then as an activist for assimilation. The second phase, from 1961 to 1965, comes with Ong the history student, discovering Java and falling in love with Javanese culture. The attempted coup of October 1965 was the start of a very difficult three years for Ong, during which he suffered a mental breakdown and was jailed for a time. Despite this, Ong pushed himself to write his final undergraduate thesis, which he successfully presented in September 1968. A few days later Ong left for America, and doctoral study at Yale University.

In September 1955, Ong Hok Ham started his university career in the law department together with another brilliant student, Harry Tjan [later a Catholic student activist, a Catholic Party leader, and prominent figure in the New Order think tank, CSIS (Centre for Strategic and International Studies)]. Why law? Ong was eventually to become a leading historian. In the mid-1950s, however, it was difficult to imagine what Indonesian history might be. It seemed so strange and new that, as Ong said, it was like studying physics in the sixteenth century; it didn't yet have an identity. Ong did not want to be in business like so many of his family (and other Chinese Indonesians) and no one could really imagine Ong as a doctor. With his readings of the great diplomatic triumphs and failures of Europe and his interest in the Versailles Conference following the World War I, he had ideas of becoming a diplomat. But could a Chinese become an Indonesian diplomat? Law was a reliable profession and might possibly be a stepping-stone to a diplomatic career.

On campus, Ong rapidly gained a reputation for eccentricity. He was already balding and wore thick glasses and he had a little motor scooter called a Mobylette (*sepeda kupu-kupu*), which he rode. Many are the tales of Ong arriving at the campus on his little Mobylette: beep beep, ring ring! "Ong, what are you doing here?", "I've come to attend Professor Hazairin's lecture". "But Ong, it's finished". "Okay". Beep, beep, off Ong would go again. His Mobylette was famed for breaking down, its owner lacking the mechanical skills to repair it.

Ong was forming friendships at university. He already knew Nugroho Notosusanto, a student leader who was to become a leading historian and one of Ong's mentors. Towards the end of the 1950s he also started socialising in Jakarta salons. One of the salons Ong frequented was run by the painter Sriyani, whose husband was a diplomat. Students would drop in from the nearby university and art centre and lengthy discussions on art, history and politics would ensue. The house of Bibsy Sunario, the daughter of the veteran Indonesian politician Agus Salim, was also a popular meeting place for Jakarta intellectuals and Ong would frequently drop in at all hours to eat and talk.[5] He was starting to make his way in the established intellectual circles of Jakarta.

In some ways this was a beginning of rather tentative starts. Although he was not a Catholic, Ong joined the Catholic student group. It was a sort of half-way house between the exclusiveness of the Chinese society on campus and the Gerakan Mahasiswa Nasional Indonesia (GMNI, Movement of Indonesian Nationalist Students), the student organisation associated with the Partai Nasional Indonesia (PNI, Indonesian Nationalist Party). He was known on campus for his garrulousness and his nomadic lifestyle. During these years Ong lived with his brother in various houses in Jakarta but he always seemed to be on the move from place to place, dropping in, eating, talking endlessly, and displaying equally great enthusiasm for all these activities.

Ong studied law for about two years. By the end of 1957, however, he had more or less abandoned his formal studies and was looking for a new direction. An opportunity to explore such a direction came when Ong began research work for the Cornell University scholar, G. William Skinner, who had just completed his major work on the Chinese in Thailand. Skinner needed a research assistant to help him with work on the Chinese of Indonesia. And who could be better as a research assistant than this clever young Chinese who was a book lover, a great reader, and with the foreign language skills to read the historical documents in Dutch. Ong soon met other Western scholars, including Betty and Herb Feith and this led on to contacts with other academics, in particular Americans and Australians.

There was another young Chinese student, Frits Tan, on campus. Older than Ong, though like him also a book lover with a great interest in economic history, Frits Tan was closely associated with P. K. Oyong, the editor of *Star Weekly* and a man with a good eye for intelligent young men with potential. *Star Weekly* was at that time virtually obligatory reading for Indonesian Chinese and covered a vast range of topics including social issues, sport, cooking, political analysis and world news.[6]

Through Frits Tan, Ong was introduced to Oyong. On the basis of Ong's research for Skinner, it was soon suggested that Ong write articles for *Star Weekly*. Ong's first contribution was an historical perspective on the Chinese in Indonesia for the special edition to celebrate Chinese New Year in 1958.

By the time *Star Weekly* was closed, in the increasingly oppressive political atmosphere in 1961, Ong had contributed 37 articles, a significant contribution for an undergraduate student. Some of these articles were rather light "fillers" to raise money, but a dozen presented more serious historical reflections on the Chinese in Indonesia, a significant deepening of Ong's identity as part of the Indonesian Chinese community. In the first half of 1959, Ong went overseas for the first time, going to the Philippines for six months. On his return, *Star Weekly* published his analysis of the Chinese there.

The climate to which Ong returned from the Philippines in the second half of 1959, was one in which the role of the Chinese in Indonesian society was being publicly debated. This debate, which centred on the question of the assimilation of the Chinese into Indonesian society, was naturally a key concern of *Star Weekly*, and of Ong himself. As an educated young Chinese who had made a conscious decision to become Indonesian in his early youth, Ong felt it was his duty to take a leading role in this debate. In articles he contributed to the *Weekly*, Ong argued strongly for the assimilation of the Indonesian Chinese, a position advocated by the periodical and by Ong's friends.

On the other side of the debate were those who argued for integration. This group, who formed Badan Permusyawaratan Kewarganegaraan

Indonesia (Baperki, Body for Consultation on Indonesian Citizenship) argued that the Chinese could not be assimilated into Indonesian society but should be regarded as a separate ethnic group like the Javanese, the Bataks, the Acehnese, the Minahasans, the Manadonese, the Balinese and so many others. In late 1959, Ong's strong views on assimilation came into conflict with those of Siauw Giok Tjan, a leading figure in Baperki. The ensuing polemic in the columns of *Star Weekly* catapulted Ong to greater prominence in the Indonesian Chinese media. His family was somewhat puzzled, but generally pleased ("he's in the papers!").

This began a short but dramatic career in which Ong was widely recognised as one of the leading advocates for the assimilation of the Indonesian Chinese. He was a signatory to a number of public statements on the issue in 1959 and 1960 and to a charter of assimilation signed in Bandungan in Central Java in 1961. Ong lost interest in this movement as it became more bureaucratic, eventually forming a body loosely associated with the military. However, his role in the assimilation debates is remembered to this day and his writings are included in all books that discuss them.

In September 1960, Ong began his studies in the History Department at the University of Indonesia's Faculty of Arts, along with a fellow student later to become a famous linguist, the Catholic Javanese Harimurti Kridalaksana, with whom he underwent the student hazing rituals. While Ong did not excel in all his first year exams in 1961, he was gradually moving back from a career mostly outside university to one that was rather immersed in it. In 1961 he first met Benedict Anderson, who was to become one of the most well-known scholars of Indonesia, and with Benedict Anderson and later Ruth McVey, another leading American scholar, he began his travels within Java. It was at this time that Ong fell in love with Javanese culture, a love which had always been present in his childhood in Surabaya, but which was now growing into one of the major themes of his life. He developed a deep fascination with Javanese art and culture, both in its aristocratic or *priyayi* form, as well as in its village and *abangan* forms. In around 1962, Ong completed a sub-thesis on the Samin movement, a peasant protest movement which flourished in north-central Java in the late nineteenth and early twentieth centuries under the charismatic leadership of an illiterate Javanese peasant named Surantika Samin. This led him on to further study.

Ong seemed to have found his niche. In the small history department, he was studying subjects that met his intellectual interests. He travelled widely in Java and to Bali, sometimes with American scholars, sometimes on his own, and becoming a collector of Javanese artefacts and Balinese paintings. He was also writing an occasional article to raise some money and expanding his substantial collection of books. At the same time, he was also broadening the range of significant figures in his life. In the history department, Ong had a great friend in A. B. Lapian, whom he had befriended in the late 1950s, and a mentor in the historian Nugroho Notosusanto. He was also involved in the Catholic conservative circles around *Star Weekly*.

Beyond that, he had become something of a follower of Soejatmoko, an intellectual associated with the Partai Sosialis Indonesia (PSI, Socialist Party). In the increasingly depressing times of guided democracy, Soejatmoko had started a study group where he gathered around him young scholars, of which Ong was one, to discuss the situation and the attitudes they should take to it. Yet at the same time, and in the other political direction, Ong also became increasingly close to the nationalist student organisation GMNI. Here he made friends such as Kartjono, a GMNI leader, and others who came from lowly Javanese village backgrounds. These friends impressed Ong with their broad knowledge and introduced him to village society.

By the mid-1960s, then, Ong had greatly expanded his social and intellectual circle. He was discussing Indonesian politics in Dutch with Soejatmoko, and nationalist approaches to Javanese culture in Javanese with Kartjono and his friends. He also had deep friendships with Ruth McVey and Benedict Anderson. With this eclectic group of friends and mentors, it was perhaps not surprising that those around Ong wondered exactly where his loyalties lay in the political environment of Guided Democracy. On the one hand his association with GMNI placed him close to the Sukarnoist leftists of the Nationalist Party. On the other hand, his friendships with foreign, in particular American, scholars aligned him with those neo-colonialist forces against whose influence president Sukarno was increasingly warning.

Then, early on the morning of 1 October 1965, Ong's world, like that of many other Indonesians, was turned upside down. In the aftermath of the attempted coup, president Sukarno's power was gradually undermined by a coalition between the military, in particular the army, and anti-Communist students, who demanded that the Communist Party and all its affiliated organisations be disbanded. This was eventually achieved with the signing of the Order of March the Eleventh (*Surat*

Perintah Sebelas Maret, Supersemar), in which Sukarno effectively ceded power to the little-known general Suharto. Ong was in one way closely associated with these events. Shortly after the attempted coup, young historians were set to work examining Communist Party files for evidence that the Party had been planning to take over the country. Although Ong found no such evidence in the files that he was set to read, he was deeply impressed by the ability of the Communist Party leadership to communicate complex historical ideas to their following. As a senior student, Ong had begun to teach classes at the university and he compared his own ability to impart ideas to his students with that of the Party leaders.

For Ong, however, the most distressing outcome of the political upheaval that dominated this period was the wave of terrible killings that took place across the countryside of Java and into Bali in late 1965 and early 1966. Ong hastened to East Java after reports of the killings there began to emerge and although many of the details have been obscured in Ong's recollection, he clearly witnessed barbaric scenes. In East Java there were stories of the rivers running red with blood; in one incident, Ong recalled witnessing a decapitated head being paraded around a village. This was linked in his mind with the horrific image of Marie Antoinette's head that he'd gained from his readings on the French Revolution. These events deeply disturbed Ong who saw it as an attack on the *abangan* culture of Java that he loved. In the light of the terrible violence of this period, Ong must also have questioned what kind of a country it was that he had chosen to call home, a country which had showed so much promise when Ong made his decision to do so soon after the end of the Revolution. Was this what "being Indonesian" involved?

Ong's experiences in late 1965 cannot be compared to the horror of those who suffered at first hand the beatings, kidnappings and killings, but they were devastating enough for a young man steeped in Javanese culture. He feared that, as had happened with the French Revolution, a "white terror" would fill Indonesia with violence for years to come. Ong was clearly in a disturbed mental state from late 1965. His behaviour both in public and in private reflected this. Friends and acquaintances remembered Ong yelling slogans such as *"Hidup PKI"* ("Long live the PKI", the Indonesian Communist Party), and all sorts of rumours circulated about him, that he was a member of the left or a CIA spy. Whatever the reasons, he was jailed around 10 March 1966 and spent some six months, until late September 1966, in very difficult conditions.

By the end of 1966, Ong was out of jail but deeply depressed as a result of the political events and his own experiences. He was particularly upset by the loss of many of his books when his small rented room was raided after his arrest and material which might provide evidence of his "guilt" confiscated. On the suggestion of Soejatmoko, Ong eventually sought psychiatric treatment for his depression. The treatment lasted for about ten weeks. After his release, Ong began to mingle more widely with the expatriate community, becoming particular friends with Blanche d'Alpuget and Tony Pratt, young Australians then in Jakarta. He says in retrospect that "they saved my life"; serving as a refuge for humour, good conversation and good food at a time when Ong was still suffering from bouts of depression and mental instability. In between teaching at the university Ong was also working towards finishing his final thesis, a massive, carefully researched document on the fall of the Dutch East Indies, later published as a book, which he completed in September 1968. Days after his thesis was examined, Ong left for Yale University where he had accepted a doctoral scholarship.

The preceding paragraphs have painted a picture of a young Indonesian scholar of Chinese background between the ages of 22 and 35, with somewhat tentative beginnings but whose early promise was already being realised. He was becoming a widely known figure both in the intellectual circles of Jakarta and amongst foreign, and in particular American, scholars of Indonesia, through whom, in part, he had "discovered" Java. He was gaining a reputation as an eccentric, a wit and a deeply knowledgeable scholar and was widely acknowledged as a pioneer figure in debates over the assimilation of the Chinese in Indonesia. Yet he was also an individual whose world had been turned upside down at the end of October 1965 and who was struggling with his horror at the political and social upheaval that had taken place, and with the depression that this, together with his own awful experiences in jail, had induced in him. Quite apart from this, however, he was also struggling with another aspect of his identity, one which dates back at least to the Revolution.

Emotional and Sexual Development

In terms of his emotional and sexual development, Ong seems to have been something of a late bloomer. He was taught to masturbate in 1945 at the age of 12 by a younger relative and during the turmoil of the Revolution became aware that he was attracted to the pictures of handsome men in photographers' shops. He also found himself drawn to the *pemuda*, the young men of the Indonesian Revolution who cast such an heroic and romantic image over the early years of Indonesia's struggle for independence. At the time, however, Ong was not able to explore these feelings further.

During his first period of freedom from his family at high school in Bandung in the early 1950s, Ong could not but notice how attractive and confident his Sundanese schoolmates were. Then, in the middle of 1955 he was plunged into the cosmopolitan world of Indonesia's greatest city Jakarta, with its great variety of lifestyles. Ong witnessed this from somewhat of a distance but as he grew more aware of his sexual orientation, he would go for long walks at night through the urban kampungs of Jakarta. He was searching, though at the time he was not quite sure for what. Occasionally, he met some of the more venerable members of the Indonesian elite out on similar strolls, rather more sure of what they were after. He also expressed regret that during his time in the Philippines in 1959 he did nothing about the many handsome men.

In those days, as now, there were two famous meeting points for homosexual encounters, at the Lapangan Banting, near the present-day Borobudur Hotel, and the park around what is now the National Monument (Monas). Ong had a few brief encounters, no doubt highly thrilling and alarming, but not really satisfactory. Sexual contact was available, but it lacked the dimensions of romance or relationships.

Ong was haunted by a sense of abnormality and sin. Everything in his background advised against homosexuality. Chinese society, like Indonesian society, tends to be hostile to the notion of homosexuality. Ong's gregarious and voluble mother sometimes mentioned homosexuality but never in a supportive way. Moreover, in Chinese families, it is the responsibility of the eldest son to marry and perpetuate the family line. Ong was his father's eldest son although amongst his mother's four children he had an older half-brother. Ong's family were also in varying degrees Catholic and Ong was a member of the Catholic student organisation. This brush with Catholicism had not given him much sense of its great morals, but it certainly helped develop in him a deep sense of guilt about his feelings. He was looking for a loving relationship but found no means by which to have one. Masturbation made him feel like a sinner.

Ong says of these years that he felt deeply troubled, and was surprised that his friends did not see it in his face. Ong remembers a small restaurant in the later half of the 1960s where a staff member asked him why he looked so haunted. Ong felt that the observation of this stranger, more percipient than his friends, was an accurate comment on his state of mind.

So, during the years from 1965 to 1968 Ong was not only struggling to come to terms with the events of 1965–66, nationally and at a more personal level, but he was also haunted by a deep sense of alienation from mainstream Indonesian and Indonesian-Chinese society.

Ong had made the serious decision to become a "real" Indonesian in 1951 or 1952, around the age of 19. By 1968, some 16 years later, this decision had become much clearer in some ways and less so in others. He had found an intellectual niche in the newly emerging field of Indonesian history. He was established as a writer, well known amongst the Jakarta intellectual elite and regarded as a pioneer in the assimilation movement. However, the political situation and the difficulties he faced with his evolving sexual identity led to a deep depression and to grave doubts about how to be a gay Chinese Indonesian in a society which under Suharto's military government was much more antipathetic to Ong's broad humanitarianism and toleration of liberalism. Ong's years in America between 1968 and 1975 were then something of a liberation.

Overseas, 1968–75: Retrieving Confidence

In September 1968 Ong left Indonesia to undertake a PhD at Yale University. When he left his mother was in a coma and he knew he was unlikely to see her again. Shortly after her death, however, Ong's father also died. The family saw this as an indication that Ong's father had truly loved his wife, despite their quarrelsomeness.

America in the late 1960s was awash with liberation movements and exciting new ideas and Ong took to it all with great enthusiasm. On arriving in America he rushed to eat an American ice-cream, which he'd been told were the best of the best. He was disappointed; it wasn't any better than Jakarta ice-creams. The gesture was significant; he was out to taste the New World.

And what a time to be in America! And on one of the most elite of American campuses. Ong arrived at Yale as George W. Bush was leaving, and studied at the same time as Hillary Rodham and Bill Clinton, Sigourney Weaver and Meryl Streep. Ong was invigorated by the doctoral experience as a whole and by his years in America, where he was supervised by major scholars: Harry Benda, Bernard Dahm, Anthony Reid and Milton Osborne. His university experience seems to me to have extended his ideas and strengthened them, rather than changed them.

American society was in turmoil in the late 1960s: Black Power, Black Panthers, Women's Liberation, Gay Liberation, hippies, love-ins, counter-culture, drugs, music, and everywhere: Vietnam! Vietnam! Vietnam! 1968, 1969 and 1970 were important years for those movements, hinted at by the following dates: the assassinations of Dr Martin Luther King Jr in April 1968, and Robert F. Kennedy in June 1968; the use of the term "Women's Liberation Front" in the magazine *Ramparts* in 1969; the birth of the Gay Liberation Front in New York city immediately after the Stonewall riots in Greenwich Village in June 1969; the Apollo II moonwalk in July 1969; the shooting of students at Kent State University in May 1970.

These events roiled onto the Yale campus in New Haven, Connecticut. President Nixon sent the National Guard into New Haven on Ong's 37th birthday (1 May 1970), not because he had heard of Ong's birthday parties, but because of massive demonstrations around the murder trial of Black Panther leaders. Tear gas was fired on rioting crowds; walking home late at night, Ong just missed being caught in an explosion.[7] His birthday present was to be a close witness of social turmoil, besides which his personal problems shrank and withered.

Ong's time at Yale roughly overlapped the Nixon presidency. Richard Nixon won the elections in late 1968, only weeks after Ong's arrival. The central issue of his early presidency was to seek solutions to the Vietnam War. Southeast Asia was a focus of American public attention as never before. In 1972 Nixon made his unprecedented visit to China, realigning world diplomatic relations. From June 1972 Ong followed the Watergate scandal that eventually brought about the president's resignation in August 1974. Watching this process Ong felt that it showed the resilience of democratic institutions, and strengthened further his preference for Western-style liberal democracy.

At Yale, Ong lived in a run-down, downtown area. He was well known for his drinking, which some people related to the trauma of his time in prison, others to the strain of his parents' death, and others again to an overwhelming appetite for life. He was famed for his humour, his garrulousness, his knowledge of Indonesia and for the haze of cigarette smoke that always seemed to surround him. He talked about his experiences in jail with some, and with others he made allusions to it. This was the period when he started experimenting with cooking. Some very odd dishes appeared along the way, but he was learning skills central to his later life.

Ong also met new and old friends at Yale, the latter being American and Australian researchers whom he had befriended in Jakarta earlier in the 1960s. He plunged into postgraduate life, and also sought out the undergraduates. He wanted to have the fullest experience of campus life. He was popular in the postgraduate community. He was seen as an Indonesian and, even more, an expert on Indonesia. After all, he had been discussing Indonesia's past, present and future with Western scholars since he had met "Bill" Skinner in Jakarta in 1957. He was studying nineteenth-century history, but when modern Indonesian politics was discussed, he had much to say. The late colonial period, the Japanese Occupation, the Revolution, the 1950s, Guided Democracy, the rise of the New Order—he had personal experience of all of them, and opinions about them all. He was seen as an Indonesian expert on Indonesia, and he spoke that way, and with that voice. He was of Chinese descent—so what? He was gay—who cared? The liberation movements urged their followers to stand up, demand their rights, and be proud.

During his time at Yale, he was also able to have a long-term relationship with a fellow student and to engage in what seems in retrospect a relatively small number of sexual experiences. He went to Holland for fieldwork and was rather disappointed there, feeling that it was like being back in primary school with the Dutch scholars as teachers. He had enjoyed writing about Dutch history in a course at Yale, treating Dutch history as an object, as he felt Dutch scholars had treated Indonesia. He was turning the tables on the Dutch. He travelled in Europe in his holidays, enjoying the customs, the cuisine, the drinks and the people—and being identified by them as Indonesian. Ong was simultaneously becoming more cosmopolitan, and more confidently Indonesian.

It is hard to exaggerate how different these seven years were to the three preceding them. From September 1965 to September 1968 he had been suffering depression and mental instability, he had been jailed for six months, and some saw him as a pariah to be feared and shunned. From September 1968 to mid-1975 he was a popular university figure, undertaking a doctoral degree at one of the most elite of Ivy League campuses. He could have stayed away from Indonesia. He was likely to have got jobs in America or Europe if he had applied. But by 1975 he wanted to come "home", to Indonesia, and to try to make a life and a career there on his own terms.

Conclusion

This discussion of Ong's life and career does not cover the years from 1975–2001 back home in Indonesia. During this quarter of a century as a public intellectual, Ong was a popular speaker and social commentator, a giver of dinners, an advisor to researchers and to those who needed pointers in living, a wit, a lover, a homemaker, a collector of objects and persons, a didactic presenter of a better Indonesian lifestyle, and, in his forties, fifties and sixties, the maker of his own life. Neither does it include an account of Ong's life from his stroke in 2001 until his death in August 2007. Much about these subsequent 32 years can be read in the "100 days" book of reminiscences referred to above.[8]

This chapter has concentrated on the early life and career of an individual whose boyhood was a thoroughly Chinese-Dutch synthesis, but who struggled throughout his later youth and much of his life to achieve a thoroughly Indonesian identity. As the discussion indicates, the decision to "become Indonesian", taken with great seriousness in the early 1950s, was at times a very difficult course and encompassed elation, depression, love, sexual yearnings, jail, psychiatric treatment and life overseas, as well as some very difficult decisions about how to live. This singular case suggests that for many people, becoming Indonesian may be a difficult project in which background, experience, emotions and sexuality are important factors.

As Ong's case shows, the development of identity may be both a gradual process, and a complex and difficult one. This chapter has not attempted to address in any comprehensive way important questions such as: what does it mean to be "Chinese", "Chinese-Indonesian" or "Indonesian" in Indonesia and what does "identity" mean? For now, these theoretical questions are best left to the experts. Yet this brief account of the life of a singular individual may provide an insight into some of the issues that individuals, be they Chinese, Javanese, Batak, Balinese or Minahasan, might face in their journey towards an achieving an "Indonesian" identity. This chapter has presented a particular example of the personal difficulties encountered by the Indonesian Chinese in establishing its identity as Indonesian. Looking back over Ong's life, this writer identifies two great factors in shaping Ong Hok Ham's desire to be Indonesian: his searching reflections on how his own family had tried to cope with Indonesia's turbulent politics from 1942, and the stimulating role of an inspiring teacher at high school.

Notes

This chapter is based on around 100 interviews conducted since 2002 as the basis for my forthcoming biography of Ong Hok Ham (also known as Onghokham), supplemented by his writings and other publications cited below.

1. The extent of "Chineseness" and "Indonesianness" are difficult to quantify, and remain largely in the eye of the beholder. But it seems largely to consist of attitude, interests, enthusiasms, "speaking position", and behaviour in society (whom one mixed with, the organisations one joined). When I asked the painter Sriyani how Ong had seemed around 1960, she said to me: "Not all the water of a thousand seas could wash away his Chinese face, but when he spoke, to me he was one hundred percent Indonesian, and Javanese".

2. Ong Hok Ham's writing was mostly published in magazines and journals. Books came more slowly. Eight articles from 1977–80, mostly from *Prisma*, were collected in *Rakyat dan Negara* (People and State) (Jakarta: Sinar Harapan, 1983). Onghokham's first degree thesis was published in 1987: Onghokham, *Runtuhnya Hindia-Belanda* (The Fall of the Dutch East Indies) (Jakarta: Gramedia, 1987). Ong's 1975 doctoral thesis at Yale University, "The Residency of Madiun: Priyayi and Peasant in the Nineteenth Century", has not yet been published, though plans come and go. Four collections of his articles were published after his stroke. First, 41 *Kompas* articles from 1980–2002 were collected in Onghokham, *Dari Soal Priyayi sampai Nyi Blorong: Refleksi Historis Nusantara* (From Javanese Aristocracy to Mythic Nyi Blorong: Indonesian Historical Reflections) (Jakarta: Kompas, 2002). Then 70 *Tempo* columns written between 1976–2002 were published in Onghokham, *Wahyu yang Hilang, Negeri yang Guncang* (The Mandate is Lost, the Nation is Tossed) (Jakarta: Tempo, Freedom Institute and LSSI, 2003). Nine scholarly articles in English from 1976–2001 are compiled in Onghokham, *The Thugs, the Curtain Thief and the Sugar Lord; Power, Politics, and Culture in Colonial Java* (Jakarta: Metafor, 2003). The fifteen articles from *Star Weekly*, 1958–60, are collected in Ong Hok Ham, *Riwayat Tionghoa Peranakan di Jawa* (The History of the Indonesian Chinese in Java) (Jakarta: Komunitas Bambu, 2005).

3. *Onze Ong: Onghokham dalam Kenangan* (Our Ong: Onghokham in Reminiscences), ed. D. Reeve, J. J. Rizal and W. Alhaziri (Jakarta: Komunitas Bambu, 2007).

4. Most members of Ong's family chose Indonesian citizenship ("after all, this is where we were born"). But other members of the family moved to Holland, Brazil and China.

5. Many people have had fantasies of running salons for Jakarta's gilded intellectual life, but so far I only know of these two. One foreign friend thought of Ong as a "walking salon", always offering an introduction to a new artist, painter, intellectual or political figure. Ong's celebrated dinners at

home, after his return from the United States, were partly a move to create civil connections between Jakarta's compartmentalised elites.

6. *Star Weekly* was one of the most prominent papers for the Indonesian Chinese population, and read by native Indonesians as well. The historical series on World War II supplied by editor P. K. Oyong was widely admired. The weekly was increasingly affected by nationalist censorship of the press from 1959, and was banned in 1961. Later P. K. Oyong was a founder of the daily *Kompas*.
7. See A. McIntyre, "Minority Men: Ong Hok Ham and Harry J. Benda in Indonesia and America", in *Onze Ong*, pp. 23–32.
8. Reeve *et al.*, *Onze Ong*.

CHAPTER 14

Indonesian Identity after the Dictatorship:
Imagining Chineseness in Recent Literature and Film

Paul Tickell

For over 30 years Indonesia's New Order government did its best to make its Chinese minority "disappear". Under the guise of assimilationist policies, Indonesian Chinese were compelled to take indigenised names, prevented from openly and publicly observing Chinese religious and cultural rituals, prohibited from importing or displaying Chinese language materials, as well as a litany of other formal and informal discriminatory policies directed at this supposedly singular and monocultural group. Assimilation in this form was a sham, which required public absence, and implied the illegitimacy of any expression of Chineseness in the context of Indonesian national public life, yet at the same time also maintained a politically convenient separation from the *pribumi* (indigenous) majority.

Conventional wisdom has *pribumi* resentment of Sino-Indonesians stemming from their power and dominance over the economy. It is a pervasive trope that extends beyond Indonesia into Western commentary, and seeks to explain why Indonesia's Chinese minority are regarded so negatively and treated with varying degrees of hostility. Frequently Western reportage will announce that the Indonesian Chinese are *x* per cent (usually between two and four per cent) of the Indonesian population and that they exercise a disproportionate control over the national economy.[1] More recently a counter-trope has emerged where it will often be noted that there are also poor Indonesian Chinese.[2] The first of these tropes clearly accepts economic jealousy as the explanation for the *pribumi* population's hostility towards Sino-Indonesians. In more sinister ways, it also provides an implicit justification for racism, discrimination and ultimately violence towards the Sino-Indonesian population. It also overly simplifies both the longer history and the more recent social and economic positioning of this population group in Indonesian society. The "some-Chinese-are-not-rich" argument is equally limiting. While it apparently contests, contradicts and lessens the economic dominance–jealousy argument, in a paradigmatic sense, both are not all that different from each other.[3] In both, the supremacy of a master narrative of the economy and relative economic status is affirmed. Sino-Indonesians and their identity are reduced to a subset of the economic. With both of these tropes we are in essence at a discursive dead end. Using either one may confront us with a continuing cycle of resentment and violence on the one hand or implied denial on the other, with neither "side" having the discursive ability to see its way out of this "problem".[4]

The dominance of "economic" explanations of the character of the Sino-Indonesian population is compounded by a persistent assertion of their alien character in the Indonesian context. Although this community has not received any significant in-migration since the first half of the twentieth century and many—especially those referred to as *peranakan*—speak Indonesian or other local Indonesian languages, are of "mixed" ancestry, and have cultures and lifestyles owing more to Indonesian rather than Chinese influences, the community is still frequently referred to as an "immigrant" one. Its "immigrant" status allows it to be depicted as essentially alien and foreign. As Heryanto has noted,[5] this "alien" character is compounded by assertions of dubious loyalty to the Indonesian nation-state, either expressed as an asserted ambiguity to the Indonesian nationalist movement or to the Indonesian republican cause during Indonesia's war of independence or under the New Order by tendencies towards unacceptable ideologies, most notably communism. As a result of these popular and widely accepted myths, singularity and essentialism characterise popular *pribumi* understandings of the Sino-Indonesian community, which in turn allows all other historic, political, cultural and linguistic affiliations to be reduced to one characteristic, viz. *Cina*.⁶

While Chineseness has always been a given and uncomplicated known for the Indonesia's *pribumi* citizens, under Suharto's New Order Chineseness was characterised more by a discursive absence rather than presence—by the unsaid rather than the said. This is best illustrated by commonly coded references to Indonesian Chinese under the New Order, where the most common, semi-official appellation for Indonesian Chinese was the acronym, WNI (*warga negara Indonesia*, Indonesian citizen). The term WNI is one that has particular historical connotations associated with post-independence debates on the citizenship status of peoples of "alien races" resident in newly independent Indonesia. The historic overtones of this term are now largely lost on the great majority of the Indonesian population and now to refer to a person as WNI is for all intents and purposes merely a code for labelling them as Chinese. A less historically laden term, but one that equally comes to mean "Chinese" in the Indonesian context is *orang keturunan* (literally, "a person of descent" with the precise nature of that descent made invisible, but discursive practice making it more than apparent that what is intended is almost always "Chinese"). In other domains reference to Chineseness was coded in similar opaque ways. For instance in the four "no-go" areas of New Order media, usually indicated by the acronym SARA (*Suku, Agama, Ras dan Antar-golongan*; Ethnicity, Religion, Race and Class), the *ras* element was generally seen as a coded reference to relations between Sino-Indonesians and the wider *pribumi* community. In all cases, there is no overt mention of the Chinese—no reference to *Cina, Tionghoa, Hoakiau* or any term that is unambiguously "Chinese". In all of these cases, literal meanings stand in marked contrast to popular understandings. Under the New Order Chinese ethnicity became unsayable and invisible.

The end of the New Order saw marked and significant changes in the representation of Sino-Indonesianness and of Sino-Indonesians. No longer is Chineseness the unsayable of Indonesian politics and culture. More often than not, Sino-Indonesians are no longer a coded absence but an openly stated fact. For Sino-Indonesians themselves self-representation and assertion of a discrete and legitimate identity has been mostly in the political realm. The 1999 general election was contested by a number of overtly Indonesian Chinese parties, with other prominent Indonesian Chinese playing a role in other mainstream, multi-racial parties. Culturally, Chinese self-representation has been far more muted. With official approval and to the apparent delight of the Indonesian Chinese community, in 2000 Chinese New Year was openly celebrated for the first time since the establishment of the New Order. With official imprimatur, such celebrations of Chineseness have been deemed acceptable. In terms of literary expression (and representation in the electronic media of cinema and television) Sino-Indonesian self-representation is still a much more uncertain phenomenon. Indonesian television stations regularly show Chinese language programs, but these are mostly from China. While this shows an acceptance of the public display of Chineseness, which was something unimaginable under the New Order, domestic expressions of Chineseness by the local Sino-Indonesian community still remain somewhat tentative.

In terms of creative literature, Sino-Indonesians appear to have concentrated on a retrospective and historical examination of their community's contribution to Indonesian literature. This has taken the form of the re-publication of a number of pre-World War II works of Sino-Indonesian (low Malay dialect) literature in what is to date a ten-volume series entitled *Kesastraan Melayu Tionghoa dan Kebangsaan Indonesia* (Sino-Malay Literature and Indonesian Nationalism/Nationhood).[7] The second part of the title of this series addresses one of the more frequently asserted characteristics of the Indonesian Chinese—their supposed dubious loyalty to the Indonesian nation-state. The series aims to put Sino-Indonesian literature into the Indonesian cultural and political mainstream. Certainly the editors maintain the uniqueness of this creative expression, but also insist on its situation within the broader social and political forces of Indonesian national awakening, nationalism and the pre-war *pergerakan* (nationalist movement). Such a re-siting of Sino-Malay literature is long overdue. What is absent in this project is, however, the presentation of issues of contemporary importance to the Sino-Indonesian community by openly, self-identifying Sino-Indonesian authors. These specific examples of Chinese political and cultural liberation are yet to manifest themselves in the contemporary literary imagination of this community. This is all the more striking because of the prominent role played in the creative arts by a number of Indonesians of Chinese descent. Since the demise of Suharto, and as far as I have been able to ascertain at the time of writing, very little creative literature has been published by Indonesians of Chinese descent which specifically addresses the Sino-Indonesian experience.[8] This stands in marked contrast to a number of works written by *pribumi* Indonesians in the post-Suharto period that—perhaps for the first time ever in the history of modern Indonesian literature[9]—begin to address problems of being Chinese in the political, social and cultural context of modern Indonesia.

Implicit in much of this new depiction/representation of the Chinese is an exploration and rejection of *pribumi* racism towards the Sino-Indonesian community. Much of this creative writing exposes and then rejects the discursive processes that have legitimised this racism and violence. The following part of this chapter will look at three Indonesian short stories and one novel of considerable length, all written by *pribumi* authors, but all of which centre on the experiences—both recent and historic—of the Sino-Indonesian community. Virtually all of the short stories discussed here arise directly out of the shocking events of May 1998, where Sino-Indonesian property was pillaged and Sino-Indonesian women were raped and murdered. Both this pillaging and the rapes were carried out ostensibly by unorganised thugs. It is also now generally believed that both the property and sexual crimes were planned and carried out by elements of the Indonesian military and their *preman* (thugs, toughs) proxies. These events—especially the rapes and to a lesser degree the lame denials of New Order apparatchiks as to the veracity of the events and the testimony of victims and witnesses—have become a singular and searing event in the consciousness of many *pribumi* Indonesians. The events of May 1998 were singular in the sense that never before has the persecution of the Sino-Indonesian community generated such a backlash and fundamental change in, and reassessment of, *pribumi* Indonesian attitudes.

A number of factors may be put forward to explain why reactions to May 1998 were so different from previous anti-Chinese pogroms. May 1998 was the first anti-Chinese pogrom in the age of the Internet. The political importance of the Internet in Indonesia should not be underestimated.[10] The role of dissident Indonesian sites, international Chinese sites, chat rooms, and feminist sites in documenting these matters and maintaining a domestic Indonesian and an international public profile cannot be discounted. The systematic sexual violence that characterised the events of May 1998 also occurred in historically and politically sensitive contexts for Indonesia. On the one hand, war in the Balkans and Bosnia in particular had (re-)sensitised the world to the use of sexual violence in war. For *pribumi* Indonesians, there was the added dimension of this sexual violence being directed against Moslem women, which gave the issue greater intensity and touched on the sensitivities of a large part of the *pribumi* population. On the other hand events of May 1998 also occurred after some 25 years of Indonesian occupation of East Timor.

The Indonesian military's use of rape as a weapon in the subjugation of the territory are well and credibly documented and widely known, though frequently denied, in Indonesia itself. For many Indonesians there was a dawning sense that barbaric tactics used on the East Timorese were now being used uncomfortably close to home.

The political "use" of rape shook the parvenu middle-class sense of an Indonesian identity. These events, seen on television, read about in newspapers and magazines, documented on the Internet and frequently in Jakarta, visible a couple of city blocks away, confronted this new middle-class's sense of what it was to be an Indonesian. Paradoxically, the New Order's ideologies of citizenship and identity—inculcated into the educated, urban middle-class and having them believe that to be Indonesian was to be *manusia yang beradab, manusia Timur* (civilised, cultured and moral Indonesian "Orientals", in implicit contrast to sexually decadent and lax Westerners)—dissolved, while another facet of the New Order, state-sponsored violence, simultaneously materialised before their eyes. Social and class changes in Indonesian society brought about by the very success of the New Order also saw the emergence of a new, urban *pribumi* middle-class. For the first time, significant numbers of *pribumi* Indonesians lived a lifestyle that had much in common with the urban, Sino-Indonesian middle-class. This new *pribumi* middle-class certainly exhibited some mutuality of interest and outlook with the Sino-Indonesian middle-class, in ways which had been rare earlier.

The violence directed at the Sino-Indonesian community also occurred at a time when the state was not just financially, but morally and ethically bankrupt. So, while in the past, anti-Chinese riots may have been sanctioned or even orchestrated by the Indonesian state, those of May 1998 have come to represent a qualitatively different level of atrocity. After these events none of the usual "othering" of the Chinese had any great level of purchase in the wider community, who no longer saw their interests as equivalent to those of the state, nor necessarily antagonistic to those of the Sino-Indonesian community. What all these factors suggest is that *pribumi* visions of Chineseness are now refracted though new prisms, as are their own senses of "Indonesian" identity. Notions of othering, of the "alien", of absolute difference which were previously formed by and understood through local filters (e.g. through ideas of "nation", ethnicity, local community, language groups, "race") are now either being internationalised or influenced by global forces of change. Global flows of information, movements of population, communications and cultural consumption mean that senses of identity are for many now in deep flux. Because these factors question notions of self and identity, powerful cross-cultural feelings of solidarity, common purpose, understanding and empathy are beginning to emerge; the concept of the "other" has become somewhat more flexible and relative.

In the light of these forces of change, the treatment of the Indonesian Chinese situation in some recent Indonesian fiction suggests that the community is no longer seen as so radically "other". What the two conventionally antagonistic poles of *pribumi* and Indonesian Chinese share and experience in common is much greater now than what divides them, and in turn, much greater than what distinguishes both from even more distant "others". By foregrounding and empathising with the Sino-Indonesian experience, these authors also interrogate their own Indonesianness. As such, these works of fiction represent a timely piece of Indonesian self-reflection.

The works examined here, Veven Sp. Wardhana's stories in *Panggil Aku Pheng Hwa* and Remy Sylado's novel and feature film, *Ca Bau Kan* address three major questions of Sino-Indonesian (and in turn, Indonesian) identity. They explore naming, absence, identity and place as one issue. They also explore the importance of arbitrary authority, and violence along with personal uncertainty and insecurity. Finally, one of the works addresses the problem of ethnicity and nationhood for the Sino-Indonesian community within the context of the Indonesian nation.

Naming/Absence/Identity/Place: Veven Sp. Wardhana's *Panggil Aku Pheng Hwa*

New Order policy did its best to make the Indonesian Chinese minority disappear. One means in particular to achieve this disappearing act was to compel Sino-Indonesians to take Indonesian-sounding names. Veven Sp. Wardhana, in several short stories in a collection entitled *Panggil Aku Pheng Hwa* (Call Me Pheng Hwa, also the title of one of the short stories) addresses this issue of naming and what it means for an individual's sense of identity and of (not-)belonging. It is important first to note the author's use of a literary conceit: Veven gives the narrator his own name (Effendy Wardhana).[11] Yet the theme as well as the narrator of the story is clearly Sino-Indonesian. Veven (the author) is not a Sino-Indonesian—as far as I can ascertain from various people who have met or know him.[12] This literary conceit and its confusion of ethnicity appear both conscious and

Indonesian Identity after the Dictatorship

intentional and as a literary device subverting the arbitrary and irrational discursive processes that make such identification important.

The story centres on naming, identity and place and how each of these change and interact with each other. It starts with the narrator telling the reader:

> "*Sejarah telah menyeretku jadi bunglon: begitu cepat berganti nama, begitu pindah tempat hinggap*".[13]
>
> [History has made me into a chameleon, as quickly as I changed names, I also changed the place where I'd perch.]

The narrator is a Sino-Indonesian, who because of historical imperatives has several names. He is Pheng Hwa, but those in his community who know him well call him Ping An. The (Indonesian) state demanded that he be called Effendy Wardhana. Others call him by the generic title *singkek* (a term of address for adult males of Chinese descent in Indonesia). Different names for different people in different contexts. His shifting of names is at times a matter of compulsion.

> "........*toh saat ke kantor Polsek atau instansi pemerintah aku harus menyebutkan nama pemberian negara itu*".[14]
>
> [..... however, when I went to the local police station or a government office, I had to use the name the state gave me.]

Later, in different contexts, first as a secondary school student in a small town, then as a university student in Yogyakarta and then as an office worker in the capital, Jakarta, it is his "official" name that he is known by, to the point where:

> "*Lalu, aku pun kemudian jadi terbiasa dengan nama Effendy Wardhana, sementara kalau ada yang memanggilku Pheng Hwa, bahkan dulu terkadang singkek, kupingku jadi mendadak gatal. Di kemudian hari, barangkali juga karena aku sudah kian jarang kontak dengan keluarga karena berbagai alasan, kesadaranku bahwa aku adalah waniktio menjadi semakin mengabur*".[15]
>
> [Then, even I later got used to the name Effendy Wardhana, to the point where if someone called me Pheng Hwa or even before that sometimes called me *singkek*, my ears suddenly got itchy. Later on, perhaps because I had less and less contact with my family for various reasons, my sense of being an Indonesian Chinese became more and more indistinct.]

The narrator then moves to Paris, where names, identities, solidarities also change. In Paris he becomes Ping An or the generic *singkek* again.

Ostensibly he assumes his *real* name and becomes his *real* self again. The Indonesian state obviously has little influence here. Yet, in a different place, with a different history, the narrator's identity is also changed. As a *pribumi* friend notes to the narrator:

> "*Tak soal, Ping: di negeri ini, tampang kayak kamu justru lebih dihargai dibandingkan aku*", *kata Gus beberapa saat menjelang acara kumpul-kumpul itu selesai dan masing-masing hendak meninggalkan resto.*
>
> *Ucapan Gus tidak salah. Dalam kereta bawah tanah, kalau misalnya, ada penumpang kereta yang menyapaku, rata-rata pertanyaan mereka adalah: Vous êtes Vietnamese?*"[16]
>
> ["It's no big deal, Ping. In this country someone who looks like you is more valued than someone who looks like me", Gus said a few moments before the social gathering broke up and the participants each were leaving the restaurant.
>
> What Gus said was not wrong. In the Metro, if for instance a passenger spoke to me, what they mostly asked was: Are you Vietnamese?]

His "Chinese" appearance, which had in part stamped his identity in Indonesia and was a liability, in France marked him again, but this time positively and in the narrator's mind, erroneously as a Vietnamese, prompting him to ask:

> "*Kenapa mereka interes pada orang Vietnam? Kenapa para Prancis itu masih juga mengulang-ulang kebebalan bule-bule lainnya, yang sering salah kira terhadap kita sebagai orang Filipina?*" *sergahku.* "*Apakah dalam zaman globalisasi dan gombalisasi ini mereka masih juga gemblung menganggap Bali itu ada di luar Indonesia, seperti yang digambarkan banyak wartawan Indonesia dari zaman ke zaman, dari orde ke orde?*" *sergahku cenderung dalam nada sengit ketimbang sekadar ingin tahu*".[17]
>
> ["Why are they interested in the Vietnamese? Why do the French keep repeating the nonsense of other whiteys when they so often mistake us for Filipinos?" I snarled. "In this age of globalisation and dumbo-isation do they still blithely regard Bali as not being part of Indonesia, as so many Indonesian reporters have shown us to be the case from one historic period to another and from one regime to another?" I snarled in combination of anger mixed with curiosity.]

From an identity in Indonesia that is clearly demarcated, that is noted on his KTP (Kartu Tanda Penduduk, citizen identity card), in France his identity is mistaken. His "otherness" is mistaken for someone else's otherness. For the French, an Asian "other" is/must be a Vietnamese. The tone of annoyance suggests that this identity confusion is shaking some of the narrator's more rigid frames of personal reference. The confusion questions who he is, how he relates to other people, how they relate to him and how he identifies others.

In his relationship with others he notes with annoyance that:

> "....semua Cina yang kutemukan di wilayah Paris distrik 13 ini tak satu pun yang bicara dalam bahasa Mandarin. Bahkan sesama Cina pun mereka ber-parlez Française".[18]
>
> [...all the Chinese I had met here in the 13th Arrondissement of Paris, not one of them spoke in Mandarin. Even with other Chinese they spoke French.]

Language as a fixed mark of ethnicity collapses before him. His attempts to converse in Chinese with people who he believes *should* be speaking Chinese also fails.[19] He is then confronted with the question *"Pakai akte kelahiran siapa?"*[20] [Whose birth certificate did you use?] While in Indonesia, the power of the state was used to deny him and others like him their real names, in France the situation is reversed. Immigrants cheat the state by assuming new identities, by taking over the birth certificate of a dead person.

Even in France, Pheng Hwa does not possess one name and with it one identity. In a formal context (an *acara syukuran*—a ceremony giving thanks for the birth of a child) and with a relatively unknown fellow countryman, Pheng Hwa becomes Effendy Wardhana again.

> "Pheng Hwa memang namaku. Namun, saat aku bertemu dengan ipar ekonomi yang disebut-sebut istriku itu, yang kusebutkan justru nama pemberian negara itu".[21]
>
> [Of course, Pheng Hwa was my name. Nevertheless when I met the economist brother-in-law (of a friend), whom my wife had mentioned, the name that I used was precisely the name the state had given me.]

His name gives others clues to his place—though again erroneous.

> "*Effendy nama Anda? Anda Muslim? Anda dari Malaya?*" tanya seorang Prancis dan seorang Italia nyaris bersamaan.
>
> "*Saya dari Indonesia, Malaya, kalau yang Anda maksudkan adalah Malaysia, itu dekat sekali dengan Indonesia*", aku mencoba menerangkan dengan penuh kesabaran.[22]
>
> ["Is Effendy your name? Are you a Muslim? Are you from Malaya?" asked a French person and an Italian almost at the same time.

"I am from Indonesia. If by Malaya, you mean Malaysia, it's near Indonesia", I tried to explain with great patience.]

Again his barely suppressed annoyance suggests that he wants and perhaps demands precision in his identity and place. His "otherness" is again mistaken for someone else's "otherness".

His sojourn in the land of the other—the remote and extremely foreign other, so much more "other" than those immediately outside his small home town Sino-Indonesian community—gives rise to a sense of ease and possession of all his names and identities.

> "*Di negeri asing ini, dengan nama Pheng Hwa atau Effendy Wardhana, aku tak lagi merasa asing atas diriku sendiri sebagaimana yang selama ini diam-diam menyelinap dan mengendap dalam benak.*
>
> *Aku tak lagi menggubris aku akan dipanggil dengan nama apa. Toh, aku sudah tidak lagi merasa ngumpet—entah dari apa—jika harus menyebutkan nama pemberian negara itu. Juga aku tak lagi perlu merasa khawatir—entah karena apa—jika kemudian ada yang memanggilku pakai nama waniktio itu.*
>
> *Aku merasa baru terlahir kembali*".²³

[In this foreign country, if I was called Pheng Hwa or Effendy Wardhana, I no longer felt alienated from myself as had been the case up to now when this alienation had seeped into and precipitated onto my brain.

I no longer cared what name people called me. However, I no longer felt the need to curse—God only knows for what reason—if I had to use the name the government gave me. I also no longer felt anxious—God only knows why—if someone used my Chinese name.

I felt as if I had been born again.]

At ease with his names, at ease with himself, Effendy/Pheng Hwa returns to Indonesia. The narrator's sense of ease and acceptance of who he is contrasts to the tense atmosphere at Jakarta-Cengkareng airport.

> "*Saat mendarat di Cengkareng, hari sudah hampir pagi. Menjelang melewati meja pemeriksaan paspor, aku mencium gelagat aneh. Entah apa. Petugas imigrasi yang memeriksa paspor pun perlu menatapku dengan tajam, sambil bercampur rasa penasaran. Entah pula karena apa*".²⁴

[When I arrived at Cengkareng, the sun was almost coming up. As I approached the passport control desk, I could sense a strange attitude. I was not quite sure what it was. Even the immigration officer checking my passport felt it necessary to stare at me sharply, mixed in with a feeling of annoyance. God only knows why?]

The description suggests both the sinophobic hostility of Indonesian officialdom, but also something more general and ominous. Phones are not working. There are no taxis to pick up passengers at the airport. He asks an official what date it is, receiving the reply, 15 May—the day of the riots in Jakarta that led to the pillaging of Indonesian Chinese property and the rape of Indonesian Chinese women. The narrator then asks what year it is, feeling as in the film the *Philadelphia Experiment*, that he has entered a time warp.

The issue of names, identities, origins, memory and (self-)recognition is explored in a slightly different way in another of Veven's short stories in the same collection. In *Déjà Vu: Kathmandu* unsayability becomes an index of the trauma suffered by Sino-Indonesians during the riots of May 1998. The story may also be read as an indictment of an initial, and widespread denial by the wider Indonesian community of the sexual violence associated with these riots. Like the previous story, its international setting provides the physical and emotional distance required to work through the trauma of these events. Memory of these events, however, always intrudes, no matter how conscious the effort to forget and to suppress that memory is.

The story is structured as an exchange between a man, fictitiously named Xu Xian, and a women, equally fictitiously named Xiao Qing. These names derive from Chinese folklore and suggest a possible relationship between the man and the woman. Throughout the story it is repeatedly suggested that the protagonists know each other, but that the precise details of their acquaintance cannot be recalled or must be consciously suppressed.

> "*Mereka sama-sama merasa saling mengenal. Mereka merasa pernah saling bertemu*".[25]
>
> [They both felt that they knew each other. They felt that they had once met each other.]

and

> "*Rasanya, pertanyaan itu adalah sebuah pernyataan. Aku juga merasakan, sebelumnya kami memang pernah berjumpa. Atau malah kami saling mengenal; kenal dengan dekat bahkan*".[26]
>
> [I felt that the question was a statement. I also felt that we had previously met. Or that we even knew each other...even knew each other intimately.]

and

> *"Apalah arti nama asli bagi pertemuan kami? Kucoba keras berpikir mengingat-ingat sosok Xiao Qing—atau siapa pun dia—yang ada di hadapanku ini di lembar-lembar masa lampau; barangkali aku bisa menemukan sosok itu, sehingga terbukti bahwa kami memang pernah saling mengenal, atau bahkan saling berdekatan.*
>
> *Usaha rekonstruksi itu sia-sia".*[27]

[What do real names mean for our meeting? I tried hard to fathom the depths of my memory to remember what Xiao Qing—or whoever she was—who stood before me, looked like. Maybe I could find this image to prove that we knew each other or had even been close to each other

This attempt at reconstruction was in vain.]

Their past is suppressed. It cannot be consciously retrieved. At times it is actively forgotten.

> *"Apakah masa lampau begitu berarti? Anda mengira aku ini benar-benar jelmaan siluman ular itu? balas perempuan itu tanpa memberi kesan bahwa dia menolak menjawab pertanyaan lelaki itu.*
>
> *"Anda berniat melupakan asal-usul dan leluhur?" lelaki itu balik bertanya, sambil diam-diam membenarkan pertanyaan retoris perempuan itu. Bukan saja nama tak lagi mempunyai arti penting, asal-usul negeri untuk melacak jejak kemungkinan mereka pernah bersama juga sama sekali tak memiliki makna".*[28]

["Is the past so important? Do you think that I am really the reincarnation of that snake spirit?" the woman replied without giving any impression that she was refusing to answer the man's question.

"Do you want to forget your origins and ancestors?" the man countered, while implicitly agreeing with the woman's rhetorical question. It wasn't just names that no longer had any importance, but also country of origin became absolutely meaningless in any attempt to trace the possibility that they had once been together.]

A person without a past, without an origin cannot be complete, cannot be pinned down. The search for a more stable and solid identity leads to an exchange concerning the man's profession. He is rather ambiguous on this score, as to whether he is a *jurnalis* (journalist) (p. 24), a *novelis* (novelist) (p. 24) or a *pencatat sejarah* (a chronicler of history). This exchange ends significantly with:

> "*Bukankah jurnalis mencatat sejarah bahkan pada saat sejarah itu sedang berlangsung? Itu bedanya dengan penyusun sejarah resmi yang memilih-milih fakta untuk kepentingan tertentu*", ucap perempuan itu lagi".[29]
>
> ["Doesn't a journalist record history precisely at the point when that history is happening? That's why official historians are different, because they selectively choose facts for particular interests", the woman said.]

History and its chroniclers record the past, but not an unbiased factual past, but a past of particular sectional interests. It is a painful past and as such must be suppressed. This "selective choosing of facts" and the problems of evidence, truth, veracity are all issues that echo official responses to the May 1998 riots and rapes. The existence of the rapes, the veracity of victims' and witnesses' evidence were all called into question, then denied by *"kepentingan tertentu"*—most notably the apparatchiks of the collapsing New Order regime.

Memory and origins can never be completely suppressed. Memory is recalled by tangential reference and unplanned events. The characters hear some music in Kathmandu, which reminds them of traditional, Jakartan-Chinese *tanjidor* music.

> "*Musik yang mereka mainkan mengingatkan aku pada tanjidor.*
>
> *Bersamaan dengan lewatnya serombongan mempelai, tangan Xiao Qing yang makin erat menggenggam tanganku kurasakan begitu dingin*".[30]
>
> [The music they were playing reminded me of *tanjidor*.
>
> As the wedding party went by, Xiao Qing's hand grasped mine even more tightly and I felt how cold it was.]

and

> "*Nama musik yang menghempaskanku ke nama negeri asal musik itulah yang membuatku kembali berkeringat dingin. Aku gemetar. Jantungku bergeletar. Aku benci negeri yang tak sempat disebutkan Xu Xian itu. Aku benci mengetahui musik itu berasal dari negeri yang kubenci itu*".[31]
>
> [The name of the music threw me back to the name of the country from where that music came and made me break out in a cold sweat. I shivered. My heart fluttered. I hate that country, whose name Xu Xian did not get to say. I hated knowing that that music came from that country that I hated.]

The country of origin cannot be named. Trauma and hatred mean that it must be actively forgotten.

"*Terus terang, aku merasa begitu tenteram bersama Xu Xian, yang nama aslinya aku tak tahu dan tak penting untuk kuketahui. Aku memang merasa tenteram berada di sampingnya. Tapi, aku ngeri mendengar nama negerinya, apalagi harus hidup bersama dengannya di negerinya. Rasa ngeri itu kembali mendesak-desak rongga dada.*

Ingin rasanya aku menghempaskan rasa ngeri itu sejauh-jauhnya, tapi aku selalu gagal mewujudkannya. Sejak berita perihal saudara kembarku tak lagi kuketahui keberadaannya—kecuali katanya dia pernah cidera dan rumahnya diporakporandakan sebelum dibakar massa—perasaanku begitu gampang bergebalau. Biasanya, jika dia sakit, aku pun ikut menderita sakit; atau ketika dia begitu ingin menyaksikan film tertentu, dan tak kesampaian, akulah yang justru kemudian menontonnya setelah kudapatkan lewat video compact disc. Kontak emosional kami tak terhalang oleh jarak yang memisahkan kami. Aku ikut Mama tinggal di Kanada, saudara kembarku ikut Papa tinggal di negeri yang namanya hendak kuhapus dari benak".[32]

[Frankly I felt so safe with Xu Xian, whose real name I didn't know and whose real name is wasn't important to know. I really felt safe and calm with him. But I was scared when I heard the name of his country, even more so if I had to live with him in that country. The sensation of fear returned and pressed down on my chest.

I think I wanted to throw that feeling of fear as far away as possible, but I always failed in making this a reality. Since the news of my twin sister, about whose existence I no longer knew anything—except for reports that she had been injured and her house trashed before being burned down by the masses—I have been easily upset. Normally if she were sick, I would also be sick as well, of when she really wanted to see a particular film, it would be me who would later watch it on after I got it on VCD. I went with Mummy to Canada, and my twin sister went with Daddy to that country whose name I want to wipe out of my brain.]

The origins of this trauma are further explained at the very end of the story, when Xu Xian opens a file on his computer when he returns to Jakarta.

"*Kalau saja nanti di Jakarta dia membuka-buka file di komputernya, dia akan menemukan tulisannya mengenai perkosaan massal yang pernah terjadi di negerinya. Dalam file yang disimpan dalam folder khusus itu, lelaki itu juga mendokumentasikan foto seorang perempuan yang wajahnya sama persis dengan Xiao Qing. Folder khusus itu menampung sejumlah tulisannya yang ditolak media massa yang tak berkehendak memuatnya*".[33]

[Only later on in Jakarta when he was skimming through files on his computer did he discover his writings on the mass rapes that had occurred in his country. In a file stored in a special folder, the man had collected photos of a woman whose face was exactly the same as Xiao Qing's as documentation. This special folder also contained a number of articles that had been rejected by the mass media that had no desire to publish them.]

Following the events of May 1998 it is "Indonesia" that becomes the unsayable, not "Chineseness". The events and especially the sexual violence are denied. The significance of this exposure of denial does not merely touch on the condition and fate of the Sino-Indonesian community, but points to a collapse in the moral legitimacy of not only Suharto's New Order Indonesia. Perhaps the whole idea of Indonesia is being brought into question. How can a state either through its official agents in the form of its military or component parts of its society in the form of the *massa* (masses) quoted above[34] perpetrate such deeds on WNI—on *warga negara Indonesia*—literally Indonesian citizens and still claim legitimacy? Significantly it is a *pribumi* Indonesian author who poses these questions and implicitly with them other broad questions regarding the basis of national integration.

Ca Bau Kan: An Acceptable Alien in an Indonesian Master Narrative

Less comprehensive and less intellectually ambitious in the questions that it poses about the position and legitimacy of the Indonesian Chinese is Remy Sylado's novel and feature film, *Ca Bau Kan* (woman, in Hokkien but a word that has come to mean whore in Indonesian). This novel/film presents issues relating to the status and legitimacy of the Indonesian Chinese, but in ways that are far more conventional and conservative than Veven Sp. Wardhana's work. Unlike Veven's short stories that are informed by a more global and post-nationalist sensibility, *Ca Bau Kan* keep the Indonesian nation-state as its main point of reference. In doing so, it does not question the fundamental legitimacy of that state. In many ways, however, Remy's novel and its subsequent transformation into a stylish and successful film make it into a far more directly influential work than Veven's stories. Like Veven Sp. Wardhana, Remy Sylado is not normally seen as a Sino-Indonesian.

Ca Bau Kan began life as a serialised novel in the Islamic-oriented daily newspaper, *Republika* in 1997. It was later republished as a book by Kepustakaan Populer Gramedia (KPG), part of the large (Sino-Indonesian,

Catholic) media conglomerate, Kompas-Gramedia. Its first edition was published in March 1999 and by May 2002 it had reached its 7th edition. The novel was filmed in 2001 and played to considerable, though not universal, critical acclaim.

Ca Bau Kan is an historical novel, covering the period 1918 to 1951. It traces the life of its main characters through the era of Dutch colonialism, to the Japanese Occupation of Indonesia during World War II, into the Indonesian revolution and ultimately to independence and national liberation. Into this master narrative of Indonesian nationhood and nationalism is woven the story of Siti Nurhayati (Tinung) and her eventual Sino-Indonesian husband, Tan Peng Liang. The story line draws both in its content and tone on pre-World War II popular *nyai* novels in the Indonesian language. These novels depict indigenous Indonesian women forced by poverty and other circumstances into becoming the wives, mistresses or concubines of European or Chinese men. The plot of *Ca Bau Kan* is circuitous, depending on misunderstanding and coincidence, scheming and plotting to propel the story forward. Life for Tinung is a series of melodramatic ups and downs. She enters a polygamous marriage at age 14 and is widowed soon after. She is tormented by her late husband's principle wife and returns to her parent's home. Driven by financial pressures, her mother's solution to their problems is surprisingly described as:

> "*Ternyata pilihan untuk mengurung diri itu pun menimbulkan masalah dalam rumahnya. Mbok Jene, sang Ibu, perempuan kebanyakan yang terbiasa berpikir cekak dan tumbuh pula dengan pertimbangan-pertimbangan pikiran yang sederhana sekali, belakang geregetan, panik dan tak dapat menahan diri untuk tidak mengomel. Dia memarahi Tinung. 'Daripade lu ngerem melulu di rume kayak tekukur kuburan, angguran lu jadi cabo, katauan juntrungannye,' katanya*".[35]

> [Obviously her choosing to lock herself away caused problems in the household. Jene, her mother—like most women—was limited in her intellect, which grew out of her simplistic considerations and had recently made her anxious, panicky and unable to stop herself from complaining. She would yell at Tinung: "Rather than just hangin' about the house like a cemetery dove, why don't ya earn ya keep by going on the game, by whoring, get to know how they do it". She said.]

Tinung becomes a prostitute, servicing Chinese men from a boat on the Kali Jodo in Batavia. She is picked up by a Chinese man, Tan Peng Liang—not to be confused with another and later Tan Peng Liang who will ultimately become her husband—and is taken into concubinage. This concubinage results in the birth of a child, but murder, violence and intrigue finally make Tinung flee and leave her first Tan Peng Liang. This first Tan Peng Liang is a cliched stereotype of a Chinese man—a stereotype to be found in much of the pre-war *nyai* literature and one that generally accords with the image of the Chinese in the Indonesian popular imagination. He is coarse, violent, criminal, corrupting, primarily interested in money and willing to be unscrupulous in his pursuit of this money. His dealings with Tinung are characterised by coarseness and violence.

After escaping Tan Peng Liang, from Tangerang, Tinung takes up with a second Tan Peng Liang, who comes from Semarang. This second Tan Peng Liang is a far more interesting and positive character. Although still fulfilling many of the stereotypical characteristics of the Chinese (he is wealthy, many of his activities are criminal or semi-criminal), he has numerous characteristics that make him a far more positive character. In terms of the Chinese community and establishment in Batavia, he is an outsider from the central Javanese city of Semarang. He has clear and unambiguous links through his family with the Indonesian nationalist movement. His father is Chinese and his mother Javanese of aristocratic birth and through his maternal side one of his cousins is a leading Indonesian nationalist (Soetardjo Rahadjo). Much of his semi-legal activity is carried out for the benefit of the nationalist movement (e.g. he smuggles guns from Thailand and the Malay peninsula for the nationalists). His politically correct affiliations with and support of the nationalist movement are amplified by his treatment of and regard for Tinung. Although he takes her as a concubine, he treats her with affection, civility and comes to love her.

In *Ca Bau Kan* Chinese characters clearly fall into two categories. Those regarded as positive and legitimate are those who have connections with and sympathy for the Indonesian nationalist movement and who treat indigenous Indonesians with affection. The illegitimate are those who fulfil the usual, predictable cliché of materialistic, business-oriented Chinese, ambivalent to political ideals and Indonesian nationalism. Such characters also treat *pribumi* Indonesians with disdain and violence. While Tinung's husband, the Semarang Tan Peng Liang is no saint, and many of his actions border on the criminal, his criminality supports the right side—the Indonesian nationalists. The novel and film appear to be saying that Chinese in Indonesia can be legitimate and can be a part of Indonesia. This legitimacy and participation merely depend on support for the nationalist ideal.

This represents a far more conservative view than the vision of belonging envisioned in Veven Sp. Wardhana's work. In part Remy Sylado's conservatism is explained by chronology. Unlike the Veven stories that were written after the shocking and socially galvanising events of May 1998, *Ca Bau Kan* is a product of the final years of the New Order. As such, it can be seen as part of the expanding, but still limited space that had opened up for Indonesian Chinese under the late New Order.[36] Although this space was probably greater than that offered to the Sino-Indonesian community at any other time during the whole of the New Order period, it was nevertheless a distinctly limited space—limited by what was ideologically acceptable within the regime and subsumed within master narratives of Indonesian nationhood and popular, conventional stereotypes about the Chinese.

In post-New Order Indonesia the events that led to the demise of Suharto have both shocked many Indonesians and left a vacuum of moral, political and economic legitimacy for the Indonesian state. New spaces opened to imagine not just what it means to be a Sino-Indonesian, but also what the future meanings of Indonesianness may come to be. It is interesting to note that it appears to have been *pribumi* Indonesian authors who have been the first to take up the literary and cinematic possibilities of sympathetically imagining the plight of Sino-Indonesians in both contemporary and more distant Indonesian historical contexts. It is somewhat paradoxical that 100 years ago at the beginning of the twentieth century, the emergence of print capitalism in the Netherlands East Indies and with it, the Malay language press, became the catalyst and provided the means by which ethnically disparate populations, both *pribumi* and ethnic Chinese, could begin to imagine new collective identities.[37] At the end of the twentieth and the beginning of the twenty-first centuries, we are perhaps seeing the way that the interaction between the old media of print, the newer media of cinema and television, the newest medium in the form of the Internet and galvanising historical events are creating new ways of imagining and new spaces where new senses of belonging and new solidarities may come into existence. These spaces may or may not draw on older, primordial, ethnicities, newer nationalisms or more recent imaginings of global solidarities. However, the questions they pose of identity, belonging and naming can no longer ever be as simple or straightforward as they once may appeared to have been.

Notes

1. For instance: M. Cohen, "Exploring a Painful Past", *Far Eastern Economic Review*, 19 Sept. 2002. "During the Suharto era, movies and TV shows preferred to uphold the cheery fiction of national unity, largely ignoring the ethnic Chinese, who account for 4 per cent of the population, but who hold a disproportionate share of the national wealth."
2. See, for instance, J. Siegel, "Early Thoughts on the Violence of May 13 and 14, 1998 in Jakarta", *Indonesia* 66 (Oct. 1998): 106.
3. This touches on the question of "thematic" and "problematic" issues, which Chatterjee raises in the context of anti-colonial nationalist discourse, where he points out that much (if not all) nationalist discourse is a thematic variation on the dominant discourse of the colonial power. As he notes: "There is, consequently, an inherent contradiction in nationalist thinking, because it reasons within a framework of knowledge, whose representational structure corresponds to the very structure of power nationalist thought seeks to repudiate". P. Chatterjee, *Nationalist Thought and the Colonial World: A Derivative Discourse* (London: Zed Books, 1986), p. 38. In the case of Sino-Indonesians, the affirmation or denial of economic privilege merely reinforces the centrality of this "thematic" and prevents an alternative problematic from shedding light on the "problem" of the Indonesian Chinese.
4. I have consciously marked the terms "side" and "problem" because I see these terms as problematic. Their unconscious use is indicative of a particular discourse, laden with what I consider fundamentally toxic, racist overtones. To say that *pribumi* and Sino-Indonesians are on opposing "sides" and that Sino-Indonesians represent a "problem" in part at least an acceptance of this racist discourse. For matters of personal conviction, it is not a discourse I wish to participate in or justify in any form whatsoever.
5. A. Heryanto, "Ethnic Identities and Erasure: Chinese Indonesians in Public Culture", in *Southeast Asian Identities: Culture and the Politics of Representation in Indonesia, Malaysia, Singapore and Thailand*, ed. J. Kahn (Singapore: ISEAS, 1998), pp. 98–101.
6. The Indonesian language has numerous ways to refer to the Chinese. Under the New Order, *Cina* became the official nomenclature for ethnic Chinese, replacing the earlier usage of *Tionghoa* (Chinese) and *Tiongkok* (China). For many ethnic Chinese, the term *Cina* is regarded as offensive and an intentional slur towards them on the part of the Suharto regime. It is worth noting that both terms—Cina and Tionghoa—have a long history in Indonesia. In post-Suharto Indonesia there has been a general move to resuscitate the use of the term "Tionghoa"—both as a mark of respect and legitimacy for Sino-Indonesians, but perhaps also as a break with a repressive and abusive past. On the relative connotations of *Cina* and *Tionghoa*, as well as debates on their contemporary usage, see: L. H. Murbandono, "Tionghoa atau Cina", available

from <http://www.rnw.nl/ranesi/html/tionghoa.html> [accessed 9 Aug. 2002]. A. Budiman, "Cina atau Tionghoa", siarlist@minihub.org, available from <http://www.minihub.org.mailinglists/siarlist/msg00699.html> [accessed 9 Aug. 2002]. Hnl, "Cina, Tionghoa atau Hoaqiau?" Satulelaki.com, available from <http://satulelaki.com/cetak/0,9341,00.html> [accessed 9 Aug. 2002].
7. A. S. Marcus and P. Benedanto, eds., *Kesastraan Melayu Tionghoa dan Kebangsaan Indonesia* (Sino-Malay Literature and Indonesian Nationhood), vol. 1 (Jakarta: KPG, 2000), 2001. There are now 10 volumes in this series (2008).
8. See, for example, "Sajak-sajak Wilson Tjandinegara": <http://cybersastra.net/edisi_mei2002/mei2002_3.htm> [accessed 26 June 2002]; "Darah Daging Sastra Wilson Tjandinegara", <http://cybersastra.net/edisi_mei2002/mei2002_1.htm> [accessed 26 June 2002]; N. Suryadi, "Tragedi Mei 1998 dalam Sajak Wison Tjandinegara", <http://cybersastra.net/edisi_mei2002/mei2002_4.htm> [accessed 26 June 2002].
9. I can think of one possible exception in the writings of Indonesia's premier novelist, Pramoedya Ananta Toer, which address issues of Chineseness and the centrality of the Sino-Indonesian population within the Indonesian national project.
10. K. Sen and D. T. Hill, "The Internet and Virtual Politics", in *Media, Culture and Politics in Indonesia*, ed. K. Sen *et al.* (Melbourne: Oxford University Press, 2000), pp. 194–217.
11. Veven is a commonly used diminutive of Effendy.
12. Personal communication, Assoc. Prof. Pam Allen, University of Tasmania, Dr Edwin Jurriëns, UNSW @ ADFA and Prof. Krishna Sen, Curtin University.
13. V. S. Wardhana, *Panggil Aku Pheng Hwa* (Call me Pheng Hwa) (Jakarta: KPG, 2002), p. 3.
14. Ibid., p. 3.
15. Ibid., p. 4.
16. Ibid., p. 5.
17. Ibid., p. 5.
18. Ibid., p. 5.
19. Ibid., p. 6.
20. Ibid.
21. Ibid., p. 7.
22. Ibid.
23. Ibid., p. 8.
24. Ibid.
25. V. S. Wardhana, in *Panggil Aku Pheng Hwa*, p. 21.
26. Ibid., p. 22.
27. Ibid., p. 24.

28. Ibid.
29. Ibid., p. 25.
30. Ibid., p. 26.
31. Ibid., p. 27.
32. Ibid., p. 31.
33. Ibid., pp. 31–2.
34. See Siegel, "Early Thoughts on the Violence of May 13 and 14, 1998 in Jakarta", pp. 78–91, for a discussion on how the terms *massa* and *rakyat* are used in the context of the May riots to delegitimise and legitimise various acts and actors.
35. R. Sylado, ed., *Ca Bau Kan* (Jakarta: KPG, 2002), p. 14.
36. Heryanto, "Ethnic Identities and Erasure", pp. 104–11.
37. B. R. O. G. Anderson, *Imagined Communities: Reflections on the Origin and Spread of Nationalism* (London: Verso, 1983), pp. 38–9.

Bibliography

Abdul Wahid, Zainal Abidin bin. "Power and Authority in the Melaka Sultanate". In *Melaka: The Transformation of a Malay Capital c 1400–1980*, ed. Kernial S. Sandhu and Paul Wheatley. Kuala Lumpur: Oxford University Press, 1983, pp. 101–12.

———. "Sejarah Melayu". *Asian Studies* 6, 3 (1966): 445–51.

Abdullah, Taufik. *Schools and Politics: The Kaum Muda Movements in West Sumatra, 1927–1933*. Ithaca: Cornell Modern Indonesia Project, 1971.

Abu Bakar, Abdul Latif, ed. *"Kesatuan dan Perpaduan" Dunia Melayu Dunia Islam*. Batu Berendam: Institute Kajian Sejarah dan Patriotisme Malaysia, 2001.

Acciaioli, Greg. "Culture as Art: From Practice to Spectacle in Indonesia". *Canberra Anthropology* 8, 1–2 (1985): 148–72.

———. "Grounds of Conflict, Idioms of Harmony: Custom, Religion, and Nationalism in Violence Avoidance at the Lindu Plain, Central Sulawesi". *Indonesia* 72 (Oct. 2001): 81–112.

———. "Re-empowering the 'Art of the Elders': The Revitalisation of Adat among the To Lindu People in Central Sulawesi and throughout Contemporary Indonesia". In *Beyond Jakarta: Regional Autonomy and Local Societies in Indonesia*, ed. Minako Sakai. Adelaide: Crawford House, 2002, pp. 217–44.

———. "From Customary Law to Indigenous Sovereignty: Reconceptualizing Masyarakat Adat in Contemporary Indonesia". In *The Revival of Tradition in Indonesian Politics: The Deployment of Adat from Colonialism to Indigenism*, ed. Jamie S. Davidson and David Henley. Abingdon and New York: Routledge, 2007, pp. 295–318.

Adhuri, Dedi S. "Hak Ulayat Laut dan Dinamika Masyarakat Nelayan di Indonesia Bagian Timur: Studi Kasus di P. Bebalang, Desa Sathean dan Demta". *Masyarakat Indonesia* 20, 1 (1993): 143–63.

———. "Selling the Sea, Fishing for Power: A Study of Conflict over Marine Tenure in the Kei Islands, Eastern Indonesia". Doctoral dissertation, The Australian National University, Canberra, 2002.

Adhuri, Dedi S. and Ary Wahyono. *Konflik-konflik Kenelayanan: Distribusi, Pola, Akar Masalah dan Resolusinya*. Jakarta: PMB-LIPI, 2004, pp. 83–117.

Adhuri, Dedi S. and Leontine Visser. "Fishing in, Fishing out: Transboundary Issues and the Territorialization of Blue Space". *Asia Pacific Forum* 36 (2007): 112–45.

Adonis, Tito. *Suku Terasing Sasak di Bayan, Daerah Propinsi Nusa Tenggara Barat*. Jakarta: Departemen Pendidikan dan Kebudayaan, 1989.

Age, The. "US President George Bush in an Interview with Bob Woodward", 20 Aug. 2002, <http://www.theage.com.au> [accessed 21 Nov. 2002].

Ahmad, Kassim, ed. *Hikayat Hang Tuah*. Kuala Lumpur: Dewan Bahasa dan Pustaka, 1966.

Allen, Pamela and Sarah Turner. "Speaking Out: Chinese Indonesians after Suharto". *Asian Ethnicity* 4, 3 (special issue, ed. Pamela Allen and Sarah Turner (Oct. 2003): 327–459.

Alter, Peter. "The Rhetoric of the Nation-State and the Fall of Empires". In *The Habsburg Legacy: National Identity in Historical Perspective*, ed. Ritchie Robertson and Edward Timms. Edinburgh: Edinburgh University Press, 1994, pp. 196–206.

Amal, Ichlasul. *Regional and Central Government in Indonesian Politics*. Yogyakarta: Gadjah Mada University Press, 1992.

Amin, S. M. *Sekitar Peristiwa Berdarah di Atjeh*. Jakarta: Soeroengan, 1956.

Andaya, Barbara Watson. "The Nature of the State in 18th Century Perak". In *Precolonial State Systems in Southeast Asia*, ed. Anthony Reid and Lance Castles. Kuala Lumpur: Malaysian Branch of the Royal Asiatic Society (MBRAS) Monograph no. 6, 1975, pp. 22–35.

———. "The Role of the Anak Raja in Malay History: A Case Study from Eighteenth Century Kedah". *Journal of Southeast Asian Studies* 7, 2 (1976): 162–87.

———. *To Live as Brothers: Southeast Sumatra in the Seventeenth and Eighteenth Centuries*. Honolulu: University of Hawai'i Press, 1993.

Andaya, Leonard. *The World of Maluku: Eastern Indonesia in the Early Modern Period*. Honolulu: University of Hawai'i Press, 1993.

Anderson, Benedict. *Imagined Communities: Reflections on the Origin and Spread of Nationalism*. London: Verso, 1983.

———. "Old State, New Society: Indonesia's New Order in Comparative Historical Perspective". *Journal of Asian Studies* 42 (1983): 477–96.

———. "The Idea of Power in Javanese Culture". In *Language and Power: Exploring Political Cultures in Indonesia*, ed. Benedict Anderson. Ithaca: Cornell University Press, 1990 (1972), pp. 17–87.

Ang, Ien. *On Not Speaking Chinese: Living Between Asia and the West*. London and New York: Routledge, 2001.

Antara (Indonesian National News Agency). "Violence in Central Kalimantan to be Stopped in Three Days". 22 May 2001.

———. "District Heads to be Authorized to Issue HPHs". 27 May 2001.

Anwar, Dewi F. "Indonesia's Strategic Culture: Ketahanan Nasional, Wawasan Nusantara and Hankamrata". Brisbane: Centre for the Study of Australia-Asia Relations, Griffith University, 1996.

Appadurai, Arjun. "Patriotism and its Futures". *Public Culture* 5, 3 (1993): 411–29.

Appiah, Kwame A. *Cosmopolitanism: Ethics in a World of Strangers*. New York: W. W. Norton, 2006.

Aragon, Lorraine V. "Communal Violence in Poso, Central Sulawesi: Where People Eat Fish and Fish Eat People". *Indonesia* 72 (2001): 45–79.

Artha, Arwan T. *Dunia Spiritual Soeharto: Menelusuri Laku Ritual, Tempat-Tempat dan Guru Spiritualnya*. Yogyakarta: Galangpress, 2007.

Aspinall, Edward and Greg Fealy, eds. *Local Power and Politics in Indonesia: Decentralisation and Democratisation*. Singapore: ISEAS, 2003.

Astaga.com. "Gereja di Irja Serukan Aparat dan OPM Tahan Diri", 30 Nov. 2000.

Auty, Richard. *Sustaining Development in the Mineral Economies: The Resource Curse Thesis*. London: Routledge, 1993.

Avonius, Leena. "Reforming Adat: Indonesian Indigenous People in the Era of Reformasi". *Asia Pacific Journal of Anthropology* 4, 1 (2003): 93–111.

———. "Reforming Wetu Telu: Islam, Adat, and the Promises of Regionalism in Post-New Order Lombok". Doctoral dissertation, Leiden University, 2004.

———. "Reconciliation and Human Rights in post-Conflict Aceh". In Birgit Bräuchler, ed., *Reconciliation from Below: Grassroots Initiatives in Indonesia and East Timor*, in press.

Azra, Azyumardi. "Mistifikasi Politik Indonesia di Awal Milenium Baru: Gus Dur dan KH Ahmad Mutamakin". *Kompas*, 31 Dec. 1999.

Badan Pusat Statistik (BPS). *Irian Jaya dalam Angka 1998*. Jayapura: BPS Propinsi Irian Jaya, 1998.

Bailey, Conner. "The Political Economy of Marine Fisheries Development Indonesia". *Indonesia* 46 (1988): 25–38.

Bailey, Conner and Charles Zerner. "Community-Based Fisheries Management Institutions in Indonesia". *Maritime Anthropological Studies* 5, 2 (1992): 1–17.

Bakker, Karen and Gavin Bridge. "Material Worlds? Resource Geographies and the 'Matter of Nature'". *Progress in Human Geography* 30, 1 (2006): 5–27.

Bakry, Sastri Yunizarti and Media Sandra Kasih, eds. *Menelusuri Jejak Melayu-Minangkabau*. Padang: Yayasan Citra Budaya, 2002.

Baland, Jean-Marie and Jean-Phillipe Platteau. *Halting Degradation of Natural Resources: Is there a Role for Rural Communities?* New York: Oxford University Press, 1996.

Bali Post. "Mega Jengkel Gus Dur Pilih Ziarah". 21 May 2001.

———. "Mega-Gus Dur Ziarah ke Makam BK". 14 Jan. 1999.

Ballard, Chris. "Citizens and Landowners: The Contest over Land and Mineral Resources in Eastern Indonesia and Papua New Guinea". In *Mining and Mineral Resource Policy Issues in Asia Pacific: Prospects for the 21st Century*, ed. Donald Denoon, Chris Ballard, Glenn Banks and Peter Hancock. Canberra: Division of Asian and Pacific History, Research School of Pacific and Asian Studies, ANU, 1997, pp. 76–81.

———. "The Denial of Traditional Land Rights in West Papua". *Cultural Survival Quarterly* 26, 3 (2002): 39–43.

Ballard, Chris and Glenn Banks. "Between a Rock and Hard Place: Corporate Strategy at the Freeport Mine in Papua, 2001–2006". In *Development and Environment in Eastern Indonesia*, ed. B. Resosudarmo and F. Jotzo (in press).

Bangunjiwo, Ki Juru. *Misteri Pusaka-Pusaka Soeharto*. Yogyakarta: Galangpress, 2007.

Banjarmasin Post. "Dayak Bakumpai Kecewa: Tak dilibatkan Rekonsiliasi". 19 Mar. 2001.

Banks, Glenn. "Mining and Environment in Melanesia: Contemporary Debates Reviewed". *The Contemporary Pacific* 14, 1 (2002): 39–67.

———. "Linking Resources and Conflict the Melanesian Way". *Pacific Economic Bulletin* 20, 1 (2005): 117–23.

———. "Globalization, Poverty, and Hyperdevelopment in Papua New Guinea's Mining Sector". *Focaal: European Journal of Anthropology* 46 (2006): 128–43.

———. "'Faces We do not Know': Mining and Migration in the Melanesian Context". In *Mining Frontiers: Comparative Perspectives on Property Relations: Social Conflicts, and Cultural Change in Boom Region*, ed. T. Grätz and K. Werthmann (in press).

Banks, Glenn and Chris Ballard, eds. The *Ok Tedi Settlement: Issues and Outcomes*. Canberra: National Centre for Development Studies, ANU, 1997.

Barber, Charles Victor. "Forest Resource Scarcity and Social Conflict in Indonesia". *Environment* 40, 4 (1998): 5–37.

Barnard, Timothy P., ed. *Contesting Malayness: Malay Identity across Boundaries*. Singapore: Singapore University Press, 2004.

Barton, Greg. *Abdurrahman Wahid: Muslim Democrat, Indonesian President: A View from Inside*. Honolulu: University of Hawai'i Press, 2002.

Basri, Hasan. "Perpindahan Orang Banjar ke Surakarta: Kasus Migrasi Inter-Etnis di Indonesia". *Prisma* 3 (1988): 42–56.
Beatty, Andrew. *Varieties of Javanese Religion: An Anthropological Account.* Cambridge: Cambridge University Press, 1999.
Benda-Beckmann, Franz and Keebet Benda-Beckmann. "Recreating the Nagari: Decentralisation in West Sumatra". Max Planck Institute for Social Anthropology Working Papers no. 31, 2002, <http://www.eth.mpg.de/pubs/wps/pdf/mpi-eth-working-paper-0031.pdf>.
Bendix, Reinhard. *Max Weber: An Intellectual Portrait.* New York: Anchor Books, 1962 (1960).
Berkes, Fikret, ed. *Common Property Resources: Ecology and Community-based Sustainable Development.* London: Belhaven Press, 1989.
Bernama (Malaysian News Agency). "Dayak-Madurese Conflict: Settling Age Old Scores". 6 Mar. 2001.
———. "Indigenous Dayaks Oppose Return of Madurese to Central Kalimantan". 7 Mar. 2001.
Bleskadit, Dance. "'Merdeka' Menurut Orang Papua". *Tifa Papua.* Aug. 2002.
Bock, Carl. *The Head-hunters of Borneo: A Narrative of Travel up the Mahakkam and down the Barito, also Journeyings in Sumatra.* Oxford: Oxford University Press, 1985 (1881).
Bonneff, Marcel. "Semar Révélé: La Crise Indonesienne et l'imaginaire Politique Javanais". *Archipel* 64 (2002): 3–37.
Boston Globe. "Beheadings on Borneo Linked to Clash over Land". 9 Mar. 2001.
Bourchier, David. *Dynamics of Dissent in Indonesia: Sawito and the Phantom Coup.* Ithaca: Cornell Modern Indonesia Project, Cornell University, 1984.
———. "Lineages of Organicist Political Thought in Indonesia". Doctoral dissertation, Politics Department, Monash University, Melbourne, 1996.
Bowen, John R. "Cultural Models for Historical Genealogies: The Case of the Melaka Sultanate." In *Melaka: The Transformation of a Malay Capital c 1400–1980*, vol. I, ed. Kernial Singh Sandhu and Paul Wheatley. Kuala Lumpur: Oxford University Press, 1983, pp. 162–79.
Braginsky, Vladimir. *The Heritage of Traditional Malay Literature: A Historical Survey of Genres, Writings and Literary Views.* Leiden: KITLV Press, 2004.
Brown, Colin C. trans. Sejarah *Melayu or Malay Annals. JMBRAS* 25, nos. 2–3 (1952): 1–276.
Brown, Donald E. Brunei: *The Structure and History of a Bornean Malay Sultanate.* Brunei: Brunei Museum, 1970.
Brown, Jacqueline N. "Rooted in the Global, Routed through the Local: Cosmopolitanism in Liverpool's Age of Sail". Paper presented at the Conference on Place, Locality and Globalisation, Center for Local, International and Regional Studies, University of California, Santa Cruz, 28 Oct. 2000.
Budiman, Arief. "Cina atau Tionghoa", <http://www.minihub.org.mailinglists/siarlist/msg00699.html> [accessed 9 Aug. 2002].

Cederroth, Sven. *The Spell of Ancestors and the Power of Mekkah: A Sasak Community of Lombok*. Göteburg: Acta Universitatis Gothoburgensis, 1981.

Cenderawasih Pos. "Papua Butuh Pejabat dan Birokrat yang Takut Tuhan: Dari Perayaan HUT 151 Injil Masuk ke Papua", 6 Feb. 2006, <http://www.cenderawasihpos.com/Utama/h.2.html>.

Chambert-Loir, Henri. "The *Sulalat al-Salatin* as Political Myth". *Indonesia* 79 (Apr. 2005): 131–60.

Chambert-Loir, Henri and Anthony Reid, eds. *The Potent Dead: Ancestors, Saints, and Heroes in Contemporary Indonesia*. Crows Nest: Allen & Unwin, 2002.

Chambert-Loir, Henri and Claude Guillot, eds. *Le Culte des Saints dans le Monde Musulman*. Paris: École française d'Extrême-Orient, 1995.

Charras, Muriel. "The Reshaping of the Indonesian Archipelago after 50 years of Regional Imbalance". In *Regionalism in Post-Suharto Indonesia*, ed. Maribeth Erb, Priyambudi Sulistiyanto and Carole Faucher. London: RoutledgeCurzon, 2005, pp. 87–108.

Chatterjee, Partha. *Nationalist Thought and the Colonial World: A Derivative Discourse*. London: Zed Books, 1986.

Chauvel, Richard. *Nationalists, Soldiers and Separatists: The Ambonese Islands from Colonialism to Revolt*. Leiden: KITLV Press, 1990.

———. *Constructing Papuan Nationalism: History, Ethnicity and Adaptation*. East-West Centre Policy Studies no. 14, Washington, D. C.: East-West Center, 2005.

———. "Refuge, Displacement and Dispossession: Responses to Indonesian Rule and Conflict in Papua". In *Dynamics of Conflict and Displacement in Papua, Indonesia*, ed. Eva-Lotta Hedman, RSC Working Paper no. 42, Oxford: Oxford University, Sept. 2007 <http://www.rsc.ox.ac.uk>.

Christie, Jan W. "States without Cities: Demographic Trends in Early Java". *Indonesia* 52 (Oct. 1991): 23–40.

Chua, Beng Huat. *Communitarian Ideology and Democracy in Singapore*. London and New York: Routledge, 1995.

Cohen, Margot. "Exploring a Painful Past". *Far Eastern Economic Review*, 19 Sept. 2002.

Collier, Paul. "Economic Causes of Civil Conflict and their Implications for Policy". In *Leashing the Dogs of War: Conflict Management in a Divided World*, ed. Chester A. Crocker, Fen O. Hampson and Pamela Aall (Washington, D. C.: U.S. Institute of Peace, 2007), pp. 219–41.

Collier, Paul and Anne Hoeffler. "Greed and Grievance in Civil War". *Oxford Economic Papers* 56, 4 (2004): 563–95.

Conklin, Beth A. "Body Paint, Feathers, and VCRs: Aesthetics and Authenticity in Amazonian Activism". *American Ethnologist* 24, 4 (1997): 711–37.

Coppel, Charles A. "Mapping the Peranakan Chinese in Indonesia". *Far Eastern History* 8 (Sept. 1973). 143–67.

———. "Patterns of Chinese Political Activity in Indonesia". In *The Chinese in Indonesia: Five Essays*, ed. Jamie A. C. Mackie. Melbourne: Nelson with The Australian Institute of International Affairs, 1976, pp. 19–76.

———. "The Origins of Confucianism as an Organized Religion in Java, 1900–1923". *Journal of Southeast Asian Studies* 12 (1981): 179–96.

———. *Indonesian Chinese in Crisis*. Kuala Lumpur: Oxford University Press, 1983.

———. "Chinese Indonesians in Crisis: 1960s and 1990s". In *Perspectives on the Chinese Indonesians*, ed. Michael R. Godley and Grayson Lloyd. Adelaide: Crawford House, 2001, pp. 20–40.

———. "Appendix I". In *Perspectives on the Chinese Indonesians*, ed. Michael R. Godley and Grayson Lloyd, pp. 302–29. Adelaide: Crawford House, 2001.

———. "The Indonesian Chinese: 'Foreign Orientals', Netherlands Subjects, and Indonesian Citizens". In *Law and the Chinese in Southeast Asia*, ed. M. Barry Hooker. Singapore: ISEAS, 2002, pp. 131–49.

———, ed. *Violent Conflicts in Indonesia: Analysis, Representation, Resolution*. London and New York: Routledge, 2006.

Cosgrove, Denis E. "Contested Global Visions: One-World, Whole-Earth, and the Apollo Space Photographs". *Annals of the Association of American Geographers* 84, 2 (1994): 270–94.

Cribb, Robert. *Historical Atlas of Indonesia*. Honolulu: University of Hawai'i Press, 2000.

Daniels, Timothy P. "Imagining Selves and Inventing Festival Sriwijaya". *Journal of Southeast Asian Studies 30*, 1 (1999): 38–53.

"Darah Daging Sastra Wilson Tjandinegara" <http://cybersastra.net/edisi_mei2002/mei2002_1.htm> [accessed 26 June 2002].

Davidson, Jamie S. "Culture and Rights in Ethnic Violence". In *The Revival of Tradition in Indonesian Politics: The Deployment of Adat from Colonialism to Indigenism*, ed. Jamie S. Davidson and David Henley. Abingdon and New York: Routledge, 2007, pp. 224–46.

Day, Tony. *Fluid Iron: State Formation in Southeast Asia*. Honolulu: University of Hawai'i Press, 2002.

———. "Ties that (Un)Bind: Families and States in Premodern Southeast Asia". *Journal of Asian Studies* 55, 2 (1996): 384–409.

Derks, Will. "Malay Identity Work". *Bijdragen tot de Taal-, Land- en Volkenkunde* (Special Issue: Riau in Rransition) 153, 4 (1997): 699–716.

DeTAK. "Misi Klenik Orde Baru", 24 Jan. 2001.

Detikcom. "Mega Ziarah ke Makam Bung Karno", 3 Apr. 2004.

Diocese of Jayapura. "Recent Developments in Papua: Papua Congress II, 29 May–4 June 2000, and the Situation Pasca-Congress", Office for Justice and Peace, Diocese of Jayapura, Jan. 2001.

di Tiro, Tengku H. M. *The Price of Freedom: The Unfinished Diary of Tengku Hasan di Tiro*. Norsborg: Information Dept., National Liberation Front Acheh Sumatra, 1984.

Djopari, John R. G. *Pemberontakan Organisasi Papua Merdeka*. Jakarta: Gramedia, 1993.

Douw, Leo, Cen Huang and Michael R. Godley, eds. *Qiaoxiang Ties: Interdisciplinary Approaches to "Cultural Capitalism" in South China*. London: Kegan Paul International with International Institute for Asian Studies, 1999.

Dove, Michael. *Swidden Agriculture in Indonesia: The Subsistence Strategies of the Kalimantan Kantu*. Berlin: Mouton, 1985.

———, ed. *The Real and Imagined Role of Culture in Development: Case Studies from Indonesia*. Honolulu: University of Hawai'i Press, 1988.

———. "'New Barbarism' or Old Agency among the Dayak: Reflections on Post-Suharto Ethnic Violence in Kalimantan". *Social Analysis* 50, 1 (2006): 192–202.

Down to Earth. "New Kalimantan Mega-Project will not Proceed". *Down to Earth* 45, May 2000.

———. "Special Report: 'Forest, People, and Rights'". *Down to Earth*, June 2002.

Drakard, Jane. *A Kingdom of Words: Language and Power in Sumatra*. Kuala Lumpur: Oxford University Press, 1999.

Dumont, Louis. *German Ideology: From France to Germany and Back*. Chicago: University of Chicago Press, 1994.

Dunia Melayu Dunia Islam (DMDI). <http://www.melayuislam.com> [accessed 14 Aug. 2008].

Durie, Mark. "Framing the Acehnese Text: Language Choice and Discourse Structures in Aceh". *Oceanic Linguistics* 35, 1 (1996): 113–37.

Economist, The. "Bloodshed in Borneo", 21 Apr. 2001.

Elson, Robert E. *Suharto: A Political Biography*. Cambridge: Cambridge University Press, 2001.

Equator. "DMDI Pacu Kemajuan Kalbar", 5 July 2006.

Erb, Maribeth, Primyambudi Sulistiyanto and Carole Faucher, eds. *Regionalism in Post-Suharto Indonesia*. London and New York: RoutledgeCurzon, 2005.

Farhadian, Charles E. *Christianity, Islam, and Nationalism in Indonesia*. New York: Routledge, 2005.

———, ed. *The Testimony Project PAPUA: A Collection of Personal Histories in West Papua*. Sentani: Penerbit Deiyai, 2007.

Fau, Nathalie. "Reviving Serumpun Identity across the Straits of Malacca". Paper presented at International Symposium "Thinking Malayness", 19–21 June 2004, Tokyo, University of Foreign Studies.

Faucher, Carole. "Popular Discourse on Identity Politics and Decentralisation in Tanjung Pinang Public Schools". *Asia Pacific Viewpoint* 46, 2 (2006): 272–85.

Featherstone, Mike et al., eds. "Special Issue on Cosmopolis". *Theory, Culture and Society* 19, 1–2 (2002).

Fine, Robert. "Taking the 'Ism' out of Cosmopolitanism: An Essay in Reconstruction". *European Journal of Social Theory* 6, 4 (2003): 451–70.
Ford, Michele. "Who are the Orang Riau? Negotiating Identity across Geographic and Ethnic Divides". In *Local Power and Politics in Indonesia: Decentralisation and Democratisation*, ed. Ed Aspinall and Greg Fealy. Singapore: ISEAS, 2003, pp. 132–47.
Fox, James J., Dedi S. Adhuri and Ida A. P. Resosudarmo. "Unfinished Edifice or Pandora's Box? Decentralisation and Resource Management in Indonesia". In *The Politics and Economics of Indonesia's Natural Resources*, ed. Budy P. Resosudarmo. Singapore: ISEAS, 2005, pp. 92–108.
Galis, Klaas W. "Geschiedenis" (History). In *Nieuw Guinea: de Ontwikkeling of Economisch Social en Cultureel Gebied, in Nederlands en Australisch Nieuw Guinea* (New Guinea: Socio-economic and Cultural Development in Netherlands and Australian New Guinea), ed. I. W. G. Klein. 's-Gravenhage: Stadtsdrukkerij, 1953.
Gatra. "Kartu di Tangan Senior Brother". 16 Oct. 1999.
———. "Meruwat Wahyu Presiden". 12 Aug. 2000.
———. "Tahlilan Kehilangan Sesajen". 12 Aug. 2000.
Geertz, Clifford. *The Religion of Java*. Glencoe: Free Press, 1960.
———. "The Integrative Revolution: Primordial Sentiments and Civil Politics in the New States". In *The Interpretation of Cultures*, ed. Clifford Geertz. New York: Basic Books, 1973 (1963).
———. *Negara: The Theatre State in Nineteenth Century Bali*. Princeton: Princeton University Press, 1980.
Gellner, Ernest. *Nations and Nationalism*. Oxford: Blackwell, 1983.
Giay, Benny. "Church and Society: The Church Leaders of Irian Jaya in the midst of Change and Conflict". Paper presented at the Eukumindo meeting, De Tiltenburg, The Netherlands, 18–19 Apr. 1996.
———. "Gereja dan Politik di Papua Barat", unpublished paper. Jayapura, Jan. 2000.
———. "'Towards a New Papua': When They Hear the Sacred Texts of the Church, Papuans See a Better Future". In *Memoria Passionis di Papua*, ed. Theo P. A. van den Broek *et al*. Jakarta: LSPP, 2001, pp. 8–9.
Go, Gien Tjwan. *Eenheid in Verscheidenheid in een Indonesisch Dorp* (Unity and Diversity in an Indonesian Village). Amsterdam: Sociologisch-Historisch Seminarium voor Zuidoost Azië, Universiteit van Amsterdam Publikatie no. 10, 1966.
Godley, Michael R. and Charles A. Coppel. "The Indonesian Chinese in Hong Kong: A Preliminary Report on a Minority Community in Transition". *Issues and Studies* 26 (1990): 94–108.
———. "The Pied Piper and the Prodigal Children: A Report on the Indonesian-Chinese Students Who Went to Mao's China". *Archipel* 39 (1990): 179–98.

Government of the Netherlands. *Netherlands Government Annual Report to the United Nations on Netherlands New Guinea*. The Hague: Government Publishing House, 1960.

Grootenhuis, G. W. "Papoea Elite en Politieke Partijen". Rapport van de Wetenschappelijk Ambtenaar G. W. Grootenhuis in NNG, Ministerie van Kolonien, ARA, Dossier 11575, 1961.

Habermas, Jürgen. "Citizenship and National Identity: Some Reflections on the Future of Europe". In *The Nationalism Reader*, ed. Omar Dalibour and Micheline R. Ishay. Atlantic Highlands: Humanities Press, 1995, pp. 333–43.

Habib, H. "Wawasan Nusantara dan Hubungannya dengan Ketahanan Nasional". In *Bunga Rampai: Wawasan Nusantara I*, ed. Lembaga Ketahanan Nasional. Jakarta: Fa. Skala Indah, 1981, pp. 21–30.

Haley, Nicole and Ron May. *Conflict and Resource Development in the Southern Highlands of Papua New Guinea*. Canberra: State, Society and Governance in Melanesia Program, ANU 2007.

Hall, John A. "How Homogeneous Need We Be? Reflections on Nationalism and Liberty Sociology". Review Essay. *Sociology* 30, 1 (1996): 163–71.

Haluan (Padang). 13 Nov. 1976.

Hamzah, Alfian, ed. *Kapok Jadi Nonpri: Warga Tionghoa Mencari Keadilan*. Bandung: Zaman, 1998.

Hardin, Garrett. "The Tragedy of the Commons". *Science* 162, 3859 (1968): 1243–8.

Harper, Krista M. "Introduction. The Environment as Master Narrative: Discourse and Identity in Environmental Problems". *Anthropological Quarterly* 74, 3 (2001): 101–3.

Harple, Todd S. "Controlling the Dragon: An Ethno-Historical Analysis of Social Engagement among the Kamoro of South-West New Guinea (Indonesian Papua/Irian Jaya)". Doctoral dissertation, The Australian National University, Canberra, 2002.

Harvey, Barbara S. *Permesta: Half a Rebellion*. Ithaca: Cornell Modern Indonesia Project, Cornell University, 1977.

Harvey, David. "Cosmopolitanism and the Banality of Geographical Evils". *Public Culture* 12, 2 (2000): 529–64.

Hasbi, Mohammad, Mochtar Naim and Damciwar Dt. Bagindo Sampono, eds. *Nagari: Desa dan Pembangunan Pedesaan di Sumatera Barat*. Padang: Yayasan Genta Budaya, 1990.

Hawkins, Mary. "Becoming Banjar: Identity and Ethnicity in South Kalimantan, Indonesia". *Asia Pacific Journal of Anthropology* 1, 1 (2000): 24–36.

———. "Market People, Mountain People: Identity in a South Kalimantan Transmigration Village". Doctoral dissertation, Department of Anthropology, University of Sydney, 1989.

Hayter, Roger, Trevor J. Barnes and Michael J. Bradshaw. "Relocating Resource Peripheries to the Core of Economic Geography's Theorizing: Rationale and Agenda". *Area* 35, 1 (2003): 15–23.

He, B., B. Galligan and T. Inoguchi, eds. *Federalism in Asia*. Cheltenham: Edward Elgar, 2007.
Hefner, Robert W., ed. *The Politics of Multiculturalism: Pluralism and Citizenship in Malaysia, Singapore, and Indonesia*. Honolulu: University of Hawai'i Press, 2001.
Heidhues, Mary F. Somers. *Bangka Tin and Mentok Pepper: Chinese Settlement on an Indonesian Island*. Singapore: ISEAS, 1992.
———. "Chinese Settlements in Rural Southeast Asia: Unwritten Histories". In *Sojourners and Settlers: Histories of Southeast Asia and the Chinese*, ed. Anthony Reid. Sydney: Asian Studies Association of Australia with Allen & Unwin, 1996, pp. 164–82.
———. "Indonesia". In *The Encyclopedia of the Chinese Overseas*, ed. Lynn Pan. Cambridge, Mass.: Harvard University Press, 1998, pp. 151–68.
———. "Kalimantan Barat 1967–1999: Violence on the Periphery". In *Violence in Indonesia*, ed. Ingrid Wessel and Georgia Wimhöffer. Hamburg: Abera Verlag, 2001, pp. 139–51.
———. *Golddiggers, Farmers, and Traders in the "Chinese Districts" of West Kalimantan, Indonesia*. Ithaca: Southeast Asia Program Publications, Cornell University, 2003.
Held, David. *Democracy and the Global Order: from the Modern State to Cosmopolitan Governance*. Cambridge: Polity, 1995.
Henley, David. *Jealousy and Justice: The Indigenous Roots of Colonial Rule in Northern Sulawesi*. Amsterdam: VU University Press, 2002.
Henley, David and Jamie S. Davidson. "Introduction: Radical Conservatism—the Protean Politics of Adat". In *The Revival of Tradition in Indonesian Politics: The Deployment of Adat from Colonialism to Indigenism*, ed. Jamie S. Davidson and David Henley. Abingdon and New York: Routledge, 2007, pp. 1–49.
———. "In the Name of Adat: Regional Perspectives on Reform, Tradition and Democracy in Indonesia". *Modern Asian Studies* 42, 4 (2008): 815–52.
Hermann, Barbara. "Could it be Worth Thinking about Kant on Sex and Marriage?" In *A Mind of Our Own*, ed. Louise Anthony and Charlotte Witt. Boulder: Westview, 1997.
Heryanto, Ariel. "Ethnic Identities and Erasure: Chinese Indonesians in Public Culture". In *Southeast Asian Identities: Culture and the Politics of Representation in Indonesia, Malaysia, Singapore and Thailand*, ed. Joel Kahn. Singapore and London: ISEAS, 1998, pp. 98–101.
Hill, A. H., trans. *Hikayat Raja Raja Pasai*. *JMBRAS* 33, 2 (1960): 134–59.
———. "Introduction". *JMBRAS* 33, 2 (1960): 7–44.
Hill, Thomas E. Jr. *Respect, Pluralism, and Justice: Kantian Perspectives*. Oxford: Oxford University Press, 2000.
Hnl, "Cina, Tionghoa atau Hoaqiau?" *Satulelaki.com*, <http://satulelaki.com/cetak/0, 9341,00.html> [accessed 9 Aug. 2002].

Hollandia. "Report on Activities, Reactions and Aims of the Autochthonic Population of Neth. New-Guinea Concerning the Future Political Status of their Country in Connection with the Dutch-Indonesian Round-Table-Talks", Sept. 1949.

———. "Manifest Politik (Political Manisfesto)", 19 Oct. 1961.

———. "Politiek Leven over Oktober 1961 (Political Developments during Oct. 1961)". Nieuw Guinea Archief, Dossier G 16725, ARA, 28 Nov. 1961.

Horowitz, L. "Daily, Immediate Conflicts: An Analysis of Villager's Arguments about a Multinational Nickel Mining Project in New Caledonia". *Oceania* 73 (2002): 35–55.

Howitt, Richard, John Connell and Philip Hirsch. "Resources, Nations and Indigenous Peoples". In *Resources, Nations and Indigenous Peoples: Case Studies from Australasia, Melanesia and Southeast Asia*, ed. Richard Howitt, John Connell and Philip Hirsch. Melbourne: Oxford University Press, 1996, pp. 1–30.

Human Rights Watch Asia. Report Excerpt. "The Horror in Kalimantan". *Inside Indonesia* 51, July–Sept., 1997.

Hurrell, Andrew. "Regionalism in Theoretical Perspective". In *Regionalism in World Politics: Regional Organization and International Order*, ed. Louise Fawcett and Andrew Hurrell. London: Oxford University Press, 1995, pp. 37–73.

Indrawasih, Ratna, Ary Wahyono and Dedi S. Adhuri. "Pengelolaan Sumberdaya Laut di Kabupaten Belitung, Provinsi Bangka Belitung". In *Pengelolaan Sumber Daya Alam Secara Terpadu: Co-Management Sumberdaya Alam Pelajaran dari Praktek Pengelolaan Sumberdaya Laut di Bangka-Belitung, Jawa Tengah, dan Jawa Timur serta Pengelolaan Taman Nasional Lore Lindu di Sulawesi Tengah*, ed. Dedi Adhuri. Jakarta: PMB-LIPI, Jakarta, 2003, pp. 20–87.

Ingleson, John. *Road to Exile: The Indonesian Nationalist Movement 1927–1934*. Singapore: Heinemann Educational Books (Asia), 1979.

International Crisis Group (ICG). "Communal Violence in Indonesia: Lessons from Kalimantan", *ICG Asia Report* no. 18, 27 June 2001.

International Labour Organisation (ILO). *Indigenous and Tribal Peoples Convention* (ILO Convention no. 107). Geneva: ILO, 1957.

———. *Indigenous and Tribal Peoples in Independent Countries* (ILO Convention no. 169), Geneva: ILO, 1989.

Jakarta Post. "Gus Dur Told to Prove His Competence", 15 June 2001.

Jawa Pos. "Gus Dur Ziarah ke Makam Syeh Damanhuri", 25 July 2000.

Jentoft, Svein. "Fisheries Co-management: Delegating Government Responsibility to Fishermen's Organizations". *Marine Policy* 13 (1989): 137–54.

Jessup, Ethan. "Beanal v. Freeport-McMoran, Inc.: Anatomy of an International Environmental Tort Case". *New England International and Comparative Law Annual* 5 (1999), <http://www.nesl.edu/intljournal/VOL5/jessup.htm>.

Johannes, Robert E. "Traditional Marine Conservation Methods in Oceania and Their Demise". *Annual Review of Ecology and Systematics* 9 (1978): 249–364.
Jones, Gavin. "Which Indonesian Women Marry Youngest, and Why?" *Journal of Southeast Asian Studies* 32, 1 (2001): 67–78.
Jorgensen, Dan. "Who and What is a Landowner? Mythology and Marking the Ground in a Papua New Guinea Mining Project". *Anthropological Forum* 7, 4 (1997): 599–627.
Josselin de Jong, P. E. de. "The Character of the 'Malay Annals'". In *Malayan and Indonesian Studies: Essays Presented to Sir Richard Winstedt on his Eighty-fifth Birthday*, ed. John Bastin and R. Roolvink. Oxford: Clarendon Press, 1964, pp. 235–41.
Kabar-Irian.com. "Appeal for a Cessation of Violence in Papua", Jayapura, 14 June 2001, <http://www.kabar-irian.com>.
———. "Letter, Ramli Sa'ud, Minister Counsellor, Embassy of the Republic of Indonesia, London, to the Rt Revd. R. D. Harries, Lord Bishop of Oxford, No. 47/IV/07/LON/05, 30 June 2005, <http://www.kabar-irian.com>.
Kahin, Audrey. *Rebellion to Integration: West Sumatra and the Indonesian Polity*. Amsterdam: University of Amsterdam Press, 1999.
Kahin, Audrey and George Kahin. *Subversion as Foreign Policy*. New York: New Press, 1995.
Kahn, Joel S. *Constituting the Minangkabau: Peasants, Culture and Modernity in Colonial Indonesia*. Oxford: Berg, 1993.
———. "Culturalizing the Indonesian Uplands". In *Transforming the Indonesian Uplands: Marginality, Power and Production*, ed. Tania Li. Amsterdam: Harwood, 1999, pp. 79–103.
———. *Modernity and Exclusion*. London: Sage, 2001.
Kaiabe, A. "Why a Hela Province!", *Post-Courier*, 14 Nov. 2006.
Kant, Immanuel. *Anthropology from a Pragmatic Point of View*. Translated, with an introduction and annotations by Mary J. Gregor. The Hague: Martinus Nijhoff, 1974.
Kartika, Sandra and Candra Gautama, eds. *Menggugat Posisi Masyarakat Adat terhadap Negara: Sarasehan Masyarakat Nusantara*. Yogyakarta: AMAN, 1999.
Kartodirdjo, Sartono. *Protest Movements in Rural Java: A Study of Agrarian Unrest in the 19th and early 20th Centuries*. Singapore: Oxford University Press, 1973.
Kato, Tsuyoshi. *Matriliny and Migration: Evolving Minangkabau Traditions in Indonesia*. Ithaca: Cornell University Press, 1982.
Kearney, Richard and Mark Dooley, eds. *Questioning Ethics: Contemporary Debates in Philosophy*. London and New York: Routledge, 1999.
Keating, Michael. *Plurinational Democracy: Stateless Nations in a Post-Sovereignty Era*. Oxford: Oxford University Press, 2001.
Khoo, Kay Jin. "The Grand Vision: Mahathir and Modernisation". In *Fragmented Vision: Culture and Politics in Contemporary Malaysia*, ed. Joel S. Kahn and Francis Loh Kok Wah. St. Leonard's: Allen & Unwin, 1992, pp. 44–76.

King, Victor T. *The Maloh of West Kalimantan: An Ethnographic Study of Social Inequality and Social Change among an Indonesian Borneo People*. Dordrecht: Foris Publications, 1985.

———. "A Question of Identity: Names, Societies and Ethnic Groups in Interior Kalimantan and Brunei Darussalam". *Sojourn: Journal of Social Issues in Southeast Asia* 16, 1 (2001): 1–36.

Kingsbury, Benedict. "Reconstructing Self-determination: A Relational Approach". In *Operationalizing the Right of Indigenous Peoples to Self-determination*, ed. Pekka Aikio and Martin Scheinin. Turku: Institute for Human Rights, Åbo Akademi University, 2000.

Kingsbury, Damien. *Peace in Aceh: A Personal Account of the Peace Process*. Jakarta: Equinox, 2006.

Kingsbury, Damien and Harry Aveling, eds. *Autonomy and Disintegration in Indonesia*. London, New York: Routledge Curzon, 2003.

Kipp, Rita S. *Dissociated Identities: Ethnicity, Religion, and Class in an Indonesian Society*. Ann Arbor: University of Michigan Press, 1993.

Kompas. "Soebadio Bertapa di Gunung Lawu", 5 Dec. 1997.

———. "Soebadio Tetap Bertapa di Gunung Lawu", 17 Dec. 1997.

———. "Buku 'Politik Dosomuko' Karya Soebadio Dilarang", 8 May 1998.

———. "Siapa Bilang Otonomi Mengkapling Laut?", 26 Feb. 2000.

———. "Presiden Ziarah ke Makam H. Mohammad Barokah", 21 May 2001.

———. "KH Salahuddin Wahid: Presiden Menganggap Enteng Megawati!", 6 June 2001.

———. "Nelayan Jakarta Protes Kehadiran Kapal 'Trawl'", 13 Aug. 2001.

———. "Buntut Bentrokan Nelayan: 2.500 Nelayan Demak tidak Berani Melaut", 12 Jan. 2002.

———. "HNSI Cilacap: Penyanderaan, Bisa Picu Konflik antar Nelayan", 23 Feb. 2002.

———. "Buntu, Pertemuan HNSI Cilacap-Ciamis", 27 Feb. 2002.

———. "Nelayan Ujungpangkah Menyita 16 Perahu Pengguna 'Mini-Trawl'", 12 Mar. 2002.

———. "Nelayan Ketapang Bakar Delapan Kapal Trawl", 21 Mar. 2002.

———. "Tak Ada Perompak, Kekerasan di Laut Ekses Otonomi Daerah", 18 Apr. 2002.

———. "Kerawanan Laut Meningkat", 21 May 2002.

———. "Masyarakat Melayu Sumut Kian Terpinggirkan", 13 June 2000.

———. "Konflik Nelayan di Musim Paceklik", 19 July 2002.

———. "Pukat Harimau akan Diizinkan Beroperasi", 14 Aug. 2002.

———. "Nelayan Tradisional Sumut Tolak Pukat Harimau", 17 Sept. 2002.

———. "Festival Seni Tari Melayu Upaya Mempertahankan Kesenian Melayu", 8 Sept. 2006.

Kontan. "Tinggal Membagi Kue", July 30, 2001 <http://www.kontan-online.com/05/44/politik/pol1.htm>.

Kontras. "Maunya Jangan Cuma Kubur yang Dipulangkan", 146, 11–17 July 2001.
———. "Solusi Gaib untuk Aceh", 146, 11–17 July 2001.
Koopmans, Ruud and Paul Statham. "Challenging the Liberal Nation State? Postnationalism, Multiculturalism and the Collective Claims of Migrants and Ethnic Minorities in Britain and Germany". *American Journal of Sociology* 105, 3 (1999): 652–96.
Korten, David. "From Empire to Earth Community". *Development* 49 (2006): 76–81.
Labrousse, Pierre. "The Second Life of Bung Karno: Analysis of the Myth (1978–1981)", *Indonesia* 57 (Apr. 1994): 175–96.
Ladjar, Leo Laba and Herman Saud. 2000, "Letter, 157/TB/00/7.2 re The Situation in Irian Jaya, Bishop Mgr. Leo Laba Ladjar OFM and Moderator, Rev. Herman Saud MTh to the Director, Indonesian National Commission for Human Rights", <http://www.kabar-irian.com> [accessed 16 Dec. 2000].
Lebovics, Herman. *True France: The Wars over Cultural Identity 1900–1945*. Ithaca and London: Cornell University Press, 1992.
Leirissa, Richard Z. *PRRI Permesta*, Jakarta: Grafiti, 1997.
Leith, Denise. *The Politics of Power: Freeport in Suharto's Indonesia*. Honolulu: University of Hawai'i Press, 2003.
Lelono, Kusumo. *Satrio Piningit: 25 Sandhi Gaib Mengenai Pemimpin Bangsa, Para Tokoh dan Situasi Politik Indonesia*. Jakarta: Gramedia, 1999.
Lestari. "Mari kita Wujudkan Pengelolaan Hutan Secara Kolaboratif dan Integratif", *Lestari: Lembar Suara Antara Mitra*, 2nd ed., July–Aug. 2006, pp. 11–2.
Li, Tania M. "Articulating Indigenous Identity in Indonesia: Resource Politics and the Tribal Slot", *Comparative Study of Society and History* 42, 1 (2000): 149–79.
———. "Masyarakat Adat, Difference and the Limits of Recognition in Indonesia's Forest Zone". *Modern Asian Studies* 35, 3 (2001): 645–76.
Lim, G. "Parliamentary Reform: Lessons for the UK and Europe". *Aliran Monthly* 22, 6 (2002).
Lindsey, Timothy C. "Concrete Ideology: Taste, Tradition, and the Javanese Past in New Order Public Space". In *Culture and Society in New Order Indonesia*, ed. Virginia M. Hooker. Kuala Lumpur: Oxford University Press, 1995, pp. 166–82.
———. "Reconstituting the Ethnic Chinese in Post-Soeharto Indonesia: Law, Racial Discrimination, and Reform". In *Chinese Indonesians: Remembering, Distorting, Forgetting*, ed. Timothy C. Lindsey and Helen Pausacker. Singapore: ISEAS, 2005, pp. 41–76.
Liow, Joseph C. Y. *The Politics of Indonesia-Malaysia Relations: One Kin, Two Nations*. London: RoutledgeCurzon, 204.
Mabbett, Hugh and Ping-ching Mabbett. "The Chinese Community in Indonesia". In *The Chinese in Indonesia, the Philippines and Malaysia*, by Charles A. Coppel,

Hugh Mabbett and Ping-ching Mabbett, pp. 10–6. London: Minority Rights Group Report no. 10, 1982 (1972).

Machiavelli, Niccolò. *The Prince and the Discourses*. New York: Modern Library, 1950.

Majalah Misteri. "Kaul Harlah Bung Karno?" <http://www.paranormal.or.id/article.php?sid=17>.

Makam Bung Karno: Proklamator Kemerdekaan dan Presiden Pertama Republik Indonesia. Panitia Pemugaran Makam Proklamator Kemerdekaan R.I., Bung Karno, (n.d.).

Malley, Michael. "Regions: Centralization and Resistance". In *Indonesia beyond Suharto: Polity, Economy, Society, Transition*, ed. D. K. Emmerson. Armonk: M. E. Sharpe with the Asia Society, 1999, pp. 71–105.

Manguin, Pierre-Yves. "Etudes Sumatranaises 1: Palembang et Sriwijaya: Anciennes Hypothèses, Recherches Nouvelles". *Bulletin de l'Ecole française d'Extrême-Orient* 76 (1987): 337–402.

Manning, C. and P. Van Dierman, eds. *Indonesia in Transition: Social Aspects of Reformasi and Crisis*. Singapore: ISEAS, 2000.

Mano, Chris. "Nasionalisme Papua Lebih Kuat di HUT RI", *Tifa Papua* (Jayapura), 2nd week Aug., 2002.

Marcus, A. S. and Pax Benedanto, eds. *Kesastraan Melayu Tionghoa dan Kebangsaan Indonesia* (Sino-Malay Literature and Indonesian Nationhood). Vols. 1–10. Jakarta: KPG, 2000–8.

Mathew, Sebastian. 1990. *Fishing Legislation and Gear Conflicts in Asian Countries: A Case Study of Selected Asian Countries*. Brussel: International Collective in Support for Fisherworkers.

Maunati, Yekti. "Contesting Dayak Identity: Commodification and the Cultural Politics of Identity in East Kalimantan". Doctoral dissertation, La Trobe University, 2000.

McCarthy, John F. *The Fourth Circle: A Political Ecology of Sumatra's Rainforest Frontier*. Stanford: Stanford University Press, 2006.

McCay, Bonnie J. and James M. Acheson, eds. *The Question of the Commons: The Culture and Ecology of Communal Resources*. Tucson: University of Arizona Press, 1987.

McGibbon, Rod. *Secessionist Challenges in Aceh and Papua: Is Special Autonomy the Solution?* Policy Studies no. 10. Washington, D. C.: East-West Centre, 2004.

McIntyre, Andrew. "Minority Men: Ong Hok Ham and Harry J. Benda in Indonesia and America". In *Onze Ong: Onghokham dalam Kenangan* (Our Ong: Onghokham in Reminiscences), ed. D. Reeve, J. J. Rizal and Wasmi Alhaziri. Jakarta: Komunitas Bambu, 2007, pp. 23–32.

McLeod, Ross H. and Andrew J. MacIntyre, eds. *Indonesia: Democracy and the Promise of Good Governance*. Singapore: ISEAS, 2007.

McNeill, William H. *Poly-ethnicity and National Unity in World History: The Donald G. Creighton Lectures*. Toronto: University of Toronto Press, 1985.
McVey, Ruth T. *The Rise of Indonesian Communism*. Ithaca: Cornell University Press, 1965.
Media Indonesia. "Yapeta Urung Buat Pernyataan Politik", 24 Feb. 1997.
———. "Gus Dur, Megawati Berdoa Khusyuk di Makam Bung Karno", 9 Oct. 1999.
———. "Mega Hasyim Ziarah Lagi ke Blitar", 5 Sept. 2004.
Media Indonesia Minggu. "Haul: Antara Zikir dan Politik", 25 June 1995.
Mehta, Uday. "Liberal Strategies of Exclusion". In *Tensions of Empire: Colonial Cultures in a Bourgeois World*, ed. Frederick Cooper and Ann Stoler. Berkeley: University of California Press, 1997, pp. 59–86.
Melaka Hari Ini. "Dunia Melayu Dunia Islam Elakkan Pergaduhan—Najib", 1 Sept. 2005.
Melville, Peter. "Kant's Dinner Party: Anthropology from a Foucauldian Point of View". *Mosaic* 35, 2 (2002): 93–109.
Mendes, Susan. "An Honest but Narrow-Minded Bourgeois?". In *Essays on Kant's Political Philosophy*, ed. Howard Williams. Chicago: University of Chicago Press, 1992.
Mietzner, Marcus. "Local Elections and Autonomy in Papua and Aceh". *Indonesia* 84 (Oct. 2007): 1–40.
Miles, Douglas. *Cutlass and Crescent Moon: A Case Study of Social and Political Change*, Sydney: Centre for Asian Studies, University of Sydney, 1976.
Milner, Anthony. *Kerajaan: Malay Political Culture on the Eve of Colonial Rule*. Tucson: University of Arizona Press for AAS, 1982.
Misteri. "Misteri Kehidupan Semu Soeharto", 5–19 Feb. 2008.
Mohamad, Lukman Z. "Transformasi Bentuk Bangsa Malaysia dan Identiti Nasional", 2001, <http://phuakl.tripod.com/pssm/conference/LukmanMohamad.doc>.
Moniaga, Sandra. "From Bumiputera to Masyarakat Adat: A Long and Confusing Journey". In *The Revival of Tradition in Indonesian Politics: The Deployment of Adat from Colonialism to Indigenism*, ed. Jamie S. Davidson and David Henley. Abingdon and New York: Routledge, 2007, pp. 275–94.
Moy, Timothy J. "The 'Sejarah Melayu' Tradition of Power and Political Structure: An Assessment of Relevant Sections of the 'Tuhfat Al-Nafis'". *JMBRAS* 48, 2 (1975): 64–78.
Muhaimin, Abdul Ghoffir. *Islam dalam Bingkai Budaya Lokal: Potret dari Cirebon*. Ciputat: Logos Wacana Ilmu with Yayasan Adikarya, IKAPI and the Ford Foundation, 2001.
Munninghof, H. F. M. "Violations of Human Rights in the Timika Area of Irian Jaya, Indonesia: A report by the Catholic Church of Jayapura", Aug. 1995, <http://www.hamline.edu/apakabar/basisdata/1995/08/31/0004.html>.

Murbandono, Leo Hs. "Tionghoa atau Cina". <http://www.rnw.nl/ranesi/html/tionghoa.html> [accessed 9 Aug. 2002].
Musi Tourism Board. "VisitMusi2008", <http://www.visitmusi2008.com/sumsel.php?a=dis>.
MWeb. "Srandil: Sejenak Menuju Nirvana", <www.mweb.co.id> [accessed 9 Aug. 2002].
Nababan, Abdon. "Masyarakat Adat dan Pembangunan Berkelanjutan". Paper presented at the discussion on "Ten Years after Rio de Janeiro Conference on Sustainable Development", Jakarta, 26 Feb. 2002.
Nagtegal, Luc. *Riding the Dutch Tiger: The Dutch East Indies Company and the Northeast Coast of Java.* Leiden: KITLV Press, 1996.
Napitupulu, Sarluhut and Fendri Jaswir. "Kepulauan Riau: Melayu Punya Susu Jakarta yang Enak". *Gamma* 2, 5 (2000).
National Aeronautics and Space Agency (NASA). Visible Earth, Earth at Night series, "Indonesia", <http://visibleearth.nasa.gov/view_rec.php?id=1438>.
New English Bible: New Testament, The. London: Oxford University Press, Cambridge University Press, 1961.
Newsweek International. "Indonesia's Island Fever", 12 Mar. 2001.
———. "Rule of the Headhunters", 5 Apr. 1999.
———. "The Bloody Birth of a 'Messy State'", 12 Mar. 2001.
Nieuw Guinea Raad (New Guinea Council). "Handelingen Eerst Buitengewone Zitting (Operations of the First Extraordinary Meeting)", 30 Oct. 1961.
Nonini, Donald M. "Shifting Identities, Positioned Imaginaries: Transnational Traversals and Reversals by Malaysian Chinese". In *Ungrounded Empires: The Cultural Politics of Modern Chinese Transnationalism*, ed. Aihwa Ong and Donald M. Nonini, pp. 203–27. New York: Routledge, 1997.
Nonini, Donald M. and Aihwa Ong. "Chinese Transnationalism as an Alternative Modernity". In *Ungrounded Empires: The Cultural Politics of Modern Chinese Transnationalism*, ed. Aihwa Ong and Donald M. Nonini. New York: Routledge, 1997, pp. 3–33.
Nuryanti, Sri, ed. *Political Parties' Performance at Local Parliament in Indonesia.* Jakarta: LIPI, 2007.
Nussbaum, Martha. "Patriotism and Cosmopolitanism". In *For Love of Country: Debating the Limits of Patriotism*, ed. Joshua Cohen and Martha Nussbaum. Cambridge, Mass.: Beacon Press, 1996, pp. 3–17.
Onghokham (Ong Hok Ham). "The Residency of Madiun: Pryayi and Peasant in the Nineteenth Century". Doctoral dissertation, Yale University, 1975.
———. *Rakyat dan Negara* (People and State). Jakarta: Sinar Harapan, 1983.
———. *Runtuhnya Hindia-Belanda* (Fall of the Dutch East Indies). Jakarta: Gramedia, 1987.
———. *Dari Soal Priyayi sampai Nyi Blorong: Refleksi Historis Nusantara* (From Javanese Aristocracy to Mythic Nyi Blorong: Indonesian Historical Reflections). Jakarta: Kompas, 2002.

———. *The Thugs, the Curtain Thief and the Sugar Lord; Power, Politics, and Culture in Colonial Java, Jakarta*: Metafor, 2003.

———. *Wahyu yang Hilang, Negeri yang Guncang* (The Mandate is Lost, the Nation is Tossed). Jakarta: Tempo, Freedom Institute and LSSI, 2003.

———. *Riwayat Tionghoa Peranakan di Jawa* (The History of the Indonesian Chinese in Java). Jakarta: Komunitas Bambu, 2005.

Ortner, Sherry. "Resistance and the Problem of Ethnographic Refusal". *Comparative Studies in Society and History* 37, 1 (1995): 173–93.

Pabottinggi, Mochtar. "Indonesia: Historicizing the New Order's Legitimacy Dilemma". In *Political Legitimacy in Southeast Asia: Quest for Moral Authority*, ed. Muthiah Alagappa. Stanford: Stanford University Press, 1995, pp. 224–56.

Pagden, Anthony. "The Genesis of 'Governance' and Enlightenment Conceptions of the Cosmopolitan World Order". *International Social Science Journal* 50, 155 (1998): 7–15.

Papua Post. "Papuanisasi Jurus Jitu dan Sederhana", Jayapura, 25 Nov. 2000.

Pateman, Carol. *The Problem of Political Obligation: A Critique of Liberal Theory*. Cambridge: Polity Press, 1985.

Paull, David *et al*. "Monitoring the Environmental Impact of Mining in Remote Locations through Remotely Sensed Data". *GeoCarto International* 21, 1 (2006) 1–9.

Pelras, Christian. "Hiérarchie et Pouvoir Traditionnel en Pays Wajo". *Archipel* 1 (1971).

Peluso, Nancy L. and Michael Watts, eds. *Violent Environments*. Ithaca: Cornell University Press, 2001.

Pemberton, John. *On the Subject of "Java"*. Ithaca: Cornell University Press, 1994.

Pengantara: Het Nieuwsblad voor Nederlands-Nieuw-Guinea (*Pengantara*: The Newspaper for Netherlands New Guinea). 21 Oct. 1961.

Perlez, Jane and Raymond Bonner. "Below a Mountain of Wealth, a River of Waste", *New York Times*, 27 Dec. 2005.

Persoon, Gerard. "Isolated Groups or Indigenous Peoples: Indonesia and the International Discourse". *Bijdragen tot de Taal-, Land- en Volkenkunde* 154, 2 (1998): 281–304.

———. "Vluchten of Veranderen: Processen van Verandering en Ontwikkeling bij Tribale Groepen in Indonesië (Flee or Change: Processes of Changes and Development amongst Indonesian Tribal Groups)". Doctoral dissertation, University of Leiden, 1994.

Piekaar, Arie J. *Atjeh en de Oorlog met Japan* (Aceh and the War with Japan). Bandung: W. Van Hoeve, 1949.

Pires, Tomé. *Suma Oriental of Tomé Pires: An Account of the East from the Red Sea to Japan, Written in Malacca and India in 1512–1515*. Trans. and ed. by Armando Cortesao. London: Hakluyt Society, 2nd series, 89, 1967.

Poeze, Harry. *Tan Malaka, Strijeder voor Indonesia's Vrijheid: Levensloop van 1897 tot 1945* (Tan Malaka, Struggle for Indonesian Freedom, 1897 to 1945). Leiden: KITLV Press, 1976.
Poffenberger, Mark. "Rethinking Indonesian Forest Policy: Beyond the Timber Barons". *Asian Survey* 37, 5 (1997): 453–70.
Pollack, Sheldon et al. "Cosmopolitanisms". *Public Culture* 12, 3 (2000).
Pomeroy Robert and Fikret Berkes. "Two to Tango: The Role of Government in Co-management". *Marine Policy* 21, 5 (1997): 465–80.
Provinsi Kepulauan Riau (Kepulauan Riau Province). <http://kepriprov.go.id/id/index.php?option=com_content&task=view&id=55&Itemid=91> [accessed 15 Aug. 2008].
Quinn, George. "The Role of a Javanese Burial Ground in Local Government". In *The Potent Dead: Ancestors, Saints and Heroes in Contemporary Indonesia*, Henri Chambert-Loir and Anthony Reid. Sydney and Honolulu: Asian Studies Association of Australia with Allen & Unwin and University of Hawai'i Press, 2002, pp. 173–82.
Rab, Tabrani. *Menuju Riau Berdaulat: Pilihan Kongres Rakyat Riau II*. Pekanbaru: Riau Cultural Institute, 2002.
Ranggawarsita, Raden Ngabei. *Zaman Edan*. Yogyakarta: Bentang Budaya, 1998.
Raffles, Sophia. *Memoir of the Life and Public Services of Sir Thomas Stamford Raffles: Particularly in the Government of Java, 1811–1816, Bencoolen and its Dependencies, 1811–1824: with Details of the Commerce and Resources of the Eastern Archipelago, and Selections from his Correspondence.* London: J. Duncan, 1835.
Ramage, Douglas. *Politics in Indonesia: Democracy, Islam and the Ideology of Tolerance.* London: Routledge, 1995.
Rapport van de Commissie Nieuw-Guinea (Irian) 1950. 3e Stuk (3rd ed.), The Hague: De Nederlands-Indonesische Unie, 1950.
Ras, Johannes J., ed. *Hikayat Bandjar: A Study in Malay Historiography*. The Hague: Martinus Nijhoff, 1968.
Reeve, David, J. J. Rizal and Wasmi Alhaziri, eds. *Onze Ong: Onghokham dalam Kenangan* (Our Ong: Onghokham in Reminiscences). Jakarta: Komunitas Bambu, 2007.
Reid, Anthony. *The Contest for North Sumatra: Atjeh, the Netherlands and Britain, 1858–1898*. London: Oxford University Press, 1969.
———, trans. "Atjeh Verslag of C. Snouck Hurgronje, 1893". In Anthony Reid, *The Contest for North Sumatra: Atjeh, the Netherlands and Britain, 1858–1898*. London: Oxford University Press, 1969.
———. "Trade and the Problem of Royal Power in Aceh, Three Stages: c. 1550–1700". In *Precolonial State Systems in Southeast Asia*, ed. Anthony Reid and Lance Castles. Kuala Lumpur: MBRAS monograph no. 6, 1975, pp. 45–55.
———. *The Blood of the People: Revolution and the End of Traditional Rule in Northern Sumatra*. Kuala Lumpur: Oxford University Press, 1979.

———. *Southeast Asia in the Age of Commerce, vol. 2: Expansion and Crisis*. New Haven: Yale University Press, 1993.

———. "Kings, Kadis and Charisma in the 17th Century Archipelago". In *The Making of an Islamic Political Discourse in Southeast Asia*, ed. Anthony Reid. Clayton: Centre of Southeast Asian Studies, Monash University, 1993, pp. 83–107.

———, ed. *Sojourners and Settlers: Histories of Southeast Asia and the Chinese*. Sydney: Asian Studies Association of Australia in association with Allen & Unwin, 1996.

———. "Inside-Out: the Colonial Displacement of Sumatra's Population". In *Paper Landscapes: Essays in the Environmental History of Indonesia*, ed. Peter Boomgaard, Freek Colombin and David Henley. Leiden: KITLV Press, 1998, pp. 61–89.

———. "National and Ethnic Identities in a Democratic Age". In *Religion, Ethnicity and Modernity in Southeast Asia*, ed. Oh Myung-Seok and Kim Hyung-Jun. Seoul: Seoul National University Press, 1998, pp. 11–43.

———. "Political 'Tradition' in Indonesia: The One and the Many". *Asian Studies Review* 22, 1 (Mar. 1998): 23–38.

———. "Sixteenth Century Turkish Influence in Western Indonesia". *Journal of Southeast Asian History* 10, 3 (1999): 395–414.

Republika. "Habibie Ziarahi Makam Moyangnya di Geger Menjangan". 29 May 1999.

———. "Hari ini Nelayan Pantura akan Demo di Jakarta". 13 Nov. 2000.

———. "SBY Ziarah ke Makam Mertuanya", 18 June 2004.

———. "Yudhoyono, Nilai Ziarah dan Rekonsiliasi", 7 Oct. 2004.

Rew, Alan and John R. Campbell. "The Political Economy of Identity and Affect". In *Identity and Affect: Experiences of Identity in a Globalising World*, ed. John R. Campbell and Alan Rew. London: Pluto Press, 1999, pp. 1–36.

Ricklefs, Merle C. *The Seen and Unseen Worlds in Java, 1726–1749: History, Literature and Islam in the Court of Pakubuwana II*. Sydney: Asian Studies Association of Australia in association with Allen & Unwin and University of Hawai'i Press, 1998.

———. "Unity and Disunity in Javanese Political and Religious Thought of the Eighteenth Century". In *Looking in Odd Mirrors: The Java Sea*, ed. Vincent J. H. Houben, Henk M. J. Maier and Willem van eer Molen. Leiden: Vakgroep Talen en Culturen van Zuidoost-Azië en Oceanië, Rijksuniversiteit te Leiden, 1992, pp. 60–75.

Rinkes, Douwe A. *The Nine Saints of Java*. Trans. H. M. Froger. Kuala Lumpur: Malaysian Sociological Research Institute, 1996.

Roolvink, Roelof. "The Variant Versions of the Malay Annals". *Bijdragen tot de Taal-, Land- en Volkenkunde* 123 (1963): 301–24.

Roshwald, Aviel. *Ethnic Nationalism and the Fall of Empires: Central Europe, Russia and the Middle East, 1914–1923*. London: Routledge, 2001.

Ross, Michael L. "The Political Economy of the Resource Curse". *World Politics* 51, 2 (1999): 297–322.

———. "The Natural Resource Curse: How Wealth Can Make You Poor". In *Natural Resources and Violent Conflict: Options and Actions*, ed. Ian Bannon and Paul Collier. Washington, D. C.: World Bank, 2003, pp. 17–42.

Rosser, Andrew. "Escaping the Resource Curse: The Case of Indonesia". *Journal of Contemporary Asia* 37, 1 (2007): 38–58.

Ruddle, Kenneth and Tomoya Akimichi, eds. *Maritime Institutions in the Western Pacific*. Osaka: National Museum of Ethnology, 1984.

Rutter, Owen. *The Pagans of North Borneo*. Oxford: Oxford University Press, 1985 (1929).

Sachs, Jeffrey and Andrew M. Warner. "The Curse of Natural Resources". *European Economic Review* 45 (2001): 827–38.

Saifuddin, Achmad F. and Zulyani Hidayah. "Etnisitas dan Proses Politik: Rekonstruksi Kemelayuan di Riau". In *Laporan Penelitian: Kebijakan Kebudayaan di Masa Orde Baru*, ed. Pusat Penelitian dan Pengembangan Kemasyarakatan dan Kebudayaan (LIPI) with Ford Foundation. Jakarta: LIPI, 2001, pp. 557–86.

"Sajak-sajak Wilson Tjandinegara", <http://cybersastra.net/edisi_mei2002/mei2002_3.htm.> [accessed 26 June 2002].

Sakai, Minako, ed. *Beyond Jakarta: Regional Autonomy and Local Societies in Indonesia*. Adelaide: Crawford House, 2002.

———. "Regional Responses to Resurgence of Adat Movements in Indonesia". In *Beyond Jakarta: Regional Autonomy and Local Societies in Indonesia*, ed. Minako Sakai. Adelaide: Crawford House, 2002, pp. 245–69.

———. "Resisting the Mainland: The Formation of the Province of Bangka Belitung (Babel)". In *Autonomy and Disintegration in Indonesia*, ed. Damien Kingsbury, pp. 189–200. London: Routledge, 2003.

Sakai, Minako and Elizabeth Morrel. "Reconfiguring Regions and Challenging the State? New Socio-economic Partnerships in the Outer Islands of Indonesia". In *Asia Reconstructed: Proceedings of the 16th Biennial Conference of the ASAA, 2006*, ed. Adrian Vickers and Margaret Hanlon. Canberra: Asian Studies Association of Australia (ASAA) and Research School of Pacific and Asian Studies, ANU, 2006 <http://coombs.anu.edu.au/SpecialProj/ASAA/biennial-conference/2006/proceedings.html>.

Sandhu, Kernial S. and Paul Wheatley. "From Capital to Municipality". In *Melaka: The Transformation of a Malay Capital c 1400–1980*, 1983, vol. II, ed. Kernial Singh Sandhu and Paul Wheatley. Kuala Lumpur: Oxford University Press, pp. 496–597.

Sanit, Arbi. "Political Parties, Society, and DPRD: The Case of Padang, Agam and Padang Pariaman". In *Political Parties' Performance at Local Parliament in Indonesia*, ed. Sri Nuryanti. Jakarta: LIPI, 2007, pp. 177–224.

Satulelaki. "Jambe Pitu, Tempat Bertapa Mantan Presiden Soeharto", <http://www.satulelaki.com> [accessed 9 Aug. 2002].

Saud, Herman and Socratez Sofyan Yoman, "Joint Statement on Regional Elections, Special Autonomy and the MRP (Papua People's Assembly)". DPRD, Jayapura, 9 June 2005, <http://www.westpapua.ca/?q=en/node/398>.

Schiller, Anne. "An 'Old' Religion in 'New Order' Indonesia: Notes on Ethnicity and Religious Affiliation". *Sociology of Religion* 57, 4 (1996): 409–15.

Schulte Nordholt, Henk. "Leadership and the Limits of Political Control: A Balinese 'Response' to Clifford Geertz". *Social Anthropology* 1, 3 (1993): 291–307.

Schulte Nordholt, Henk and Gerry van Klinken, eds. *Renegotiating Boundaries: Local Politics in Post Soeharto Indonesia*. Leiden: KITLV Press, 2007.

Schrauwers, Albert. *Colonial "Reformation" in the Highlands of Central Sulawesi, Indonesia, 1892–1995*. Toronto, Buffalo and London: University of Toronto Press, 2000.

Scott, James C. "Freedom and Freehold: Space, People and State Simplification in Southeast Asia". In *Asian Freedoms: The Idea of Freedom in East and Southeast Asia*, ed. David Kelly and Anthony Reid. Cambridge: Cambridge University Press, 1998, pp. 37–64.

Sejarah Melayu: The Malay Annals MS. Raffles no. 18. Romanised by Abdul Rahman Haji Ismail. Kuala Lumpur: MBRAS repr. no. 17, 1998, pp. 65–313.

Sen, Krishna and David T. Hill. "The Internet and Virtual Politics". In *Media, Culture and Politics in Indonesia*, Krishna Sen and David T. Hill. Melbourne: Oxford University Press, 2000, pp. 194–217.

Siauw, Tiong Djin and Hay Djoen Oey, eds. *Sumbangsih Siauw Giok Tjhan dan Baperki dalam Sejarah Indonesia*. Jakarta: Hasta Mitra, 2000.

Siegel, James. "Early Thoughts on the Violence of May 13 and 14, 1998 in Jakarta". *Indonesia* 66 (Oct. 1998).

Sindhunata. *Bayang-Bayang Ratu Adil*. Jakarta: Gramedia Pustaka Utama, 1999.

Sinode Gereja Kristen Indonesia (GKI). *Keputusan dan Ketetapan, Sidang Sinode XIV GKI di Tanah Papua, Tahun 2000*. Sorong: Panitia Sidang Sinode XIV GKI di Tanah Papua, 2000.

Skinner, G. William. "Creolized Chinese Societies in Southeast Asia". In *Sojourners and Settlers: Histories of Southeast Asia and the Chinese*, ed. Anthony Reid. Sydney: Asian Studies Association of Australia in association with Allen & Unwin, 1996, pp. 51–93.

Slater, Dan. "Indonesia's Accountability Trap: Party Cartels and Presidential Power after Democratic Transition", *Indonesia* 79 (Oct. 2004): 61–92.

Smith, Anthony. "Is Indonesia Breaking Up?". *New Zealand International Review* 26, 5 (2001): 19–22.

Smith, Claire Q. *The Roots of Violence and Prospects for Reconciliation: A Case Study of Ethnic Conflict in Central Kalimantan, Indonesia*. Social Development Papers no. 23, Conflict Prevention and Reconstruction Unit. Washington, D. C.: World Bank, 2005.

Soekarno. *Indonesia Menggugat: Pidato Pembelaan Bung Karno di Muka Hakim Kolonial.* Jakarta: S. K. Seno, 1960.
Soewarno, Mohd Hari. *Ramalan Jayabaya Versi Sabda Palon.* Jakarta: Yudha Gama (n.d.).
Somer, J. M. *De Korte Verklaring* (The Short Declarations). Published Utrecht Dissertation. Breda: Corona, 1934.
Somers, Mary F. A. "Peranakan Chinese Politics in Indonesia". Doctoral dissertation, Cornell University, 1965.
Sriwijaya Post. "Silsilah SMB III Dapat Dipertanggungjawabkan", 28 Mar. 2003.
Steedly, Mary M. *Hanging Without a Rope: Narrative Experience in Colonial and Postcolonial Karoland.* Princeton: Princeton University Press, 1993.
Suara Karya. "Pesertanya Didominasi Sumsel", 29 Nov. 2001.
Suara Merdeka. "Paku Buwono Hadiri Peringatan HUT Tokoh PSI", 28 May 1998.
―――. "Dibahas, Rencana Pemindahan Makam", 21 June 1998.
―――. "Bung Karno Milik Kita Semua...", 21 June 2001.
―――. "Nyekar ke Makam Ayah", 26 July 2001.
―――. "Meriah, Peringatan Malam 1 Sura", 16 Mar. 2002.
―――. "Satu Jam Mega di Makam Bung Karno", 7 June 2002.
―――. "Senantiasa Diselimuti Dunia Mistik", 12 Jan. 2008.
Suara Papua. "Sidang Sinode GKI XIV Membahas Akar Permasalahan Aspirasi M", (Sorong), 25 Oct.–1 Nov. 2000.
Suara Pembaruan. "Mega dan Gus Dur Ziarah Bersama", 9 Oct. 1999.
―――. "Gus Dur Ziarah ke Makam Kakek dan Ayahnya", 23 Oct. 1999.
Sudiyono and J. Haba. "Konflik-konflik Perikanan di Mataram". In *Konflik-konflik Kenelayanan: Distribusi, Pola, Akar Masalah dan Resolusinya,* ed. Dedi Adhuri. Jakarta: PMB-LIPI, 2004, pp. 11–55.
Sularso, Aji, Ali Supardan, Ali Rokhman, P. Mulyono, M. Hermawan and A. A. Zaelany, "Konflik antar Nelayan di Indonesia". Paper presented in 2002 at the doctoral program at Bogor Agriculture Institute, Bogor, <http://tumoutou.net/702_05123/group_d_123.htm> [accessed 12 Aug. 2008].
Sumule, Agus. "Swimming against the Current: The Drafting of the Special Autonomy Bill for the Province of Papua and its Passage through the National Parliament of Indonesia". *Journal of Pacific History* 38, 3 (2003): 353–69.
Surabaya Post. "Soal Rencana Pemindahan Makam BK: Warga Bentuk Paguyuban", 28 July 1998.
Suryadi. "Identity, Media and the Margins: Radio in Pekanbaru, Riau (Indonesia)". *Journal of Southeast Asian Studies* 36, 1 (2005): 131–51.
Suryadi, Nanang. "Tragedi Mei 1998 dalam Sajak Wison Tjandinegara", <http://cybersastra.net/edisi_mei2002/mei2002_4.htm> [accessed 26 June 2002].
Suryadinata, Leo, ed. *Political Thinking of the Indonesian Chinese 1900–1995: A Sourcebook,* 2nd ed. Singapore: Singapore University Press, 1997.

Sweeney, P. L. Amin. "The Connection between the Hikayat Raja2 Pasai and the Sejarah Melayu". *JMBRAS* 40, 2 (1967): 94–105.
Switzer, Jason. "Armed Conflict and Natural Resources: The Case of the Minerals Sector". Mining Minerals and Sustainable Development Report no. 12. London: International Institute for Environment and Development, July 2001.
Sylado, Remy. *Ca Bau Kan*. Jakarta: KPG, 2002.
Tadjoedin, Mohammad Z. "A Future Resource Curse in Indonesia: The Political Economy of Natural Resources, Conflict and Development". CRISE Working Paper no. 35, Oxford: Oxford University, 2007.
Tapol. "West Papua: Brimob Violence Engulfs Manokwari", *Tapol: The Indonesia Human Rights Campaign Bulletin Online* 162, Aug. 2001, <http://tapol.gn.apc.org/bulletin/2001/bull162.htm>.
Tay, Elaine. "Global Chinese Fraternity and the Indonesian Riots of May 1998: The Online Gathering of Dispersed Chinese", Sept. 2000, <http://intersections.anu.edu.au/issue4/tay.html>.
Taylor, Charles. *Multiculturalism and "The Politics of Recognition": An Essay by Charles Taylor*, ed. Amy Guttman. Princeton: Princeton University Press, 1994.
Teeuw, Andries. "Hikayat Raja Raja Pasai and Sejarah Melayu". In *Malayan and Indonesian Studies: Essays Presented to Sir Richard Winstedt on his Eighty-fifth Birthday*, ed. John Bastin and Roelof Roolvink. Oxford: Clarendon Press, 1964.
Tempo. "Menunggu Kata Putus Para Kiai Waskita", 27, 11–17 Oct. 1999.
———. "Di Balik Pencopotan Itu", 29, 1–7 May 2000.
———. "Menunggu Keajaiban dari Langit", 19–25 Mar. 2001.
———. "Akibat Pergaulan Gaib", 31, 26 Aug.–1 Sept. 2002.
Tempo Interaktif. "Gus Dur Minta Theys Dibebaskan", 7 Dec.2000.
Thung, Ju-lan. "Identities in Flux: Young Chinese in Jakarta". Doctoral dissertation, La Trobe University, 1998.
Tifa Papua. 3rd week of May, 2002.
Time International. "The Darkest Season", 12 Mar. 2001.
Timura, Christopher. "'Environmental Conflict' and the Social Life of Environmental Discourse". *Anthropological Quarterly* 74, 3 (2001): 104–13.
Tokoh. "Michael Menufandu, Senior Advisor Masalah Otonomi Daerah untuk Irian Jaya", Denpasar, 20–26 Dec. 1999.
Tønnesson, Stein and Hans Antlöv, ed. *Asian Forms of the Nation*. Richmond: Curzon, 1996.
Toulmin, Stephen E. *Cosmopolis: The Hidden Agenda of Modernity*. New York: Free Press, 1990.
Tsing, Anna L. *In the Realm of the Diamond Queen: Marginality in an Out-of-the-Way Place*. Princeton: Princeton University Press, 1993.
———. *Friction: An Ethnography of Global Connection*. Princeton: Princeton University Press, 2005.

Twang, Peck Yang. *The Chinese Business Elite in Indonesia and the Transition to Independence 1940–1950*. Kuala Lumpur: Oxford University Press, 1998.
United Nations Development Programme (UNDP), Yayasan Lembaga Bantuan Hukum (YLBH) Indonesia and the Commission on the Legal Empowerment of the Poor. *Legal Empowerment of the Poor: Lessons Learned from Indonesia*, July 2007, <http://www.undp.org/legalempowerment> [accessed 18 Feb. 2008].
van Dijk, Cornelis. *Rebellion under the Banner of Islam: The Darul Islam in Indonesia*. The Hague: Martinus Nijhoff, 1981.
van Eek, J. W. "Bestuursverslag van de Afdeeling Fak Fak over de Maand Oktober, 1961 (Administration Report of the Fakfak Residency for Oct. 1961)". Resident of Fakfak, Nieuw Guinea Archief , Dossier G 16721, ARA, 1961.
———. "Bestuursverslag van de Afdeeling Fak Fak over de Maand December, 1961 (Administration Report of the Fakfak Residency for Dec. 1961)". Resident of Fakfak, Nieuw Guinea Archief , Dossier G 16721, ARA, 14 Feb. 1962.
———. "Politiek Overzicht van de Afdeeling Fak Fak over de Maand December 1961" (Political Report of the Fakfak Residency for Dec. 1961). Nieuw Guinea Archief, Dossier G 16721, ARA, 5 Jan. 1962.
———. "Politiek Overzicht van de Afdeeling Fak Fak over de Maand Januari 1962" (Political Report of the Fakfak Residency for Jan. 1962), Nieuw Guinea Archief, Dossier G 16721, ARA, 8 Feb. 1962.
van Klinken, Gerry. "Indonesia's New Ethnic Elites". In *Indonesia: In Search of Transition*, ed. Henk Schulte Nordholt and Irwan Abdullah. Yogyakarta: Pustaka Pelajar, 2002, pp. 67–106.
———. "Return of the Sultans: Local Community and the Rejection of Modernity after Suharto". In *The Revival of Tradition in Indonesian Politics: The Deployment of Adat from Colonialism to Indigenism*, ed. Jamie Davidson and David Henley. London: Routledge, 2007, pp. 146–69.
Vertovec, Steven and Robin Cohen, eds. *Conceiving Cosmopolitanism: Theory, Context, and Practice*. Oxford and New York: Oxford University Press, 2002.
Visser, Louise. "Remaining Poor on Natural Riches? The Fallacy of Community Development in Irian Jaya/Papua". *Asia Pacific Journal of Anthropology* 2, 2 (Oct. 2001): 68–88.
"Vraaggesprek met Kaisiepo and Jouwe". Kabinet van de Gouverneur van Nederlands Nieuw Guinea, dossier 35, ARA, 13 Oct. 1961.
Wade, Geoffrey. "The Ming Shi-lu (Veritable Records of the Ming Dynasty) as a Source for Southeast Asian History: Fourteenth to Seventeenth Centuries", 8 vols. Doctoral dissertation, University of Hong Kong, 1994.
Wagner, Peter. *A Sociology of Modernity: Liberty and Discipline*. London and New York: Routledge, 1994.
———. "The Resistance that Modernity Constantly Provokes: Europe, America and Social Theory". *Thesis Eleven* 58 (1999).

Wahid, Abdurrahman. "Islam: Apakah Bentuk Perlawanannya?". *Kompas*, 7 June 2002.
Wahyono, Ary. "Konflik-konflik Kenelayanan di Riau Kepulauan". In *Konflik-konflik Kenelayanan: Distribusi, Pola, Akar Masalah dan Resolusinya*, ed. Ratna Indrawasih. Jakarta: PMB-LIPI, 2006, pp. 55–69.
Wake, Christopher H. "Melaka in the Fifteenth Century: Malay Historical Traditions and the Politics of Islamisation". In *Melaka: The Transformation of a Malay Capital c 1400–1980*, vol. II, ed. Kernial Singh Sandhu and Paul Wheatley. Kuala Lumpur: Oxford University Press, 1983, pp. 128–62.
Walker, John H. "Autonomy, Diversity and Dissent: Conceptions of Power and Sources of Action in the *Sejarah Melayu* (Raffles MS 18)". *Theory and Society* 33 (2004): 213–55.
Walker, Peter. "Political Ecology: Where is the Ecology?" *Progress in Human Geography* 2, 1 (2006): 73–82.
Walls, C. "Legacy of the Fathers: Testamentary Admonitions and the Thematic Structure of the Sejarah Melayu". Doctoral dissertation, Yale University, New Haven, 1974.
Wang, Gungwu. "A Single Chinese Diaspora? Some Historical Reflections". In *Imagining the Chinese Diaspora: Two Australian Perspectives*, ed. Wang Gungwu and Annette Shun Wah. Canberra: Centre for the Study of the Chinese Southern Diaspora, Research School of Pacific and Asian Studies, ANU, 1999, pp. 1–17.
Wardhana, Veven Sp. *Panggil Aku Pheng Hwa*. Jakarta: KPG, 2002.
Waters, Kristin. "Women in Kantian Ethics: A Failure of Universality". In *Modern Engendering: Critical Feminist Readings in Modern Western Philosophy*, ed. Bat-Ami Bar On. Albany: State University of New York Press, 1994, pp. 117–25.
Watson, Conrad W. "Islamic Books and their Publishers: Notes on the Contemporary Indonesian Scene". *Journal of Islamic Studies* 16, 2 (2005): 177–210.
Wayne, H. "Give Services or Forget Pipeline: Hela", *The National*, 22 July 2002.
Weber, Eugene. *Peasants into Frenchmen: The Modernization of Rural France, 1870–1914*. Stanford: Stanford University Press, 1976.
Website Resmi Pemerintah Kabupaten Pacitan. "SBY Melakukan Ziarah ke Makam Orang Tuanya", 7 Oct. 2004, <http://www.pacitan.go.id/berita.php?id=111>.
Wee, Vivienne. "Political Fault-Lines in Indonesia: Atavistic Movements in Riau, Aceh and Beyond". Paper presented at the Panel on Political Fault-lines in Southeast Asia: Premodern Atavisms in Post-colonial Nation-states, Annual Meeting of the Association for Asian Studies, Chicago, 22–25 Mar. 2001.
———. "Ethno-nationalism in Process: Ethnicity, Atavism and Indigenism in Riau, Indonesia". *Pacific Review* 15, 4 (2002): 497–516.

Weldon, Peter. "Indonesian and Chinese Status Differences in Urban Java". Singapore: University of Singapore, Department of Sociology Working Paper no. 7, 1973.
Werbner, Pnina. "Global Pathways: Working Class Cosmopolitans and the Creation of Transnational Ethnic Worlds". *Journal of Ethnic and Migration Studies* 28, 1 (1999): 119–33.
———, ed. *Anthropology and Cosmopolitanism: Rooted, Feminist, Demotic, and Vernacular Perspectives.* Oxford: Berg, 2008.
Werbner, Richard. "Cosmopolitan Ethnicity: Entrepreneurship and the Nation: Minority Elites in Botswana". *Journal of Southern African Studies* 28, 4 (2002): 731–53.
Whittington, Floyd L. "The West Sumatran Political Scene". Airgram to Department of State from Floyd L. Whittington, Counselor of Embassy for Political Affairs, No. A-69, 19 July 1963.
Wibowo, Ignatius, ed. *Harga yang Harus Dibayar: Sketsa Pergulatan Etnis Cina di Indonesia,* Jakarta: Gramedia Pustaka Utama bekerja sama dengan Pusat Studi Cina, 2000.
———. *Retrospeksi dan Rekontekstualisasi "Masalah Cina".* Jakarta: Gramedia Pustaka Utama and Pusat Studi Cina, 1999.
———. "Exit, Voice and Loyalty: Indonesian Chinese after the Fall of Soeharto". *Sojourn* 16 (2001): 125–40.
Wibowo, Wahyu. "Gus Dur: Mega Sebagai 'Simbol'". *Suara Pembaruan,* 11 Nov. 1999.
Widen, Kumpriadi. "The Resurgence of Dayak Identities: The Symbols of their Struggle for Regional Autonomy are Self-Evident". In *Beyond Jakarta: Regional Autonomy and Local Societies in Indonesia,* ed. Minako Sakai. Adelaide: Crawford, 2002, pp. 102–20.
Wiener, Margaret. *Visible and Invisible Realms: Power, Magic and Conquest in Bali.* Chicago: University of Chicago Press, 1995.
Wilkinson, Richard J. "The Malacca Sultanate". *JMBRAS* 13, 2 (1935): 22–67.
———. "The Pengkalan Kempas 'Saint'". *JMBRAS* 9, 1 (1931): 134–5.
Willmott, Donald E. *The National Status of the Chinese in Indonesia 1900–1958.* Rev. ed. Ithaca: Cornell University Modern Indonesia Project, 1961.
Winichakul, Thongchai. "Writing at the Interstices: Southeast Asian Historians and Postnational Histories in Southeast Asia". In *New Terrains in Southeast Asian History,* ed. Abu Talib Ahmad and Tan Liok Ee. Athens: Ohio University and Singapore: Singapore University Press, 2003, pp. 3–29.
Witoelar, Wimar. *No Regrets: Reflections of a Presidential Spokesman.* Jakarta: Equinox, 2002.
Wolters, Oliver W. *History, Culture and Region in Southeast Asian Perspectives.* Rev. ed. Singapore: ISEAS, 1999 (1982).

———. *The Fall of Srivijaya in Malay History*. Kuala Lumpur: Oxford University Press, 1975 (1970).

———. "What Else May Ngo Si Lien Mean? A Matter of Distinctions in the Fifteenth Century". In *Sojourners and Settlers: Histories of Southeast Asia and the Chinese*, ed. Anthony Reid. Sydney: Asian Studies Association of Australia in association with Allen & Unwin, 1996, pp. 94–114.

Wood, Allan W. *Kant's Ethical Thought*. Cambridge: Cambridge University Press, 1999.

World Bank Group, Operations Evaluation Department. *Transmigration in Indonesia*. Jakarta: World Bank, 2001.

World Press Review. "Headhunting Again in Borneo", 44 (5), 1997 (orig. in *The Australian*).

Yu, Insun. "Le Van Huu and Ngo Si Lien: Their Perception of Vietnamese History". In *Viet Nam: Borderless Histories*, ed. Nhung Tran and Anthony Reid. Madison: University of Wisconsin Press, 2006), pp. 45–71.

Zammito, John H. *Kant, Herder, and the Birth of Anthropology*. Chicago and London: University of Chicago Press, 2002.

Zed, Mestika. *Somewhere in the Jungle. Pemerintah Darurat Republik Indonesia: Sebuah Mata Rantai Sejarah yang Terlupakan*. Jakarta: Grafiti, 1997.

Zed, Mestika, Alfan Miko and Emeraldy Chatra, eds. *Perubahan Sosial di Minangkabau*. Padang: Universitas Andalas, 1992.

Zhou, Fuyuan. "Where Do We Belong?" *Asian Ethnicity* 4, 3, special issue, ed. Pamela Allen and Sarah Turner (2003): 453–9.

Zook, Darren C. "Decolonizing Law: Identity Politics, Human Rights and the United Nations". *Harvard Human Rights Journal* 19 (2006): 95–122.

Index

Abdurrahman Wahid/Gus Dur
  pilgrimages of, 173–5, 176, 177, 183–8, 191, 193
  presidency of, 113, 192
Abdurra'uf of Singkel, 95
Abu Sofyan Daud, 186
Acciaioli, Greg, 224, 229
Aceh, 89, 91
  conflict/ violence in, 7, 8, 15, 16, 23, 31, 33, 94–5, 102, 112–3, 120–1, 186
  devolution of power and, 3
  DMDI and, 66
  elections in, 112–3
  elites of, 95
  Islam and, 93, 95
  nation-state and, 91, 92–7
  precolonial period in, 46, 89, 93
  rebellion, 7, 94–5
  regional identity and, 39
  resources of, 1, 7, 8, 120
  secession movement of, 3, 112–3
  trade and, 93
adat communities, 9, 107, 219–39
adat guards, 231
adat law, 9, 41, 68, 103, 165–6, 219, 224, 231
Adhuri, D., 145
Africa, 5, 8, 19, 94
Ahmad Mutamakin, 184–5, 187
Al Azhar, 77
Alexander the Great, *see* Iskander Dzu'l-Karnain
Ali Sadikin, 182
Aliansi Masyarakat Adat Nusantara, 9, 219, 221, 222–6, 229, 233, 235
Alomang, Mama Yosepha, 129
AMAN, *see* Aliansi Masyarakat Adat Nusantara

Ambon, 101, 202, 213, 215
America, *see* United States
Amungme people, 124–7, 128–9
Andaya, Barbara, 46, 54
Andaya, Leonard, 88
Anderson, Benedict, 23, 87–8, 91, 102–3, 263–4
Ang, Ien, 243–4, 247, 249, 250
animism, 77
anticolonial nationalism, 5–6, 22, 85, 94, 95, 104–8, 192
Apong, 50
Aria Magatsari, 53
As'ad Syamsul Arifin, 185–6
Asia, 19, 28
see also Southeast Asia
Asian Indigenous Peoples Pact, 221, 226
Asian nationalism, 84, 85
assimilation, 242, 244–5, 247, 260, 262–3, 268, 274
Attabik Ali, 188
Australia, 2, 247, 262, 266, 270
Austro-Hungarian empire, 85
autonomy, *see* regional autonomy
Azyumardi Azra, 187

Badan Permusyawaratan Kewarganegaraan Indonesia (Baperki), 248, 263
Bahasa Indonesia, 9–10, 83, 176, 241, 245
Bakker, Karen, 129–30
Balanan, 53
Bali, 1, 15, 67, 87, 88, 154, 167, 179, 219–21, 264–5
Bali bombings, 15
Baliem Valley, 205, 208
Balinese people, 154, 167–8, 179, 200, 249, 263
Balkanization, 15, 85
Banda Sea, 136
Bandung, 259, 267
Bangka Belitung, 66, 81, 82, 245
Bangka Island, 145, 149, 245, 247
Banjar people, 156, 164–5, 168

Banjarmasin, 154–5
Banten, 90, 93, 108, 109
Baperki, *see* Badan Permusyawaratan Kewarganegaraan Indonesia
Barton, Greg, 176
Basic Forestry Law (1967), 166–7
Batak, 30, 91, 92, 200, 263, 271
Batam, 77
Batee Kureng Declaration, 95
Banteng Council, 108, 109
Bayan, 228
Beanal, Thom, 128–9
Belitung, 145, 245
Bendahara dynasty, 40, 44–5, 47, 48, 49, 50
Bendahara Paduka Raja, *see* Tun Perak
Bendahara Puteh, 48
Bendahara Sriwa Raja, 52
Bendan Duwur, 180–1
Bengkalis, 66
Bengkulu, 141, 144, 145
Benny Giay, Dr, 205–6, 207–8, 214
Bentan, 47, 51
Bentan Karangan, 50
Bhinneka Tunggal Ika, 240, 250
Biak, 212, 213
Bibsy Sunario, 261
Bintan, 77
Bintang Kejora flag, 201, 202, 203, 207
Blitar, 173, 186, 188–90, 191, 194
Bock, Carl, 158, 159
Bogor, 189, 190, 191, 245
Bonneff, Marcel, 177
Borneo, 35, 158–60, 161–2, 163
see also Kalimantan
Borobudur, 175, 267
Bougainville, 117, 122
Brebes, 143
Bridge, Gavin, 129–30
Britain, 93–4
British Empire, 24, 161, 162
Brooke, James, 161
Brunei, 65, 70, 72, 161
Buddhism, 77, 226
Buginese people, 138–40, 201, 249
Bugis, 87

Index **327**

Bukit Seguntang, 42, 70
Bukit Tinggi, 66, 73
bureaucracy, 86, 89, 90
Burma, 85, 122
Buru, 50
Bush, George W., 18, 21, 25, 28, 268
Butonese people, 139, 140

Ca Bau Kan, 280, 289–93
cannibalism, 157, 159
cargo cult traditions, 207
Catholic Church, 208, 209, 260, 261, 264, 267, 290
censorship, 90
Central Europe, 25, 84, 85
Central Java, 141–3, 167, 175, 178, 180–1, 184, 185, 186, 193, 246, 257, 263, 291
Central Kalimantan, 79, 157, 158, 160, 165
Central Sulawesi, 226, 229
Central Sumatra, 1, 76
centralised government, 3–4, 8, 9, 39, 63, 77, 103, 108, 110–4, 135–6, 146–9, 150
charisma, 87, 88, 158
child mortality, 119, 227
China, 85, 86, 90, 93, 241–2, 243, 248
Chinese culture, 243, 274, 275, 277
Chinese diaspora, 243–4, 247, 248
Chinese identity, 10, 240–73, 275, 276, 274–95
Chinese Indonesians, 30
 alienation of, 10
 allegiance/loyalty of, 9, 242, 243, 275, 277
 assimilation policy and, 242, 244–5, 247, 260, 262–3, 268, 274
 citizenship and, 241, 242, 249, 259
 diversity among, 245–6, 250
 economic dominance of, 274, 275
 hybridisation and, 244, 247, 248, 249, 250
 language and, 10, 241, 243, 245, 246, 258, 259, 274, 275, 277, 283
 legal rights of, 240–1

 literature of, 277, 280–93
 marginalisation of, 9
 national status of, 242
 New Order and, 10, 242, 248, 250, 274, 275, 276, 278, 280, 283, 292
 Papua and, 211
 plurality of, 10
 pogroms against, 278
 religion and, 245–6, 256, 261, 267, 274
 transmigration and, 246–7
 violence against, 10, 155, 242, 243, 246, 249, 258, 275, 278, 279, 285
 see also Ong Hok Ham
Chinese language, 243, 245, 274, 277
Chinese nationality, 241–2
Chineseness, 242, 246, 248–9, 250, 274–95
Christians and Christianity, 7, 9, 16, 28, 31, 77, 137, 154, 155, 202, 203, 204–15, 267, *see also* missionaries
Christie, Jan, 88–9
Cilacap, 141, 142, 180, 182
Cirebon, 141, 144
citizenship, 241, 242, 249, 259, 276, 279, 289
civic integration, 25, 33
civic nationalism, 18–21, 24–6, 27–8
civil society, 33
clash of civilisations, 19
Collier, Paul, 119–20, 129, 130
colonialism, 64, 70, 225
 Chinese Indonesians and, 240, 241, 254, 255
 cultural diversity and, 24
 dual, 202
 exclusivism and, 28
 fight against, 2, 22, 104, 106, 106–8
 nation-building after, 19–20, 23, 24
 nation-states and, 85, 92, 93–4
 nationalism and, 6, 201–3, 207, 212, 213
 power and, 90
 statelessness and, 87

see also British Empire; Dutch colonial rule
communal identities, 50
communal violence, *see* conflict/violence
communism, 20, 105, 109, 110, 181, 192, 228, 242, 264–5, 275
community-building, 28
community identity, 8
   see also Chinese identity; cultural identity; ethnic identity; local identity; Malay identity
conflict/violence, 21
   Aceh and, 7, 8, 31, 33, 94–5, 96, 102, 120–1
   Ambon, 101
   Bengkulu, 141, 145
   Central Europe, 85
   Central Sulawesi, 226
   Chinese Indonesians and, 10, 155, 242, 243, 246, 249, 258, 275, 278, 279, 285
   colonial era, 94, 96
   East Java and, 139–40, 142, 143
   East Timor and, 278–9
   environmental security and, 121–2
   identity and, 124–9, 130
   indigenous people and, 122–3, 124–9, 208, 210, 211, 213
   Java, 102, 139–40, 141, 142, 143, 144, 145
   Kalimantan and, 9, 15, 16, 23, 31, 79, 120, 141, 143, 147, 153–61, 250
   Kei Islands and, 137–9
   Lampung, 141
   Madura, 141
   Maluku, 16, 31
   maritime resources and, 137–49, 150
   Masalembo, 141, 142, 145
   migration and, 121, 124–6, 250
   North Lombok, 228, 231
   North Sumatra, 141
   Pangandaran, 141, 143
   Papua, 7, 8, 15, 23, 31, 33, 112, 120–1, 124–6, 127, 128, 129, 208, 210, 211, 213

Pontianak, 141, 143
post-New Order, 7, 8, 9, 15, 16–7, 18, 20, 23, 24, 31
regions and, 15, 16–7, 18, 33
resources and, 8, 117, 118, 119–23, 124–31, 135–6, 141, 145, 148
Revolution and, 265
South Sulawesi, 102
state, 89
Sulawesi, 102, 226
Sumatra, 102, 141
USA, 269
West Java, 102
   see also counter-centre movements; global conflicts; human rights abuses
Confucianism, 245–6
Connell, John, 122
Constitution (1945), 193, 240–1
copper, 121, 127
corruption, 73, 112, 113–4, 121, 233
cosmopolitanism, 28–32, 33
counter-centre movements, 117, 123
counter-global trends, 123–4
cultural aims, 231–2
cultural capital, 243
cultural community, 86
cultural diversity, 15, 19, 23–4, 25, 30, 31, 32, 164
cultural essentialism, 23–4
cultural homogeneity, 22, 23, 24, 25, 91
cultural identity, 4, 23–4, 29, 32, 122, 124
cultural networks, 65
   see also Malay culture
cultural neutrality, 24–8, 33
cultural particularism, 30
cultural pluralism, 250
cultural racism, 19
cultural traditions, 231–2
   see also Chinese culture; Javanese culture; Malay culture
cultural unity, 9
cultural values, 22, 206–7
customary law
   see adat law
Cut Nya' Dien, 186

Dai Sejuta Umat, 68
d'Alpuget, Blanche, 266
dangdut, 153, 154
Dani people, 125, 126, 213–4
Darul Islam movement, 101, 102
Datuk Abdul Latif Abu Bakar, 65–6
Datuk Ismail Hussein, 65
Datuk Seri Haji Mohd Ali bin Mohd Rustam, 64, 65
Day, Tony, 89
Dayak people, 8–9, 16, 23, 79, 153–61, 162–5, 167, 168, 169–70
decentralisation, 2, 3–4, 63–4, 102, 103, 112–4, 141, 160, 170, 176, 193, 221, 232, see also regionalism
Decentralisation Law 22/99, 3, 113, 222
decolonisation, 29, 234
Déjà Vu: Kathmandu, 285–9
de Jong, P.E. de Josselin, 40
Demak, 142, 184
Demang Lebar Daun, 42–3, 47, 48, 50
democracy, 22, 85, 91, 97, 103, 111, 113, 187, 192, 193, 226, 232, 233–5
democratic nationalism, 23
democratisation, 85, 91, 92, 222, 226, 233, 235
Department of Marine Affairs and Fisheries, 146–7
derhaka, 40, 41, 43
Dewan Bahasa dan Pustaka, 73
Dewan Papua, 201
Dewan Perwakilan Rakyat Daerah, 114
diaspora, 120, 243–4, 247, 248, 249
diasporic nationalism, 244
Diniyyah Schools, 104
Dove, Michael, 161, 162
Drakard, Jane, 88
dual nationality, 241, 242
Dullah Laut, 139, 140
Dunia Melayu Dunia Islam, *see* Malay and Islamic World Movement
Durie, Mark, 96
Dutch colonial rule, 2, 8, 24, 67, 74, 87, 88, 90, 92, 102, 103, 104–5, 107–8, 109, 111, 159, 160, 162, 201–3, 207, 212–3, 240, 241–2, 245–6, 254, 255, 257, 258–9, 266, 290
Dutch disease, 119
Dutch East India Company, 90
dwi-tunggal, 174

East Java, 257
 conflict/ violence and, 139–40, 156, 265
 fisheries of, 139–40
 pilgrimages to, 173–4, 177–8, 188–90
 transmigration and, 156, 160, 167
East Kalimantan, 120, 166
East Nusa Tenggara, 145
East Timor, 7, 39, 209, 278–9
Eastern Europe, 19, 84
economic conditions, 106
economic dependence, 118–9
economic development, 7–8, 63, 78, 110, 121
economic management, 192, 193, 194
economic growth, 118–9
education, 84, 85, 90, 104, 119, 202–3, 205, 212, 227, 231, 257, 258, 259
Elsham, 208, 209
Elson, Bob, 176
emancipatory nationalism, 21, 22, 23, 30
empire, 28–9
England, 93
environmental determinism, 120
environmental impact, 128, 129
environmental security, 121–2, 130
ethnic cleansing, 23
ethnic diversity, 7, 119–20, 157
 see also cultural diversity
ethnic dominance, 23, 26
ethnic homogeneity, 85
ethnic identity, 126, 200–1, 204, 206, 214, 240–72
ethnic integration, 25, 33
 see also integration problems
ethnic nationalism, 25, 26, 28, 206
ethnicity, 24, 30, 76, 137–40, 141, 146–9, 150, 165, 280

ethno-claims, 148
ethnographic refusal, 160–1
ethnographies, 161–5
ethno-nationalism, 84–5, 91
Europe
  empire and, 29
  ethno-nationalism in, 84–5
  immigrants from, 28
  nation-state in, 17, 18, 20, 21, 25
  nationalism in, 26, 84–5
  new immigrants to, 19
  transformation of, 84–5
  universalism in, 19
  see also colonialism
Evangelical Christian Church, 206, 207, 208, 209–1, 211, 213
exclusions, 2, 28, 30, 32
  see also politics of exclusion
Eyang Lengkung Saweri, 182

failed state, 17, 33
Fakfak, 202, 212
federalism, 95
Feith, Betty and Herb, 262
feminism, 29
feudalism and patrimonialism, 39–61
fisheries, 121, 226
  access, social identity and, 134–52
  co-management of, 148–9, 150
  ethnicity and, 137–40, 141, 146–9, 150, 165
  licences for, 135
  policies regarding, 135–6, 141, 145, 146–9, 150
  politics of exclusion and, 141–6
  regionalism and, 141–9, 150
  sustainability of, 148
  technology and, 135, 136, 138, 139, 140, 141, 142–4, 145, 146, 147, 149, 150
fishing ground violations, 141, 142–4
fishing zones, 135, 136, 142, 146, 147, 149
Flores Sea, 136
forestry concessions, 166–7
forests, 121, 130, 135, 226, 232–3

Foucault, Michel, 29
France, 84, 91, 93, 94
Free Aceh Movement, 3
Free Papua Movement, 3
Freeport, 1, 121, 124–6, 128–9, 208
French republic, 19, 20, 25
Frits Tan, 262

Gajahmungkur, 180
GAPENA, 64, 65–6
Garuda, 179
Gayo, 94
Geertz, Clifford, 19–20, 87, 88, 168
Geissler, J.G., 204, 205
Gerakan Aceh Merdeka, 3, 112, 186
Giribangun, 193
global communication, 85
global influences, 127, 128
global security, 21
globalisation, 6, 14, 15–6, 17, 30, 66, 92, 118, 123–4, 129, 131, 235, 247, 279–80
GMNI, 261, 264
GMPKM, 72–3
Gobe project, 127
Godley, Michael, 246
gold, 121, 127
Goldman Environmental prize, 129
Golkar, 72, 155
good governance, 15–6, 21
governance systems, 4, 21, 107
governing elites, 20
government (central)
  devolution of power of, 3–4
  fisheries and, 135–6, 141, 145, 146–9, 150
  forestry concessions and, 166–7
  hegemonic claims by, 39
  independence and, 108
  Javanese beliefs and, 103
  local and regional identity and, 39
  local power politics and, 4
  New Order and, 110–1
  resource control and, 8, 135–6, 141, 145, 146–9, 150, 166–7

Index

social development and, 9
see also decentralisation; transmigration
Grasberg mine, 129
Gresik, 143
Guided Democracy, 39, 192, 264
Gunung Gundul, 167–8
Gunung Srandil, 182
Gyu gun, 106

Habibie, BJ, 111, 112, 174, 175, 205, 222
Hall, John, 25, 28
Hamzah Fansuri, 95
Han Loen Nio, 257
Han Siong Kong, 257
Hang Khoja, 48
Hang Nadim, 49
Hang Tuah, 48–9, 50
Hapsburg empire, 84
Harimurti Kridalaksana, 263
Harper, Krista, 128
Harun Zain, 110
Hasan Basri, 164–5
Hasan Tiro, 94, 95, 96
Hasballah M. Saad, 186
Hasyim Asy'ari, 173–4
Hasyim Muzadi, 191
headhunting, 157, 158–60, 164
Heidhues, Mary Somers, 246–7
Hela Province, 127
Helsinki Memorandum of Understanding, 96
Henley, David, 87
Herman Awom, Rev., 208–10
Herman Saud, 209–10
Heryanto, A., 275
Hides gas project, 127
Hikayat Raja Pasai, 40, 53
Hirsch, Philip, 122
Hoeffler, Anke, 119, 120
Hollandia, 201, 202
homosexuality, 267
Hong Kong, 246
Howitt, Richard, 122
Huaren, 248
Huli people, 127

human reason, 29, 30, 32
human rights, 221, 222, 225, 226, 234, 235
abuses, 119, 120, 126–7, 128, 130, 206, 208–9, 211
Hurgronje, C. Snouck, 93
hybridisation, 244

Iban, 162, 163
Ibrahim Yaacob, 66
ICMI, 79
identity, *see* Chinese identity; cultural identity; ethnic identity; local identity; Malay identity; national identity; regional identity
identity formation, 15
identity politics, 16, 17, 19, 30, 124–6, 127, 128, 130, 131
Idul Fitri, 188
IKSEP, 64
Imbi Square, Jayapura, 201
independence, 2, 106–8, 200, 201, 259, 267
India, 85, 93, 225
indigenous people, 7, 8–9, 22, 64, 91, 122–3, 124–6, 128, 156, 168, 170, 221–35, 248, 249–50, 274, 275, *see also* Dayak people
indoctrination classes, 90
Indonesia-Malaysia-Thailand Growth Triangle, 78
Indonesia Menggugat, 179
Indonesian Borneo, *see* Kalimantan
Indonesian elite, 111–2
Indonesian Islamic State, 95
Indonesian military, *see* military power/forces
Indonesian Republic, 95, 96, 101, 103, 106, 108, 240
Indonesianists, 85, 87
Indonesianness, 6, 10, 256, 271, 280, 292
Indragiri, 56
Indramayu, 141, 144
Indrawasih, R., 145
industrialisation, 84

Ingleson, John, 104–5
INS, 104
integration problems, 101–16
  see also national integration
integrative revolution, 20, 25
international community, 91
internationalisation, 29
Internet, 278, 279, 292
Irene A. Muslim, 163
Irian, 154, 168
  see also Papua
Iskander Dzu'l-Karnain, 42, 45, 47, 49, 54, 55, 70
Islam
  Aceh and, 93, 95
  Chinese Indonesians and, 242
  conversion to, 53, 54, 164
  education and, 104
  Javanised variants of, 184
  Kalimantan and, 153, 154, 155, 164, 165, 168
  legalism and, 187
  Malays and, 62, 63–7, 68, 69, 72, 73, 77
  Maluku and, 16, 137
  Minangkabau and, 31, 72
  nationalist movements and, 105
  New Order and, 110
  North Lombok and, 226, 227–8, 229, 234
  Papua and, 7, 207, 210, 211, 212, 213–4, 215
  Sasak culture and, 226, 234
  strength of, 102
  the West and, 15
  transmigration and, 168
  Waktu Lima, 228, 230
  West Sumatra and, 7, 102, 104, 105
  Wetu Telu, 226, 227–8, 229, 230
  see also pilgrimages
Islamic cultural practices, 9
Islamic movements, 16, 113
  see also Malay and Islamic World Movement
Islamic world, 104, 105
Islamisation, 4, 79

Ismeth Abdullah, 78
Italy, 93, 94
IWGIA, 221, 226

Jaka Tingkir, 185
Jakarta, 62, 63, 64, 78, 79, 80, 94, 96, 101, 102, 108, 112, 114, 142
Jakarta bombing, 15, 246–7, 267
Jalan Kapasan, 246
Jambi, 53, 66, 72, 76
Jangka Jayabaya, 178–9
Japanese occupation, 90, 94, 106, 179, 255, 258, 259, 270, 290
Japen island, 212
Java, 1, 93, 263–4
  Chinese Indonesians and, 247
  conflict in, 139–40, 141, 142, 143, 145, 265
  language in, 241, 245
  maritime resources of, 139–40, 141, 142, 143, 145
  nationalist movements in, 104–5
  political power and, 1, 7
  resources of, 7, 139–40, 141, 142, 143, 144, 145
  transmigration programmes from, 8, 9, 167–8
  West Sumatran invasion by, 108, 109
  see also Central Java; East Java; Jakarta
Javanese culture, 4, 9, 20, 73, 79, 260, 263, 264
Javanese kingdoms, 88–9
Javanese people, 102–3, 154, 156, 166, 167–8, 175, 249
Javanese sacred sites, see pilgrimages
Jayabaya, 177–80
Jayapura, 201, 207, 208, 211, 212, 214
Johor, 77
Jombang, 173
Jusuf Kalla, 185

Kadilangu, 184
Kaharingan, 154
Kajen, 184
Kali Garang, 180

Kali Sadeng, 180
Kalimantan, 1, 245
  conflict/violence in, 9, 15, 16, 23, 31, 79, 120, 141, 143, 147, 153–61
  DMDI and, 66
  ethnographies of, 161–5
  fisheries and, 141, 143, 165
  forestry and, 165–8
  GMPKM and, 72
  headhunting in, 157, 158, 160, 166–9
  Malaysian States on, 2
  plantations of, 154, 160, 168–9
  political economy of, 165–9
  population of, 160
  religion and, 153, 154, 164, 165, 168
  resources of, 7, 120, 141, 143, 147
  transmigration to, 8–9, 16, 154, 158, 160, 166–9
  see also Central Kalimantan; Dayak people; East Kalimantan; Madurese people; Malays; North Kalimantan; South Kalimantan; West Kalimantan
Kamoro people, 124–8
Kampar, 54, 55, 56
Kant, Immanuel, 28–9, 30, 31, 32
Kapuas, 163
Karimun, 77
Kartjono, 264
Kayan people, 162
kebatinan, 246
Kei Islands, 137–9, 140
Kei Kecil Island, 137–9
Keiese people, 202
Kenyah people, 162
Kepulauan Riau, 145
Kerukunan Keluarga Palembang, 68
Kesastraan Melayu Tionghoa dan Kebangsaan Indonesia, 277
Ketonggo Forest, 175
Kimbin, 213
King, Victor, 162–3
Kingsbury, Benedict, 234
kinship, 86, 88, 89, 125, 138

Kintamani, 219–21
Klang, 52
Koibur, Beatrix, 208
Komite Nasional, 201–2, 203
Konfrontasi, 74
Koppo, 257–8
Korea, 86
Kroya, 186
Kuala Kapuas, 156
Kutubu project, 127

Lake Batur, 219–21
Laksamana, 50–1, 55
Laksamana Nadim, 51
Laksamana Sukardi, 185
Lampung, 141
land clearance, 160, 165
land reform, 226
land rights, 229
language(s), 9–10, 23, 26, 68, 78, 91, 92, 95–6, 104, 164, 176, 221, 231, 241, 243, 245, 246, 258, 259, 274, 275, 283
Lapian, A.B., 264
Lasi Suroharjo, 177
Latin America, 222
Lebaran, *see* Idul Fitri
Ledo, 153
legal pluralism, 224
legal system, 224, 231
  see also adat law
legitimacy, political, 14, 191–4
Lembaga Musyawarah Desa, 233
Lembar, 145
Li, Tania, 123, 124, 222, 223, 235
Lide, 56
Liem Yoe Tik, 257
Lingga, 56
literature, 277, 280–93
local culture, 9, 231–2
  see also cultural diversity
local government, *see* decentralisation
local history, 192
local identity, 3, 4, 8, 39, 52, 123–8
local loyalties, 39
local pilgrimages, 193–4

local power, 4
local practice, 192–3
local resources, 8, 118, 128, 130
  see also resources, natural
local values, 68
logging, 160, 166, 226, 228, 232
Lombok, 219, 220, 221
  see also North Lombok
Lore Lindu National Park, 226
loyalty
  family-based, 51–2
  local, 39
  Malay rulers and, 45, 51–2
  primordial, 25
  regional, 15, 19, 39
  SM and, 41, 43
  see also Chinese Indonesians

Mabbett, Hugh, 246
Mabbett, Ping-Ching, 246
Madagascar, 66
Madura, 9, 16, 141, 153, 160, 166, 167, 176, 184
Madurese people, 9, 79, 139–40, 143, 153–61, 165, 166, 167, 168, 169, 170, 249, 250
Maharaja Isak, 51
Maharaja Permaisura, 54
Majapahit, 50, 67, 88
Majelis Adat Budaya Melayu Indonesia, 74
Majelis Adat Sasak, 232
Makasar, 90, 93
Malang, 245, 248
Malay
  Malay and Islamic World Movement, 6, 64–7, 68, 69–70, 73, 74
  Malay Annals, 39–61
  Malay culture, 62, 63, 64, 65–6, 67–71, 72–3, 77, 80
  Malay identity, 62, 63, 64, 66, 72, 76, 77, 79
  Malay/ Indonesian language, 95, 96
  Malay royal authority, 40, 42–3, 74
  Malay rulers, 40–1, 42–55

Malay sovereignty, 6
Malay world, 6, 40, 41, 65, 68, 73, 79, 104
Malayness, 62–3, 64–7, 71, 74, 75, 77, 78–9
Malays, 24, 40, 62–3, 65, 66, 70, 72, 73, 76, 78, 79, 155, 156, 159, 160, 163, 164–5, 168, 169
Malaysia, 5, 24, 62, 63, 64, 66, 72, 74, 117, 123, 161
Malaysian Malays, 62
Maloh, 162, 163–4
Maluku, 15, 16, 31, 53, 88, 137, 202, 212, 213
Maluku Sea, 136
Manchuria, 258
Manokwari, 215
marginalisation, 2, 6, 9, 65, 68, 74, 76, 78, 79, 160, 167, 170, 215, 230
Margoyoso, 184
marine resource management, 146–9
maritime resources, 134–52
Maritime Study Group, 145
Marizal Umar, 72–3
Markus Kaisiepo, 203
Marxism, 20, 85, 89
Masalembo, 141, 145
mass media, 92
masyarakat adat, 9, 221, 222, 233, 224–6, 235
masyarakat terasing, 222, 225, 228
Masyumi, 110
Mataram, 145, 178, 229, 230
Mbah Lengkung Kusuma, 182
McNeill, William, 85
McVey, Ruth, 263, 264
Me people, 206, 208
Medan, 62, 66, 74–5, 78, 91, 144, 202, 245, 246
media, 90, 92, 292
Media Sandra Kasih, Dr, 73
Megawati Sukarnoputri, 68–9, 187, 189, 190
  pilgrimages of, 173–4, 175, 177, 186–7, 188, 190, 191, 193
  presidency of, 113, 191, 192

Melaka, 40, 49, 50, 53–6, 64, 65, 70, 78
Melaka-Johor rulers, 40
Melakan kingship, 42–5, 47–9, 54
Melakan power structure, 47–8
Melanesian cultural values, 206
Melayu Raya, 6
Melayu Riau Sejati, 75
Menang, 177
Mendi people, 127
Mentawaian people, 30
Merah Silu, 53
Meratus Dayak, 162
Merba, 50
Mesjid Agung, 68
Michael Menufandu, 204
Middle East, 19, 25
migration, 124–6, 127
    see also Chinese Indonesians; transmigration
Miles, Doug, 162
military power/forces, 33, 110, 113, 119, 125, 126, 127, 208, 210, 211, 213, 278–9
Milner, Anthony, 88
Mimika, 202
Minangkabau, 47, 54, 92
Minangkabau people, 30–1, 53, 72–3, 76, 102, 103, 104, 105, 106, 107–8, 109, 111
Mining, Minerals and Sustainable Development project, 121
mining and minerals, 7, 62, 75, 118, 119, 135, 226
missionaries, 202, 203, 204, 205–6, 213, 245
modernisation, 85, 92
Mohammad Hatta, 105, 106–7, 109, 174
Mohammed Iskander Shah, 45
Moluccas, see Maluku
Moran project, 127
Mount Geulis, 191
Mount Kare gold project, 127
Mount Lawu, 175–6, 193, 194
Mount Muria, 175, 184

Mount Selok, 180, 182
Mount Tidar, 175
Moy, Timothy, 40–1
Mugo, 186
Muhammad Barokah, Haji, 186–7
Muhammad Yamin, 180
Muhammadiah, 105
multiculturalism, 19, 24, 29, 225, 250
multinational resource corporations, 11, 128, 129
Munninghof, Mgr H.F.M., 208
Musi River, 70
Muslim religion, see Islam; Islamic cultural practices
mysticism, 176, 184, 190, 194

nagari, 4, 103, 107, 111
Nagtegal, Luc, 88
Nahdlatul Ulama, 173
nation-building, 5, 15, 18, 19–20, 21, 24, 25, 123
nation content, 21–3
nation-states, 5, 6, 14–5, 17–8, 21, 22, 23, 29, 64, 84–92, 102, 163, 224, 235
national consciousness, 90
national cultures, 9
national history writing projects, 3, 86
national homogeneity, 21, 22–3
national identity, 26, 163, 200, 241–2
national integration, 3, 5, 7, 17, 18, 23, 25
    see also integration problems
national integrity, 17, 21
national liberation, 20
national particularism, 22, 23
national power, 14
national sovereignty, 85
national symbols, 192, 194
nationalism, 2, 3, 6, 7, 16, 18, 19, 22, 23, 24, 25–8, 30, 84–6, 90, 91, 92, 97, 108, 112, 200–18, 241, 244, 248, 277, 290, 291
nationalist movements, 85, 104–6, 107, 108, 275, 277, 291–2
Natuna, 77

natural gas, 1, 7, 62, 77, 127
natural resources, *see* resources, natural
Nederlandsche Zendingsvereeniging, 245
Negara Bahagian Aceh, 95
neo-Kantians, 30
Netherlands, 101, 270
  see also Dutch colonial rule
Netherlands East Indies, 102, 104, 292
Netherlands Indies, 90
Netherlands New Guinea, *see* Papua
Netherland subjects, 240, 241–2
New Guinea Council, 203, 207
new history-writing, 3, 86
New Order, 147
  airline routes under, 78
  assimilation program of, 242, 245
  attacks on, 175–6
  centralisation and, 103, 110–1
  Chinese Indonesians and, 10, 242, 248, 250, 274, 275, 276, 278, 280, 283, 292
  fall of, 5, 39, 63
  Indonesian diversity and, 24
  Javanese culture and, 4
  legitimacy of, 192, 193
  North Lombok and, 220, 221, 222, 224, 227–8, 230, 232, 233
  Papua and, 205, 208, 214
  pilgrimages and, 175–6, 181, 183, 188–9, 193
  unitary village systems and, 4
  see also sexual violence; transmigration
new security paradigm, 121
Ngadju Dayak, 162
NGOs, 9, 11, 128, 129, 221–2, 223, 226, 228, 229, 235
Nonini, Donald, 248
Nordholt, Henk Schulte, 88
North Kalimantan, 153–4, 162
North Lombok, 219, 225–6, 227–33, 234
North Sulawesi, 212
North Sumatra, 74–5, 141, 144, 246
  see also Medan

Nucleus Estate/Smallholder Scheme, 169
Nugroho Notosusanto, 261, 264
Numbing Island, 145
Nuruddin ar-Raniry, 95
Nusakambangan island, 182

Obed Komba, Rev., 205, 214
ocean resources, *see* maritime resources
Ohoisaran, 137–9
Ohoislam, 137–9, 140
oil, 1, 7, 62, 75, 118, 119, 121, 127
Ok Tedi mine, 128
Ong Hok Hai, 258
Ong Hok Ham, 10, 254–72
Ong Ik Sien, 257
Ong Thuan Hian, 257–8, 268
Ong Thwan Tjiang, 257
Orang Kaya, 46
Organisasi Papua Merdeka, 3, 205, 211
Ortner, Sherry, 160
otherness, 139, 140, 141
Ottoman Turkey, 93
Ottow, Carl W., 204, 205
Oyong, P.K., 262

Padang, 62, 72–3, 78
Padangbai, 219
Padhepokan Jambe Lima, 182, 183
Padhepokan Jambe Pitu, 182, 183
Paduka Tuan, 49, 50, 51
Pagar Ruyong, 54, 55
Pagden, Anthony, 28–9
Pahang, 50, 54, 55, 56
Pajang, 185
Pak Cilik Cakrawangsa (Nalagareng), 182
Pak Cilik Cari Sukmayarengga (Petruk), 182
Pakage, Zacheus, 206
Pakistan, 85
Palangkaraya, 156, 157, 165
Palar, 178, 180
Palembang, 42, 47, 48, 50, 62, 66, 67–71, 78

Palembang Darussalam Festival, 68
Pamuksan Sri Aji Jayabaya, *see* Jayabaya
Pancasila, 110, 179, 193, 224
Panchur Serapong, 50
Panciran, 143
Panembahan Senapati, 184
Pangandaran people, 141, 142
Panggil Aku Pheng Hwa, 280–9
Pangkal Pinang, 66
Pangkalangbun, 157
Paniai, 205–6, 208
Pan-Papuan identity, 203, 212
Papua
  Asian population of, 211
  asylum-seekers from, 2
  Christianity in, 9, 202, 203, 204–11
  colonialism and, 7, 201–3, 207, 212, 213
  conflict/violence in, 7, 8, 15, 23, 31, 33, 112, 120–1, 124–6, 127, 128, 129, 208, 210, 211, 213
  CoW areas of, 124–6, 127
  culture and, 9, 206–7
  demographic transformation of, 211–4
  devolution of power and, 3
  education in, 202–3
  elections in, 113
  ethnicity and, 206, 211–4
  human rights and, 206, 208–9, 211
  identity in, 200–1, 204, 206, 214, 215
  Islam in, 207, 210, 211, 212, 213–4, 215
  migration and, 8, 124–6, 202, 211–4, 215
  missionaries and, 202, 203, 204, 205–6, 213
  nation-state and, 92
  nationalism in, 200–18
  New Order and, 205, 208, 214
  regional identity and, 39
  resources of, 1, 7, 8, 120, 124–6, 128, 208
  secession movements of, 2, 3, 205, 209, 214
  special autonomy status of, 112, 204, 206, 214, 215
Papua New Guinea, 2
  conflict in, 121, 127
  cultural identity in, 121, 123, 125, 126
  peripheral provinces of, 117
  resources of, 117, 127, 128
Papuan values, 206–7
Parangkusumo, 184
Parangtritis, 175
Partai Golongan Karya, 72, 155
Partai Rakyat Indonesia, 105
particularism, 21, 22, 25, 28
Pasai, 93, 95
Pasangan river, 53
Pasuruan, 257
Patani, 54
Pati people, 142
patrimonialism and feudalism, 39–61
patriotism, 25
PDI-P, 190
PDP, 206, 208, 212, 214
PDRI, 107
Pedir, 56
Pekanbaru, 66, 77, 78
pembina adat, 232
Pemerintah Revolusioner Republik Indonesia, 102, 108–9
pemuda, 267
Penang, 93
Pendidikan Nasional Indonesia, 105
People's Republic of China, *see* China
Perak, 51, 55
Perak chiefs, 46
peranakan Chinese, 245, 247, 275, 279
Perekat Ombara, 229–33
Perigi, 139–40
peripheral regions, 1–13
Permesta rebels, 102
perpetual peace, 31
Persatuan Muslimin Indonesia, 105
PERZIM, 64
Petaka, 53
Petalangan, 77
Philippines, 72, 117, 262, 267

pilgrimages, 79, 173–91, 193–4
Pires, Tomé, 55–6
PKI, 105
plantations, 154, 160, 167, 168–9, 226
pluralism, 14, 85, 86, 187, 233, 247, 250
PNI, 261
PNI (Baru), 105
political ecology, 122
political integration, 18, 19, 20, 21, 28, 33
political legitimacy, 191–4
political pilgrimages, *see* pilgrimages
political universalisation, 18–21
politics of exclusion, 141–6, 148, 150
politics of recognition, 33
Pontianak, 66, 141, 143, 155, 157, 169, 245, 247
populist politics, 84–5
Porgera gold project, 127
Portuguese colonists, 40, 51
postcolonial theory, 19, 29
postnationalism, 18
post-nationalist globalised order, 85
poststructuralism, 29
poverty, 122, 227
power, 87–8, 89–90, 92, 122
Pratt, Tony, 266
Presidium Dewan Papua, *see* PDP
pribumi Indonesians, 274, 275–6, 277–8, 279, 280, 283, 291, 292
primordialism, 193
print capitalism, 84
PRRI, 102, 108–9
PSI, 175, 264
PSSI, 105
PT Freeport Indonesia, 1, 121, 124–6, 128–9, 208
PT Perkebunan Nusantara II, 74–5
Purjm, 56
Putussibau, 162

racial homogeneity, 22, 23
racism, 10, 19, 275, 278
Raden Haji Muhammad Sjafei Prabu Diradja, 71, 104

Raden Ngabei Ranggawarsita, 178–9, 180
Raffles, Stamford, 87, 93
Raffles MS 18, *see Sejarah Melayu*
Raja Abdullah, 55
Raja Ampat Islands, 212
Raja Kecik, 77
Raja Muhammad, 54
Raja of Kedah, 54
Raja people, 202
rajas, 90
Rama Sudiyat, 181–2, 183
rape, 278–9, 285
rationality, 27
Reformasi era, 111–4, 200, 201, 220, 222, 228, 231
regional autonomy, 2, 3–4, 62, 63, 65, 68, 70, 78, 79, 80, 96, 108, 222, 224, 226, 228, 230, 232, 233, 247, 249
  see also Decentralisation Law 22/99
regional conflict, *see* conflict/violence
regional dissidence, 101–2
  see also conflict/violence
regional identity, 8, 39, 40, 52, 118, 148, 164, 176, 193, 200, 214
regional loyalties, 15, 19, 39
regional politics, 15–8
regionalism, 5, 15–8, 21, 33, 34, 117, 131, 141–9, 150, 193, 220, 221, 230
Reid, Anthony, 41, 46
Rekan, 53
relative peace, 31
religio-cultural diversity, 24, 25
religio-cultural neutrality, 20, 33
religio-cultural particularism, 21
religion, 7, 9, 16, 77, 119–20, 137, 154, 155, 157, 274, *see also* Buddhism; Chinese Indonesians; Christians and Christianity; Islam
religious identity, 16
Remy Sylado, 280, 289–93
Republik Maluku Selatan, 101
resource conflict, 7, 8, 16, 117, 119–23, 124–31, 137–49, 150
resource control, 8, 117, 118, 119–23, 124–31, 135–6, 141, 145, 148

Index **339**

resource curse thesis, 118
resource dependence, 118–9
resource rents, 8
resource scarcity, 121
resource sovereignty, 122
resources, natural
   access, social identity and, 134–52
   Aceh, 1, 7, 8, 120–1
   Asia-Pacific, 117
   Bengkulu, 141, 145
   co-management of, 148–9, 150
   diaspora and, 120
   economic dependence on, 118–9, 120
   ethnicity and, 137–40, 141, 146–9
   environmental security and, 121–2
   export of, 119, 120
   globalisation and, 123–4
   grievance and greed models of, 119–20
   identity and, 123–8
   indigenous people and, 122–3, 126–8, 226, 232–3
   Jakarta, 142
   Java, 7, 139–40, 141, 142, 143, 144, 145
   Kalimantan, 7, 120, 141, 143, 147, 165–8, 169
   Kei Islands, 137–9, 140
   Lampung, 141
   Madura, 141
   maritime, 134–52
   Masalembo, 141, 142, 145
   migration and, 124–6, 127, 168
   nations and, 122–3
   ownership of, 7–9, 122, 128
   Pangandaran, 141, 142
   Papua, 1, 7, 8, 120–1, 124–6, 127, 128, 208
   Papua New Guinea, 117, 127, 128
   politics of exclusion and, 141–6, 148, 150
   Pontianak, 141, 143
   regionalism and, 141–9, 150
   revenues from, 16, 126
   Sumatra, 62, 75, 76, 77–8, 141

Riau, 63, 66, 72, 73, 75–8
Riau Airlines, 78
Riau Archipelago, 75, 77–8, 245
Riau Movement, 75–6, 77
Riau Province, 75–6, 78
Riau Vision for 2020, 78
Ricklefs, Merle, 88
Rokan, 56
Roni Hanan, 68
Rosario, Brother, 259
Roshwald, Aviel, 25–6
Rosihan Arsyad, 68, 69–70
Ross, Michael, 118, 119
royal absolutism, 40, 42, 44, 45, 56
royal alliances, 87
royal authority, 40, 42
rubber, 168, 169
Rumainum, Rev., 208
Rumbati, 202
Rusli Zainal, 78
Rutter, Owen, 158–9

Sabah, 161
Sachs, Jeffrey, 119
sacred sites, *see* pilgrimages
Saidin, O.K., 75
Sakai people, 77
Salahuddin Wahid, K.H., 188
Samagat Yuliana Anna, 163
Samin Movement, 263
Sampang, 160
Sampit, 155, 156, 157–8, 160, 169
Sanggau, 154
SARA, 276
Sarawak, 161, 162
Sarikat Rakyat, 105
Sasak people, 225–6, 231, 232, 234
Sathean, 137–9
Sawito Kartowibowo, 175
Sawu Sea, 136
Sayong, 50
Scott, James, 41, 45
sea resources, *see* maritime resources
secession movements, 2, 3, 112–3, 205, 209, 214
security cooperation treaty, 2

security forces, *see* military power/
    forces
Sejarah Melayu, 39–61
Sekotong Barat, 145
self-determination, 232, 234
self-identification, 225
self-representation, 276–7
Semar, 182, 183
Semarang, 180–1, 245
Sening Ujong, 50, 52
Seram Sea, 136
Serang, 141, 144
Serui, 212
serumpun Melayu, 62, 63, 64, 69, 70,
    78, 79
sexual violence, 278–9, 285
Siak, 55, 56, 77
Siantan, 50–1
Siauw Giok Tjan, 263
Simbur Cahaya, 68
Simuh, Dr, 184
Sindhunata, 177, 178
Singapore, 5, 40, 50, 51, 63, 65, 70, 72,
    77, 107
Singkawang, 153, 155
Singkep, 77
Sino-Indonesians, *see* Chinese
    Indonesians
Sintang, 169
Siti Hartinah, 193
Situbondo, 186
Sjafri Sairin, 184
Skinner, G. William, 261–2, 270
Slater, Daniel, 114
slaves, 159
Smith, Claire, 155–6
social revolution, 74
Soejatmoko, 264, 266
Solo, 246
Sorong, 1, 212
South Africa, 66
South Kalimantan, 154–5, 164–5
South Sulawesi, 87, 102, 144
South Sumatra, 67–71
    see also Palembang
Southeast Asia, 269

education in, 84
ethno-nationalism in, 84, 85–6
independence movements in, 5
industrialisation of, 84
population shifts in, 84
post-colonial power in, 87, 89–90
power management in, 89
transformation of, 84
urbanisation and, 84
sovereignty, 8, 22, 42, 47, 54, 70, 85,
    103, 107
Soviet empire, 19
special autonomy, 204, 206, 214, 215
spontaneous migrants, 125, 246
Sri Agar Raja, 51
Sri Bija diraja, 50, 51, 54
Sri Lanka, 65
Sri Nara 'diraja, 51–2
Sri Rama, 48
Sri Tri Buana, 42–3, 45, 47, 50, 54
Sriwijaya, 67, 88, 89
Sriyani, 261
Star Weekly, 262, 263, 264
statelessness, 87
Strait of Melaka, 6, 62, 63, 88, 136
Subadio Sastrosatomo, 175–6
Sudar, 50
Sudjai, Colonel, 181–2
Sudjono Humardhani, 180
Suharto
    centralisation and, 95
    democracy and, 192
    pilgrimages of, 176, 177, 180–3, 189,
        193
    pilgrimages to tomb of, 193, 194
Suharto government, 4, 9, 103, 112,
    265, 292
    centralisation and, 110–1
    forestry resources and, 166, 167
    national consciousness and, 90
    transport and communication
        system and, 80
    transmigration programmes of, 8,
        168
    see also New Order
Suir, 50

Sukabumi, 245
Sukarno, 106, 107, 258, 264
  centralisation and, 96
  democracy and, 192
  Konfrontasi and, 74
  pilgrimages by, 177–80, 188–91, 193
  pilgrimages to tomb of, 173–4, 175, 186, 188–91, 194
Sukarno government, 103–4, 112
  nation-state and, 90
  PRRI rebellion and, 109
  transmigration under, 167–8
Sulawesi, 87, 93, 102, 108, 144, 168, 212, 213, 226, 229
Sultan Adiwijaya, 185
Sultan Ahmad, 49
Sultan Ahmad Shah, 54
Sultan Ala'u'd-din, 45, 51, 54, 55, 56
Sultan Ibrahim of Siak, 54, 55
Sultan Iskander Shah, 50
Sultan Mahmud Badaruddin II, 67
Sultan Mahmud Badaruddin III, 71
Sultan Mahmud of Palembang, 45
Sultan Mahmud Shah, 48, 49, 54, 55
Sultan Mansur Shah, 45, 49, 50, 51, 52, 54
Sultan Menawar Shah, 54, 55
Sultan Muhammad of Pahang, 55
Sultan of Brunei, 161
sultanates, 90, 93, 94
Sumatra, 102, 108, 245
  colonial period in, 93
  culture and cultural symbols of, 62, 63, 64, 67–75, 76
  DMDI and, 64, 66
  economy of, 62, 63, 78
  government in, 4
  Japanese occupation of, 106
  Malay heritage and culture in, 64, 68, 67–75, 76
  pre-colonial period in, 87, 88
  regional autonomy and, 62, 63, 65, 68, 70
  resources of, 62, 75, 76, 77–8, 141
  sultanates of, 67–8, 69, 71, 74–5
  tourism and, 70

  see also Aceh; North Sumatra; West Sumatra
Sumatra Thawalib schools, 104
Sumedang, 186
Sunan Kalijaga, 175, 184
Sundanese people, 249, 267
Sungai Liat, 145, 149
Sungei Raya, 50
Surabaya, 246, 257, 258, 259, 263
Surakarta, 185
Surantika Samin, 263
Susilo Bambang Yudhoyono/SBY, 112, 113, 177, 193
Susuhunan Pakubuwana II, 185
Switzer, Jason, 121
Syiah Kuala, 95

Tabalung, 53
Tabernacle Bible Church of Indonesia, 208
Tabrani Rab, 77
Tan Hie Sioe, 257
Tan Malaka, 105
Tan Siang Leon, 257
Tan Siang Tjia, 257–8, 268
Tanjong Pura, 47
Tanjung, 229
Taufik Kiemas, 69
Tay, Elaine, 244
Tebuireng Islamic Centre, 173
technology, *see* fisheries
Tegal, 142, 143
Teluk Tomini Bay, 136
Tengkal, 56
Tengku Rizal Nurdin, 74, 75
Terengganu, 53, 55
territorial integrity, 2, 3
Teuku Umar Djohan, 186
Teungku Daud Beureu'eh, 94, 95
Teweh river, 159
Thaha Al Hamid, 207, 212
Thailand, 72, 117, 262
Thambun Anyang, 163
theatre-state, 88
Theosophy, 246
Thongchai Winichakul, 3

Thung Ju-lan, 245, 246
Tides Foundation Award, 129
timber, 7, 8, 165–8, 169
timber companies, 167, 170
timber concessions, 166–7
Timor, 168
  see also East Timor
Tjan, Harry, 260
tomb pilgrimages, 173–91, 193–4
tourism, 70, 80, 226, 227, 232, 233
trade, 80, 86, 87, 89, 92, 93, 102, 107, 160, 165, 169, 245
translocal conflicts, 16
translocalism, 16
transmigration, 8–9, 16, 125, 154, 158, 160, 166–9, 202, 211–4, 215, 246–7, 249, 250
transnational nationalism, 243–4, 248
tribalisation, 18, 24
Tsing, Anna, 128, 130, 162, 165
Tuanku Luckman Sinar Basyarsyah II, 74
Tuanku Muhammad Daud, 94, 95
Tubagus Ali Imran, KH, 190
Tugu Suharto, 181
Tun 'Ali Hati, 49
Tun Aria Bija, 51
Tun Isak, see Paduka Tuan
Tun Mai Ulat Bulu, 49
Tun Muhammad Rahang, 49
Tun Narawangsa, 51
Tun Pawah, 44
Tun Perak, 44–5, 48, 49, 52
Tun Pikrima, 50
Tun Telanai, 55
Tun Zainal, 44
Turkey, 85, 93, 94

unitary village systems, 4
United Nations Declaration on the Rights of Indigenous People, 225
United Nations Working Group on Indigenous Populations, 221
United States, 19, 25, 26–7, 28, 93, 94, 109, 205, 256–7, 260, 266, 268–71
universal values, 5, 26

universalism, 18–21, 25, 26–8, 32, 33, 123
Universitas Indonesia, 260–6
urbanisation, 84, 91
Ut Island, 139

values, 14, 22, 68, 206–7
van Eechoud, J.P.K., 203
Vanishing Place of King Jayabaya, 177
Veven Sp. Wardhana, 280–9
Vietnam, 86
Vietnam War, 269
Village Law (1979), 110–1
violence, see conflict/violence

Wagner, Peter, 26–7
Wahid Hasyim, 173–4
Wahyono, A., 145
Waktu Lima, 228, 230
Walesi, 213
Walls, C., 41, 43–4
Wang Gungwu, 244, 247
war on terrorism, 106, 107
Warner, Andrew, 119
Wasior, 210, 211
Watergate scandal, 269
Wawasan Nusantara, 134, 149–50
wayang clowns, 182–3
Wee, Vivienne, 79
West Java, 101, 142, 144, 165, 245–6
West Kalimantan, 143, 147, 158, 162, 169, 245, 247, 250
West Nusa Tenggara, 227
West Papua, see Papua
West Sumatra, 7
  centralisation and, 73, 110–1
  colonial rule of, 73, 104, 105, 107
  corruption in, 114
  culture in, 72, 73
  governance unit of, 4
  guerilla war in, 108, 109
  identity in, 72–3
  Japanese occupation of, 106
  national integrity and, 7
  nationalist struggle in, 103, 104–6, 107

New Order and, 111
rebellions in, 108–10
Reformasi era in, 111
regional autonomy in, 108
see also Minangkabau people;
 Padang
Western lifestyle, 232
Wetu Telu, 225–6, 227–8, 229, 230
Wiener, Margaret, 88
Wijayakusuma flower, 182
Willem Rumsarwir, 207, 211
Wimar Witoelar, 176
WNI, 276, 289
Wolters, O.W., 88, 89
World Bank, 169

World Huaren Federation, 243
World Social Forum, 226

Yayasan Melayu Raya, 75
Yogyakarta, 106, 107
Yoman, Rev. Socratez Sofyan, 205
Yos Soedarso, 201, 202
Youth Pledge, 241

Zainal Abidin, 40, 42, 43
Zainal Bakar, 72, 73
Zainuddin MZ, K.H., 68
Zhou Fuyuan, 249
Zook, Darren, 234